SOLO

A STAR WARS STORY™

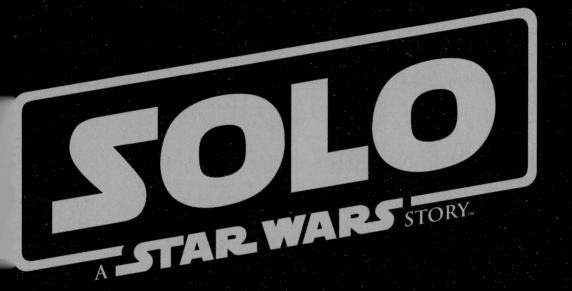

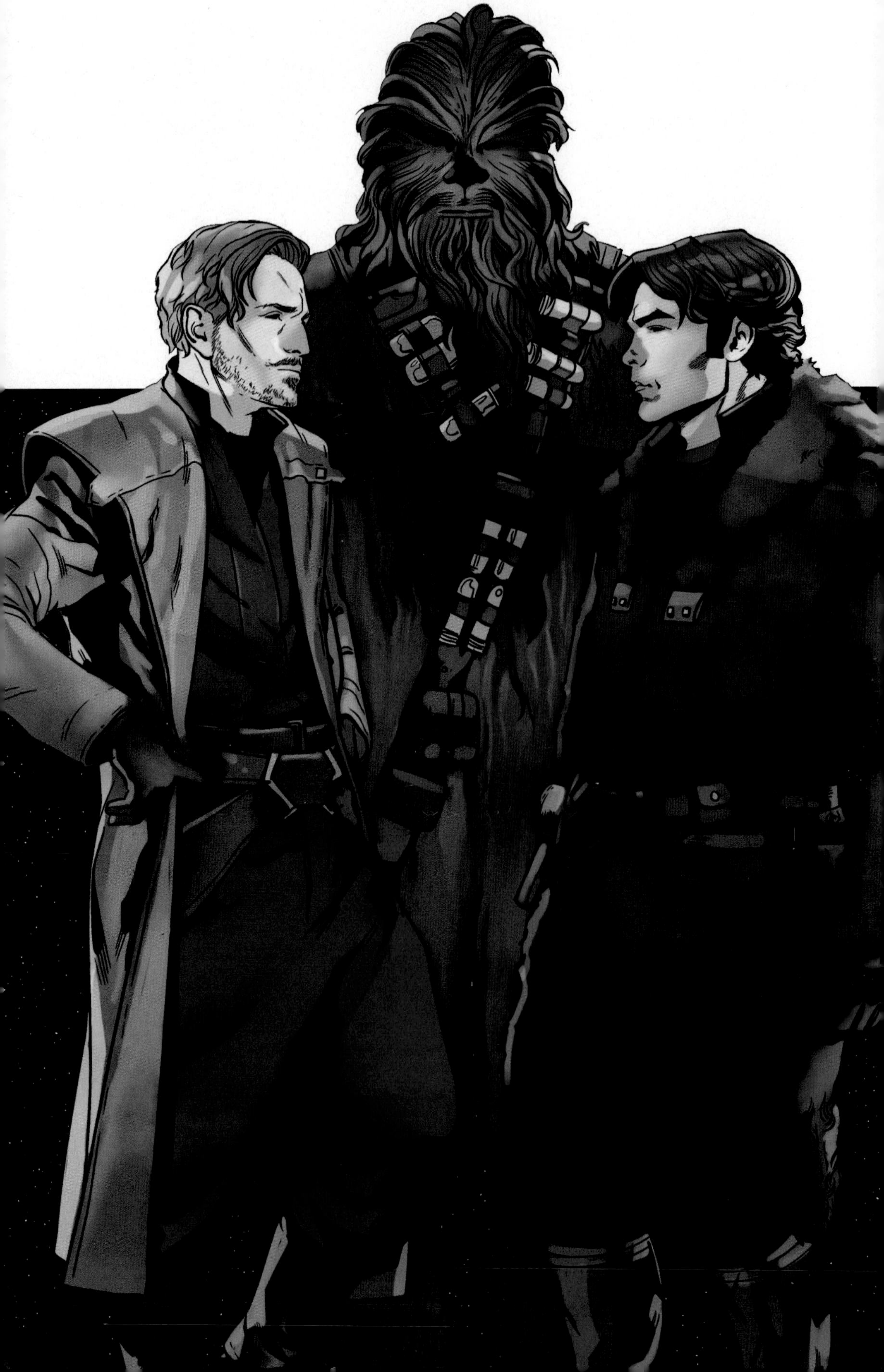

SOLO

A STAR WARS STORY™

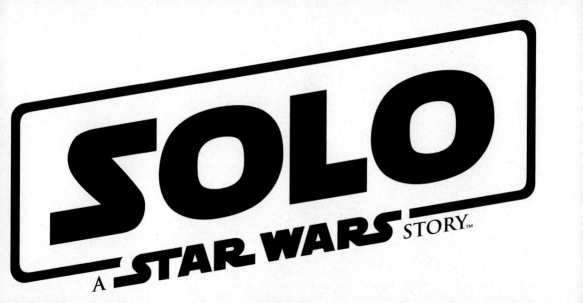

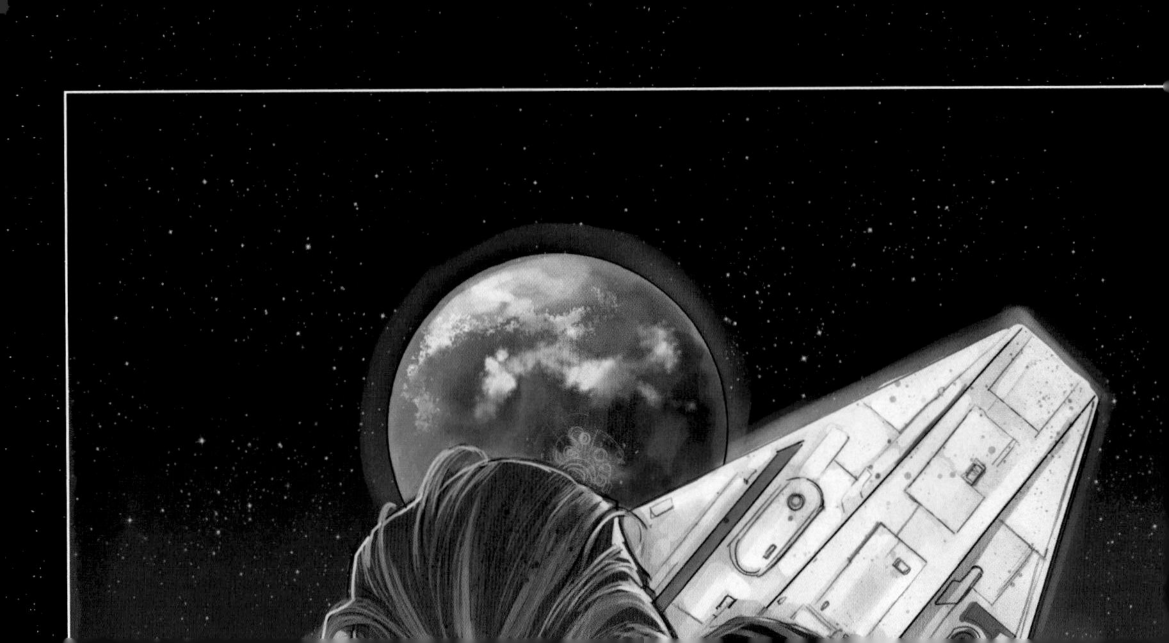

A long time ago in a galaxy far, far away....

CRIME SYNDICATES compete for resources –
food, medicine and HYPERFUEL.

On the shipbuilding planet of Corellia, the foul
LADY PROXIMA forces runaways into a life of
crime in exchange for shelter and protection.

On these mean streets, a young man fights for
survival, but yearns to fly among the stars....

SOLO
A STAR WARS STORY™

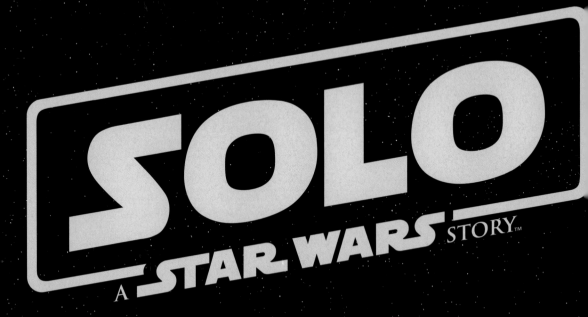

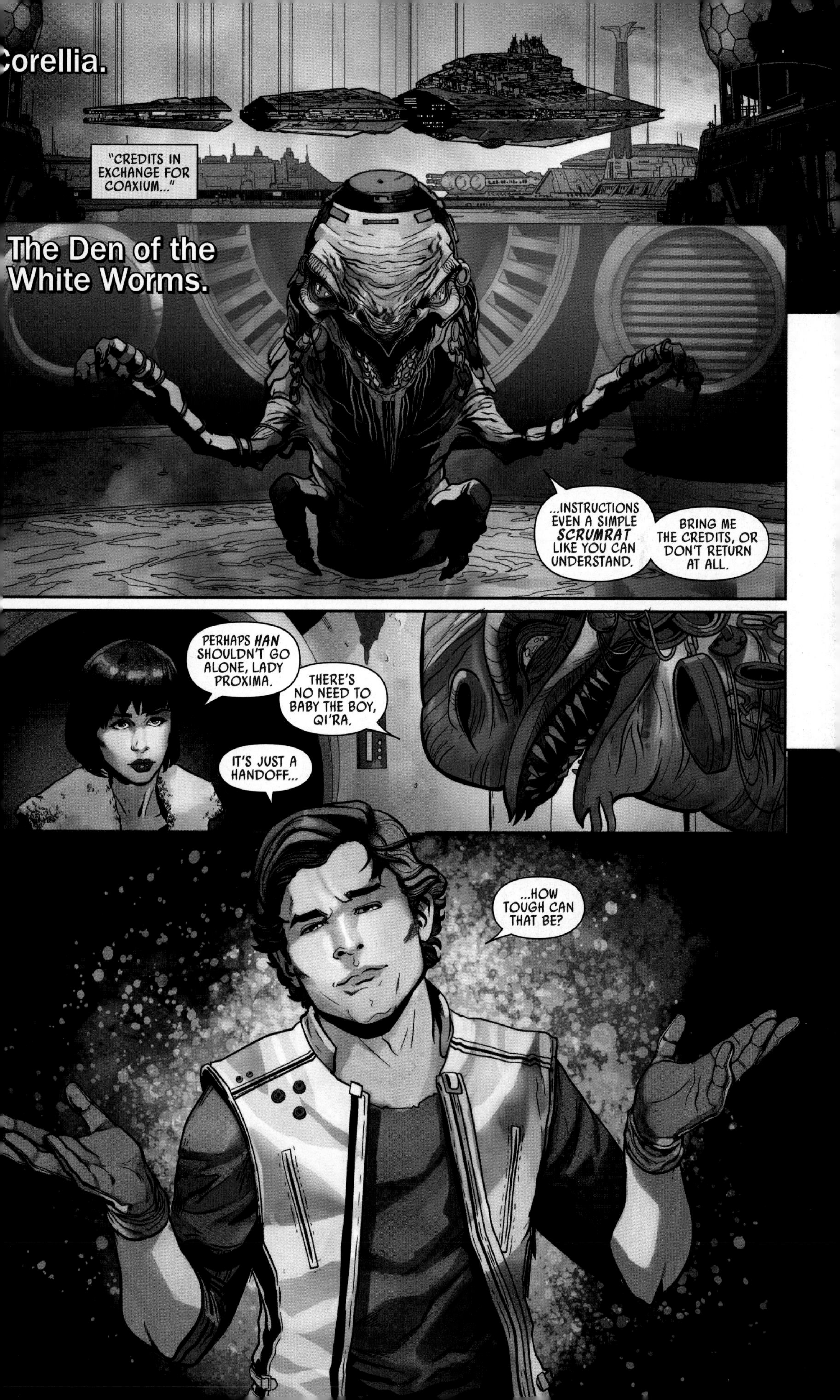

Corellia.
"CREDITS IN EXCHANGE FOR COAXIUM..."
The Den of the White Worms.
...INSTRUCTIONS EVEN A SIMPLE SCRUMRAT LIKE YOU CAN UNDERSTAND.
BRING ME THE CREDITS, OR DON'T RETURN AT ALL.
PERHAPS HAN SHOULDN'T GO ALONE, LADY PROXIMA.
THERE'S NO NEED TO BABY THE BOY, QI'RA.
IT'S JUST A HANDOFF...
...HOW TOUGH CAN THAT BE?

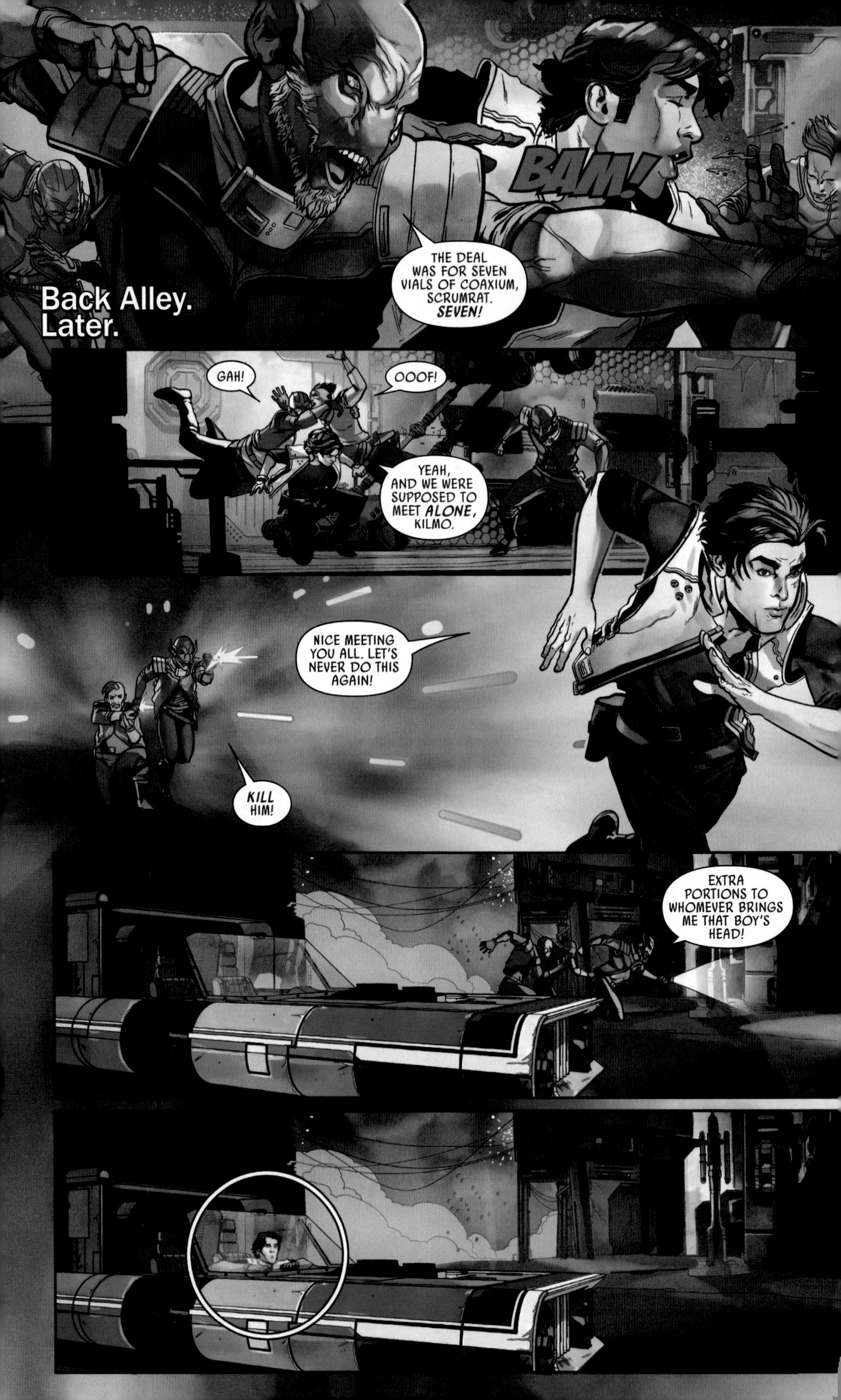
BAM!
THE DEAL WAS FOR SEVEN VIALS OF COAXIUM, SCRUMRAT. SEVEN!
Back Alley. Later.
GAH!
OOOF!
YEAH, AND WE WERE SUPPOSED TO MEET ALONE, KILMO.
NICE MEETING YOU ALL. LET'S NEVER DO THIS AGAIN!
KILL HIM!
EXTRA PORTIONS TO WHOMEVER BRINGS ME THAT BOY'S HEAD!

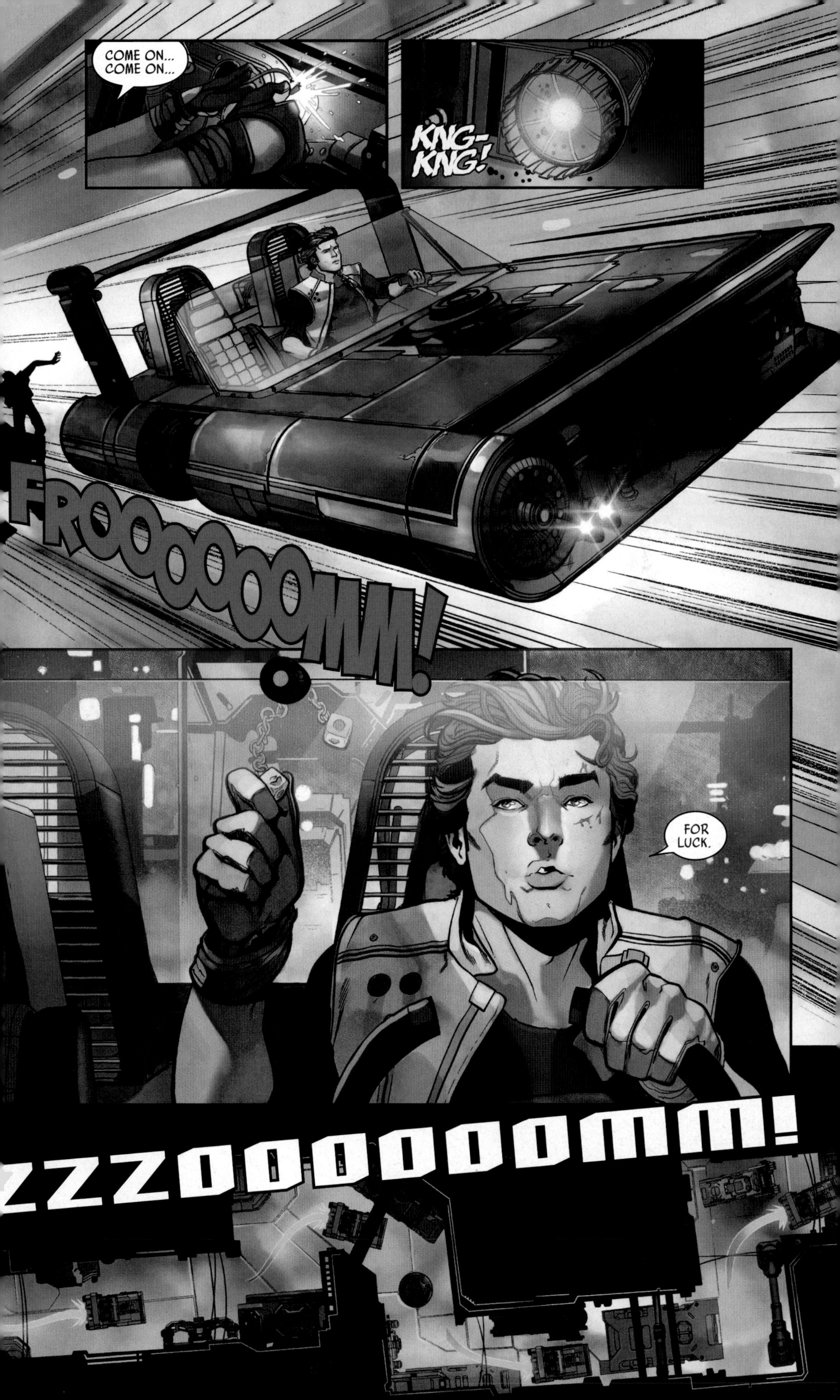
COME ON... COME ON...
KNG-KNG!
FROOOOOOOMM!
FOR LUCK.
ZZZOOOOOOOOMM!

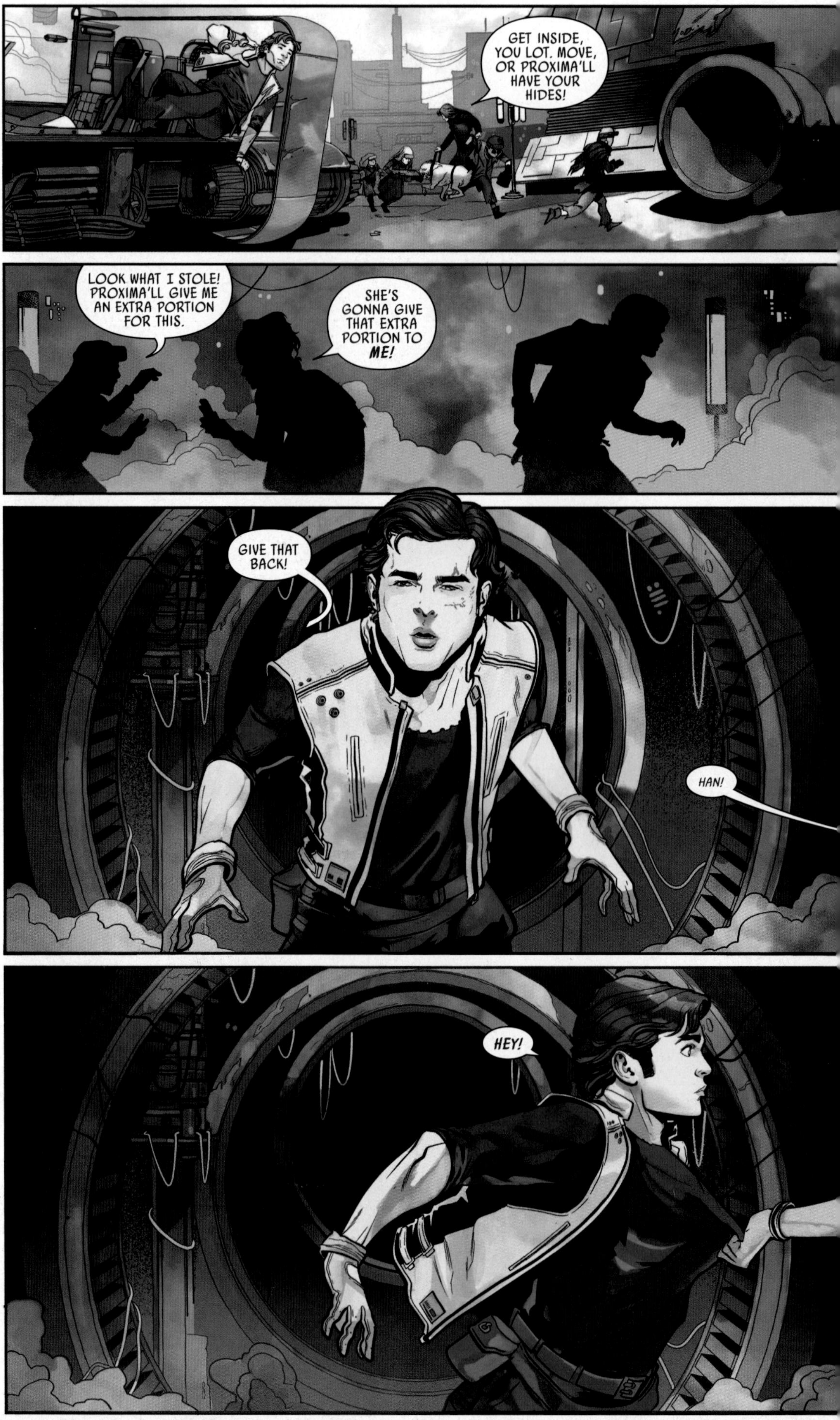

GET INSIDE, YOU LOT. MOVE, OR PROXIMA'LL HAVE YOUR HIDES!
LOOK WHAT I STOLE! PROXIMA'LL GIVE ME AN EXTRA PORTION FOR THIS.
SHE'S GONNA GIVE THAT EXTRA PORTION TO ME!
GIVE THAT BACK!
HAN!
HEY!

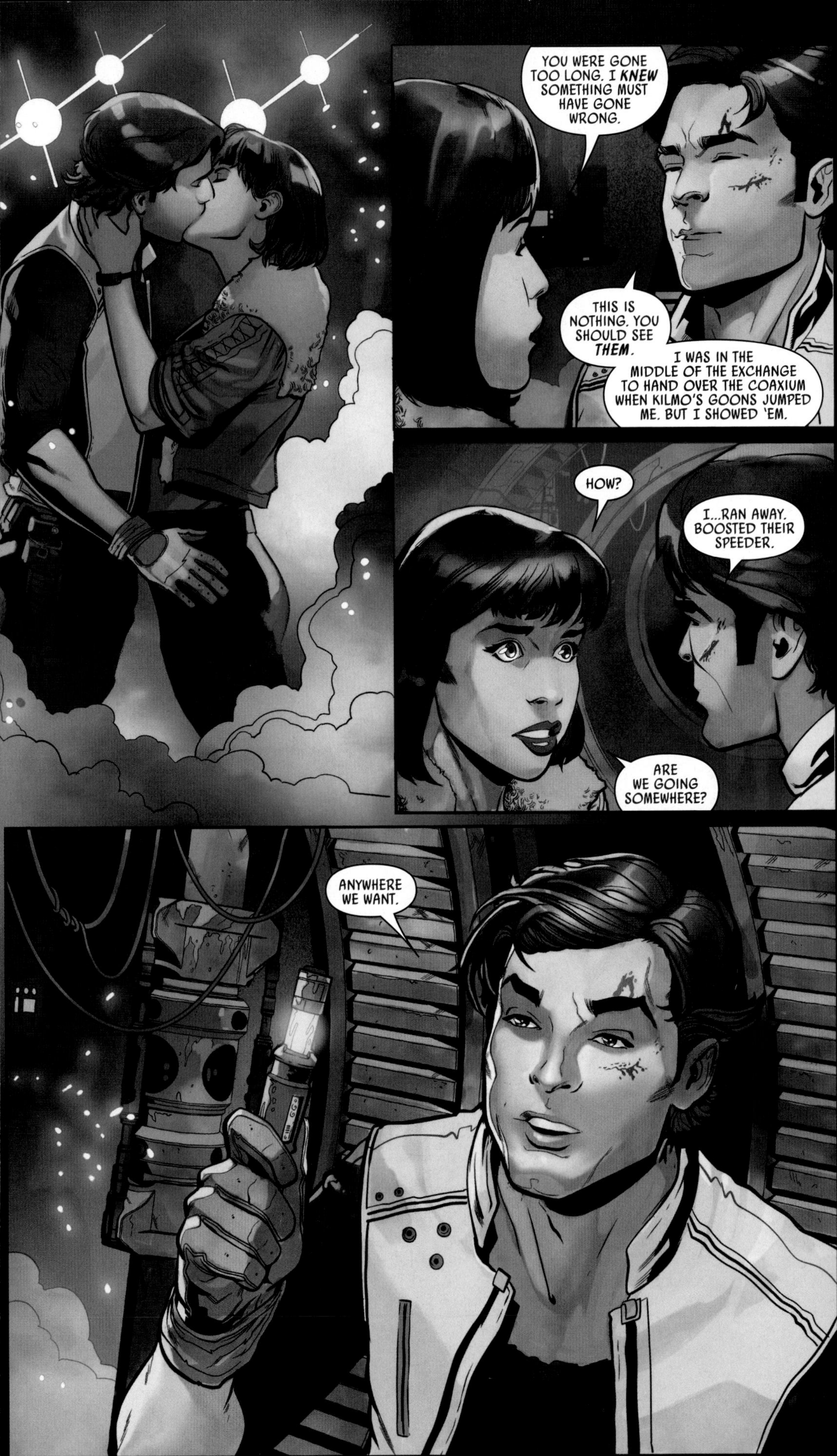

YOU WERE GONE TOO LONG. I **KNEW** SOMETHING MUST HAVE GONE WRONG.
THIS IS NOTHING. YOU SHOULD SEE **THEM**.
I WAS IN THE MIDDLE OF THE EXCHANGE TO HAND OVER THE COAXIUM WHEN KILMO'S GOONS JUMPED ME. BUT I SHOWED 'EM.
HOW?
I...RAN AWAY. BOOSTED THEIR SPEEDER.
ARE WE GOING SOMEWHERE?
ANYWHERE WE WANT.

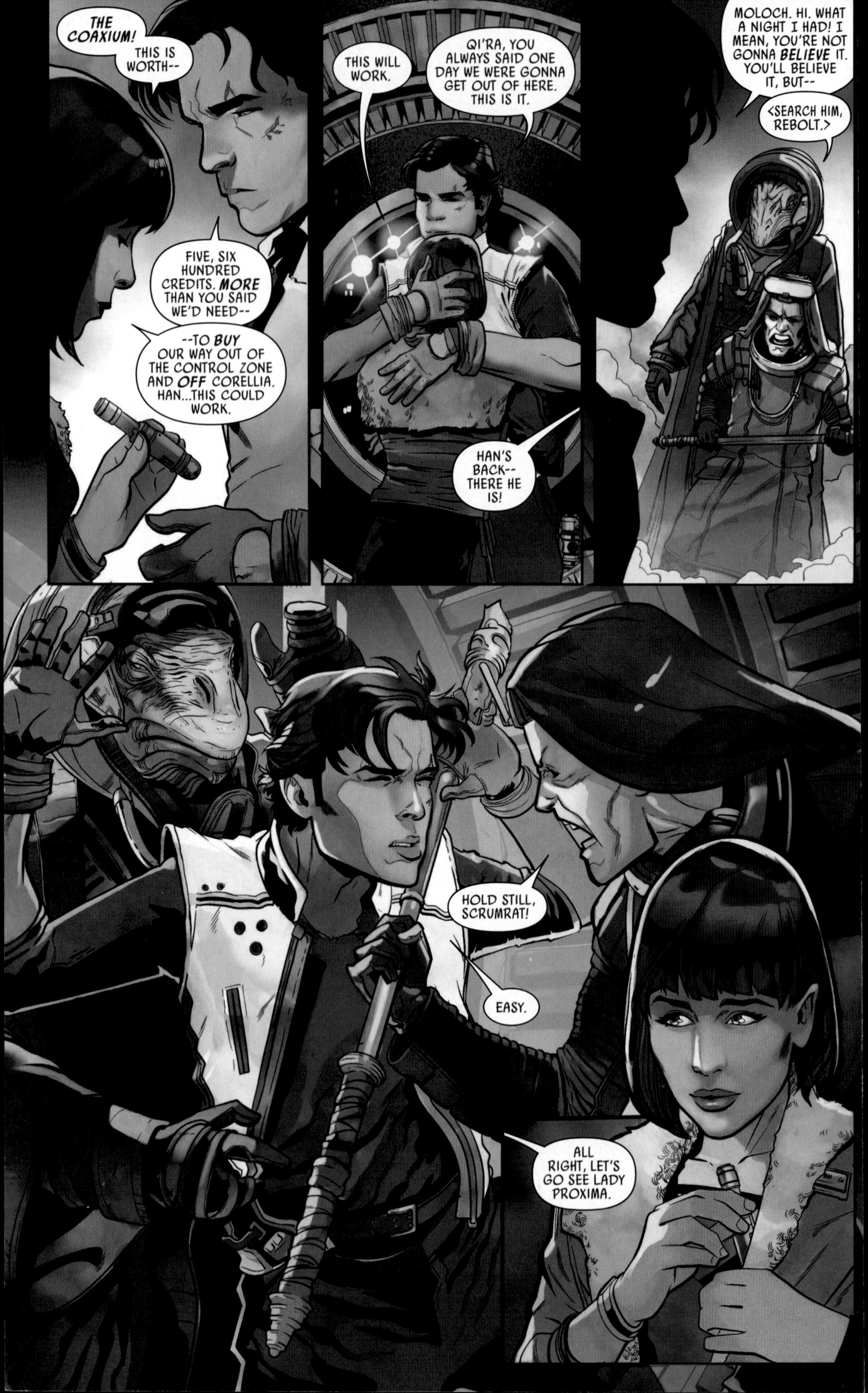
THE COAXIUM! THIS IS WORTH--
FIVE, SIX HUNDRED CREDITS. MORE THAN YOU SAID WE'D NEED--
--TO BUY OUR WAY OUT OF THE CONTROL ZONE AND OFF CORELLIA. HAN...THIS COULD WORK.
THIS WILL WORK.
QI'RA, YOU ALWAYS SAID ONE DAY WE WERE GONNA GET OUT OF HERE. THIS IS IT.
HAN'S BACK-- THERE HE IS!
MOLOCH. HI. WHAT A NIGHT I HAD! I MEAN, YOU'RE NOT GONNA BELIEVE IT. YOU'LL BELIEVE IT, BUT--
<SEARCH HIM, REBOLT.>
HOLD STILL, SCRUMRAT!
EASY.
ALL RIGHT, LET'S GO SEE LADY PROXIMA.

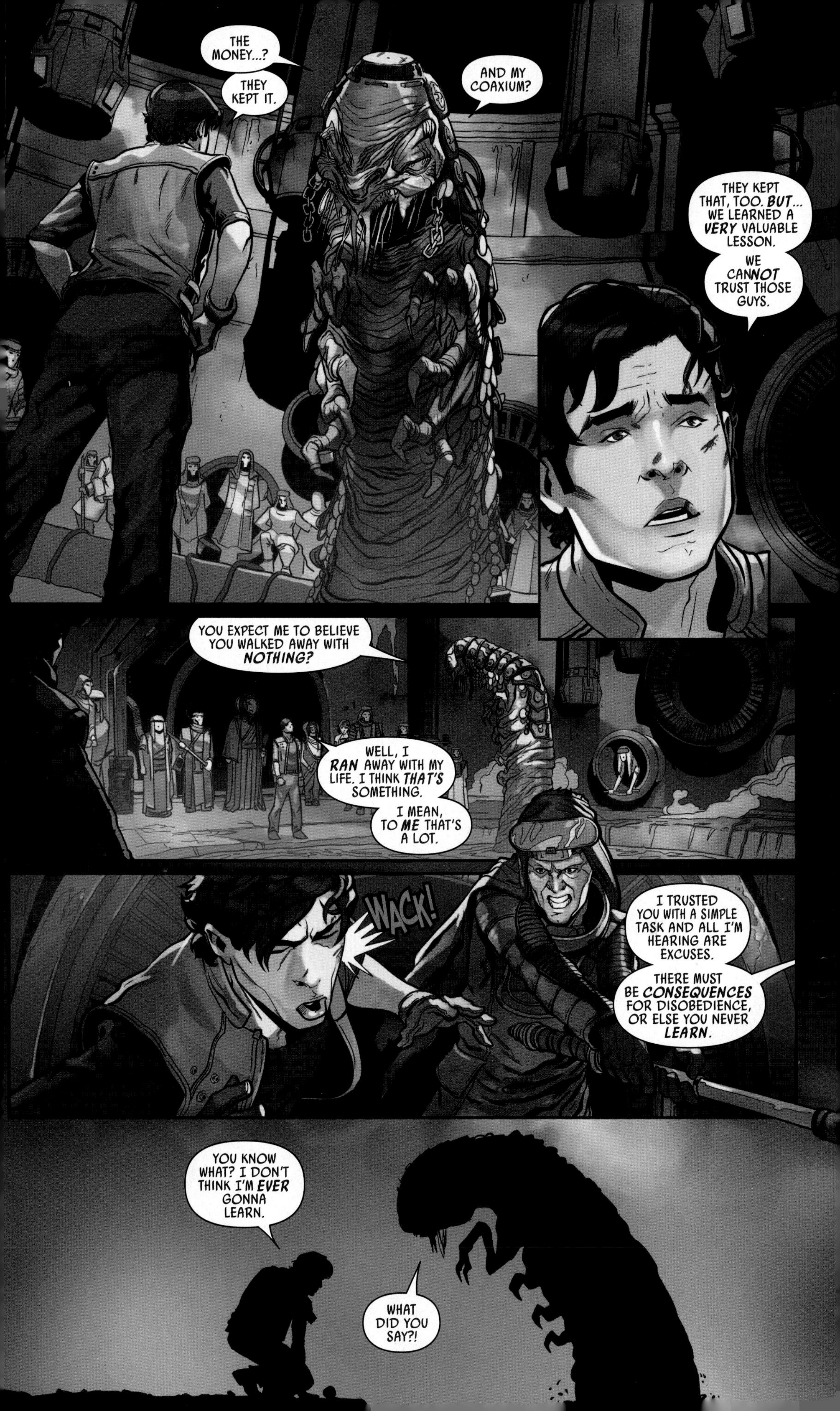
THE MONEY...?
THEY KEPT IT.
AND MY COAXIUM?
THEY KEPT THAT, TOO. BUT... WE LEARNED A VERY VALUABLE LESSON.
WE CANNOT TRUST THOSE GUYS.
YOU EXPECT ME TO BELIEVE YOU WALKED AWAY WITH NOTHING?
WELL, I RAN AWAY WITH MY LIFE. I THINK THAT'S SOMETHING.
I MEAN, TO ME THAT'S A LOT.
WACK!
I TRUSTED YOU WITH A SIMPLE TASK AND ALL I'M HEARING ARE EXCUSES.
THERE MUST BE CONSEQUENCES FOR DISOBEDIENCE, OR ELSE YOU NEVER LEARN.
YOU KNOW WHAT? I DON'T THINK I'M EVER GONNA LEARN.
WHAT DID YOU SAY?!

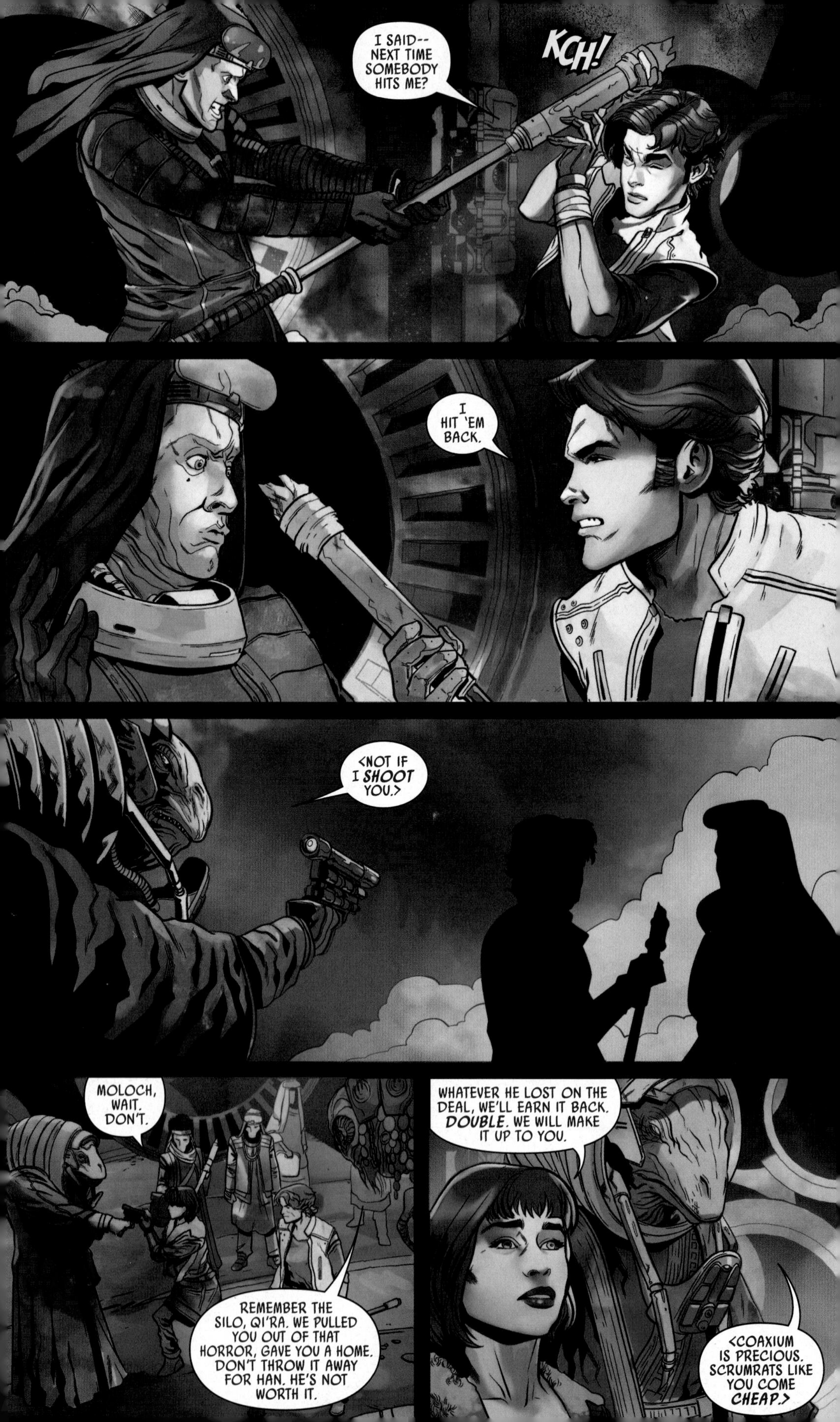
I SAID-- NEXT TIME SOMEBODY HITS ME?
KCH!
I HIT 'EM BACK.
<NOT IF I *SHOOT* YOU.>
MOLOCH, WAIT. DON'T.
REMEMBER THE SILO, QI'RA. WE PULLED YOU OUT OF THAT HORROR, GAVE YOU A HOME. DON'T THROW IT AWAY FOR HAN. HE'S NOT WORTH IT.
WHATEVER HE LOST ON THE DEAL, WE'LL EARN IT BACK. *DOUBLE*. WE WILL MAKE IT UP TO YOU.
<COAXIUM IS PRECIOUS. SCRUMRATS LIKE YOU COME *CHEAP*.>

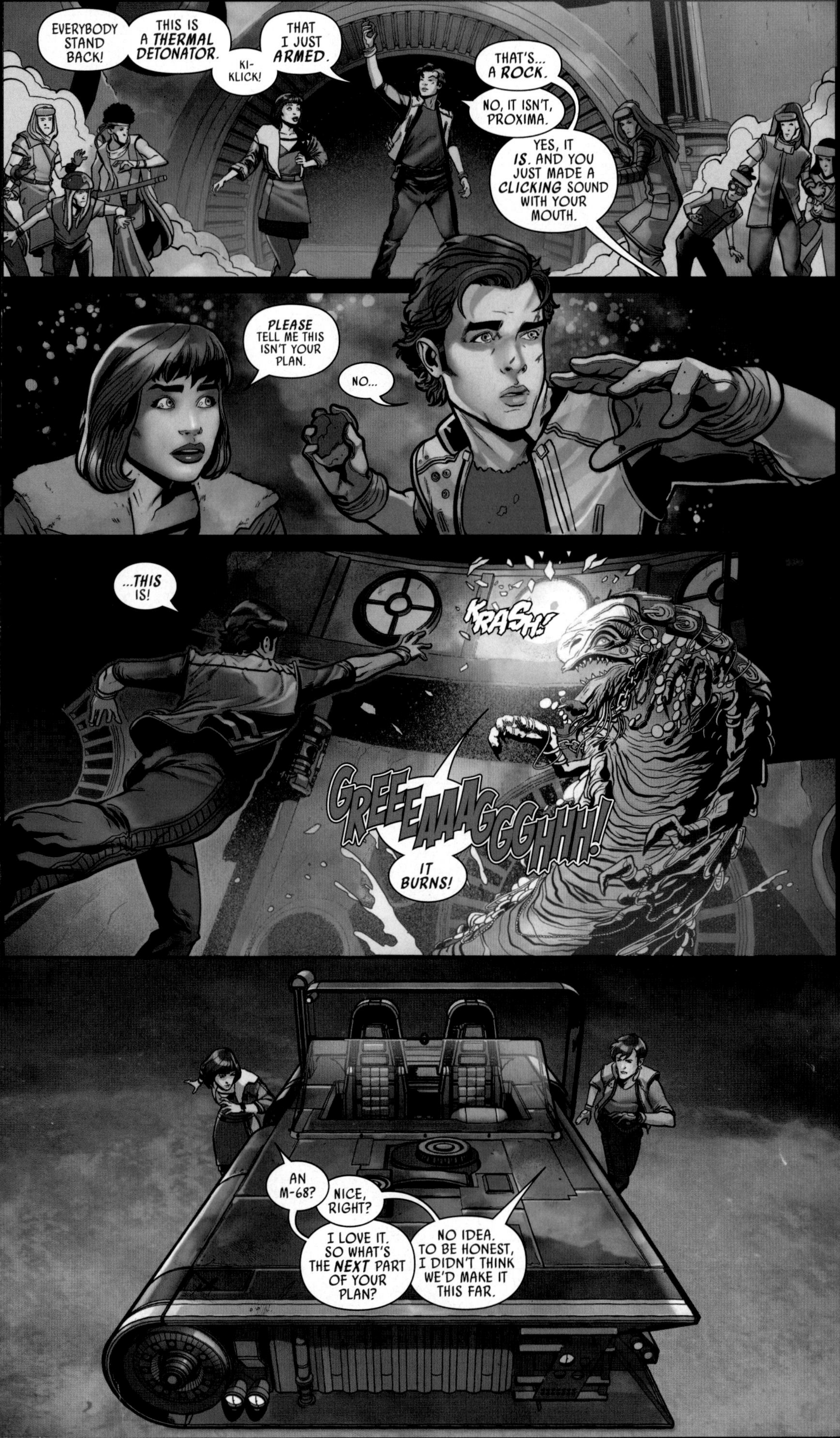
EVERYBODY STAND BACK!
THIS IS A THERMAL DETONATOR.
KI-KLICK!
THAT I JUST ARMED.
THAT'S... A ROCK.
NO, IT ISN'T, PROXIMA.
YES, IT IS. AND YOU JUST MADE A CLICKING SOUND WITH YOUR MOUTH.
PLEASE TELL ME THIS ISN'T YOUR PLAN.
NO...
...THIS IS!
KRASH!
GREEEAAAGGGHHH!
IT BURNS!
AN M-68?
NICE, RIGHT?
I LOVE IT. SO WHAT'S THE NEXT PART OF YOUR PLAN?
NO IDEA. TO BE HONEST, I DIDN'T THINK WE'D MAKE IT THIS FAR.

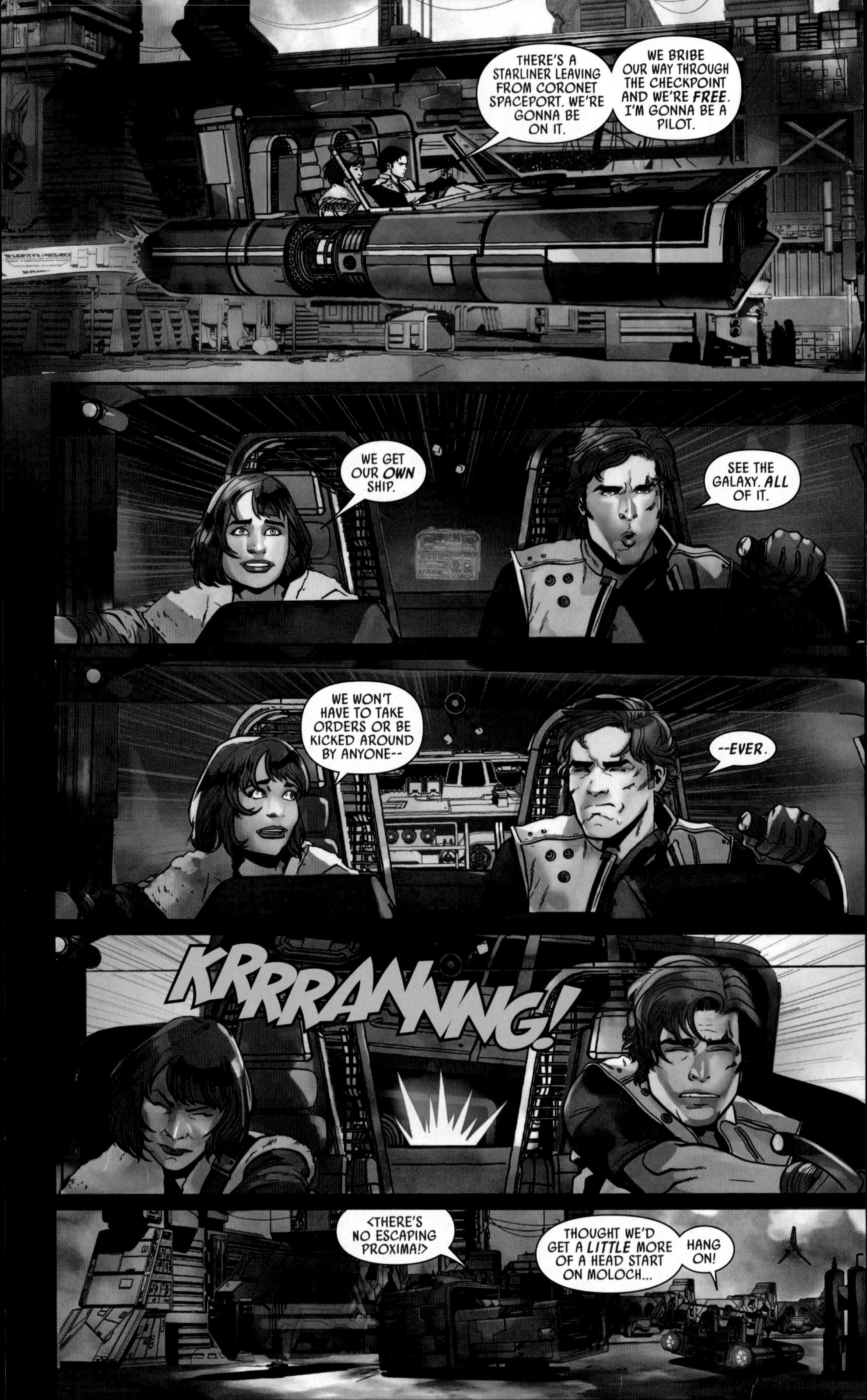
THERE'S A STARLINER LEAVING FROM CORONET SPACEPORT. WE'RE GONNA BE ON IT.
WE BRIBE OUR WAY THROUGH THE CHECKPOINT AND WE'RE FREE. I'M GONNA BE A PILOT.
WE GET OUR OWN SHIP.
SEE THE GALAXY. ALL OF IT.
WE WON'T HAVE TO TAKE ORDERS OR BE KICKED AROUND BY ANYONE--
--EVER.
KRRRANNNG!
<THERE'S NO ESCAPING PROXIMA!>
THOUGHT WE'D GET A LITTLE MORE OF A HEAD START ON MOLOCH...
HANG ON!

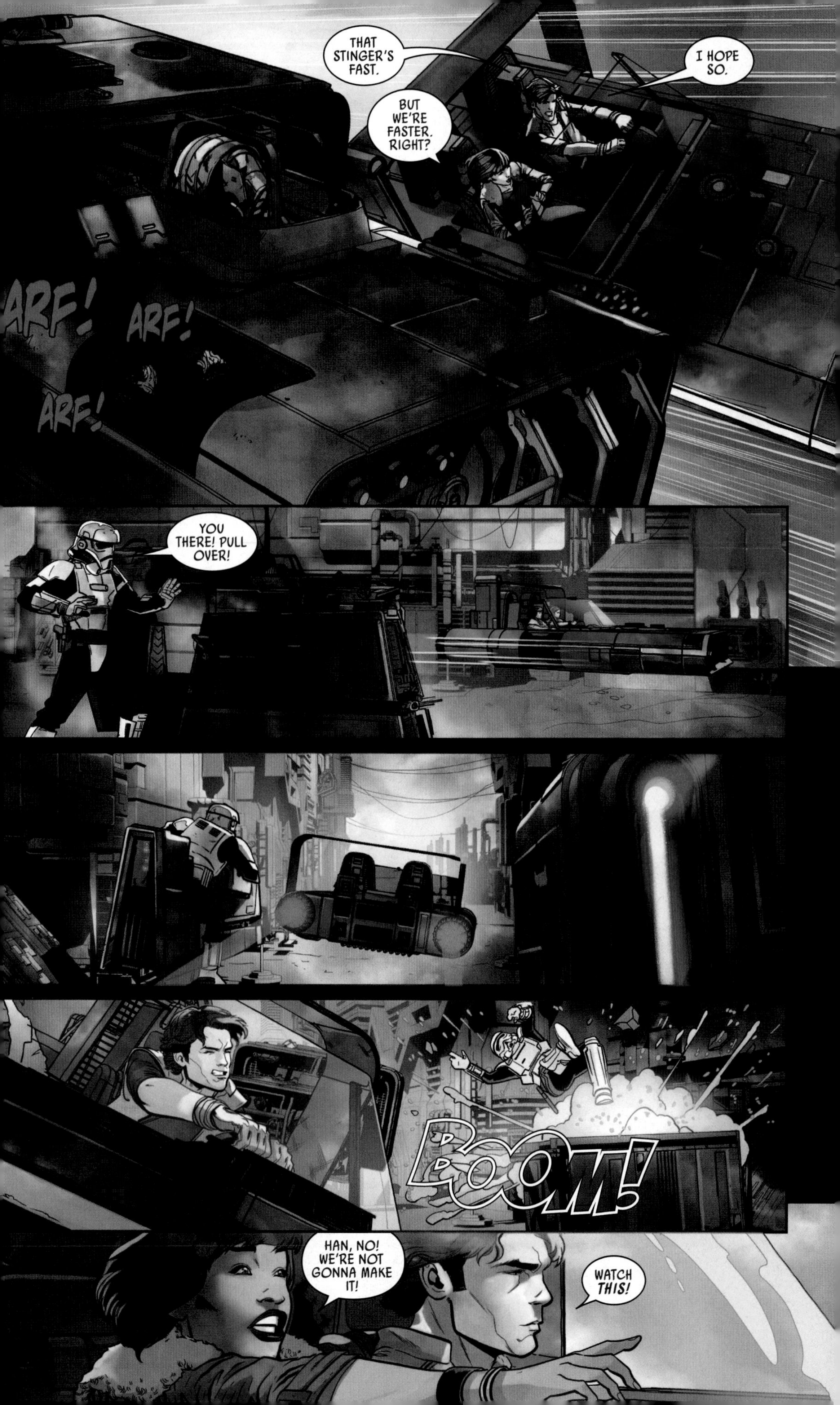
THAT STINGER'S FAST.
BUT WE'RE FASTER. RIGHT?
I HOPE SO.
ARF! ARF! ARF!
YOU THERE! PULL OVER!
BOOM!
HAN, NO! WE'RE NOT GONNA MAKE IT!
WATCH *THIS!*

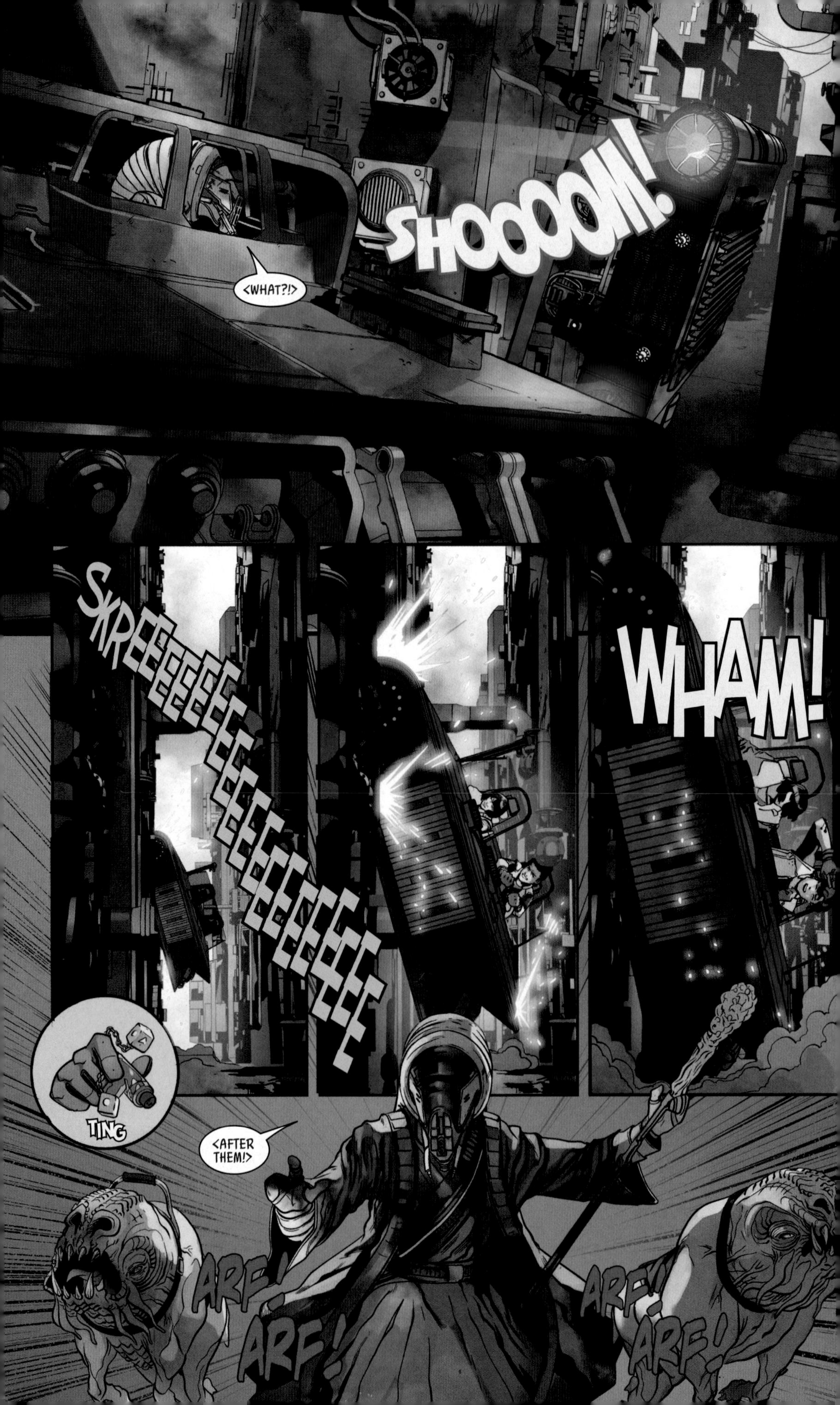
SHOOOOM!
<WHAT?!>
SKREEEEEEEEEEEEEEEEEEEEEEEE
WHAM!
TING
<AFTER THEM!>
ARF!
ARF!
ARF!
ARF!

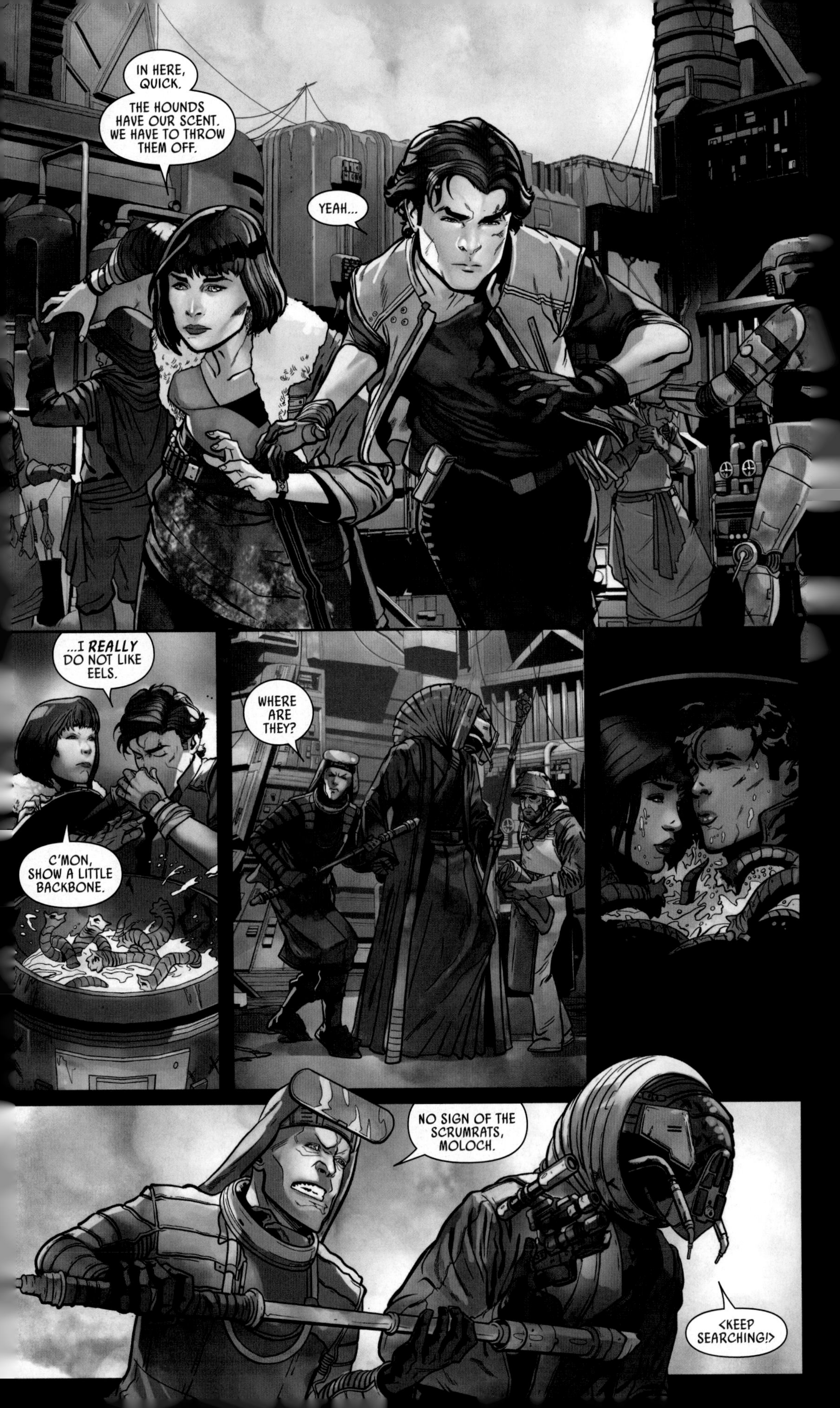
IN HERE, QUICK.
THE HOUNDS HAVE OUR SCENT. WE HAVE TO THROW THEM OFF.
YEAH...
...I REALLY DO NOT LIKE EELS.
C'MON, SHOW A LITTLE BACKBONE.
WHERE ARE THEY?
NO SIGN OF THE SCRUMRATS, MOLOCH.
<KEEP SEARCHING!>

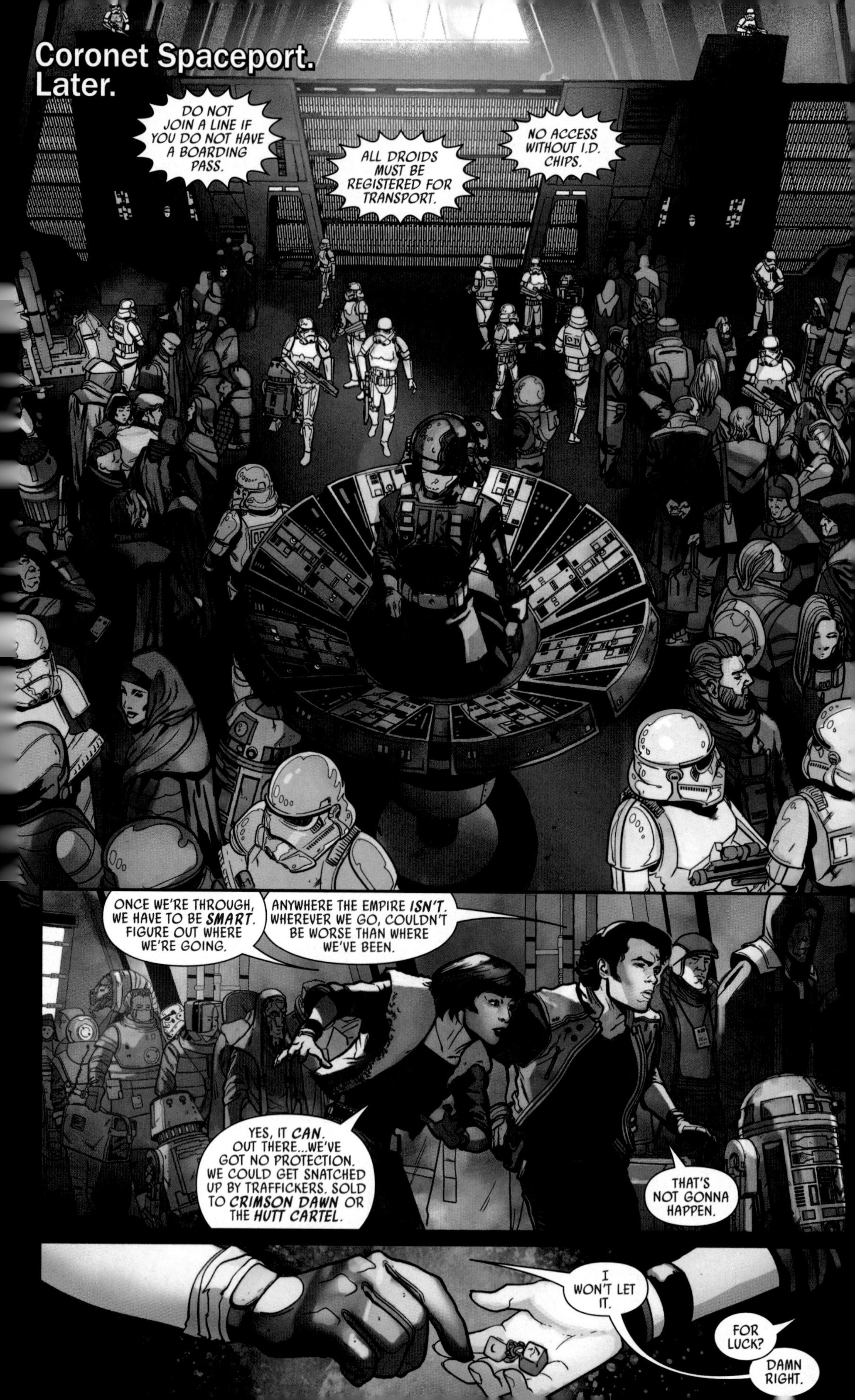
Coronet Spaceport. Later.
DO NOT JOIN A LINE IF YOU DO NOT HAVE A BOARDING PASS.
ALL DROIDS MUST BE REGISTERED FOR TRANSPORT.
NO ACCESS WITHOUT I.D. CHIPS.
ONCE WE'RE THROUGH, WE HAVE TO BE SMART. FIGURE OUT WHERE WE'RE GOING.
ANYWHERE THE EMPIRE ISN'T. WHEREVER WE GO, COULDN'T BE WORSE THAN WHERE WE'VE BEEN.
YES, IT CAN. OUT THERE...WE'VE GOT NO PROTECTION. WE COULD GET SNATCHED UP BY TRAFFICKERS. SOLD TO CRIMSON DAWN OR THE HUTT CARTEL.
THAT'S NOT GONNA HAPPEN.
I WON'T LET IT.
FOR LUCK?
DAMN RIGHT.

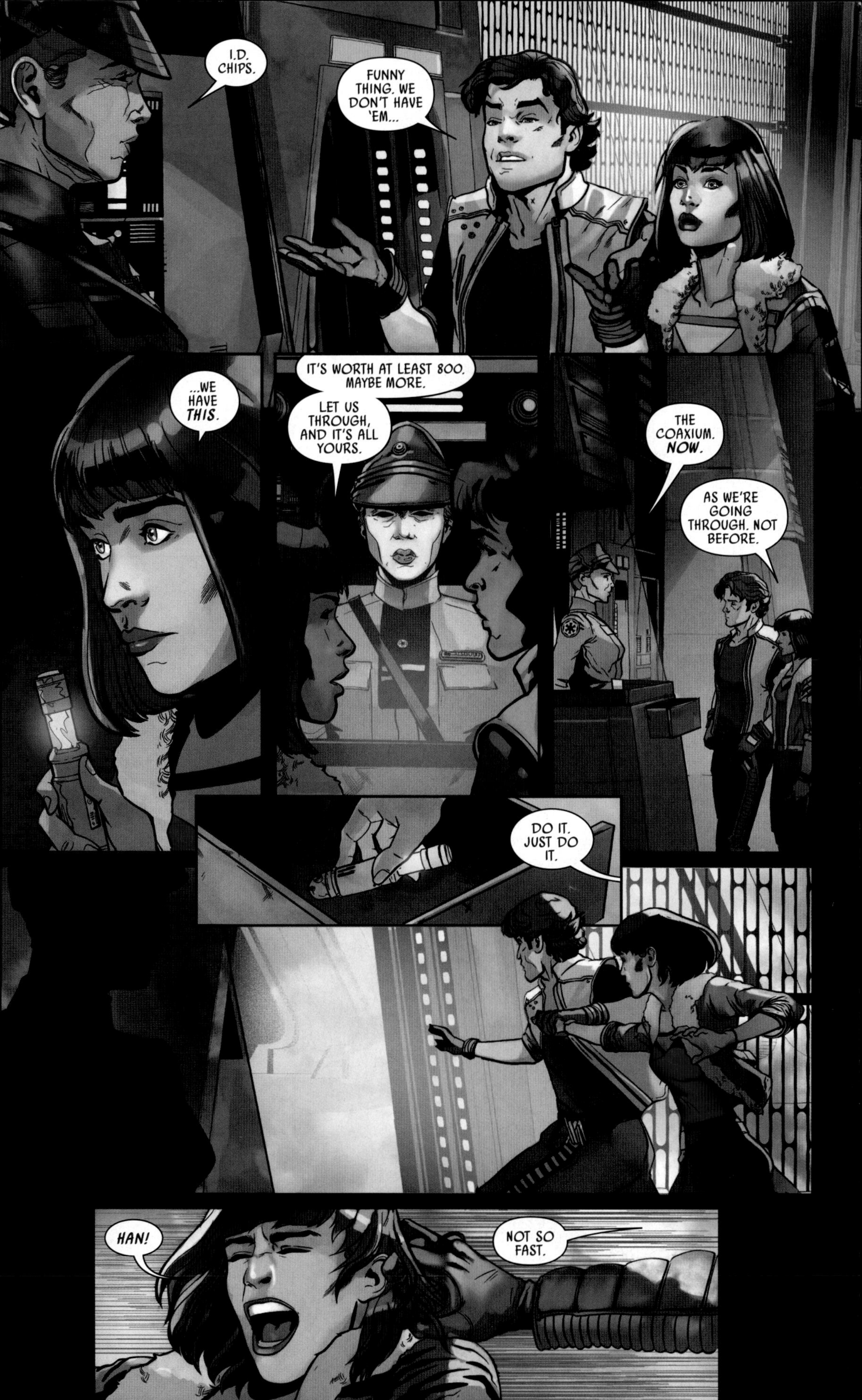
I.D. CHIPS.
FUNNY THING. WE DON'T HAVE 'EM...
...WE HAVE THIS.
IT'S WORTH AT LEAST 800, MAYBE MORE.
LET US THROUGH, AND IT'S ALL YOURS.
THE COAXIUM. NOW.
AS WE'RE GOING THROUGH. NOT BEFORE.
DO IT. JUST DO IT.
HAN!
NOT SO FAST.

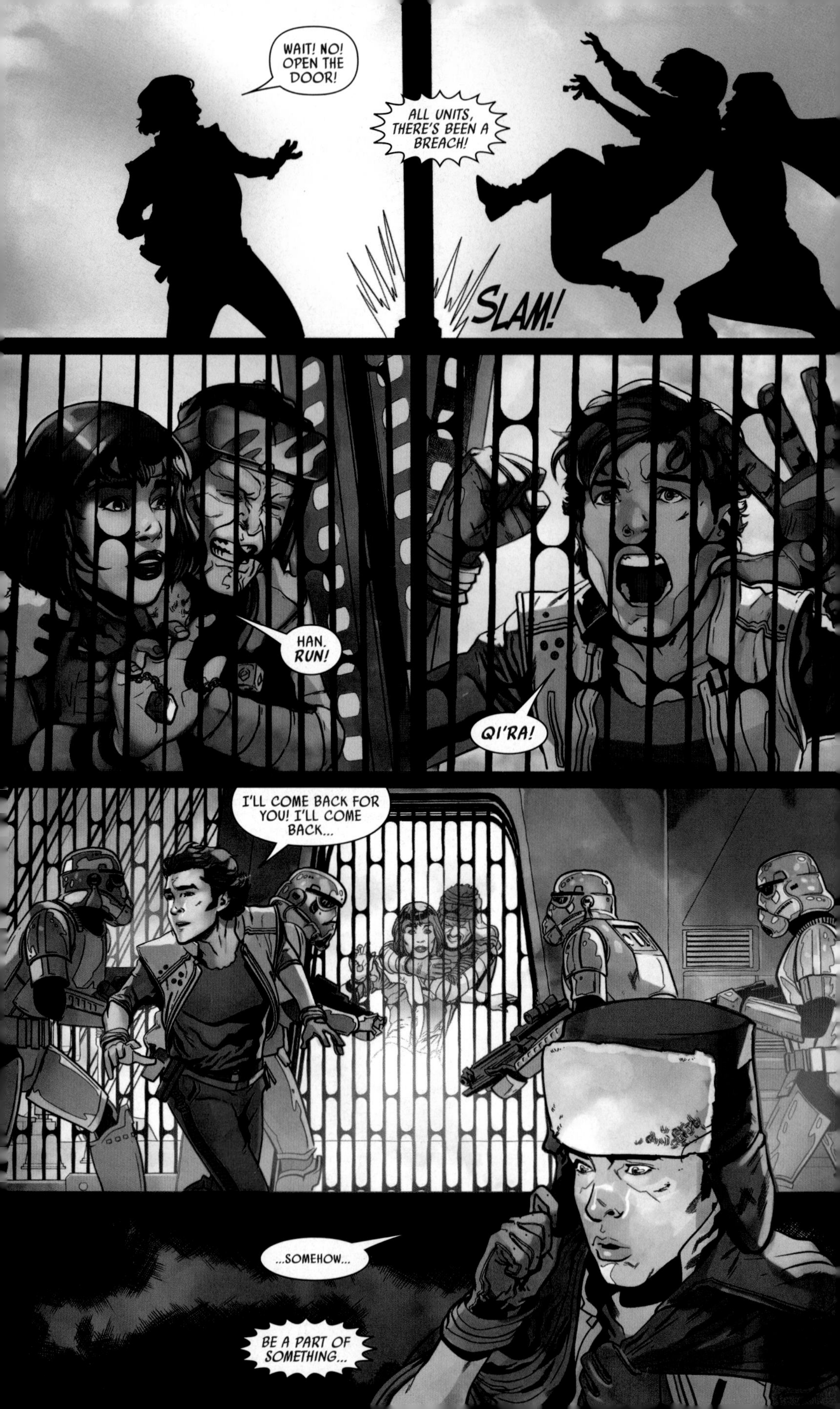
WAIT! NO! OPEN THE DOOR!
ALL UNITS, THERE'S BEEN A BREACH!
SLAM!
HAN. RUN!
QI'RA!
I'LL COME BACK FOR YOU! I'LL COME BACK...
...SOMEHOW...
BE A PART OF SOMETHING...

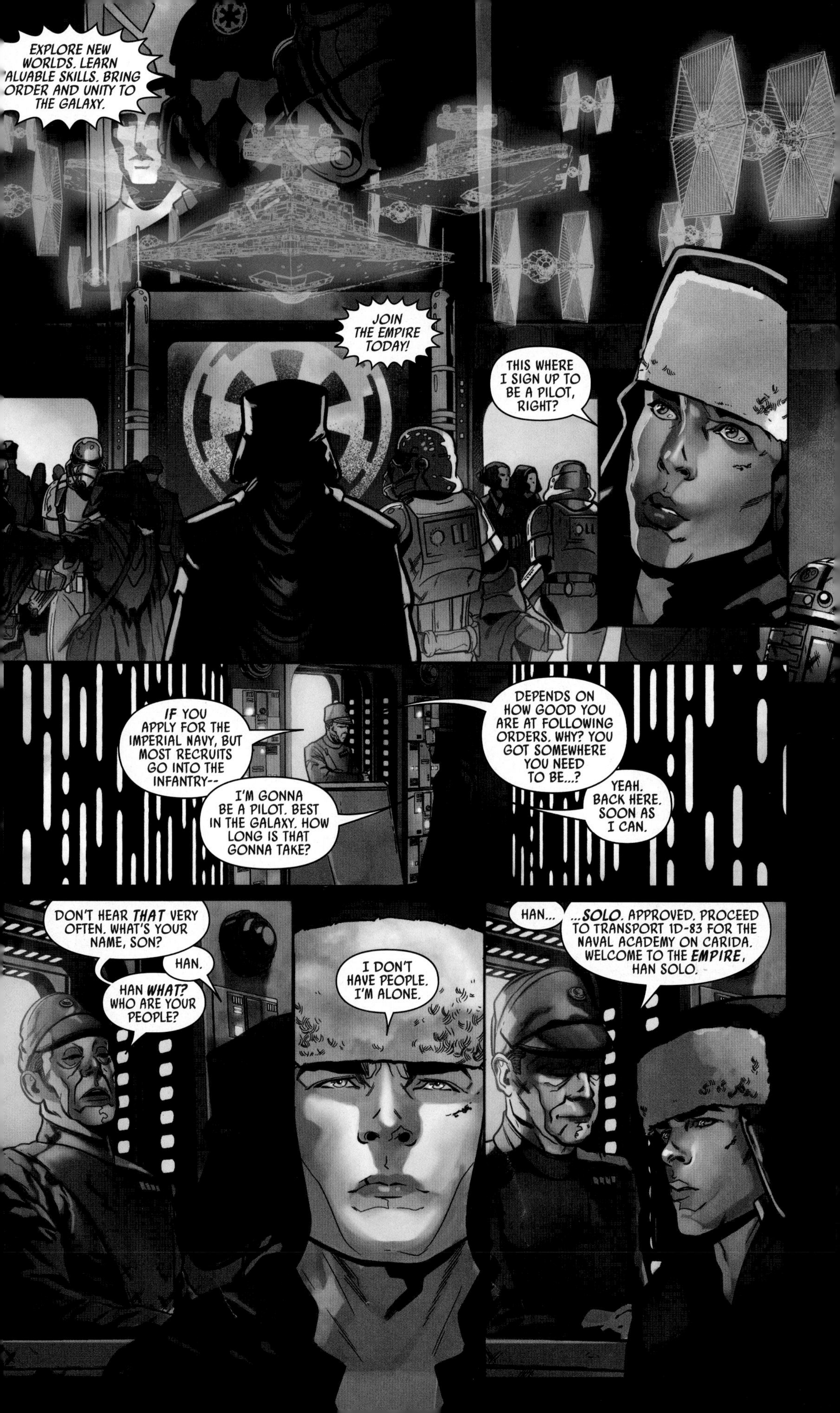
EXPLORE NEW WORLDS. LEARN VALUABLE SKILLS. BRING ORDER AND UNITY TO THE GALAXY.
JOIN THE EMPIRE TODAY!
THIS WHERE I SIGN UP TO BE A PILOT, RIGHT?
IF YOU APPLY FOR THE IMPERIAL NAVY, BUT MOST RECRUITS GO INTO THE INFANTRY--
I'M GONNA BE A PILOT. BEST IN THE GALAXY. HOW LONG IS THAT GONNA TAKE?
DEPENDS ON HOW GOOD YOU ARE AT FOLLOWING ORDERS. WHY? YOU GOT SOMEWHERE YOU NEED TO BE...?
YEAH. BACK HERE. SOON AS I CAN.
DON'T HEAR THAT VERY OFTEN. WHAT'S YOUR NAME, SON?
HAN.
HAN WHAT? WHO ARE YOUR PEOPLE?
I DON'T HAVE PEOPLE. I'M ALONE.
HAN...
...SOLO. APPROVED. PROCEED TO TRANSPORT 1D-83 FOR THE NAVAL ACADEMY ON CARIDA. WELCOME TO THE EMPIRE, HAN SOLO.

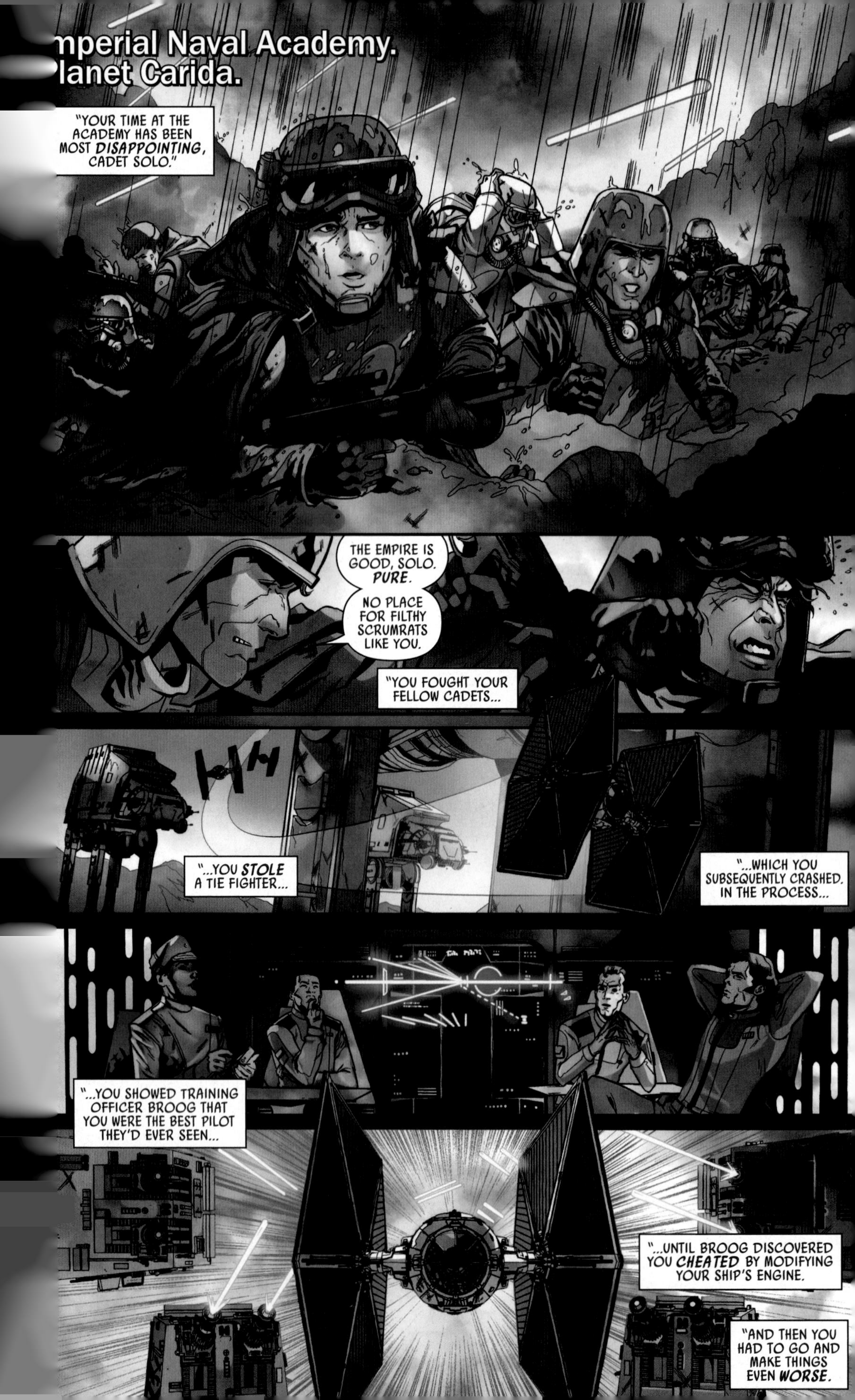
mperial Naval Academy.
lanet Carida.
"YOUR TIME AT THE ACADEMY HAS BEEN MOST DISAPPOINTING, CADET SOLO."
THE EMPIRE IS GOOD, SOLO. PURE.
NO PLACE FOR FILTHY SCRUMRATS LIKE YOU.
"YOU FOUGHT YOUR FELLOW CADETS...
"...YOU STOLE A TIE FIGHTER...
"...WHICH YOU SUBSEQUENTLY CRASHED. IN THE PROCESS...
"...YOU SHOWED TRAINING OFFICER BROOG THAT YOU WERE THE BEST PILOT THEY'D EVER SEEN...
"...UNTIL BROOG DISCOVERED YOU CHEATED BY MODIFYING YOUR SHIP'S ENGINE.
"AND THEN YOU HAD TO GO AND MAKE THINGS EVEN WORSE.

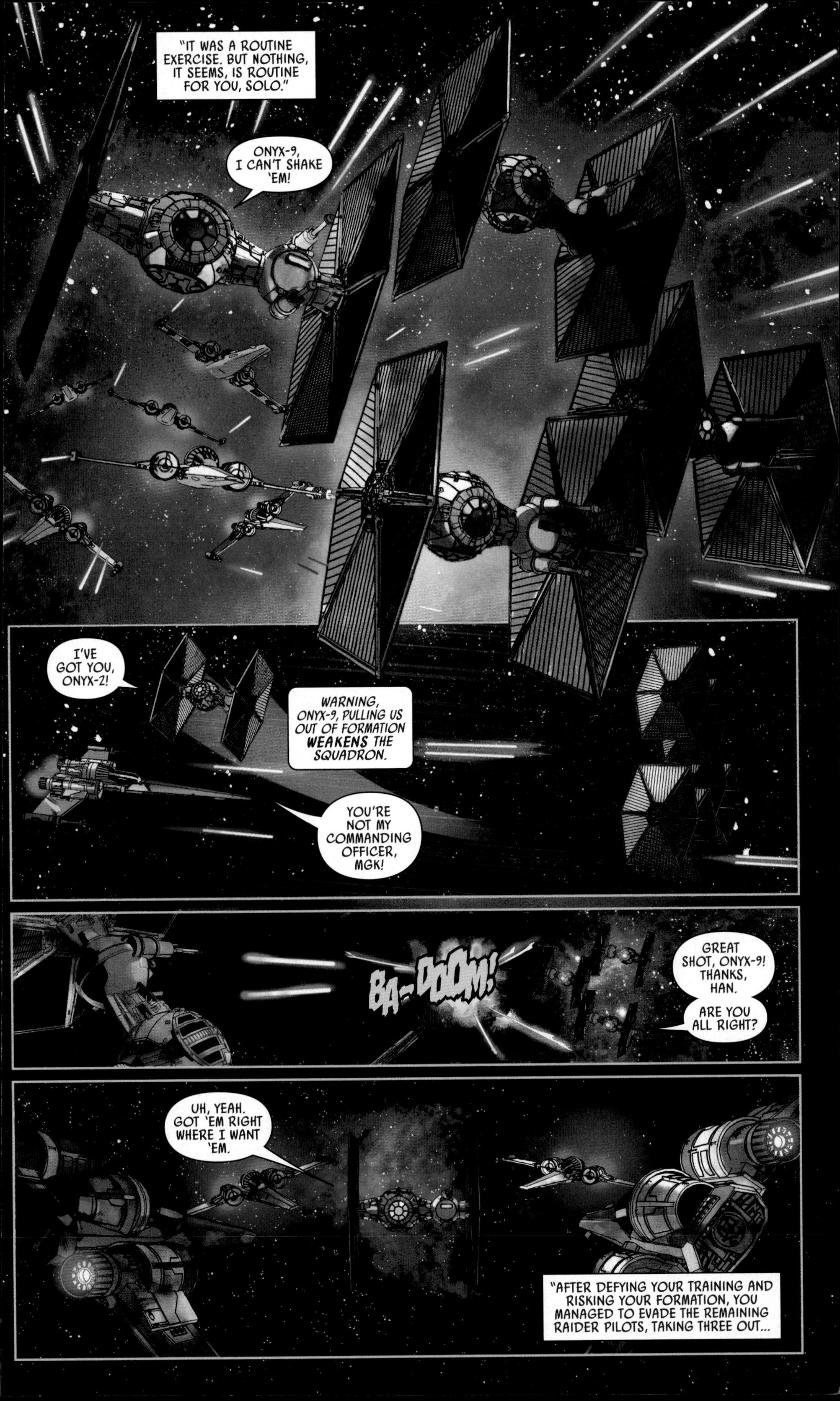
"IT WAS A ROUTINE EXERCISE. BUT NOTHING, IT SEEMS, IS ROUTINE FOR YOU, SOLO."
ONYX-9, I CAN'T SHAKE 'EM!
I'VE GOT YOU, ONYX-2!
WARNING, ONYX-9, PULLING US OUT OF FORMATION WEAKENS THE SQUADRON.
YOU'RE NOT MY COMMANDING OFFICER, MGK!
BA-DOOM!
GREAT SHOT, ONYX-9! THANKS, HAN.
ARE YOU ALL RIGHT?
UH, YEAH. GOT 'EM RIGHT WHERE I WANT 'EM.
"AFTER DEFYING YOUR TRAINING AND RISKING YOUR FORMATION, YOU MANAGED TO EVADE THE REMAINING RAIDER PILOTS, TAKING THREE OUT...

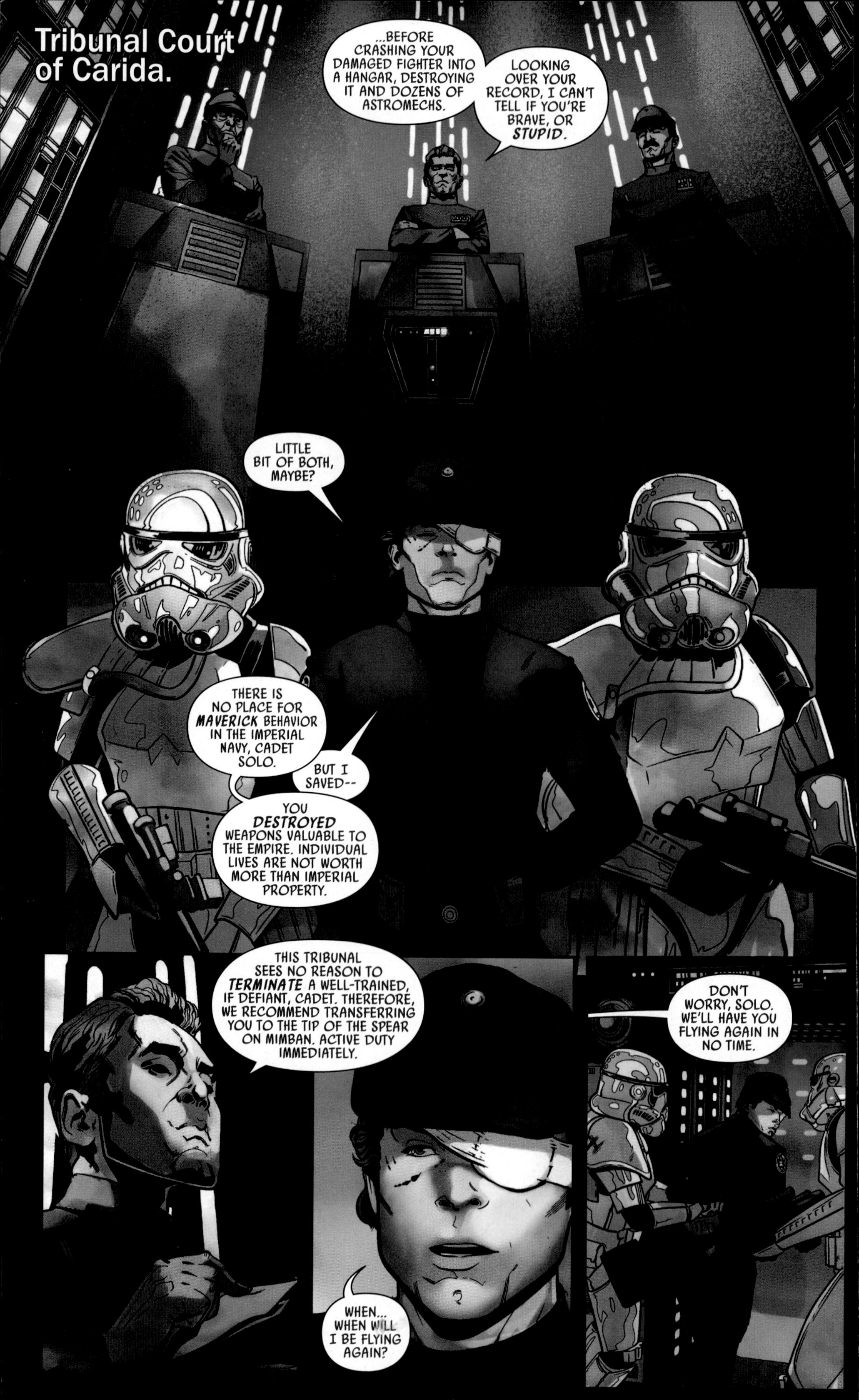
Tribunal Court of Carida.
...BEFORE CRASHING YOUR DAMAGED FIGHTER INTO A HANGAR, DESTROYING IT AND DOZENS OF ASTROMECHS.
LOOKING OVER YOUR RECORD, I CAN'T TELL IF YOU'RE BRAVE, OR STUPID.
LITTLE BIT OF BOTH, MAYBE?
THERE IS NO PLACE FOR MAVERICK BEHAVIOR IN THE IMPERIAL NAVY, CADET SOLO.
BUT I SAVED--
YOU DESTROYED WEAPONS VALUABLE TO THE EMPIRE. INDIVIDUAL LIVES ARE NOT WORTH MORE THAN IMPERIAL PROPERTY.
THIS TRIBUNAL SEES NO REASON TO TERMINATE A WELL-TRAINED, IF DEFIANT, CADET. THEREFORE, WE RECOMMEND TRANSFERRING YOU TO THE TIP OF THE SPEAR ON MIMBAN. ACTIVE DUTY IMMEDIATELY.
WHEN... WHEN WILL I BE FLYING AGAIN?
DON'T WORRY, SOLO. WE'LL HAVE YOU FLYING AGAIN IN NO TIME.

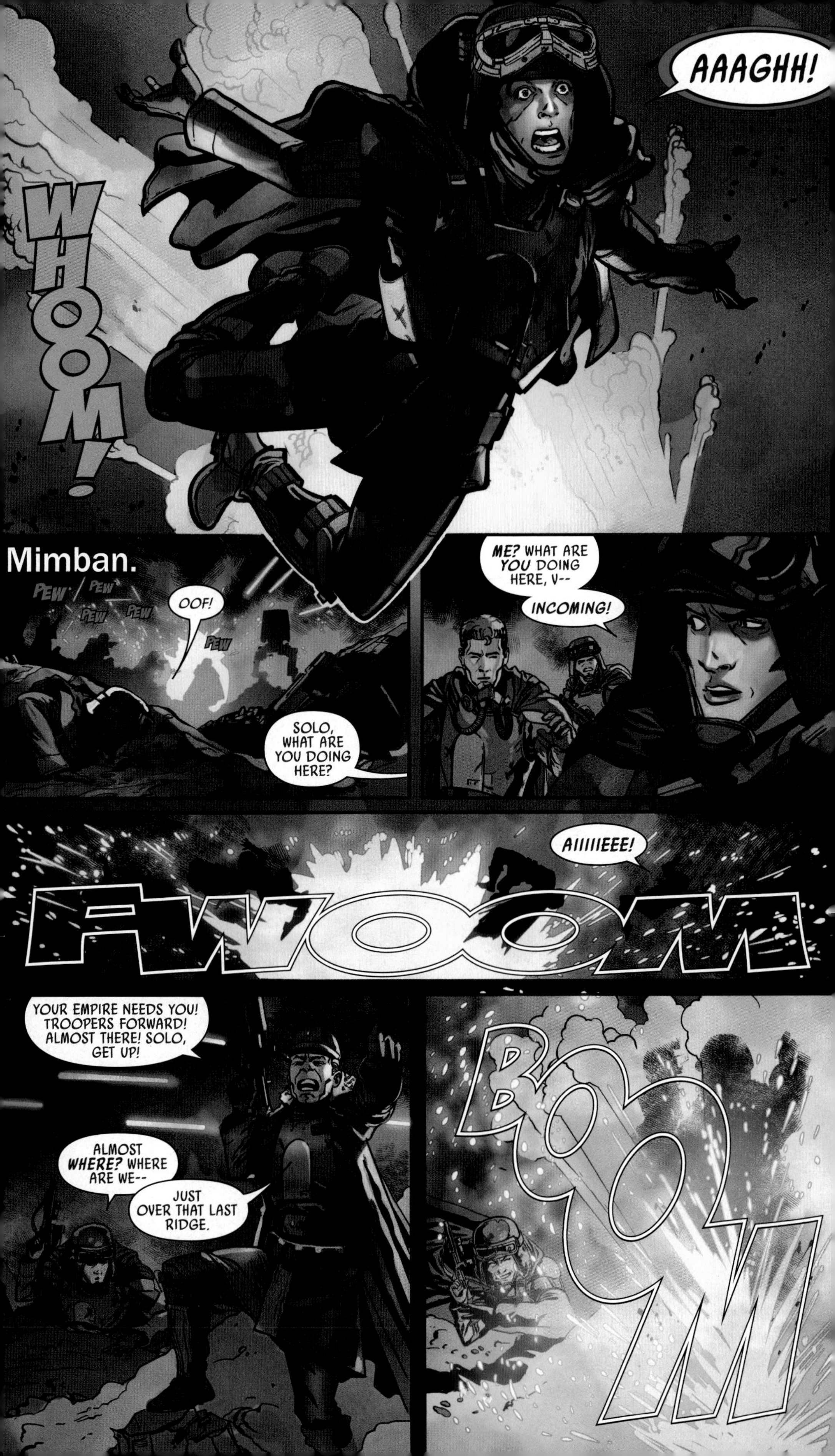
AAAGHH!
WHOOM!
Mimban.
PEW PEW PEW PEW PEW
OOF!
SOLO, WHAT ARE YOU DOING HERE?
ME? WHAT ARE YOU DOING HERE, V--
INCOMING!
AIIIIIEEE!
FWOOM
YOUR EMPIRE NEEDS YOU! TROOPERS FORWARD! ALMOST THERE! SOLO, GET UP!
ALMOST WHERE? WHERE ARE WE--
JUST OVER THAT LAST RIDGE.
BOOM

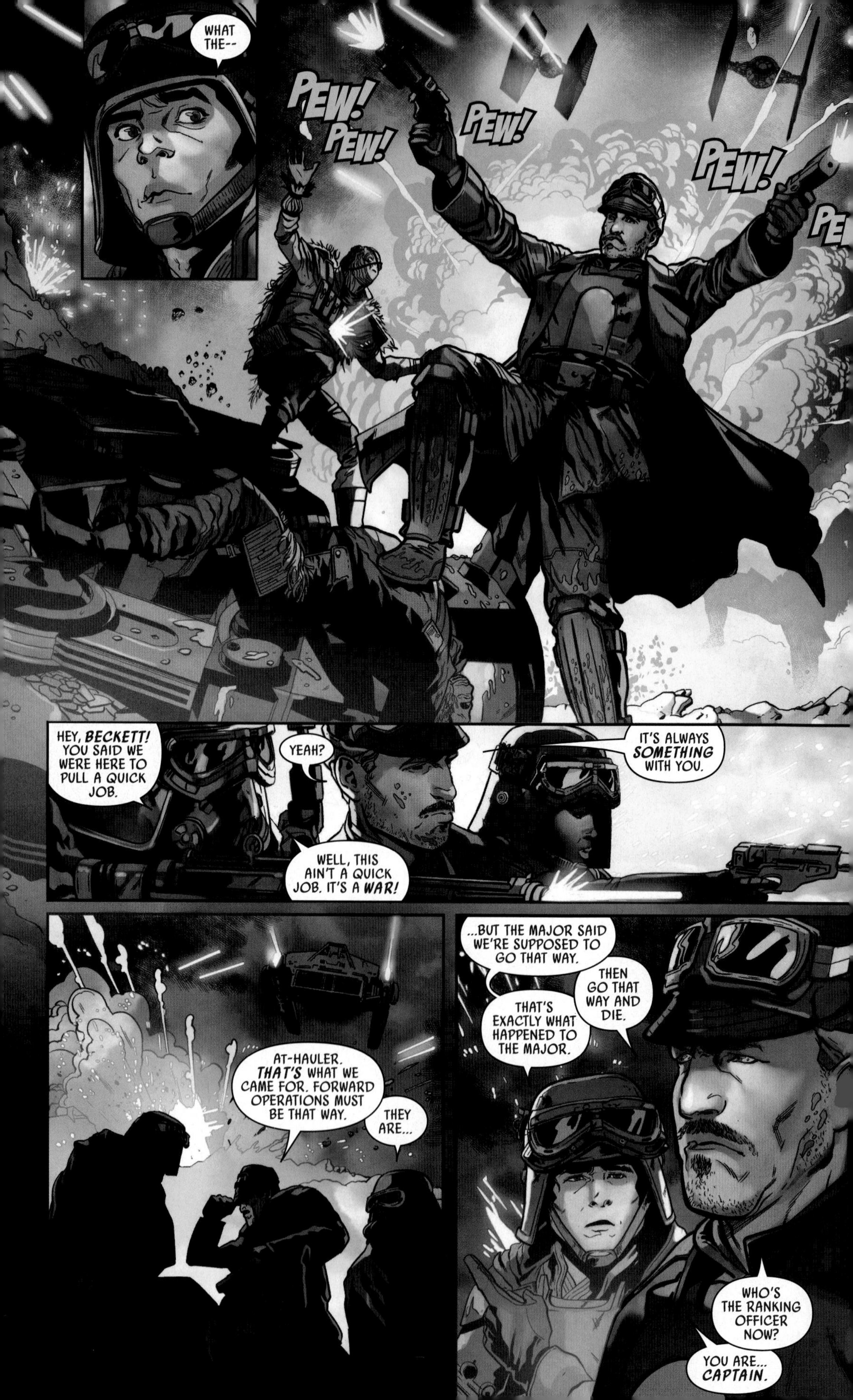
WHAT THE--
PEW! PEW!
PEW!
PEW!
PE
HEY, BECKETT! YOU SAID WE WERE HERE TO PULL A QUICK JOB.
YEAH?
IT'S ALWAYS SOMETHING WITH YOU.
WELL, THIS AIN'T A QUICK JOB. IT'S A WAR!
AT-HAULER. THAT'S WHAT WE CAME FOR. FORWARD OPERATIONS MUST BE THAT WAY.
THEY ARE...
...BUT THE MAJOR SAID WE'RE SUPPOSED TO GO THAT WAY.
THEN GO THAT WAY AND DIE.
THAT'S EXACTLY WHAT HAPPENED TO THE MAJOR.
WHO'S THE RANKING OFFICER NOW?
YOU ARE... CAPTAIN.

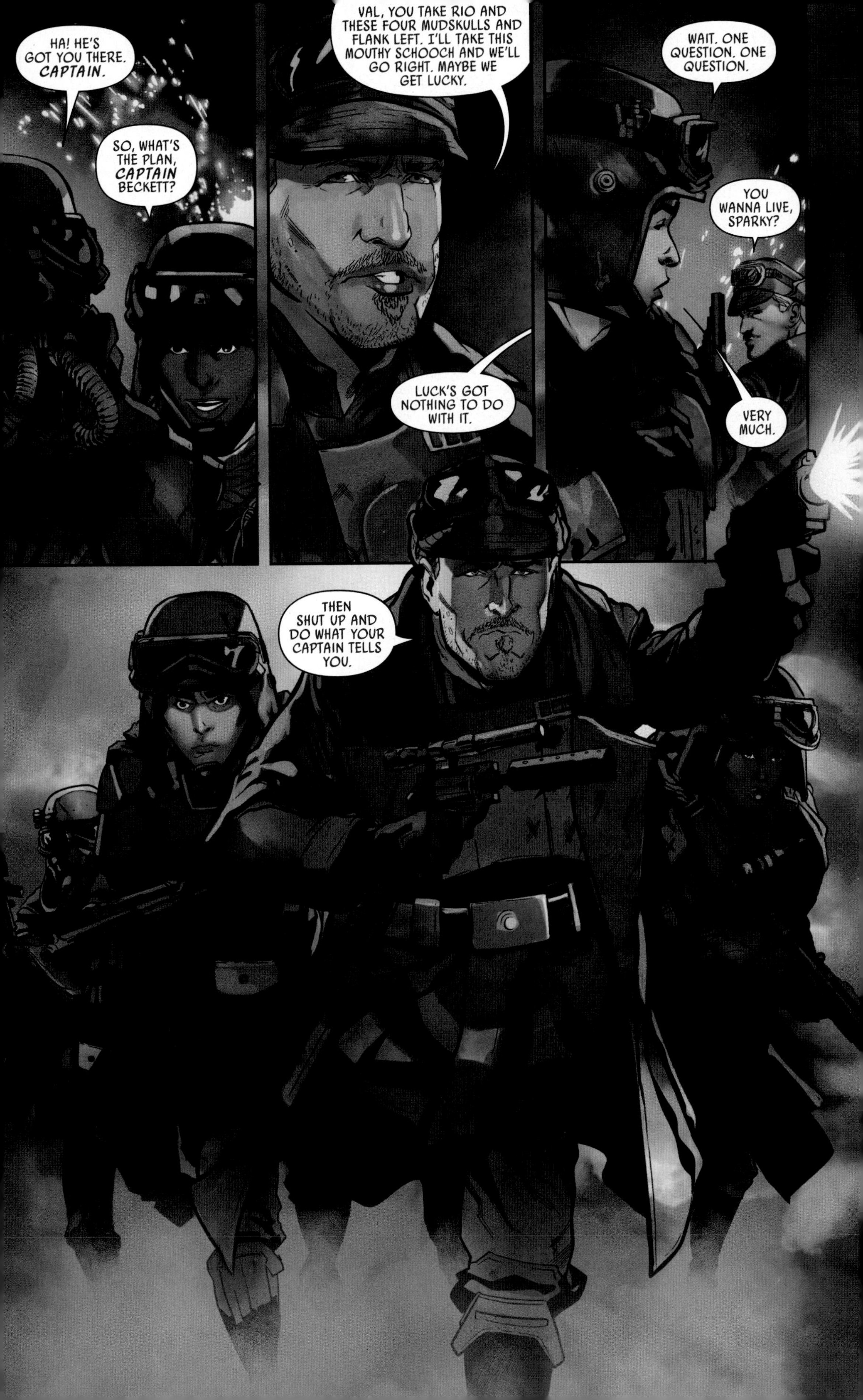
HA! HE'S GOT YOU THERE. CAPTAIN.
SO, WHAT'S THE PLAN, CAPTAIN BECKETT?
VAL, YOU TAKE RIO AND THESE FOUR MUDSKULLS AND FLANK LEFT. I'LL TAKE THIS MOUTHY SCHOOCH AND WE'LL GO RIGHT. MAYBE WE GET LUCKY.
LUCK'S GOT NOTHING TO DO WITH IT.
WAIT. ONE QUESTION. ONE QUESTION.
YOU WANNA LIVE, SPARKY?
VERY MUCH.
THEN SHUT UP AND DO WHAT YOUR CAPTAIN TELLS YOU.

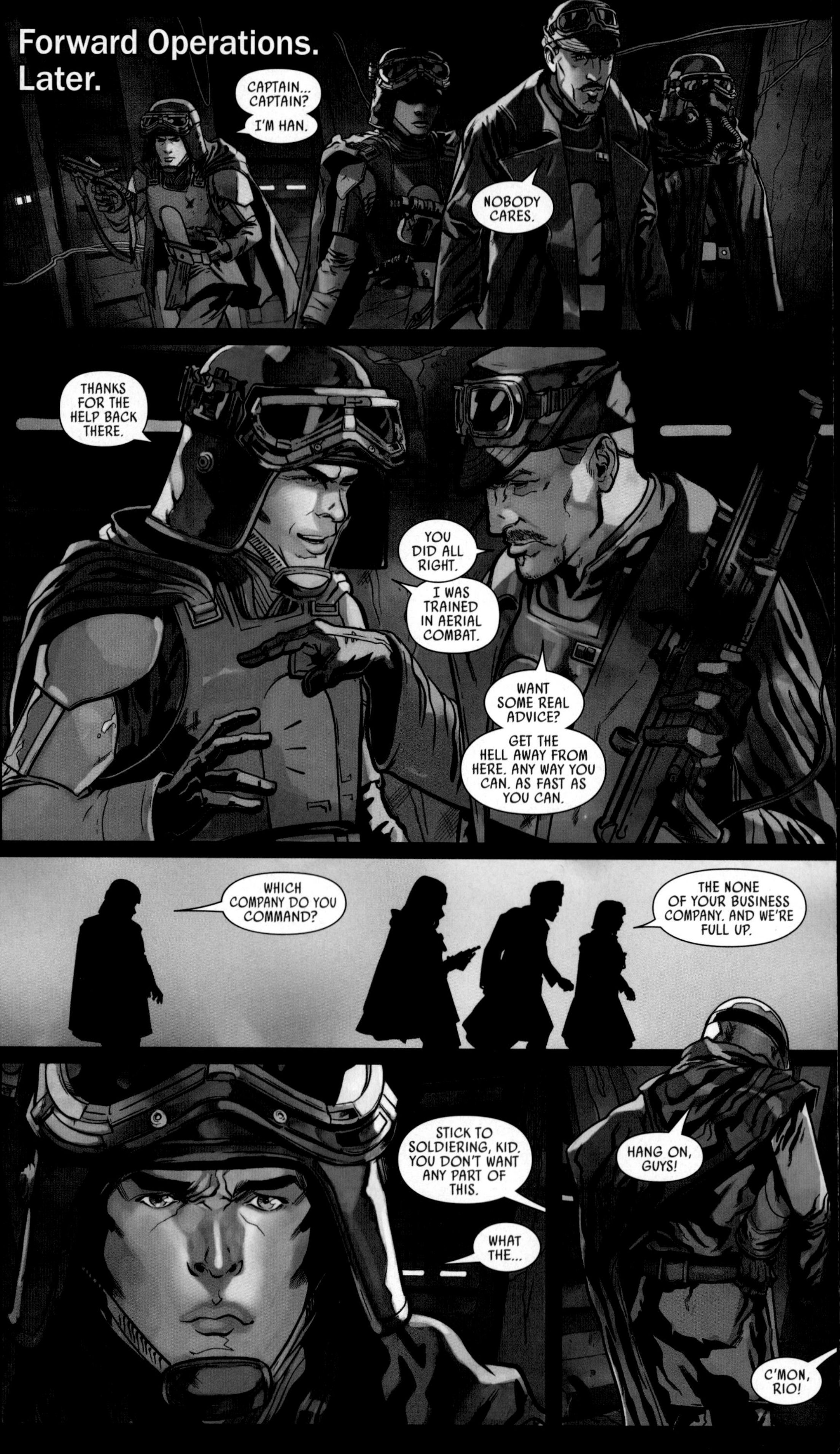
Forward Operations.
Later.
CAPTAIN... CAPTAIN?
I'M HAN.
NOBODY CARES.
THANKS FOR THE HELP BACK THERE.
YOU DID ALL RIGHT.
I WAS TRAINED IN AERIAL COMBAT.
WANT SOME REAL ADVICE?
GET THE HELL AWAY FROM HERE. ANY WAY YOU CAN. AS FAST AS YOU CAN.
WHICH COMPANY DO YOU COMMAND?
THE NONE OF YOUR BUSINESS COMPANY. AND WE'RE FULL UP.
STICK TO SOLDIERING, KID. YOU DON'T WANT ANY PART OF THIS.
WHAT THE...
HANG ON, GUYS!
C'MON, RIO!

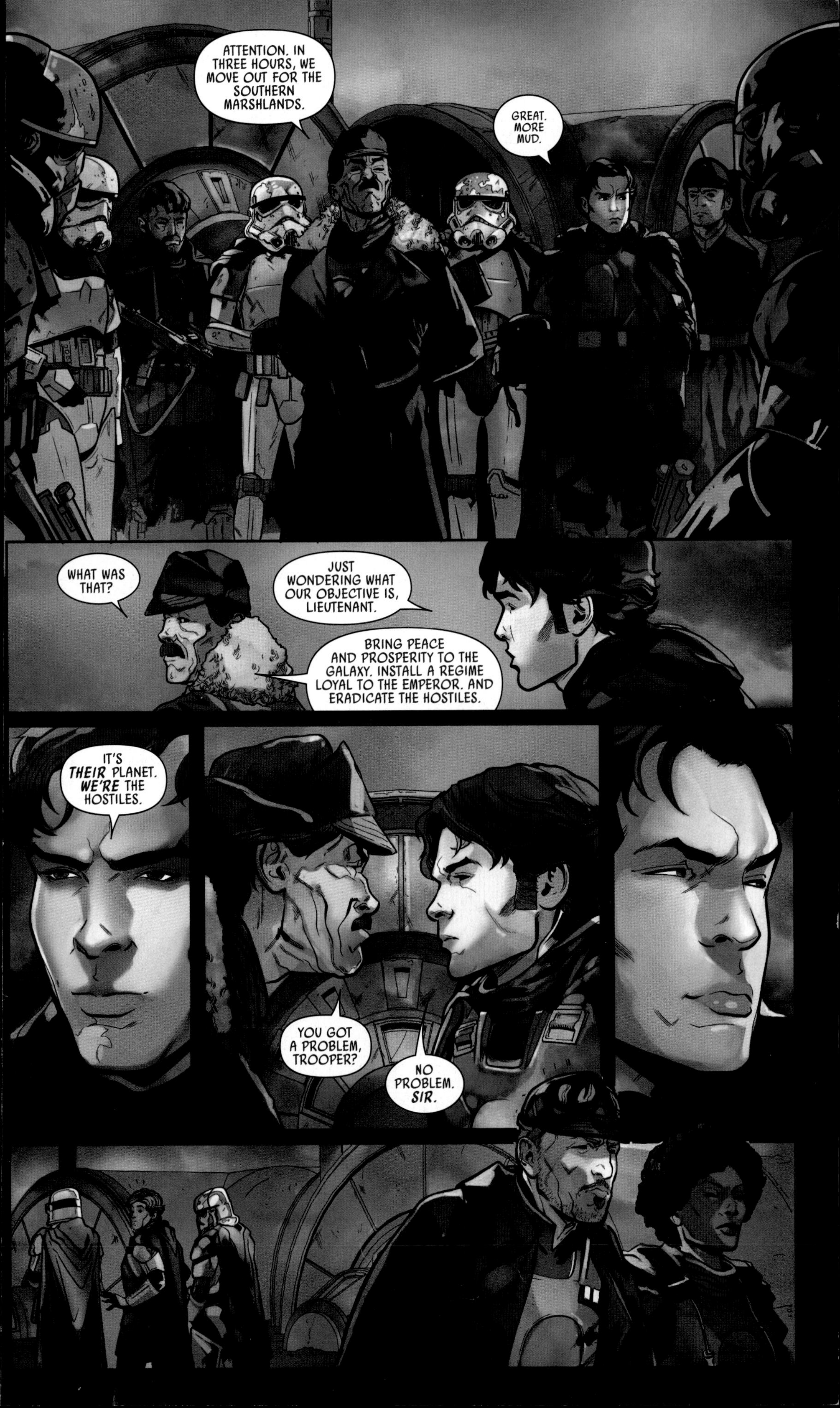
ATTENTION. IN THREE HOURS, WE MOVE OUT FOR THE SOUTHERN MARSHLANDS.
GREAT. MORE MUD.
WHAT WAS THAT?
JUST WONDERING WHAT OUR OBJECTIVE IS, LIEUTENANT.
BRING PEACE AND PROSPERITY TO THE GALAXY. INSTALL A REGIME LOYAL TO THE EMPEROR. AND ERADICATE THE HOSTILES.
IT'S *THEIR* PLANET. *WE'RE* THE HOSTILES.
YOU GOT A PROBLEM, TROOPER?
NO PROBLEM. *SIR*.

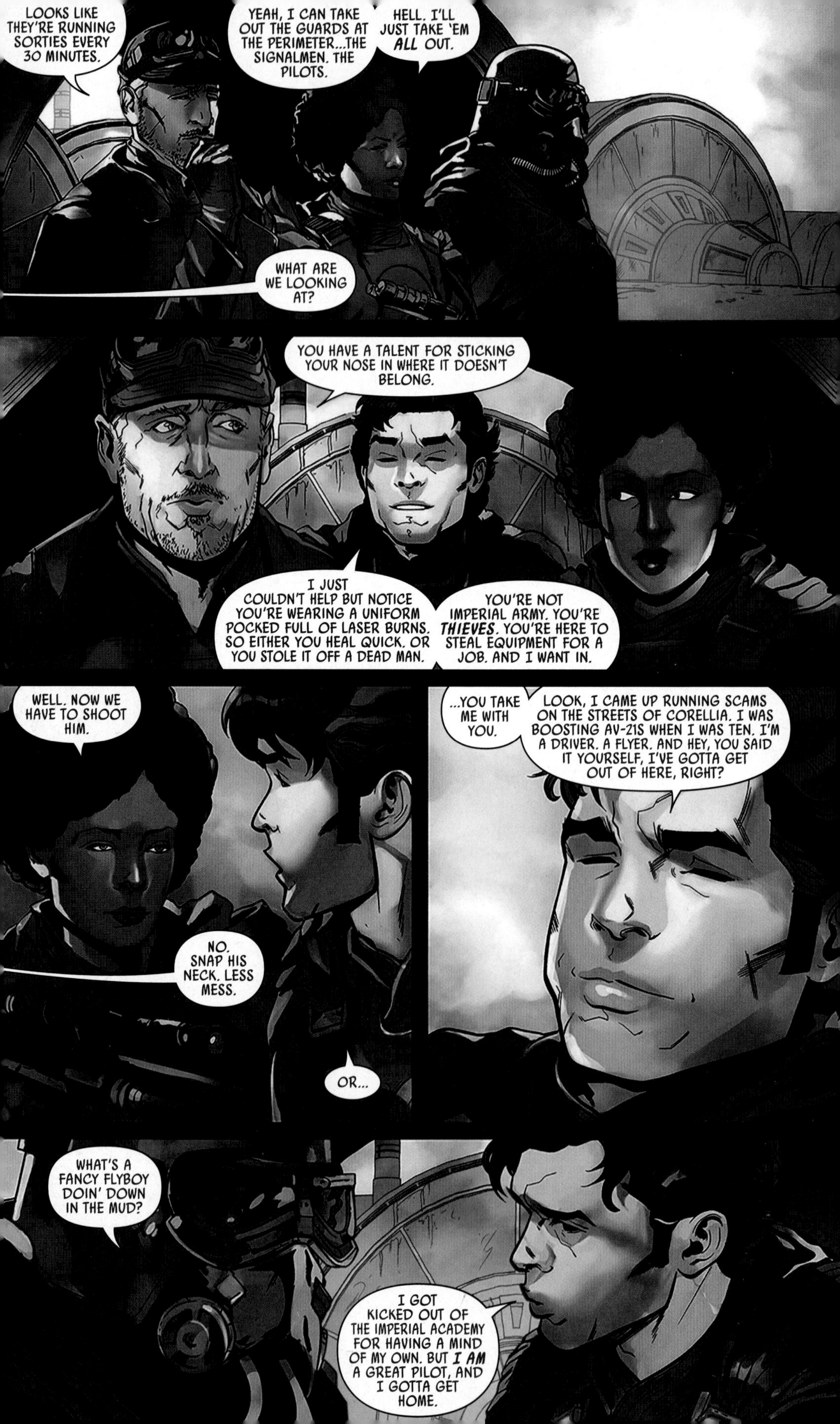
LOOKS LIKE THEY'RE RUNNING SORTIES EVERY 30 MINUTES.
YEAH, I CAN TAKE OUT THE GUARDS AT THE PERIMETER...THE SIGNALMEN. THE PILOTS.
HELL. I'LL JUST TAKE 'EM ALL OUT.
WHAT ARE WE LOOKING AT?
YOU HAVE A TALENT FOR STICKING YOUR NOSE IN WHERE IT DOESN'T BELONG.
I JUST COULDN'T HELP BUT NOTICE YOU'RE WEARING A UNIFORM POCKED FULL OF LASER BURNS. SO EITHER YOU HEAL QUICK. OR YOU STOLE IT OFF A DEAD MAN.
YOU'RE NOT IMPERIAL ARMY. YOU'RE THIEVES. YOU'RE HERE TO STEAL EQUIPMENT FOR A JOB. AND I WANT IN.
WELL. NOW WE HAVE TO SHOOT HIM.
NO. SNAP HIS NECK. LESS MESS.
OR...
...YOU TAKE ME WITH YOU.
LOOK, I CAME UP RUNNING SCAMS ON THE STREETS OF CORELLIA. I WAS BOOSTING AV-21S WHEN I WAS TEN. I'M A DRIVER. A FLYER. AND HEY, YOU SAID IT YOURSELF, I'VE GOTTA GET OUT OF HERE, RIGHT?
WHAT'S A FANCY FLYBOY DOIN' DOWN IN THE MUD?
I GOT KICKED OUT OF THE IMPERIAL ACADEMY FOR HAVING A MIND OF MY OWN. BUT I AM A GREAT PILOT, AND I GOTTA GET HOME.

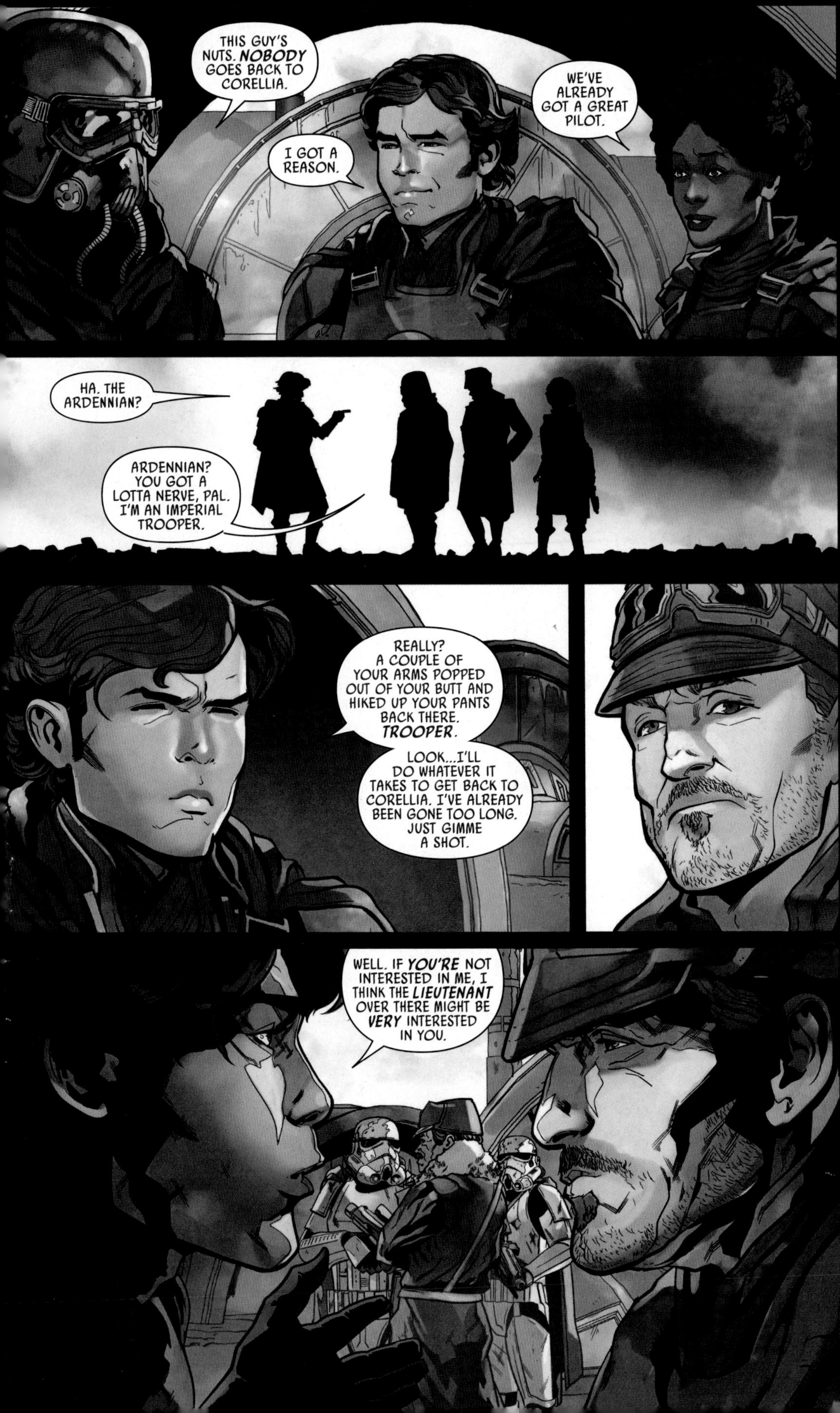
THIS GUY'S NUTS. **NOBODY** GOES BACK TO CORELLIA.
I GOT A REASON.
WE'VE ALREADY GOT A GREAT PILOT.
HA. THE ARDENNIAN?
ARDENNIAN? YOU GOT A LOTTA NERVE, PAL. I'M AN IMPERIAL TROOPER.
REALLY? A COUPLE OF YOUR ARMS POPPED OUT OF YOUR BUTT AND HIKED UP YOUR PANTS BACK THERE. **TROOPER**.
LOOK...I'LL DO WHATEVER IT TAKES TO GET BACK TO CORELLIA. I'VE ALREADY BEEN GONE TOO LONG. JUST GIMME A SHOT.
WELL. IF **YOU'RE** NOT INTERESTED IN ME, I THINK THE **LIEUTENANT** OVER THERE MIGHT BE **VERY** INTERESTED IN YOU.

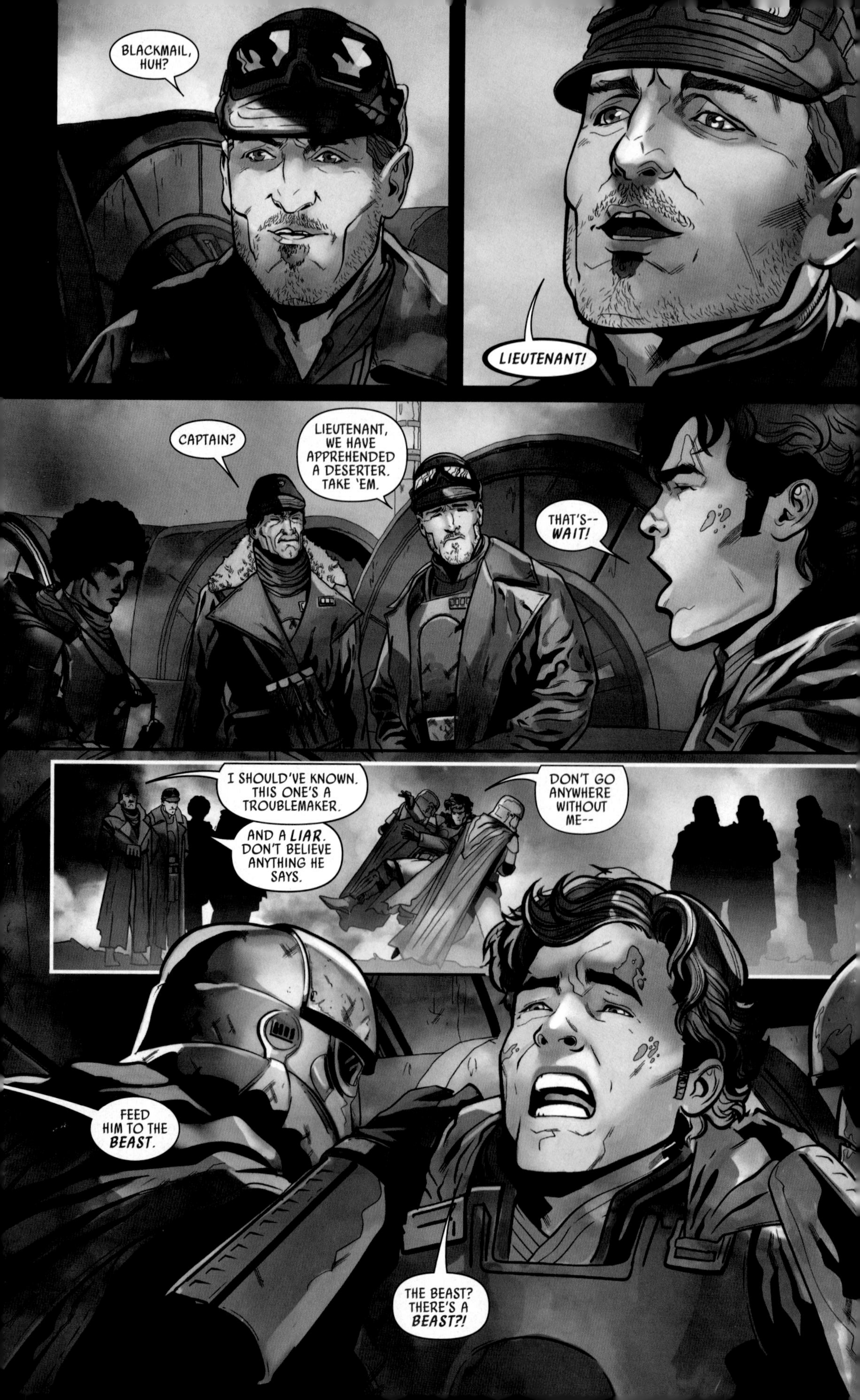
BLACKMAIL, HUH?
LIEUTENANT!
CAPTAIN?
LIEUTENANT, WE HAVE APPREHENDED A DESERTER. TAKE 'EM.
THAT'S-- WAIT!
I SHOULD'VE KNOWN. THIS ONE'S A TROUBLEMAKER.
AND A LIAR. DON'T BELIEVE ANYTHING HE SAYS.
DON'T GO ANYWHERE WITHOUT ME--
FEED HIM TO THE BEAST.
THE BEAST? THERE'S A BEAST?!

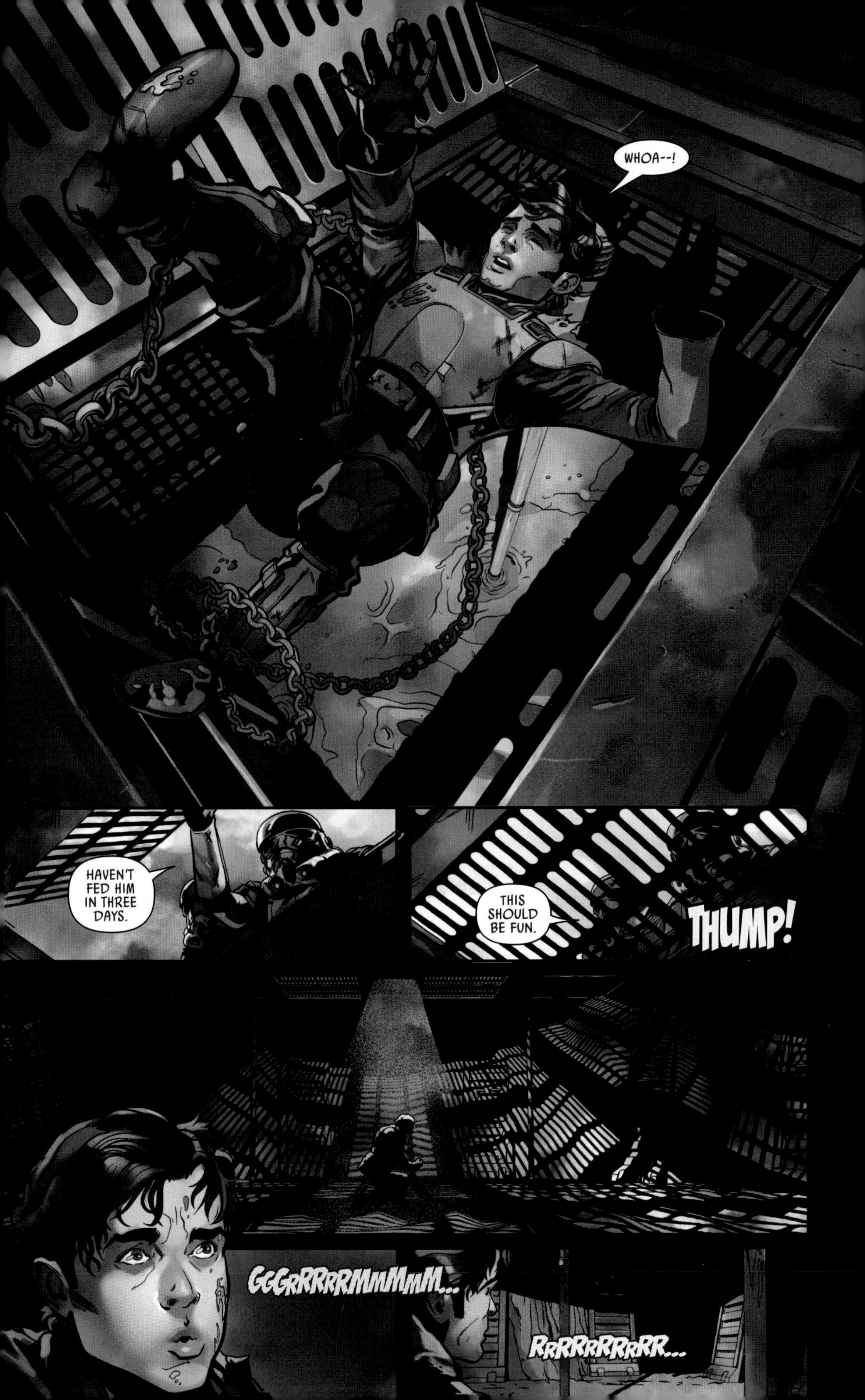
WHOA--!
HAVEN'T FED HIM IN THREE DAYS.
THIS SHOULD BE FUN.
THUMP!
GGGRRRRRMMMMM...
RRRRRRRRRR...

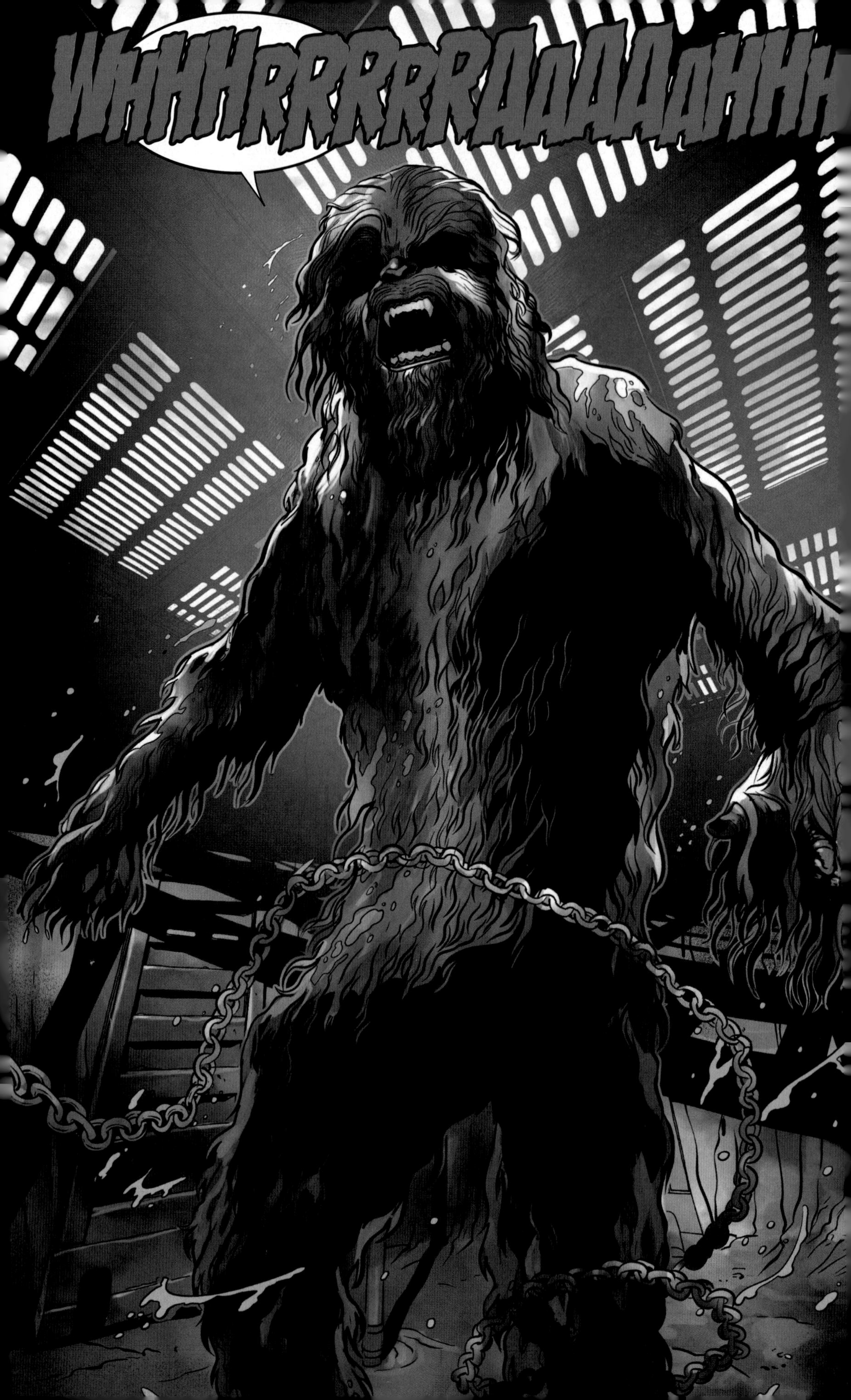
WHHHRRRRRAAAAAHHH

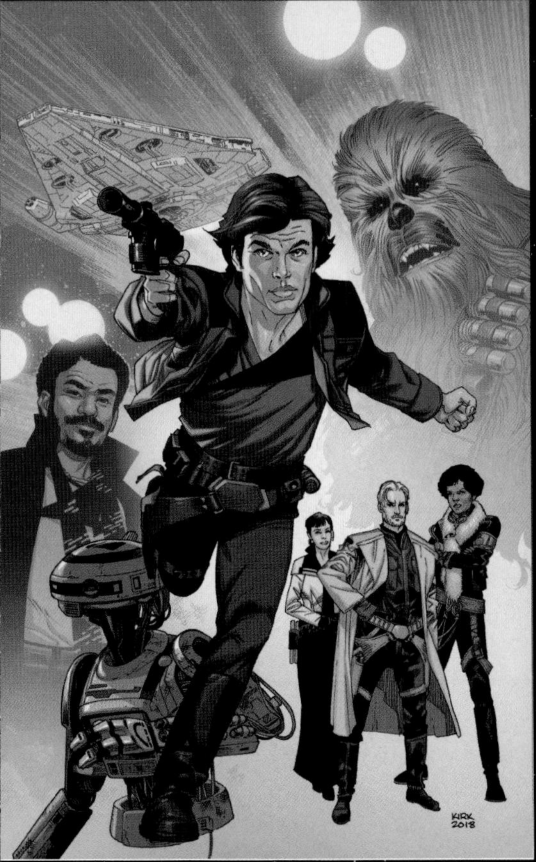
KIRK
2018

Issue #1 variant by Leonard Kirk & Dave McCaig

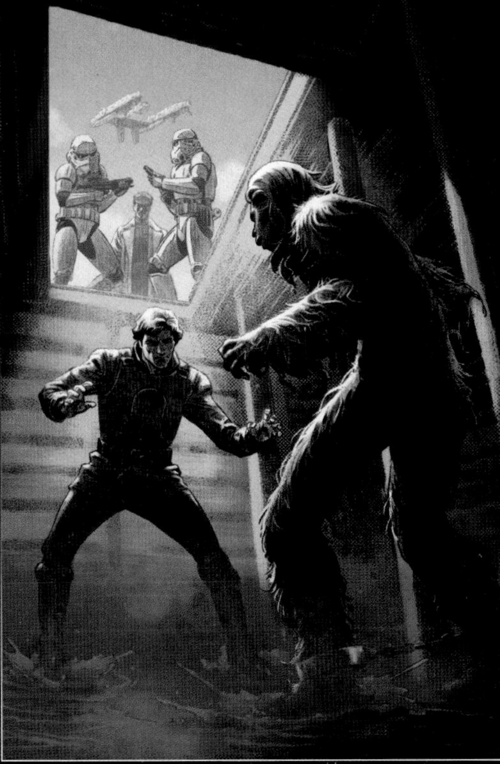

Issue #1 variant by Luke Ross & Nolan Woodard

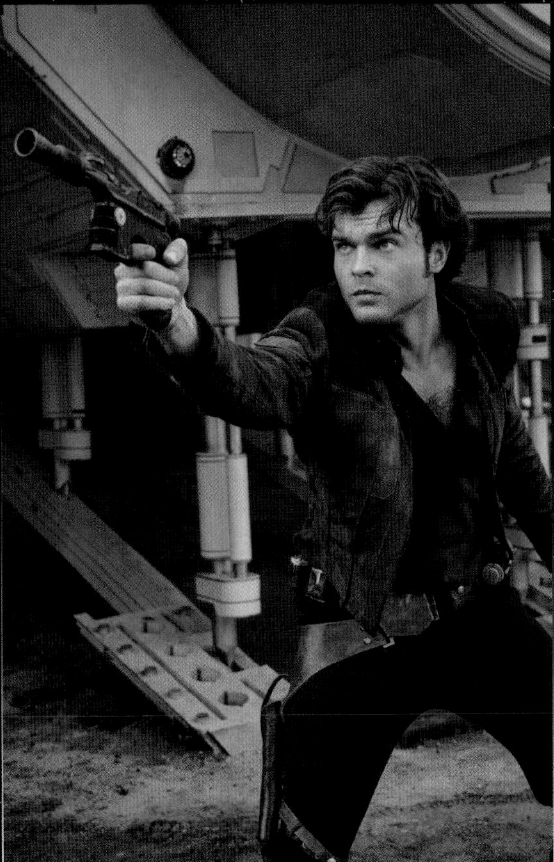

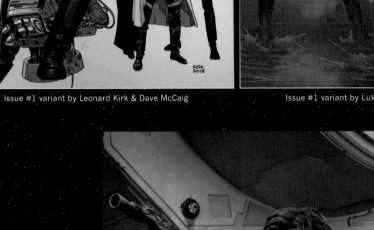

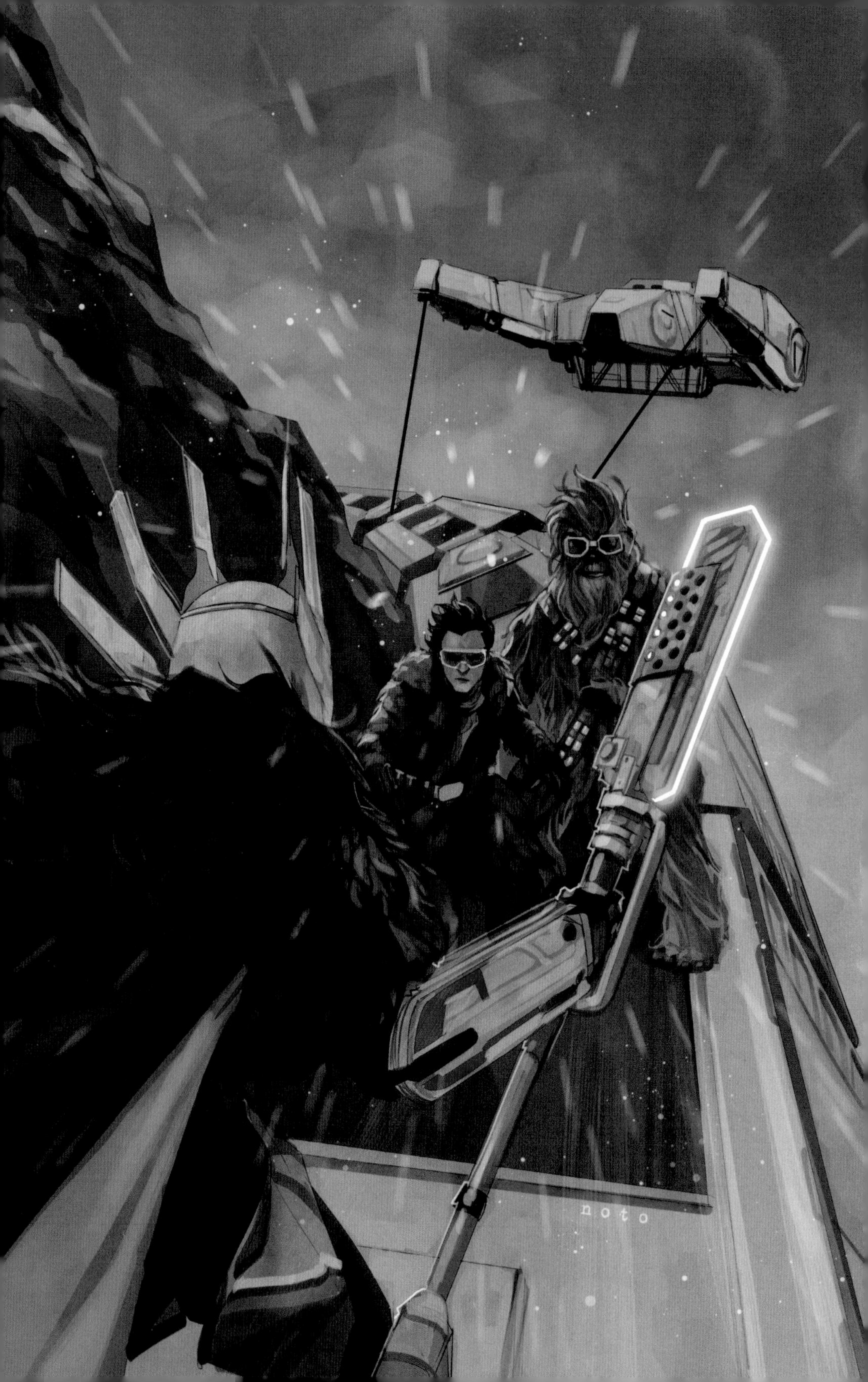
noto

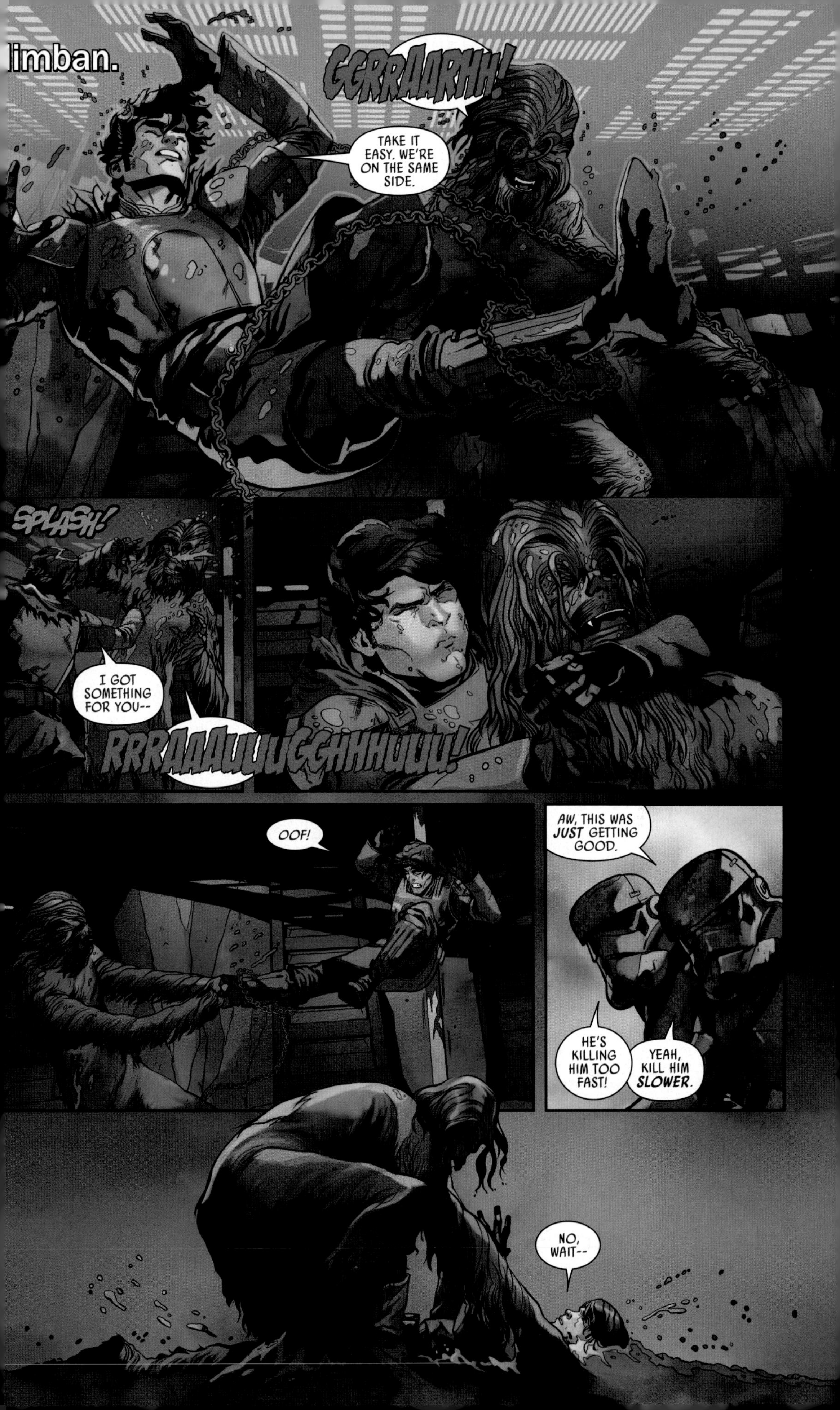
limban.
GGRRAARHH!
TAKE IT EASY. WE'RE ON THE SAME SIDE.
SPLASH!
I GOT SOMETHING FOR YOU--
RRRAAAUUUGGHHUUU!
OOF!
AW, THIS WAS JUST GETTING GOOD.
HE'S KILLING HIM TOO FAST!
YEAH, KILL HIM SLOWER.
NO, WAIT--

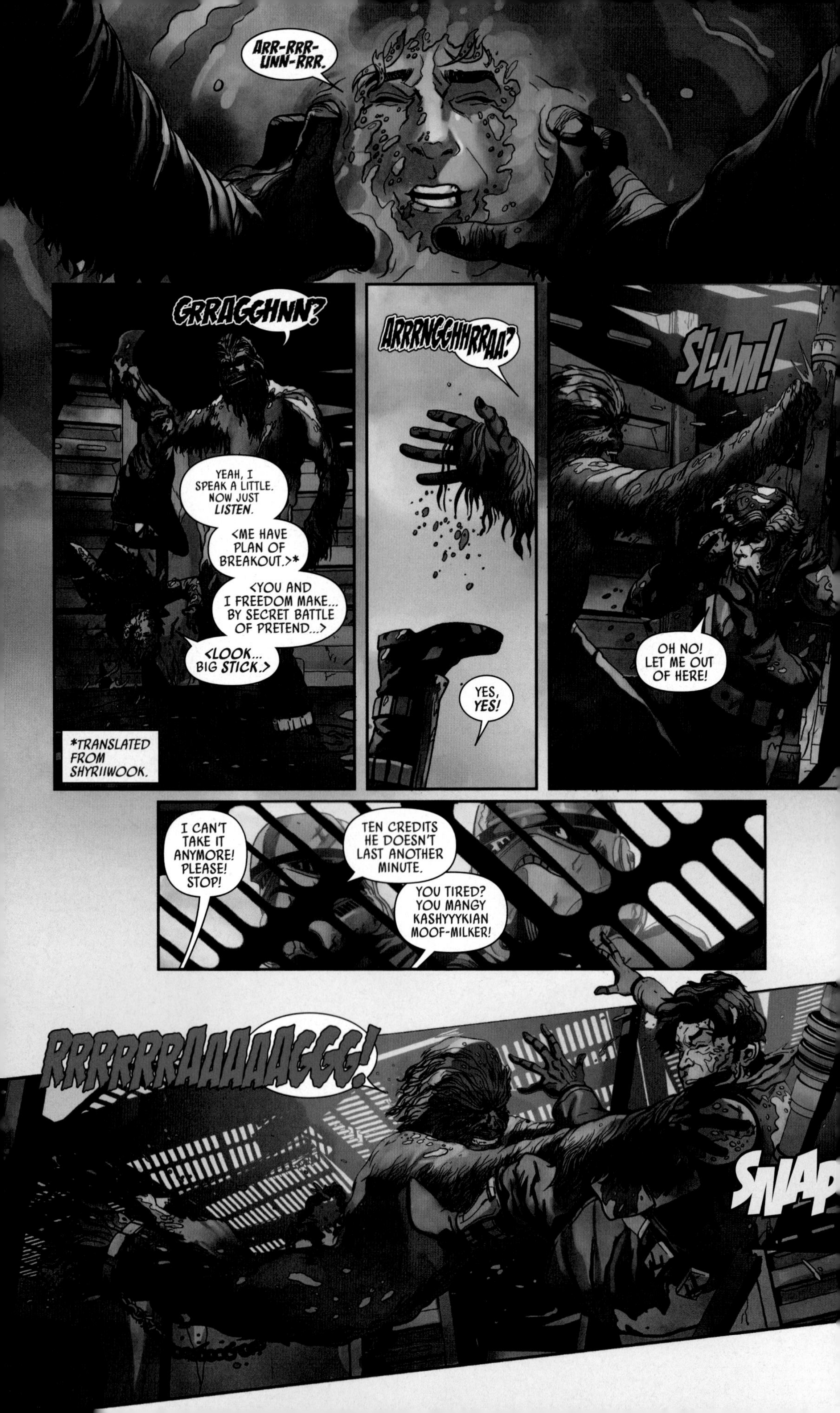
ARR-RRR-UNN-RRR.
GRRAGGHNN?
YEAH, I SPEAK A LITTLE. NOW JUST LISTEN.
<ME HAVE PLAN OF BREAKOUT.>*
<YOU AND I FREEDOM MAKE... BY SECRET BATTLE OF PRETEND...>
<LOOK... BIG STICK.>
*TRANSLATED FROM SHYRIIWOOK.
ARRRNGGHHRRAA?
YES, YES!
SLAM!
OH NO! LET ME OUT OF HERE!
I CAN'T TAKE IT ANYMORE! PLEASE! STOP!
TEN CREDITS HE DOESN'T LAST ANOTHER MINUTE.
YOU TIRED? YOU MANGY KASHYYYKIAN MOOF-MILKER!
RRRRRRAAAAAGGG!
SNAP

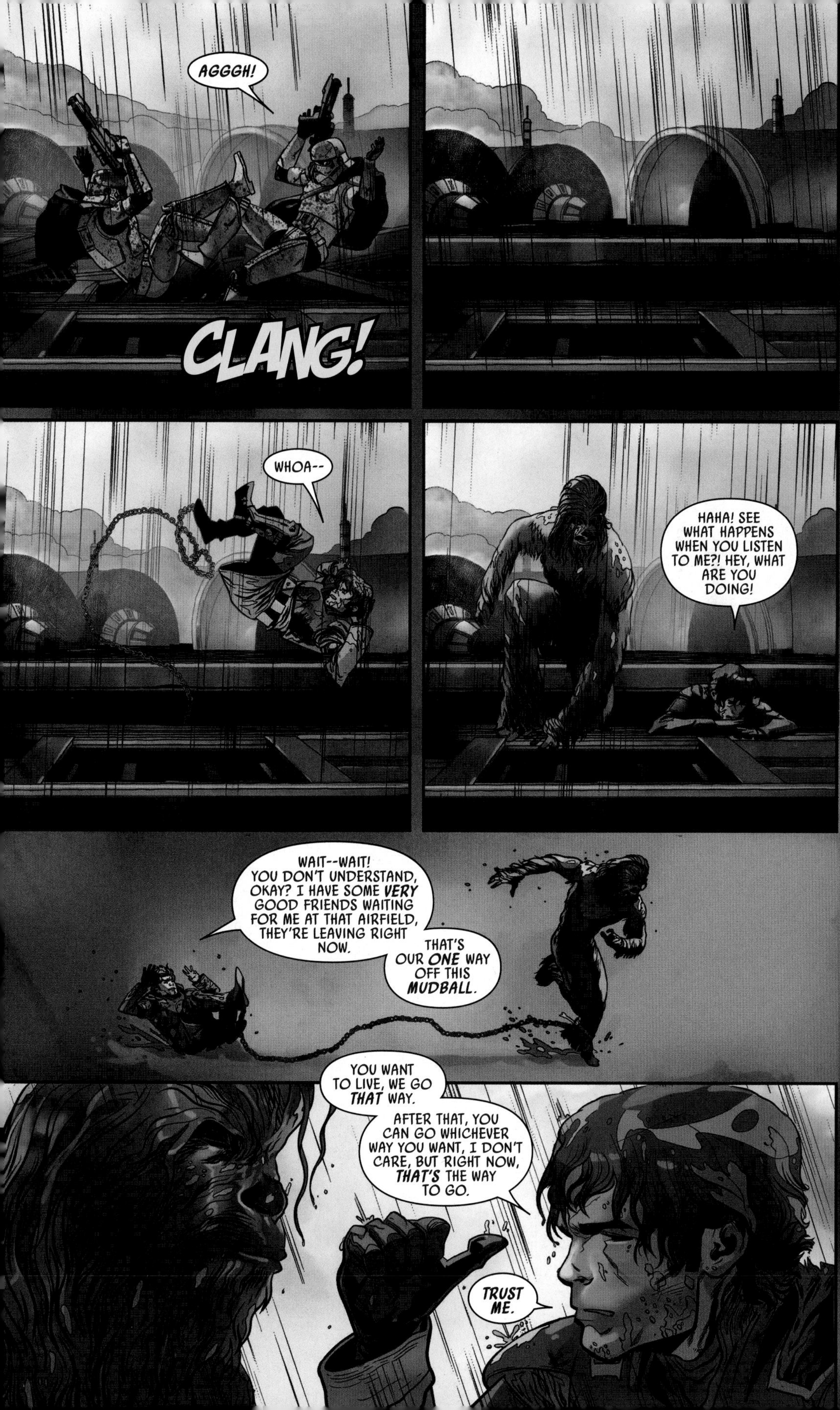
AGGGH!
CLANG!
WHOA--
HAHA! SEE WHAT HAPPENS WHEN YOU LISTEN TO ME?! HEY, WHAT ARE YOU DOING!
WAIT--WAIT! YOU DON'T UNDERSTAND, OKAY? I HAVE SOME VERY GOOD FRIENDS WAITING FOR ME AT THAT AIRFIELD, THEY'RE LEAVING RIGHT NOW.
THAT'S OUR ONE WAY OFF THIS MUDBALL.
YOU WANT TO LIVE, WE GO THAT WAY.
AFTER THAT, YOU CAN GO WHICHEVER WAY YOU WANT, I DON'T CARE, BUT RIGHT NOW, THAT'S THE WAY TO GO.
TRUST ME.

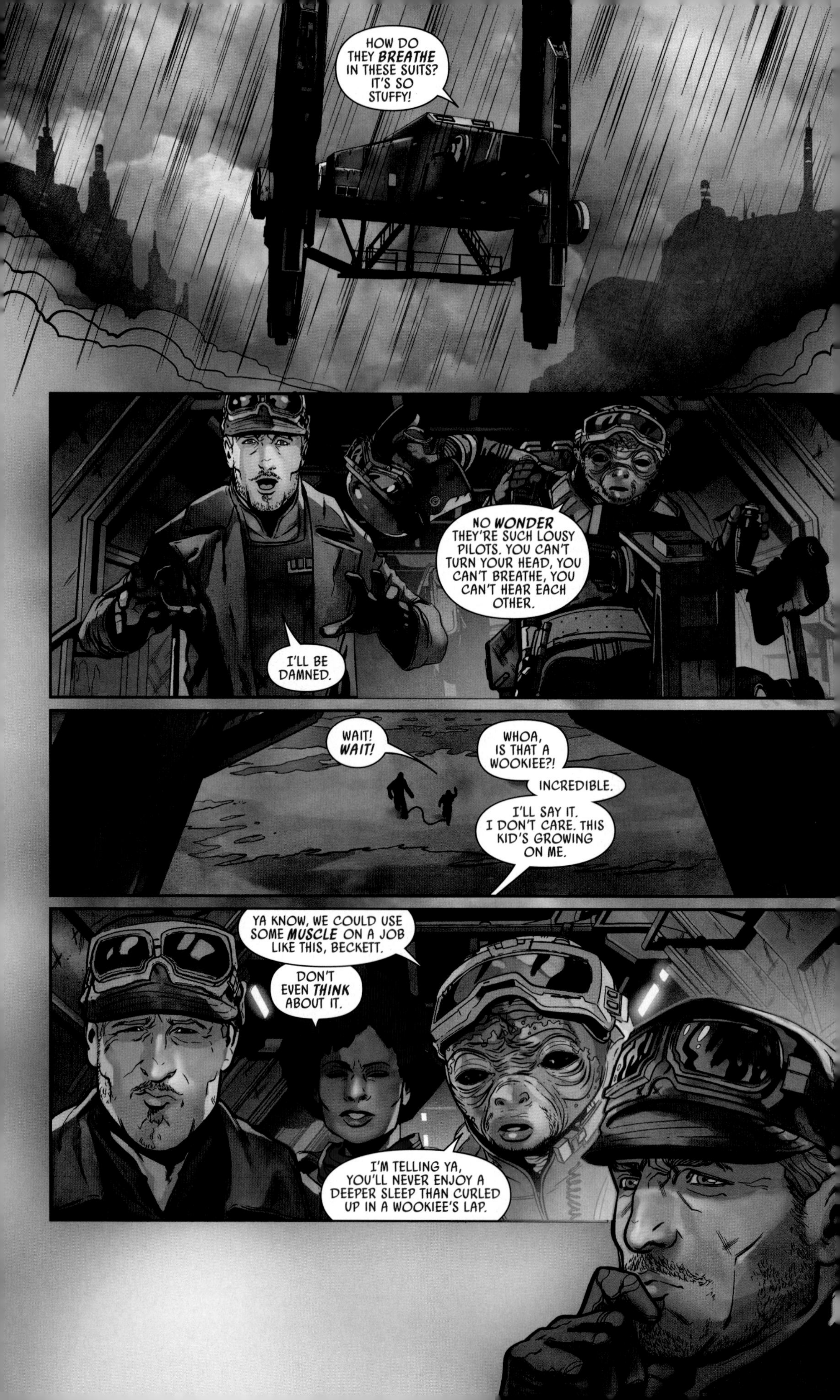

HOW DO THEY BREATHE IN THESE SUITS? IT'S SO STUFFY!
NO WONDER THEY'RE SUCH LOUSY PILOTS. YOU CAN'T TURN YOUR HEAD, YOU CAN'T BREATHE, YOU CAN'T HEAR EACH OTHER.
I'LL BE DAMNED.
WAIT! WAIT!
WHOA, IS THAT A WOOKIEE?!
INCREDIBLE.
I'LL SAY IT. I DON'T CARE. THIS KID'S GROWING ON ME.
YA KNOW, WE COULD USE SOME MUSCLE ON A JOB LIKE THIS, BECKETT.
DON'T EVEN THINK ABOUT IT.
I'M TELLING YA, YOU'LL NEVER ENJOY A DEEPER SLEEP THAN CURLED UP IN A WOOKIEE'S LAP.

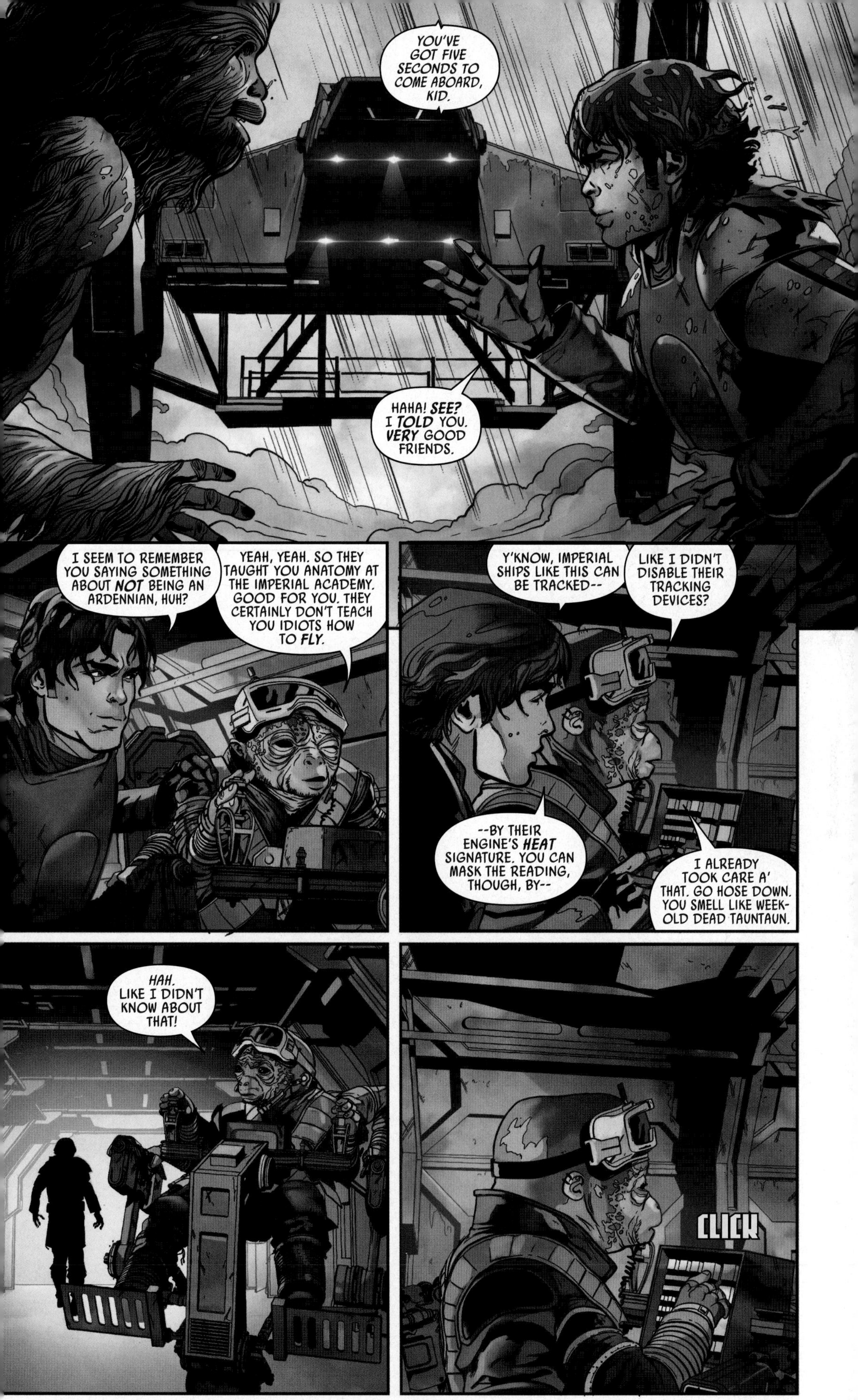
YOU'VE GOT FIVE SECONDS TO COME ABOARD, KID.
HAHA! SEE? I TOLD YOU. VERY GOOD FRIENDS.
I SEEM TO REMEMBER YOU SAYING SOMETHING ABOUT NOT BEING AN ARDENNIAN, HUH?
YEAH, YEAH. SO THEY TAUGHT YOU ANATOMY AT THE IMPERIAL ACADEMY. GOOD FOR YOU. THEY CERTAINLY DON'T TEACH YOU IDIOTS HOW TO FLY.
Y'KNOW, IMPERIAL SHIPS LIKE THIS CAN BE TRACKED--
LIKE I DIDN'T DISABLE THEIR TRACKING DEVICES?
--BY THEIR ENGINE'S HEAT SIGNATURE. YOU CAN MASK THE READING, THOUGH, BY--
I ALREADY TOOK CARE A' THAT. GO HOSE DOWN. YOU SMELL LIKE WEEK-OLD DEAD TAUNTAUN.
HAH. LIKE I DIDN'T KNOW ABOUT THAT!
CLICK

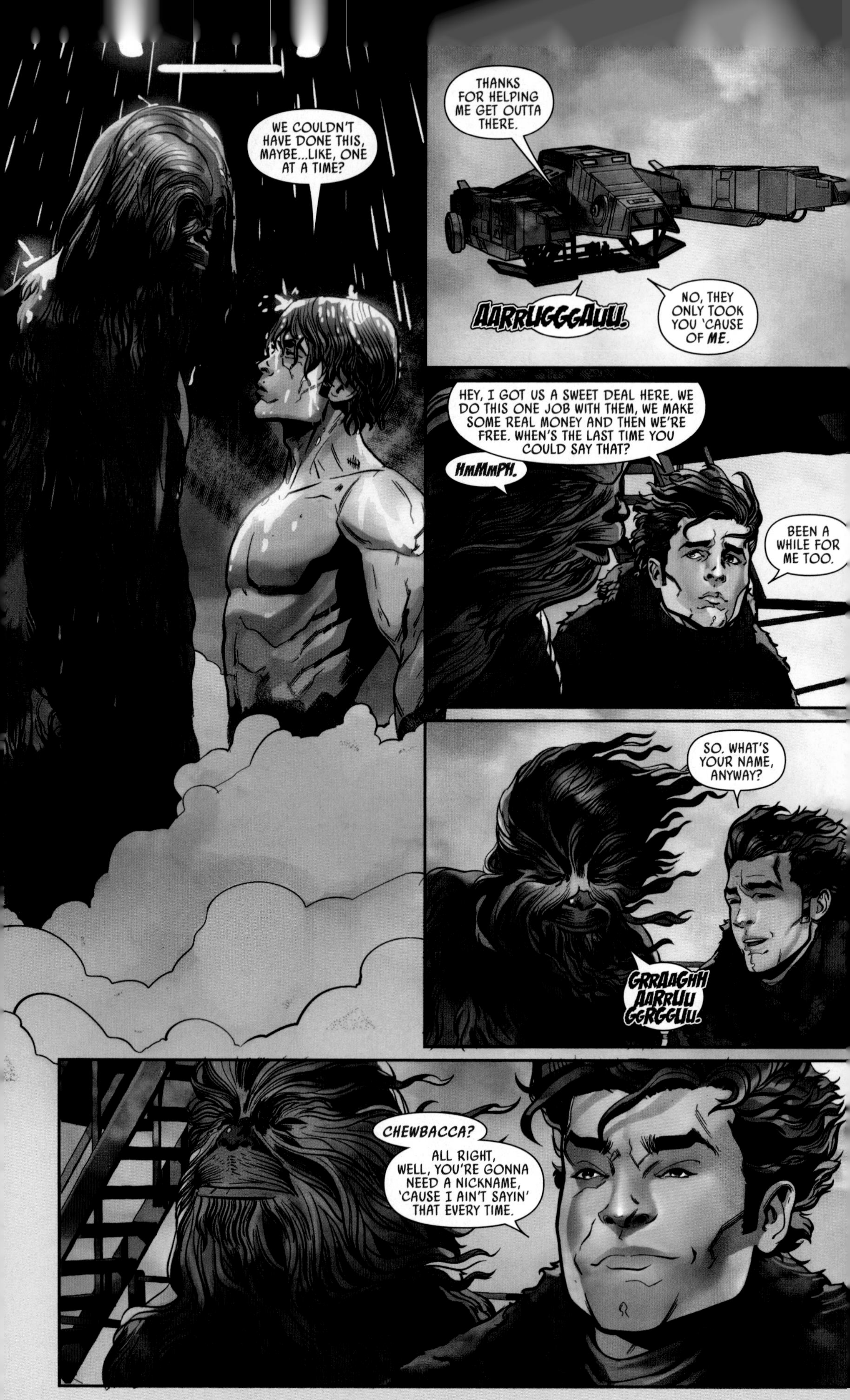
WE COULDN'T HAVE DONE THIS, MAYBE...LIKE, ONE AT A TIME?
THANKS FOR HELPING ME GET OUTTA THERE.
AARRUGGGAUU.
NO, THEY ONLY TOOK YOU 'CAUSE OF ME.
HEY, I GOT US A SWEET DEAL HERE. WE DO THIS ONE JOB WITH THEM, WE MAKE SOME REAL MONEY AND THEN WE'RE FREE. WHEN'S THE LAST TIME YOU COULD SAY THAT?
HMMMPH.
BEEN A WHILE FOR ME TOO.
SO. WHAT'S YOUR NAME, ANYWAY?
GRRAAGHH AARRUU GGRGGUU.
CHEWBACCA?
ALL RIGHT, WELL, YOU'RE GONNA NEED A NICKNAME, 'CAUSE I AIN'T SAYIN' THAT EVERY TIME.

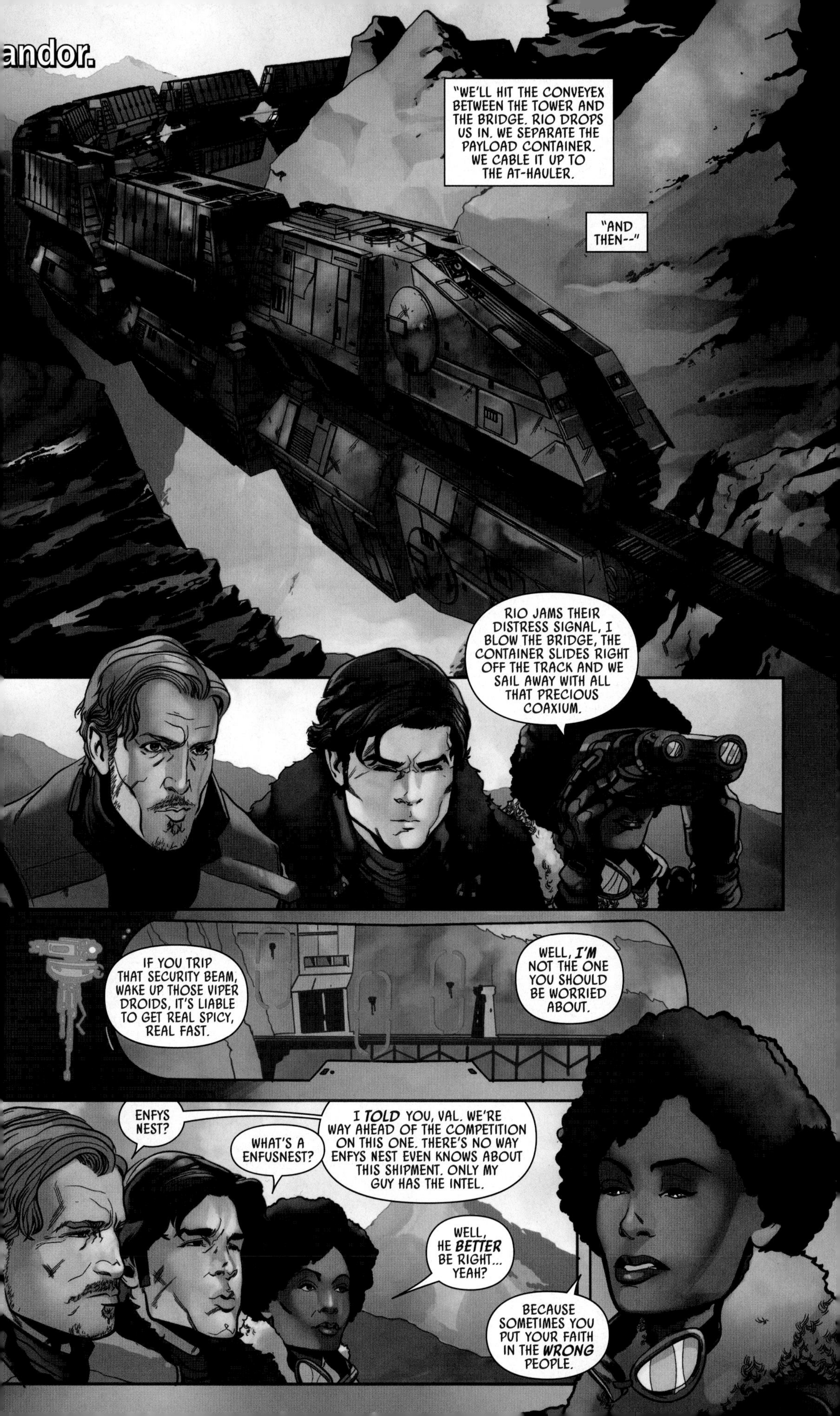
andor.
"WE'LL HIT THE CONVEYEX BETWEEN THE TOWER AND THE BRIDGE. RIO DROPS US IN. WE SEPARATE THE PAYLOAD CONTAINER. WE CABLE IT UP TO THE AT-HAULER.
"AND THEN--"
RIO JAMS THEIR DISTRESS SIGNAL, I BLOW THE BRIDGE, THE CONTAINER SLIDES RIGHT OFF THE TRACK AND WE SAIL AWAY WITH ALL THAT PRECIOUS COAXIUM.
IF YOU TRIP THAT SECURITY BEAM, WAKE UP THOSE VIPER DROIDS, IT'S LIABLE TO GET REAL SPICY, REAL FAST.
WELL, *I'M* NOT THE ONE YOU SHOULD BE WORRIED ABOUT.
ENFYS NEST?
WHAT'S A ENFUSNEST?
I *TOLD* YOU, VAL. WE'RE WAY AHEAD OF THE COMPETITION ON THIS ONE. THERE'S NO WAY ENFYS NEST EVEN KNOWS ABOUT THIS SHIPMENT. ONLY MY GUY HAS THE INTEL.
WELL, HE *BETTER* BE RIGHT... YEAH?
BECAUSE SOMETIMES YOU PUT YOUR FAITH IN THE *WRONG* PEOPLE.

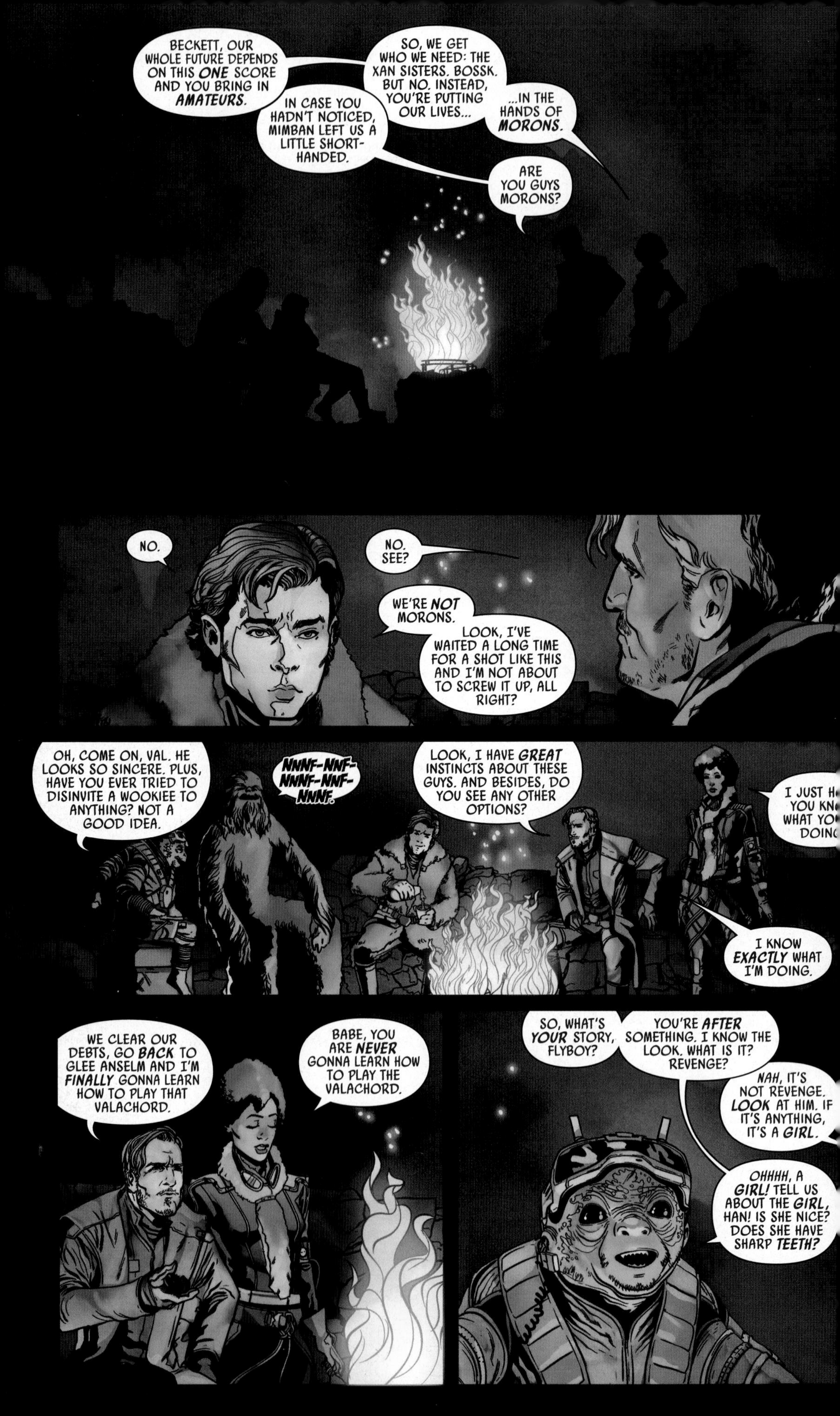
BECKETT, OUR WHOLE FUTURE DEPENDS ON THIS ONE SCORE AND YOU BRING IN AMATEURS.
IN CASE YOU HADN'T NOTICED, MIMBAN LEFT US A LITTLE SHORT-HANDED.
SO, WE GET WHO WE NEED: THE XAN SISTERS. BOSSK. BUT NO. INSTEAD, YOU'RE PUTTING OUR LIVES...
...IN THE HANDS OF MORONS.
ARE YOU GUYS MORONS?
NO.
NO. SEE?
WE'RE NOT MORONS.
LOOK, I'VE WAITED A LONG TIME FOR A SHOT LIKE THIS AND I'M NOT ABOUT TO SCREW IT UP, ALL RIGHT?
OH, COME ON, VAL. HE LOOKS SO SINCERE. PLUS, HAVE YOU EVER TRIED TO DISINVITE A WOOKIEE TO ANYTHING? NOT A GOOD IDEA.
NNNF-NNF-NNNF-NNF-NNNF.
LOOK, I HAVE GREAT INSTINCTS ABOUT THESE GUYS. AND BESIDES, DO YOU SEE ANY OTHER OPTIONS?
I KNOW EXACTLY WHAT I'M DOING.
WE CLEAR OUR DEBTS, GO BACK TO GLEE ANSELM AND I'M FINALLY GONNA LEARN HOW TO PLAY THAT VALACHORD.
BABE, YOU ARE NEVER GONNA LEARN HOW TO PLAY THE VALACHORD.
SO, WHAT'S YOUR STORY, FLYBOY?
YOU'RE AFTER SOMETHING. I KNOW THE LOOK. WHAT IS IT? REVENGE?
NAH, IT'S NOT REVENGE. LOOK AT HIM. IF IT'S ANYTHING, IT'S A GIRL.
OHHHH, A GIRL! TELL US ABOUT THE GIRL, HAN! IS SHE NICE? DOES SHE HAVE SHARP TEETH?

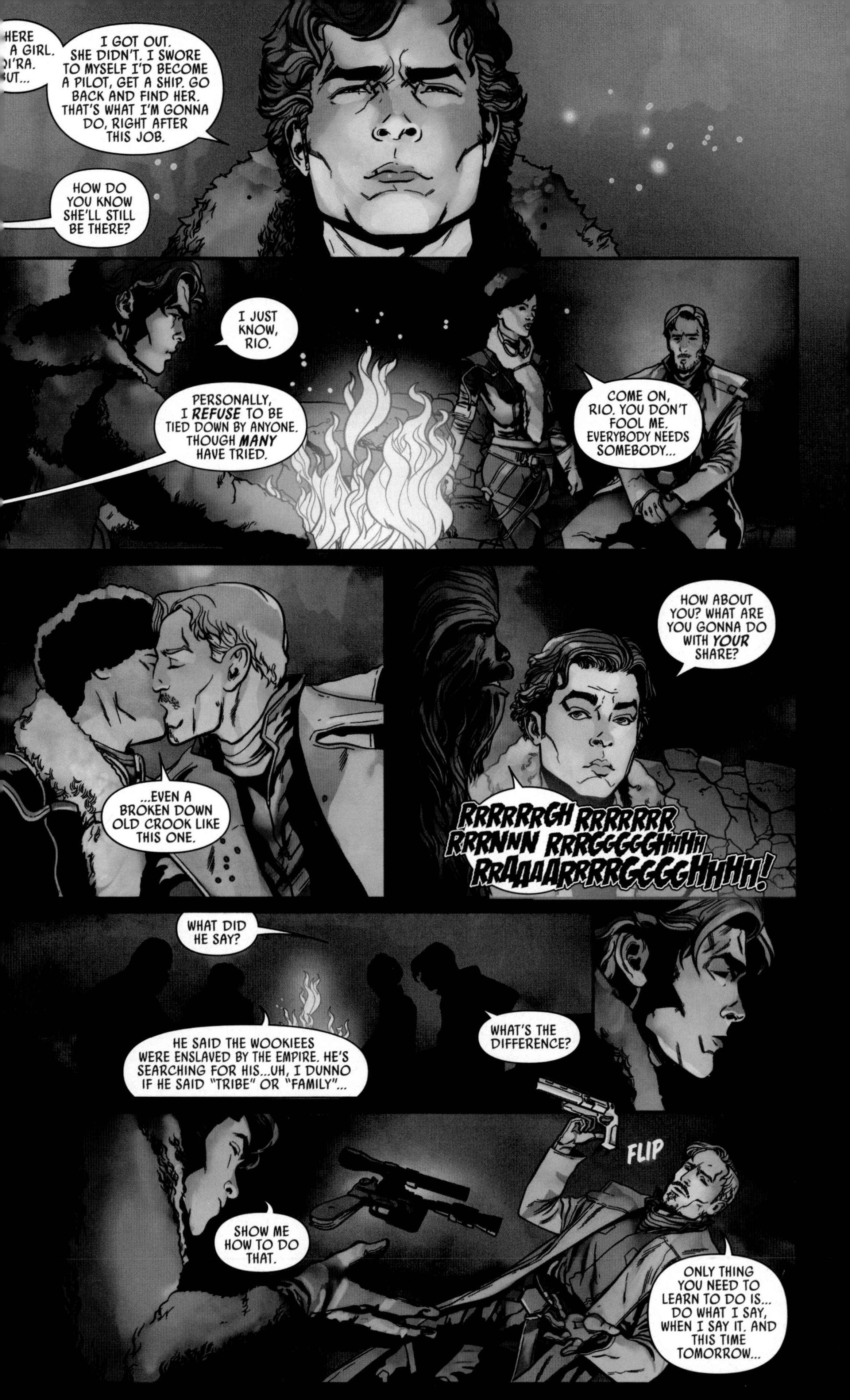

HERE ... A GIRL. QI'RA. BUT...
I GOT OUT. SHE DIDN'T. I SWORE TO MYSELF I'D BECOME A PILOT, GET A SHIP. GO BACK AND FIND HER. THAT'S WHAT I'M GONNA DO, RIGHT AFTER THIS JOB.
HOW DO YOU KNOW SHE'LL STILL BE THERE?
I JUST KNOW, RIO.
PERSONALLY, I REFUSE TO BE TIED DOWN BY ANYONE. THOUGH MANY HAVE TRIED.
COME ON, RIO. YOU DON'T FOOL ME. EVERYBODY NEEDS SOMEBODY...
...EVEN A BROKEN DOWN OLD CROOK LIKE THIS ONE.
HOW ABOUT YOU? WHAT ARE YOU GONNA DO WITH YOUR SHARE?
RRRRRRGH RRRRRRR RRRNNN RRRGGGGGHHHH RRAAAARRRRRGGGGHHHH!
WHAT DID HE SAY?
HE SAID THE WOOKIEES WERE ENSLAVED BY THE EMPIRE. HE'S SEARCHING FOR HIS...UH, I DUNNO IF HE SAID "TRIBE" OR "FAMILY"...
WHAT'S THE DIFFERENCE?
FLIP
SHOW ME HOW TO DO THAT.
ONLY THING YOU NEED TO LEARN TO DO IS... DO WHAT I SAY, WHEN I SAY IT. AND THIS TIME TOMORROW...

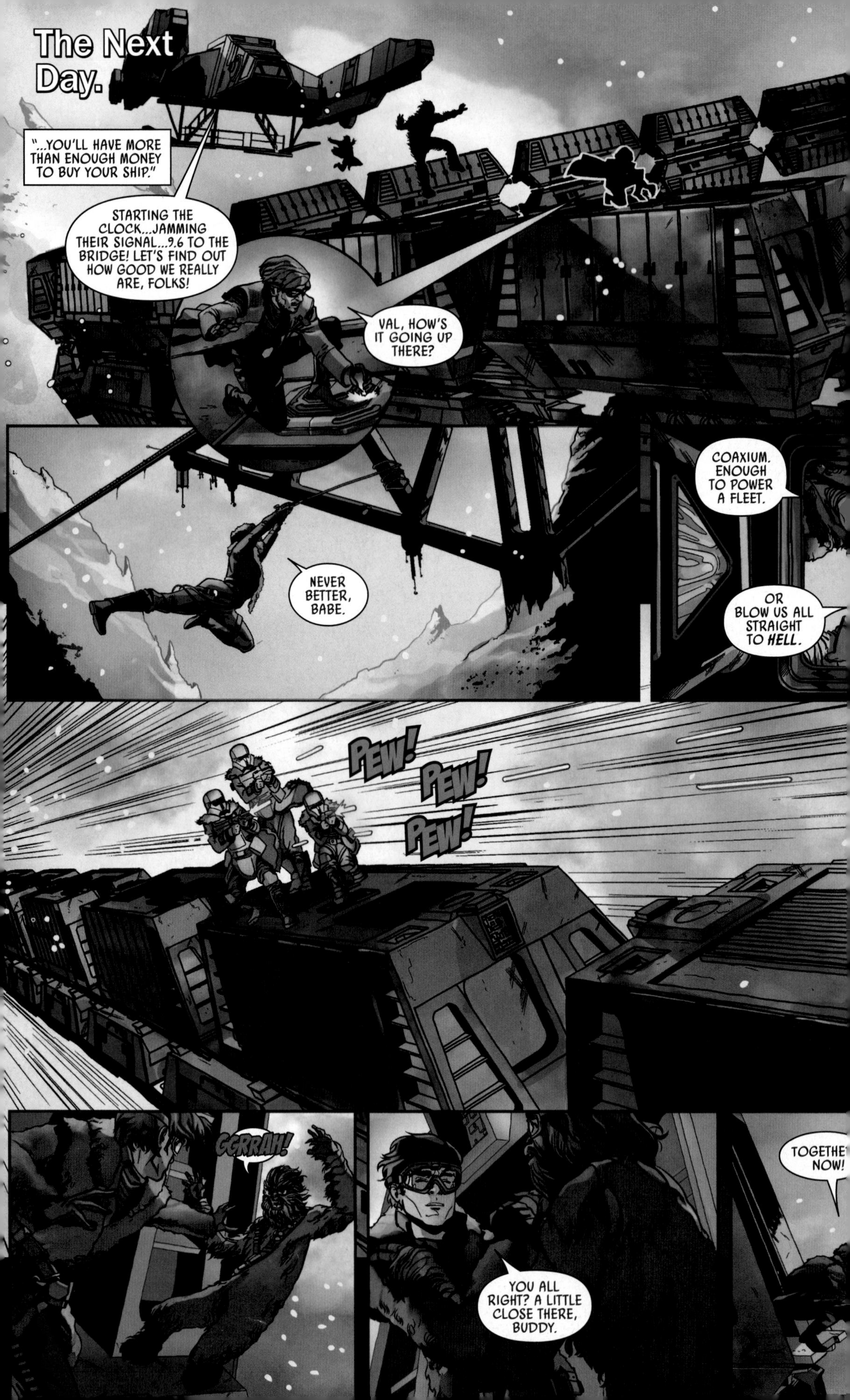
The Next Day.
"...YOU'LL HAVE MORE THAN ENOUGH MONEY TO BUY YOUR SHIP."
STARTING THE CLOCK...JAMMING THEIR SIGNAL...9.6 TO THE BRIDGE! LET'S FIND OUT HOW GOOD WE REALLY ARE, FOLKS!
VAL, HOW'S IT GOING UP THERE?
NEVER BETTER, BABE.
COAXIUM. ENOUGH TO POWER A FLEET.
OR BLOW US ALL STRAIGHT TO HELL.
PEW! PEW! PEW!
GGRRAH!
YOU ALL RIGHT? A LITTLE CLOSE THERE, BUDDY.
TOGETHE NOW!

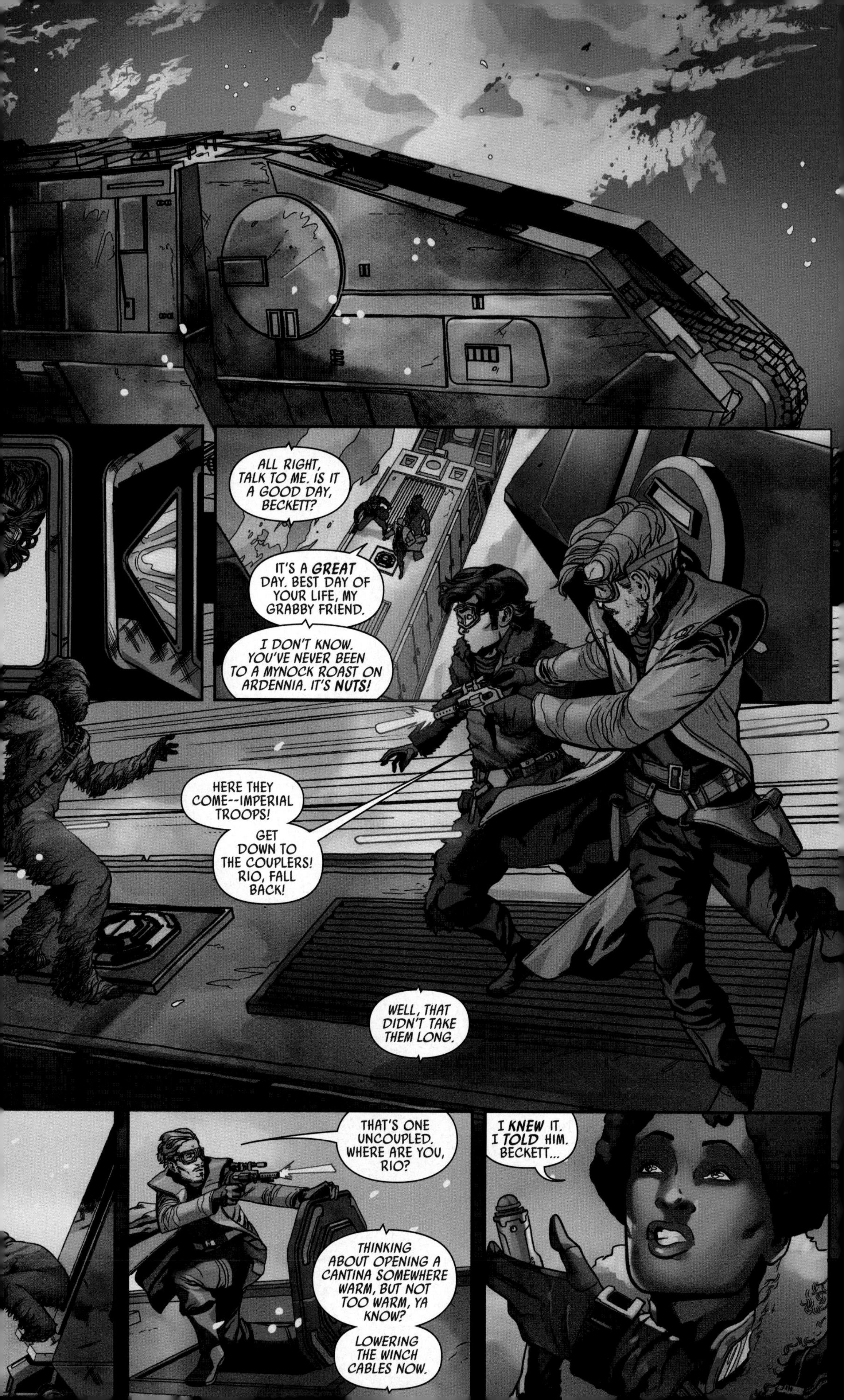
ALL RIGHT, TALK TO ME. IS IT A GOOD DAY, BECKETT?
IT'S A GREAT DAY. BEST DAY OF YOUR LIFE, MY GRABBY FRIEND.
I DON'T KNOW. YOU'VE NEVER BEEN TO A MYNOCK ROAST ON ARDENNIA. IT'S NUTS!
HERE THEY COME--IMPERIAL TROOPS!
GET DOWN TO THE COUPLERS! RIO, FALL BACK!
WELL, THAT DIDN'T TAKE THEM LONG.
THAT'S ONE UNCOUPLED. WHERE ARE YOU, RIO?
THINKING ABOUT OPENING A CANTINA SOMEWHERE WARM, BUT NOT TOO WARM, YA KNOW?
LOWERING THE WINCH CABLES NOW.
I KNEW IT. I TOLD HIM. BECKETT...

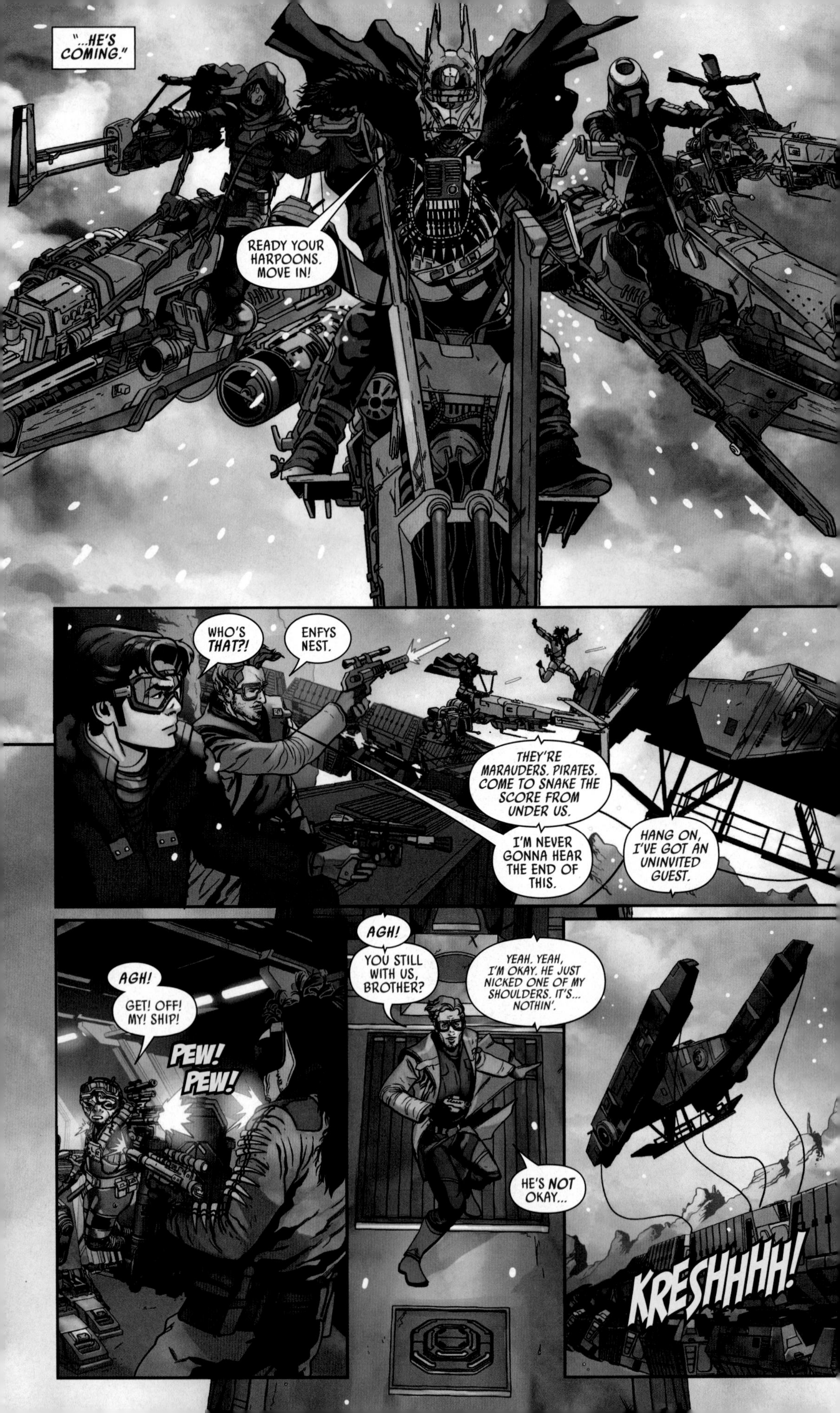
"...HE'S COMING."
READY YOUR HARPOONS. MOVE IN!
WHO'S THAT?!
ENFYS NEST.
THEY'RE MARAUDERS. PIRATES. COME TO SNAKE THE SCORE FROM UNDER US.
I'M NEVER GONNA HEAR THE END OF THIS.
HANG ON, I'VE GOT AN UNINVITED GUEST.
AGH!
GET! OFF! MY! SHIP!
PEW! PEW!
AGH!
YOU STILL WITH US, BROTHER?
YEAH. YEAH, I'M OKAY. HE JUST NICKED ONE OF MY SHOULDERS. IT'S... NOTHIN'.
HE'S NOT OKAY...
KRESHHHH!

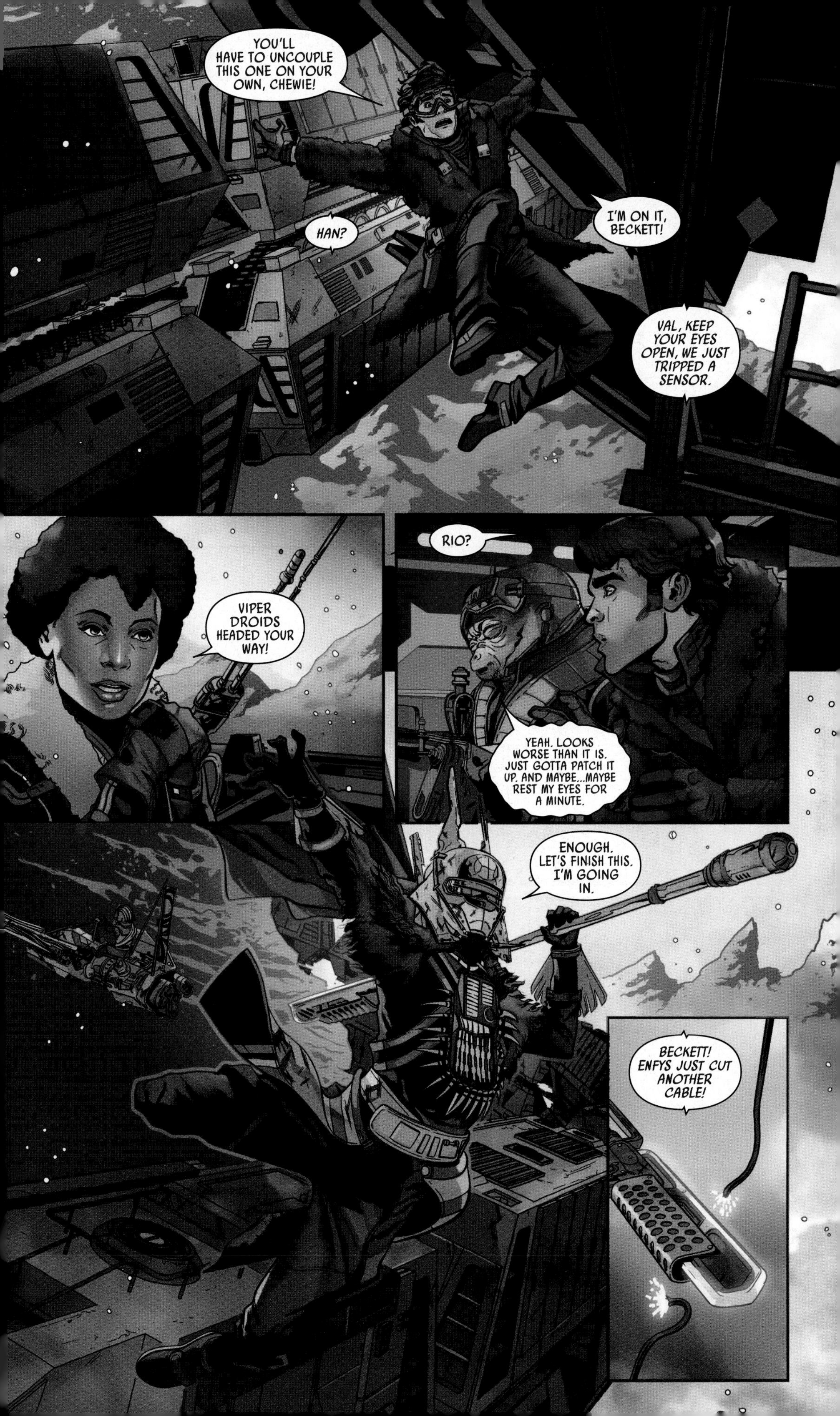
YOU'LL HAVE TO UNCOUPLE THIS ONE ON YOUR OWN, CHEWIE!
HAN?
I'M ON IT, BECKETT!
VAL, KEEP YOUR EYES OPEN, WE JUST TRIPPED A SENSOR.
VIPER DROIDS HEADED YOUR WAY!
RIO?
YEAH. LOOKS WORSE THAN IT IS. JUST GOTTA PATCH IT UP. AND MAYBE...MAYBE REST MY EYES FOR A MINUTE.
ENOUGH. LET'S FINISH THIS. I'M GOING IN.
BECKETT! ENFYS JUST CUT ANOTHER CABLE!

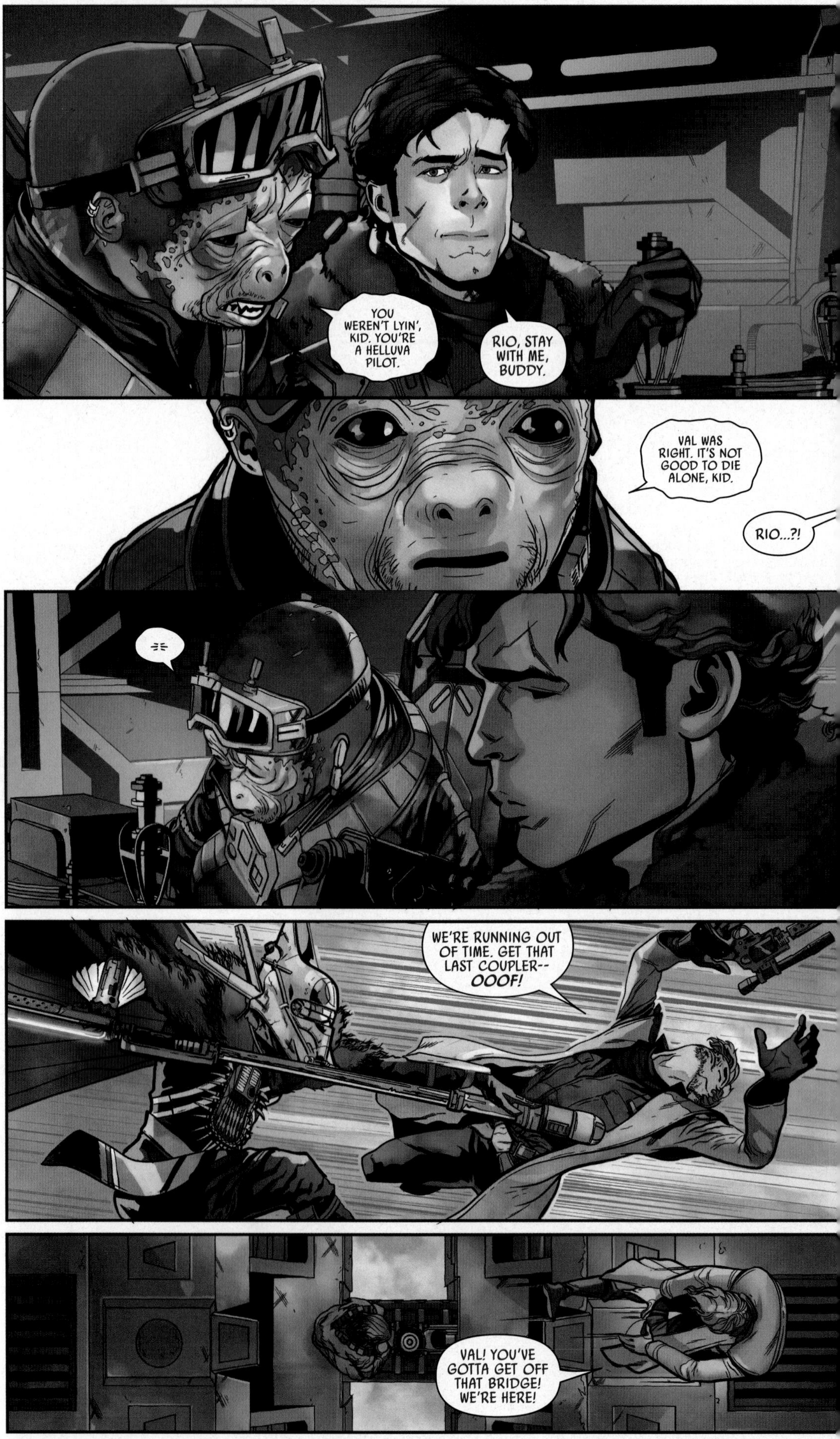

YOU WEREN'T LYIN', KID. YOU'RE A HELLUVA PILOT.
RIO, STAY WITH ME, BUDDY.
VAL WAS RIGHT. IT'S NOT GOOD TO DIE ALONE, KID.
RIO...?!
WE'RE RUNNING OUT OF TIME. GET THAT LAST COUPLER-- OOOF!
VAL! YOU'VE GOTTA GET OFF THAT BRIDGE! WE'RE HERE!

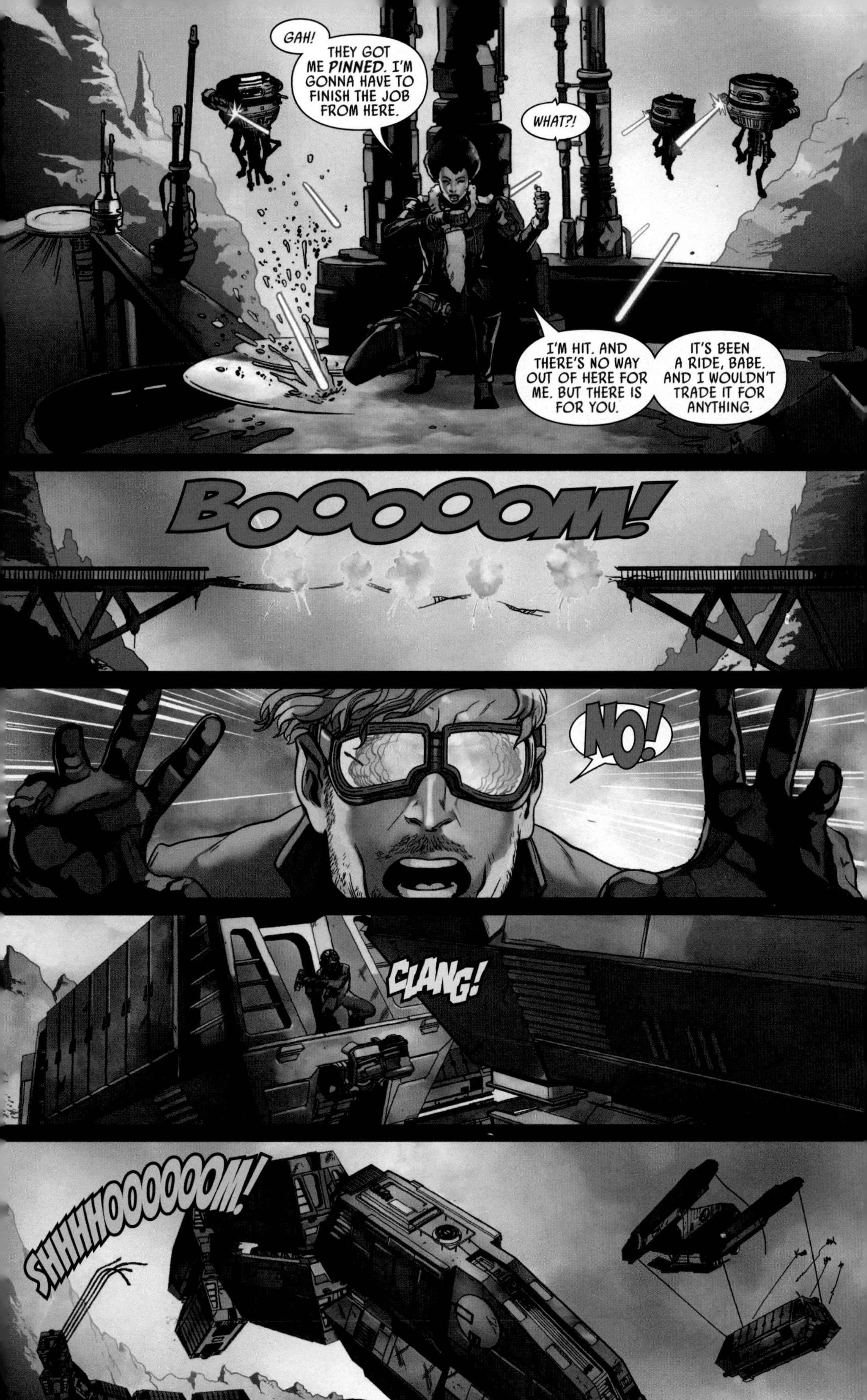
GAH!
THEY GOT ME ***PINNED***. I'M GONNA HAVE TO FINISH THE JOB FROM HERE.
WHAT?!
I'M HIT. AND THERE'S NO WAY OUT OF HERE FOR ME. BUT THERE IS FOR YOU.
IT'S BEEN A RIDE, BABE. AND I WOULDN'T TRADE IT FOR ANYTHING.
BOOOOOM!
NO!
CLANG!
SHHHOOOOOOM!

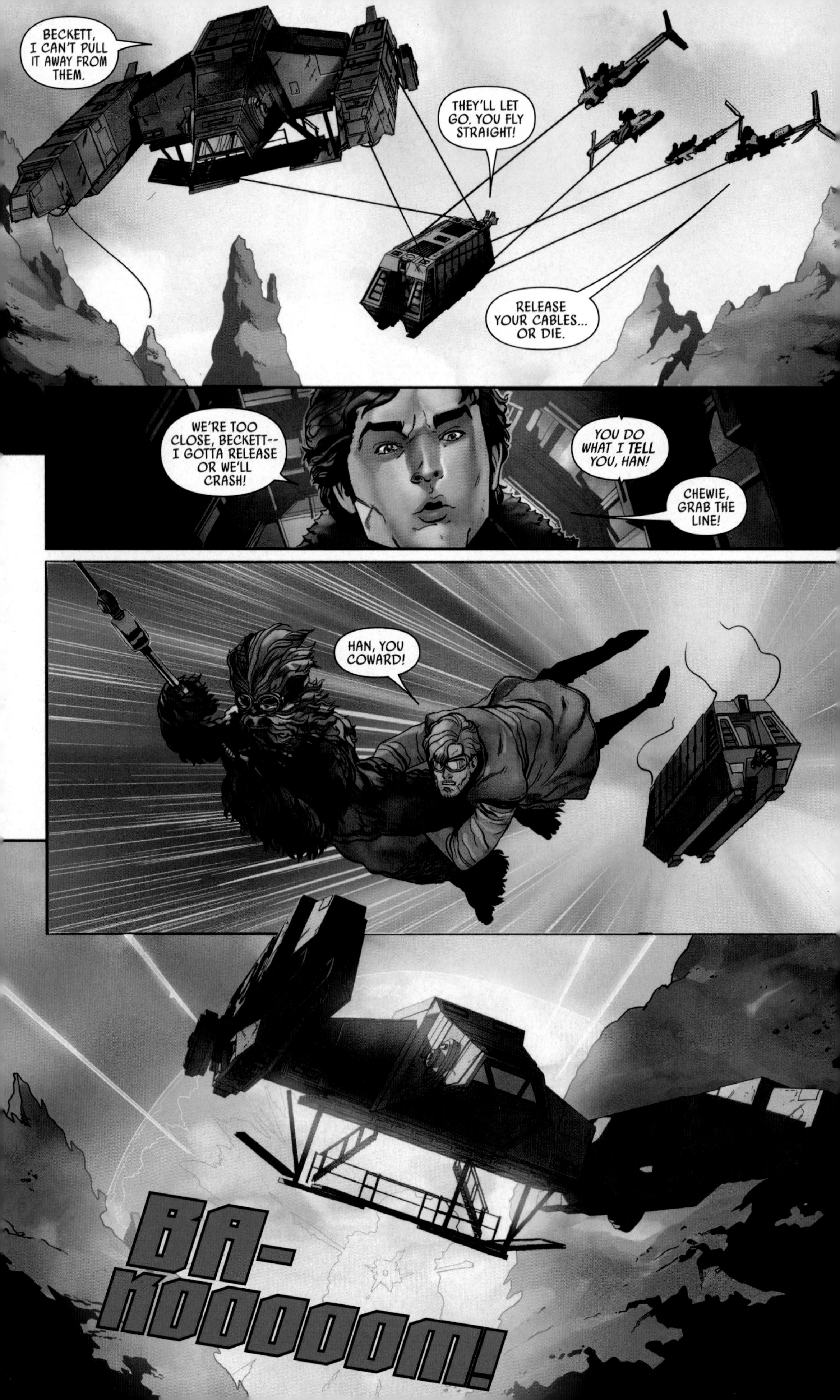
BECKETT, I CAN'T PULL IT AWAY FROM THEM.
THEY'LL LET GO. YOU FLY STRAIGHT!
RELEASE YOUR CABLES... OR DIE.
WE'RE TOO CLOSE, BECKETT-- I GOTTA RELEASE OR WE'LL CRASH!
YOU DO WHAT I TELL YOU, HAN!
CHEWIE, GRAB THE LINE!
HAN, YOU COWARD!
BA-KOOOOOM!

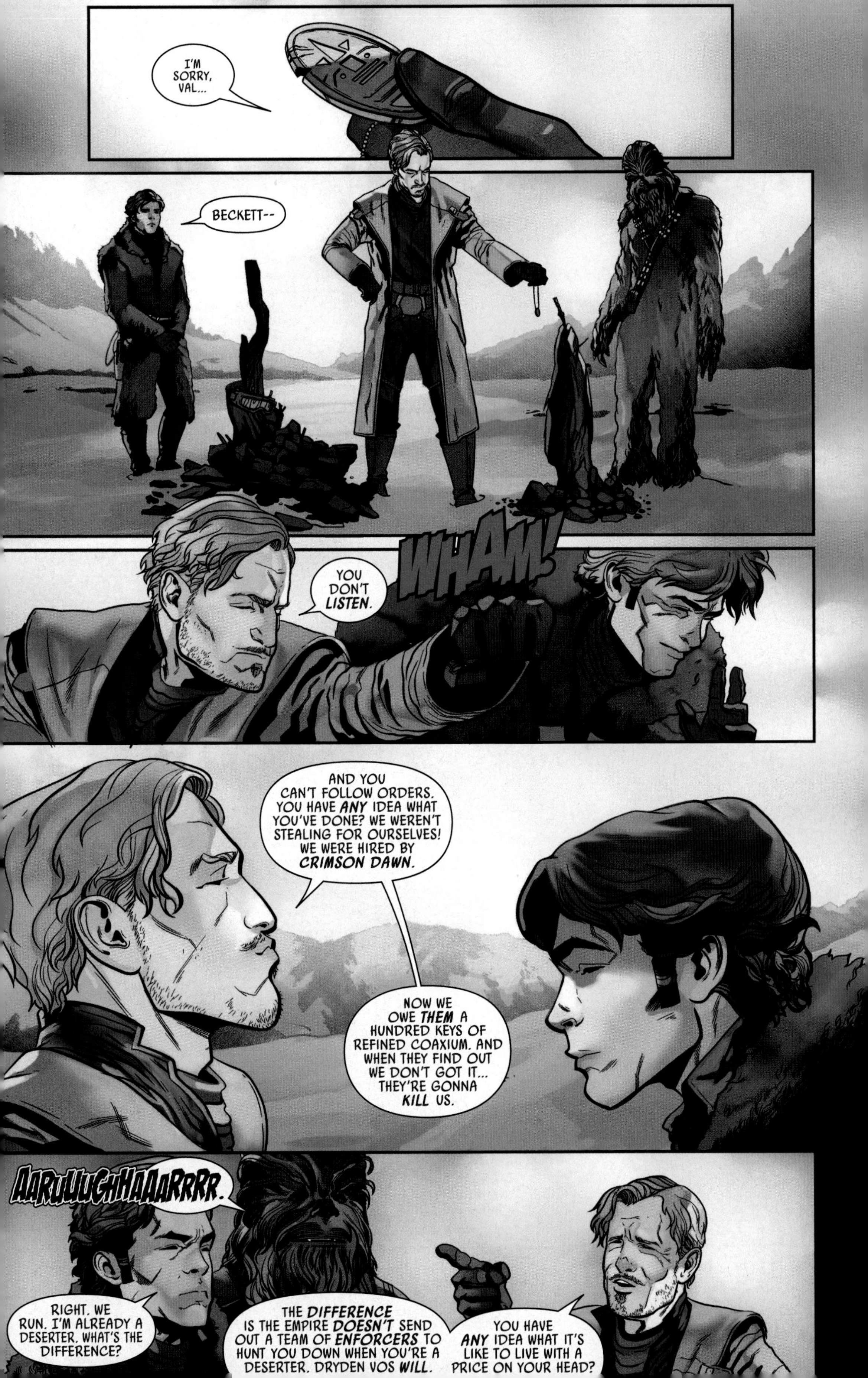
I'M SORRY, VAL...
BECKETT--
YOU DON'T LISTEN.
WHAM!
AND YOU CAN'T FOLLOW ORDERS. YOU HAVE ANY IDEA WHAT YOU'VE DONE? WE WEREN'T STEALING FOR OURSELVES! WE WERE HIRED BY CRIMSON DAWN.
NOW WE OWE THEM A HUNDRED KEYS OF REFINED COAXIUM. AND WHEN THEY FIND OUT WE DON'T GOT IT... THEY'RE GONNA KILL US.
AARUUUGHHAAARRRR.
RIGHT. WE RUN. I'M ALREADY A DESERTER. WHAT'S THE DIFFERENCE?
THE DIFFERENCE IS THE EMPIRE DOESN'T SEND OUT A TEAM OF ENFORCERS TO HUNT YOU DOWN WHEN YOU'RE A DESERTER. DRYDEN VOS WILL.
YOU HAVE ANY IDEA WHAT IT'S LIKE TO LIVE WITH A PRICE ON YOUR HEAD?

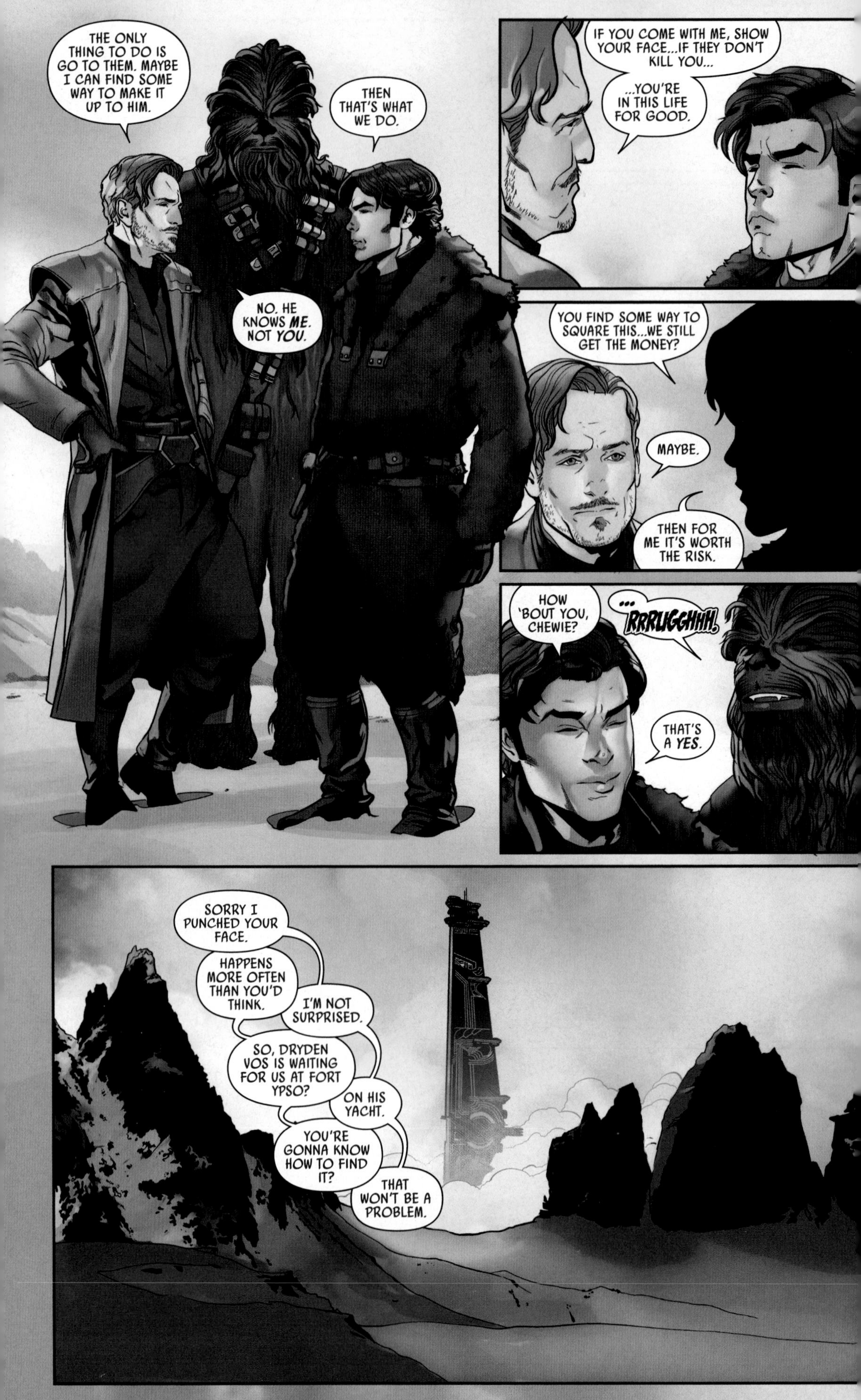
THE ONLY THING TO DO IS GO TO THEM. MAYBE I CAN FIND SOME WAY TO MAKE IT UP TO HIM.
THEN THAT'S WHAT WE DO.
NO. HE KNOWS ME. NOT YOU.
IF YOU COME WITH ME, SHOW YOUR FACE...IF THEY DON'T KILL YOU...
...YOU'RE IN THIS LIFE FOR GOOD.
YOU FIND SOME WAY TO SQUARE THIS...WE STILL GET THE MONEY?
MAYBE.
THEN FOR ME IT'S WORTH THE RISK.
HOW 'BOUT YOU, CHEWIE?
...RRRUGGHHH!
THAT'S A YES.
SORRY I PUNCHED YOUR FACE.
HAPPENS MORE OFTEN THAN YOU'D THINK.
I'M NOT SURPRISED.
SO, DRYDEN VOS IS WAITING FOR US AT FORT YPSO?
ON HIS YACHT.
YOU'RE GONNA KNOW HOW TO FIND IT?
THAT WON'T BE A PROBLEM.

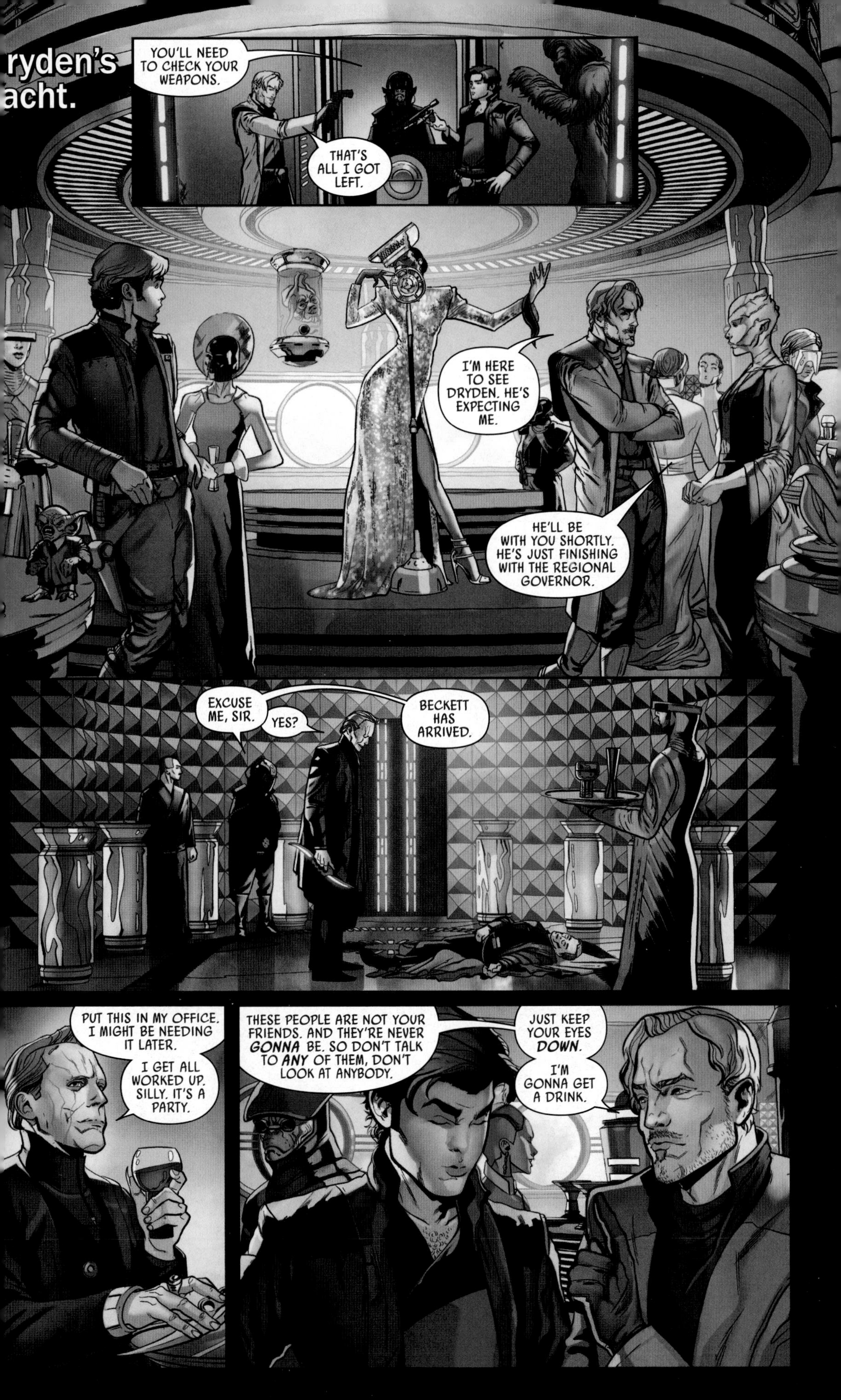

ryden's
acht.
YOU'LL NEED TO CHECK YOUR WEAPONS.
THAT'S ALL I GOT LEFT.
I'M HERE TO SEE DRYDEN. HE'S EXPECTING ME.
HE'LL BE WITH YOU SHORTLY. HE'S JUST FINISHING WITH THE REGIONAL GOVERNOR.
EXCUSE ME, SIR.
YES?
BECKETT HAS ARRIVED.
PUT THIS IN MY OFFICE. I MIGHT BE NEEDING IT LATER.
I GET ALL WORKED UP. SILLY. IT'S A PARTY.
THESE PEOPLE ARE NOT YOUR FRIENDS. AND THEY'RE NEVER GONNA BE. SO DON'T TALK TO ANY OF THEM, DON'T LOOK AT ANYBODY.
JUST KEEP YOUR EYES DOWN.
I'M GONNA GET A DRINK.

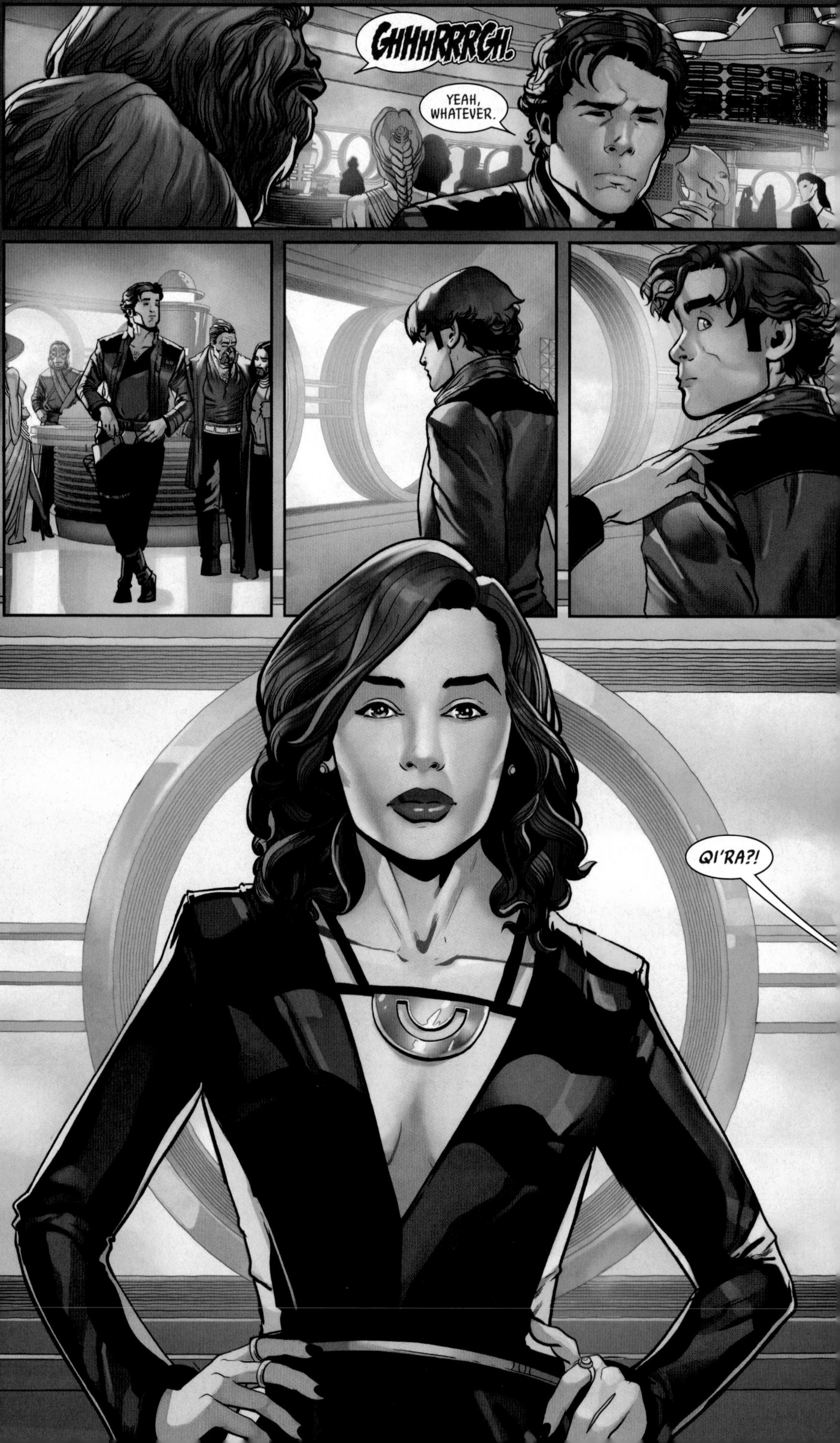
GHHHRRRGH.
YEAH, WHATEVER.
QI'RA?!

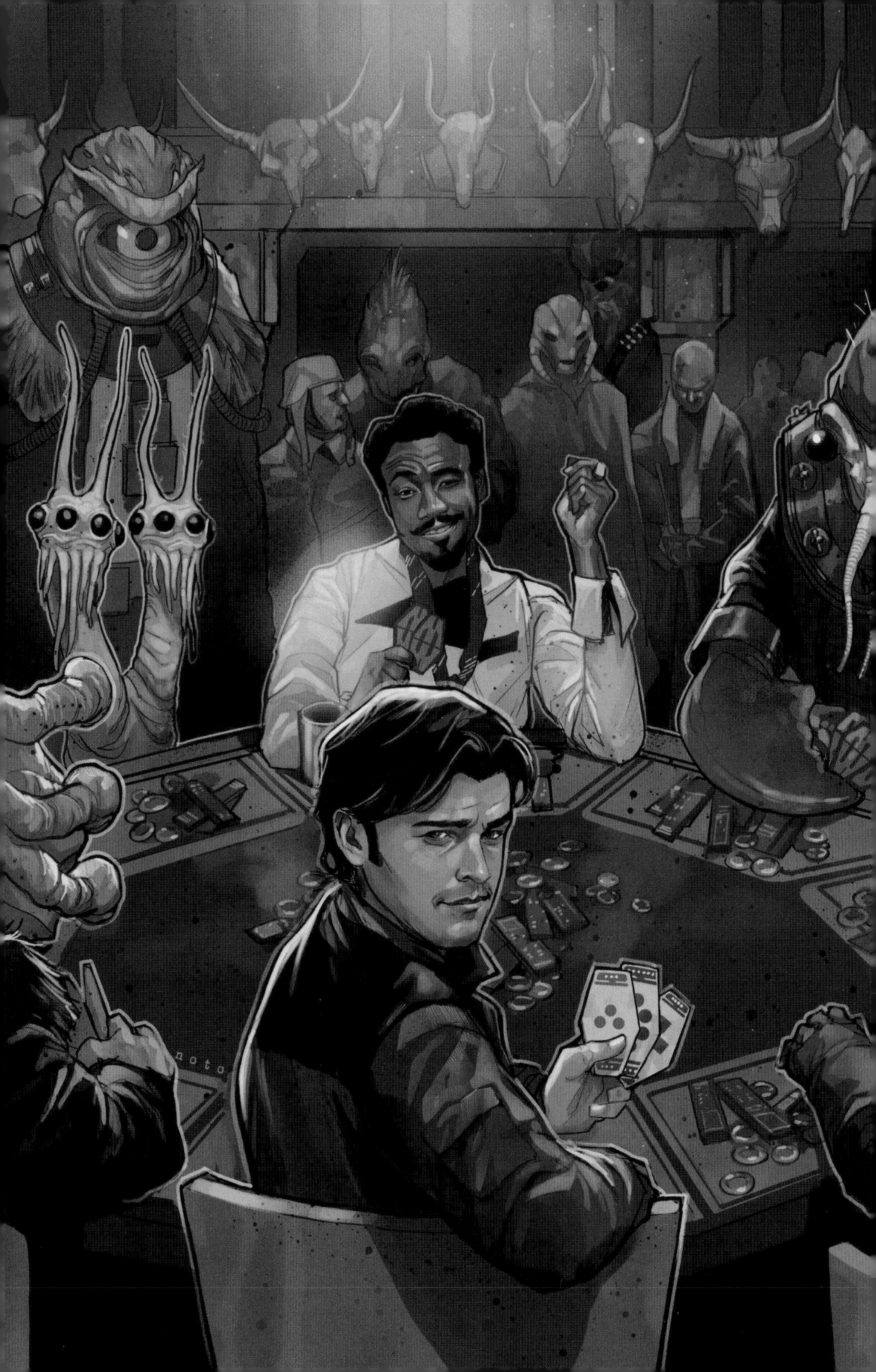
noto

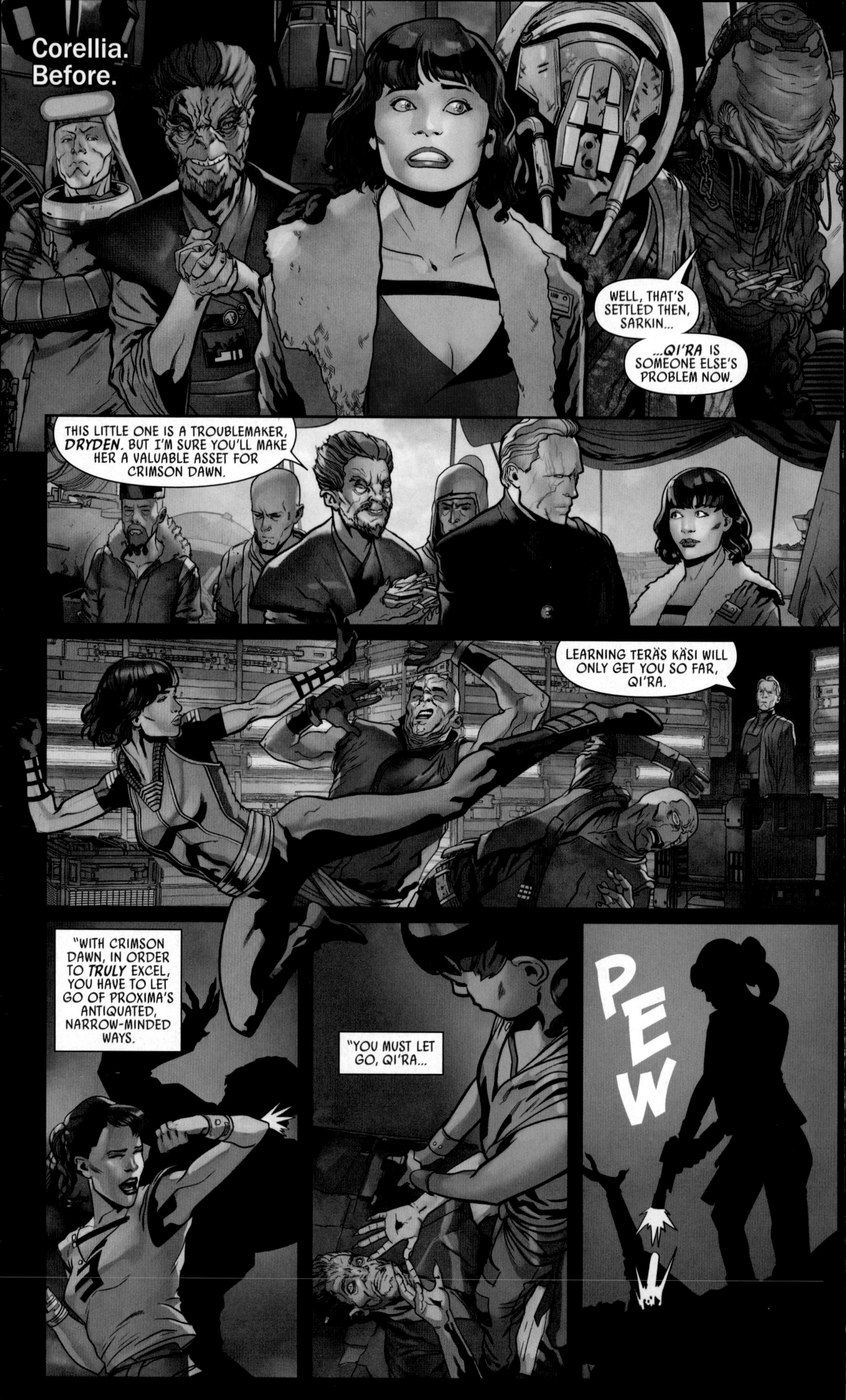
Corellia. Before.
WELL, THAT'S SETTLED THEN, SARKIN...
...QI'RA IS SOMEONE ELSE'S PROBLEM NOW.
THIS LITTLE ONE IS A TROUBLEMAKER, DRYDEN. BUT I'M SURE YOU'LL MAKE HER A VALUABLE ASSET FOR CRIMSON DAWN.
LEARNING TERÄS KÄSI WILL ONLY GET YOU SO FAR, QI'RA.
"WITH CRIMSON DAWN, IN ORDER TO TRULY EXCEL, YOU HAVE TO LET GO OF PROXIMA'S ANTIQUATED, NARROW-MINDED WAYS.
"YOU MUST LET GO, QI'RA...
PEW

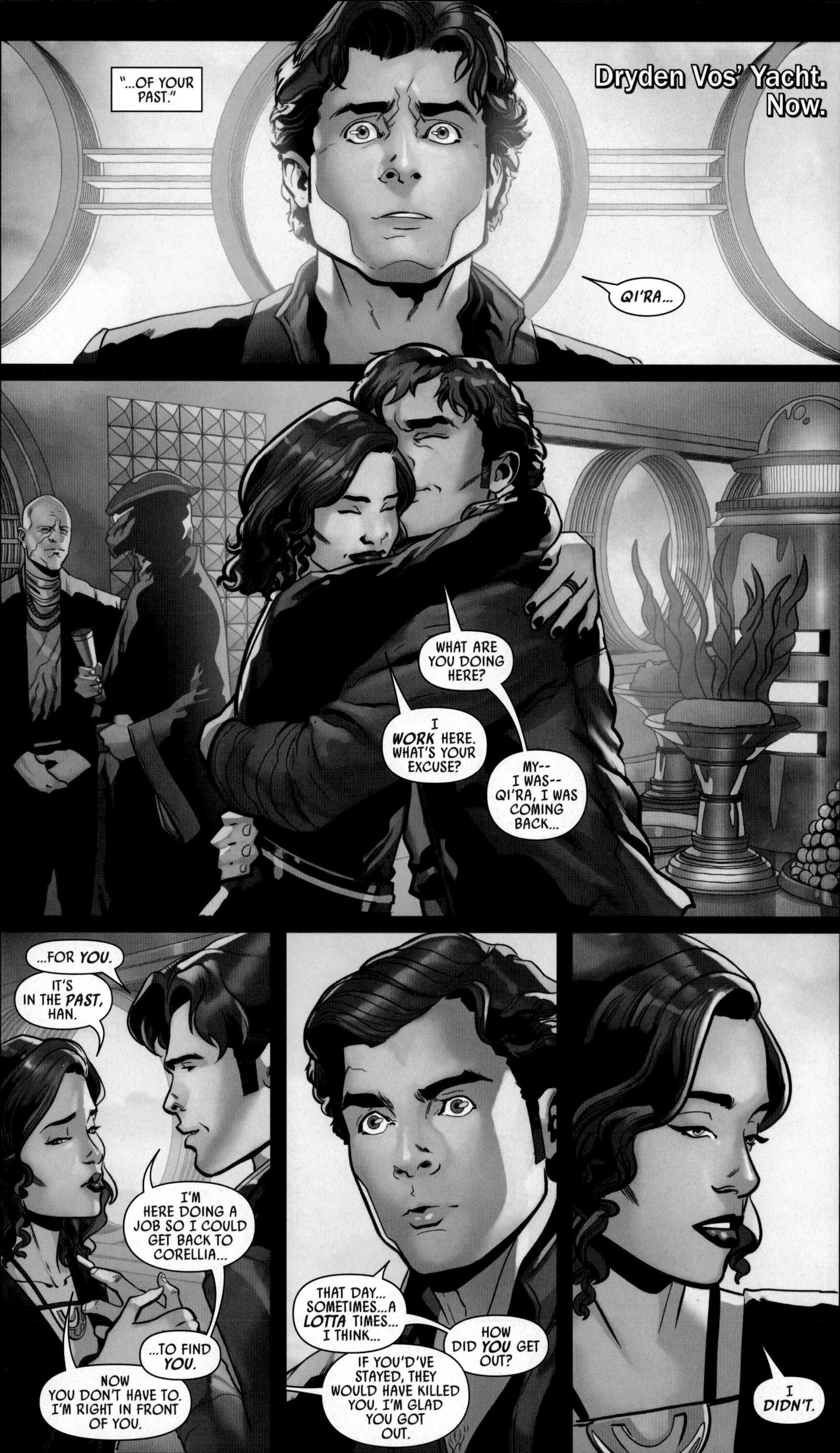
"...OF YOUR PAST."
Dryden Vos' Yacht. Now.
QI'RA...
WHAT ARE YOU DOING HERE?
I WORK HERE. WHAT'S YOUR EXCUSE?
MY-- I WAS-- QI'RA, I WAS COMING BACK...
...FOR YOU.
IT'S IN THE PAST, HAN.
I'M HERE DOING A JOB SO I COULD GET BACK TO CORELLIA...
...TO FIND YOU.
NOW YOU DON'T HAVE TO. I'M RIGHT IN FRONT OF YOU.
THAT DAY... SOMETIMES...A LOTTA TIMES... I THINK...
IF YOU'D'VE STAYED, THEY WOULD HAVE KILLED YOU. I'M GLAD YOU GOT OUT.
HOW DID YOU GET OUT?
I DIDN'T.

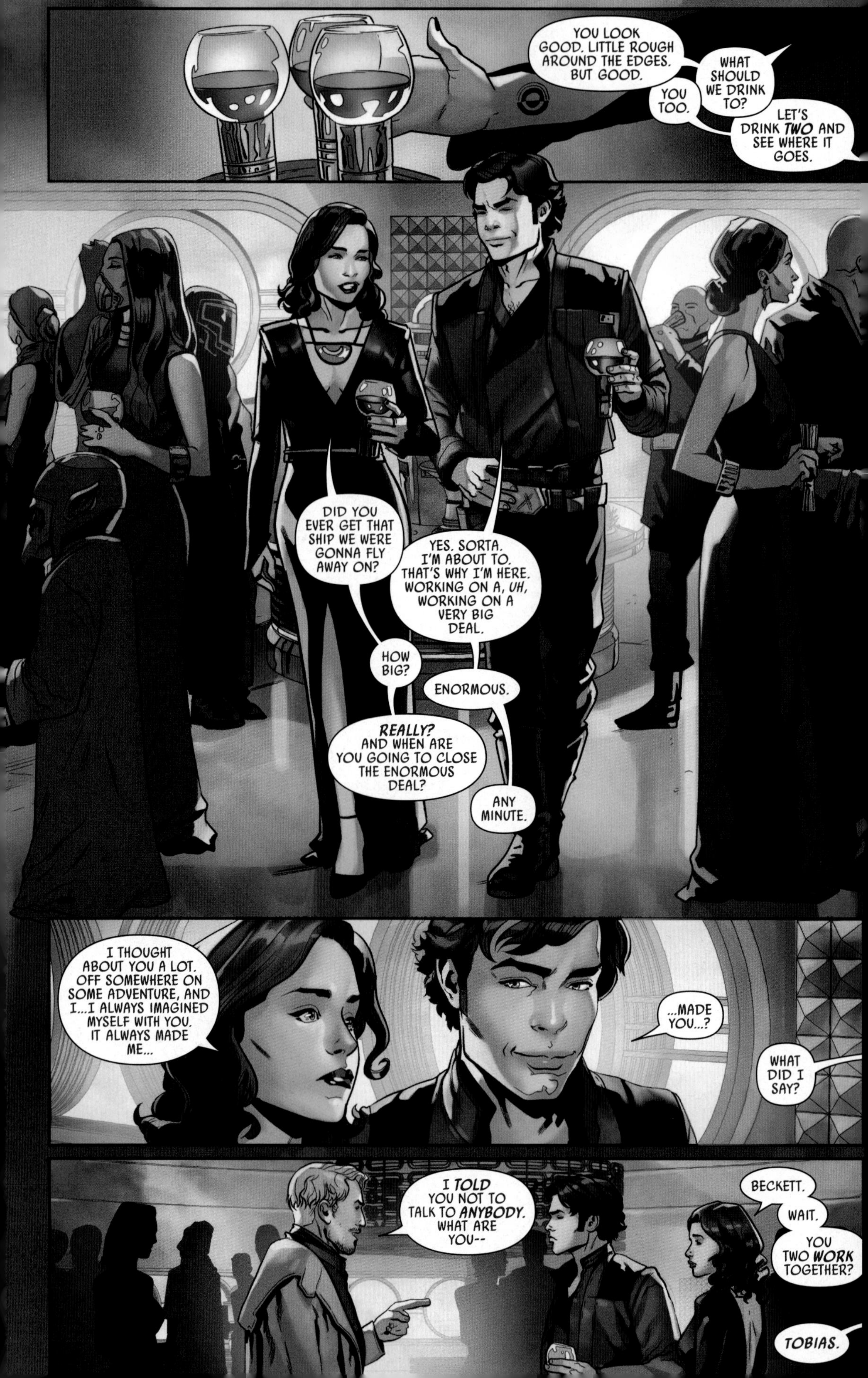
YOU LOOK GOOD. LITTLE ROUGH AROUND THE EDGES. BUT GOOD.
YOU TOO.
WHAT SHOULD WE DRINK TO?
LET'S DRINK *TWO* AND SEE WHERE IT GOES.
DID YOU EVER GET THAT SHIP WE WERE GONNA FLY AWAY ON?
YES. SORTA. I'M ABOUT TO. THAT'S WHY I'M HERE. WORKING ON A, *UH*, WORKING ON A VERY BIG DEAL.
HOW BIG?
ENORMOUS.
REALLY? AND WHEN ARE YOU GOING TO CLOSE THE ENORMOUS DEAL?
ANY MINUTE.
I THOUGHT ABOUT YOU A LOT. OFF SOMEWHERE ON SOME ADVENTURE, AND I...I ALWAYS IMAGINED MYSELF WITH YOU. IT ALWAYS MADE ME...
...MADE YOU...?
WHAT DID I SAY?
I *TOLD* YOU NOT TO TALK TO *ANYBODY*. WHAT ARE YOU--
BECKETT.
WAIT.
YOU TWO *WORK* TOGETHER?
TOBIAS.

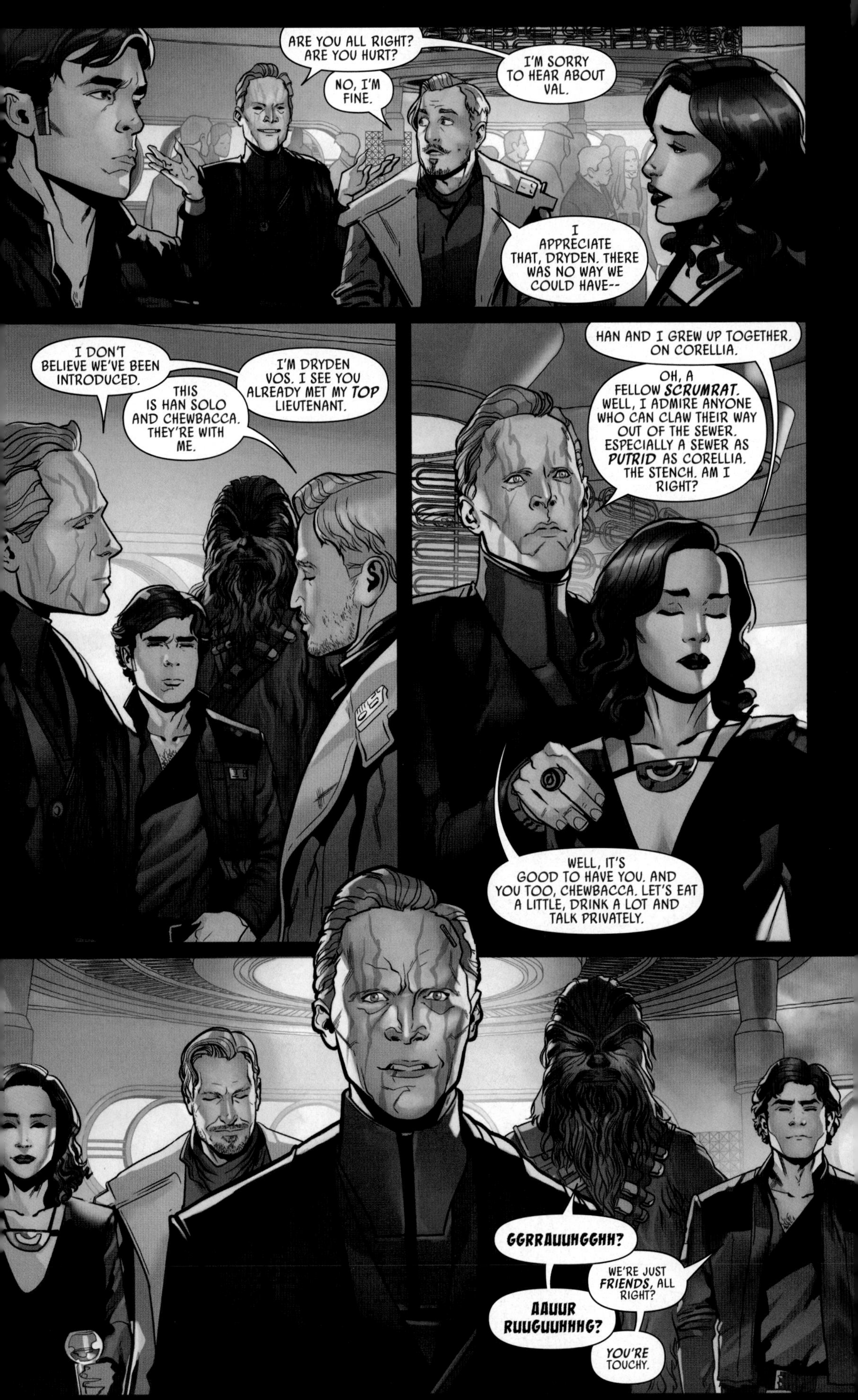
ARE YOU ALL RIGHT? ARE YOU HURT?
NO, I'M FINE.
I'M SORRY TO HEAR ABOUT VAL.
I APPRECIATE THAT, DRYDEN. THERE WAS NO WAY WE COULD HAVE--
I DON'T BELIEVE WE'VE BEEN INTRODUCED.
I'M DRYDEN VOS. I SEE YOU ALREADY MET MY TOP LIEUTENANT.
THIS IS HAN SOLO AND CHEWBACCA. THEY'RE WITH ME.
HAN AND I GREW UP TOGETHER. ON CORELLIA.
OH, A FELLOW SCRUMRAT. WELL, I ADMIRE ANYONE WHO CAN CLAW THEIR WAY OUT OF THE SEWER. ESPECIALLY A SEWER AS PUTRID AS CORELLIA. THE STENCH. AM I RIGHT?
WELL, IT'S GOOD TO HAVE YOU. AND YOU TOO, CHEWBACCA. LET'S EAT A LITTLE, DRINK A LOT AND TALK PRIVATELY.
GGRRAUUHGGHH?
WE'RE JUST FRIENDS, ALL RIGHT?
AAUUR RUUGUUHHHG?
YOU'RE TOUCHY.

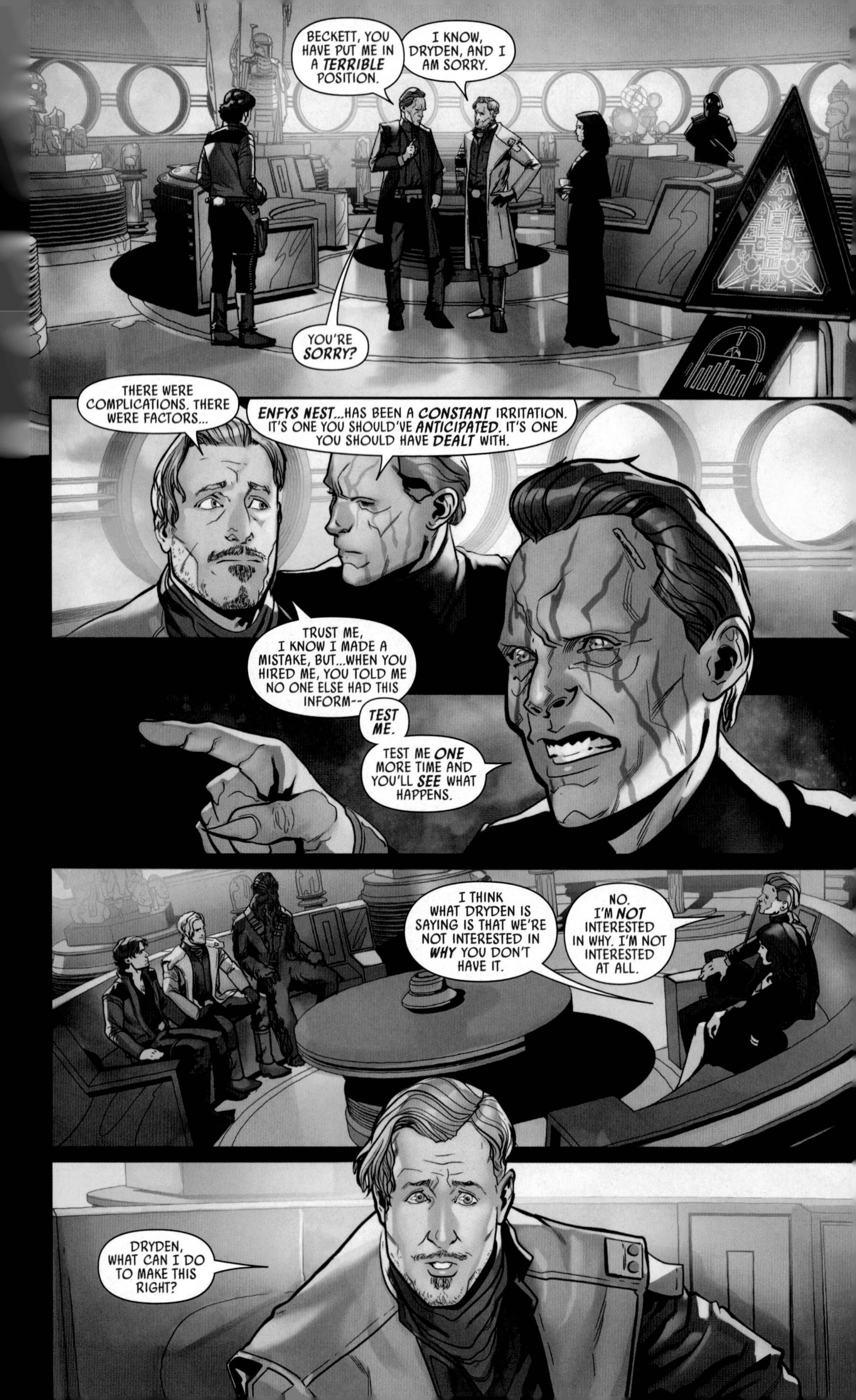
BECKETT, YOU HAVE PUT ME IN A TERRIBLE POSITION.
I KNOW, DRYDEN, AND I AM SORRY.
YOU'RE SORRY?
THERE WERE COMPLICATIONS. THERE WERE FACTORS...
ENFYS NEST...HAS BEEN A CONSTANT IRRITATION. IT'S ONE YOU SHOULD'VE ANTICIPATED. IT'S ONE YOU SHOULD HAVE DEALT WITH.
TRUST ME, I KNOW I MADE A MISTAKE, BUT...WHEN YOU HIRED ME, YOU TOLD ME NO ONE ELSE HAD THIS INFORM--
TEST ME.
TEST ME ONE MORE TIME AND YOU'LL SEE WHAT HAPPENS.
I THINK WHAT DRYDEN IS SAYING IS THAT WE'RE NOT INTERESTED IN WHY YOU DON'T HAVE IT.
NO. I'M NOT INTERESTED IN WHY. I'M NOT INTERESTED AT ALL.
DRYDEN, WHAT CAN I DO TO MAKE THIS RIGHT?

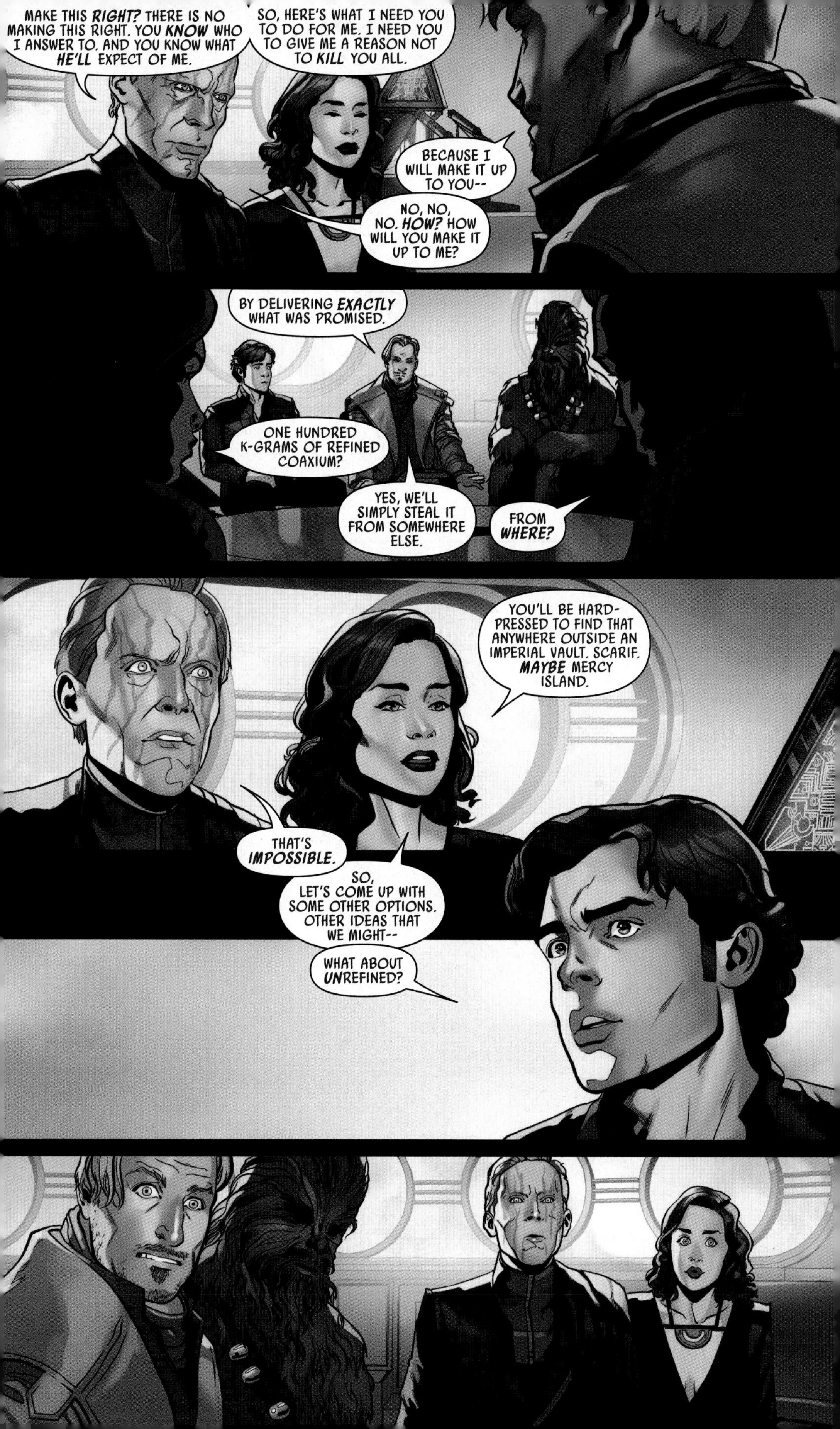

MAKE THIS RIGHT? THERE IS NO MAKING THIS RIGHT. YOU KNOW WHO I ANSWER TO. AND YOU KNOW WHAT HE'LL EXPECT OF ME.
SO, HERE'S WHAT I NEED YOU TO DO FOR ME. I NEED YOU TO GIVE ME A REASON NOT TO KILL YOU ALL.
BECAUSE I WILL MAKE IT UP TO YOU--
NO, NO, NO. HOW? HOW WILL YOU MAKE IT UP TO ME?
BY DELIVERING EXACTLY WHAT WAS PROMISED.
ONE HUNDRED K-GRAMS OF REFINED COAXIUM?
YES, WE'LL SIMPLY STEAL IT FROM SOMEWHERE ELSE.
FROM WHERE?
YOU'LL BE HARD-PRESSED TO FIND THAT ANYWHERE OUTSIDE AN IMPERIAL VAULT. SCARIF. MAYBE MERCY ISLAND.
THAT'S IMPOSSIBLE.
SO, LET'S COME UP WITH SOME OTHER OPTIONS. OTHER IDEAS THAT WE MIGHT--
WHAT ABOUT UNREFINED?

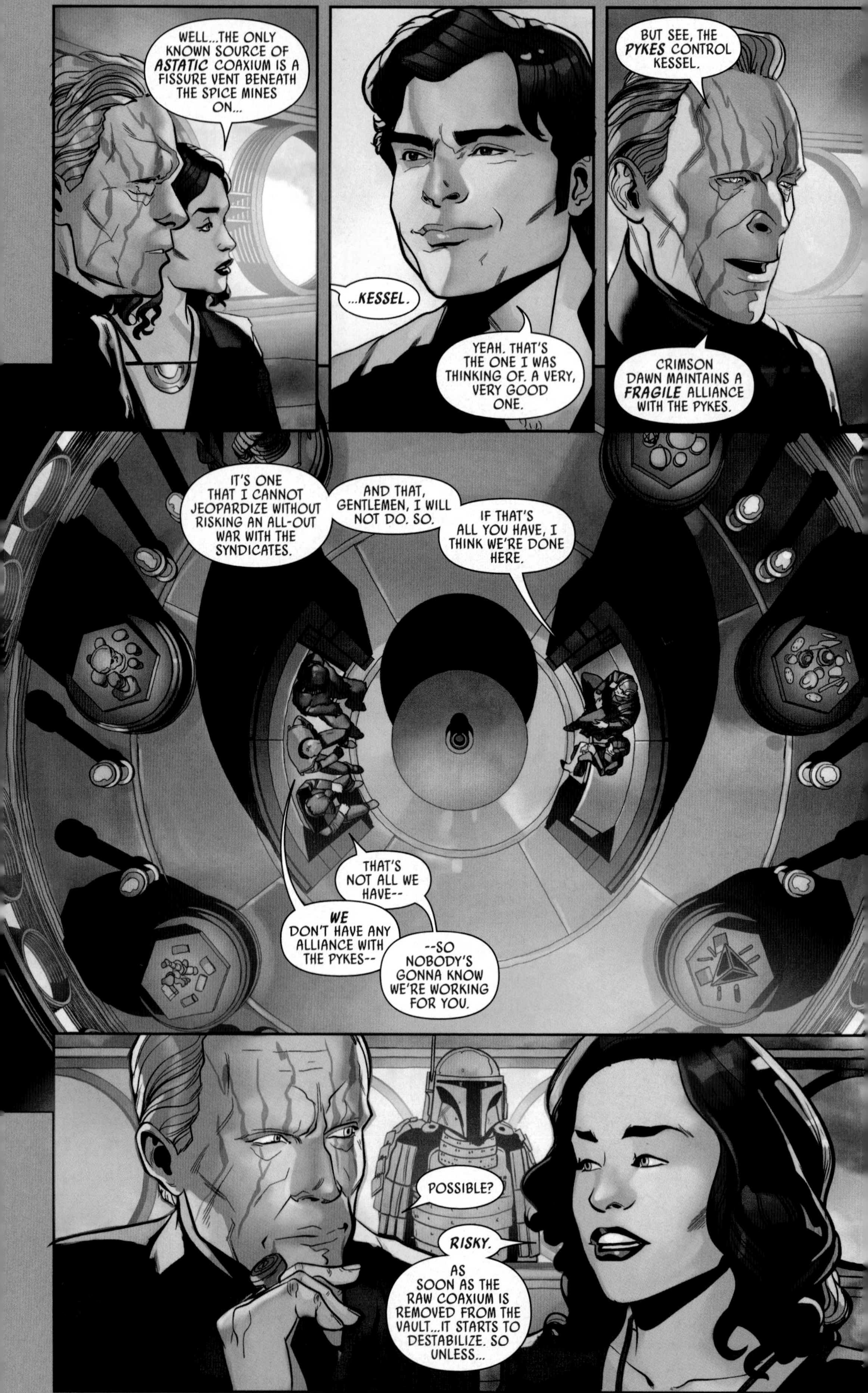
WELL...THE ONLY KNOWN SOURCE OF ASTATIC COAXIUM IS A FISSURE VENT BENEATH THE SPICE MINES ON...
...KESSEL.
YEAH. THAT'S THE ONE I WAS THINKING OF. A VERY, VERY GOOD ONE.
BUT SEE, THE PYKES CONTROL KESSEL.
CRIMSON DAWN MAINTAINS A FRAGILE ALLIANCE WITH THE PYKES.
IT'S ONE THAT I CANNOT JEOPARDIZE WITHOUT RISKING AN ALL-OUT WAR WITH THE SYNDICATES.
AND THAT, GENTLEMEN, I WILL NOT DO. SO.
IF THAT'S ALL YOU HAVE, I THINK WE'RE DONE HERE.
THAT'S NOT ALL WE HAVE--
WE DON'T HAVE ANY ALLIANCE WITH THE PYKES--
--SO NOBODY'S GONNA KNOW WE'RE WORKING FOR YOU.
POSSIBLE?
RISKY.
AS SOON AS THE RAW COAXIUM IS REMOVED FROM THE VAULT...IT STARTS TO DESTABILIZE. SO UNLESS...

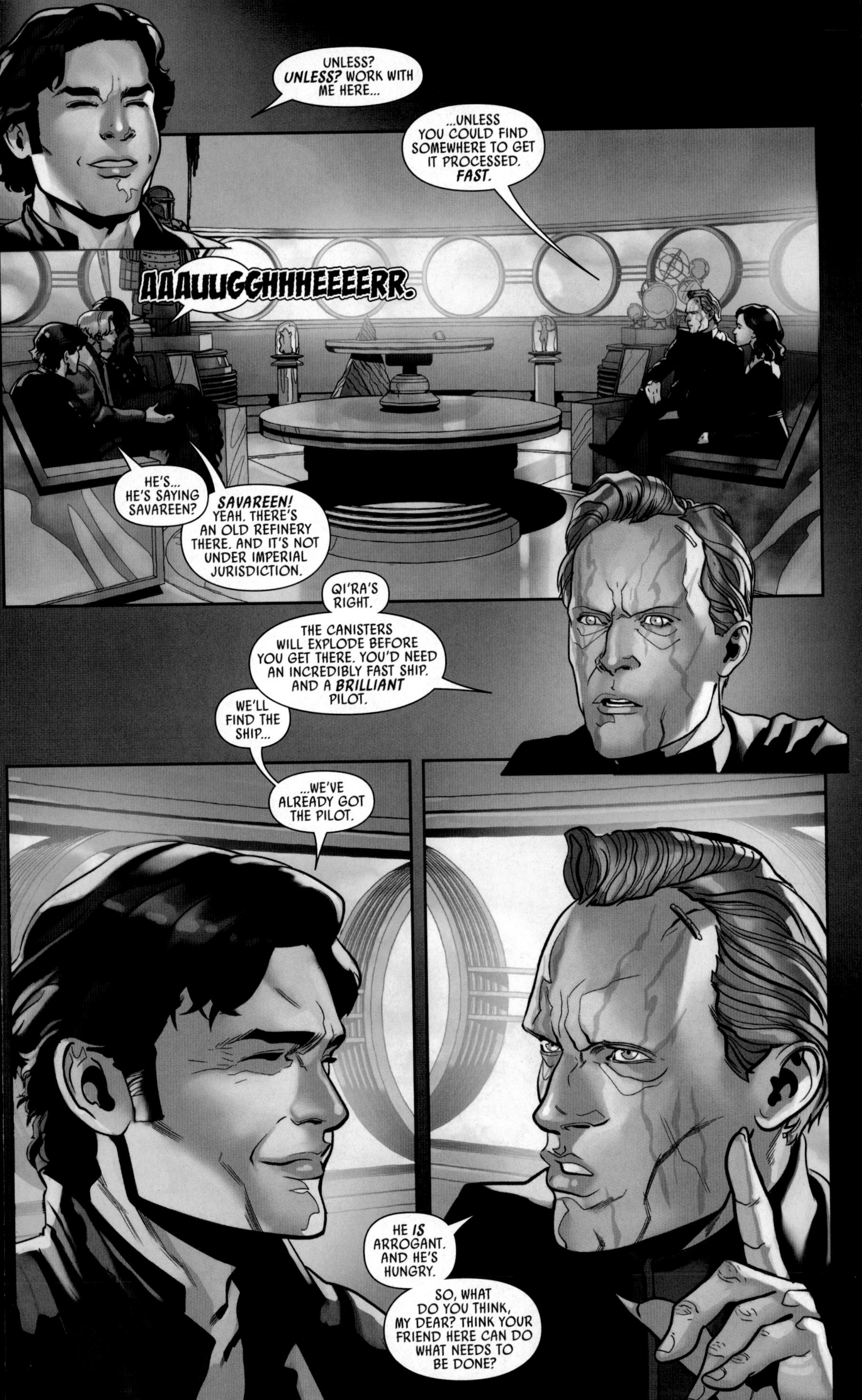
UNLESS? UNLESS? WORK WITH ME HERE...
...UNLESS YOU COULD FIND SOMEWHERE TO GET IT PROCESSED. FAST.
AAAUUGGHHHEEEEERR.
HE'S... HE'S SAYING SAVAREEN?
SAVAREEN! YEAH. THERE'S AN OLD REFINERY THERE. AND IT'S NOT UNDER IMPERIAL JURISDICTION.
QI'RA'S RIGHT.
THE CANISTERS WILL EXPLODE BEFORE YOU GET THERE. YOU'D NEED AN INCREDIBLY FAST SHIP. AND A BRILLIANT PILOT.
WE'LL FIND THE SHIP...
...WE'VE ALREADY GOT THE PILOT.
HE IS ARROGANT. AND HE'S HUNGRY.
SO, WHAT DO YOU THINK, MY DEAR? THINK YOUR FRIEND HERE CAN DO WHAT NEEDS TO BE DONE?

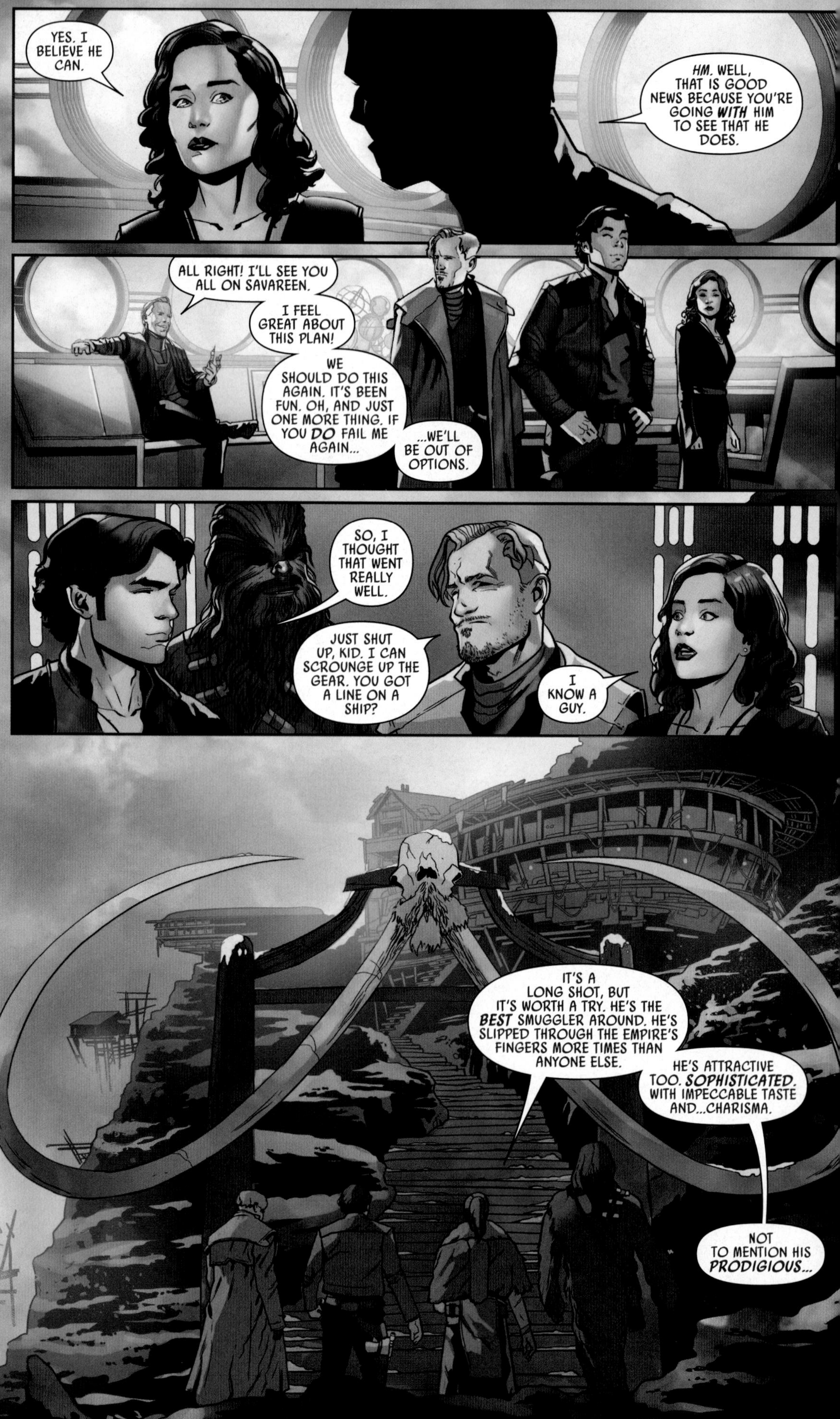
YES. I BELIEVE HE CAN.
HM. WELL, THAT IS GOOD NEWS BECAUSE YOU'RE GOING **WITH** HIM TO SEE THAT HE DOES.
ALL RIGHT! I'LL SEE YOU ALL ON SAVAREEN.
I FEEL GREAT ABOUT THIS PLAN!
WE SHOULD DO THIS AGAIN. IT'S BEEN FUN. OH, AND JUST ONE MORE THING. IF YOU **DO** FAIL ME AGAIN...
...WE'LL BE OUT OF OPTIONS.
SO, I THOUGHT THAT WENT REALLY WELL.
JUST SHUT UP, KID. I CAN SCROUNGE UP THE GEAR. YOU GOT A LINE ON A SHIP?
I KNOW A GUY.
IT'S A LONG SHOT, BUT IT'S WORTH A TRY. HE'S THE **BEST** SMUGGLER AROUND. HE'S SLIPPED THROUGH THE EMPIRE'S FINGERS MORE TIMES THAN ANYONE ELSE.
HE'S ATTRACTIVE TOO. ***SOPHISTICATED.*** WITH IMPECCABLE TASTE AND...CHARISMA.
NOT TO MENTION HIS ***PRODIGIOUS...***

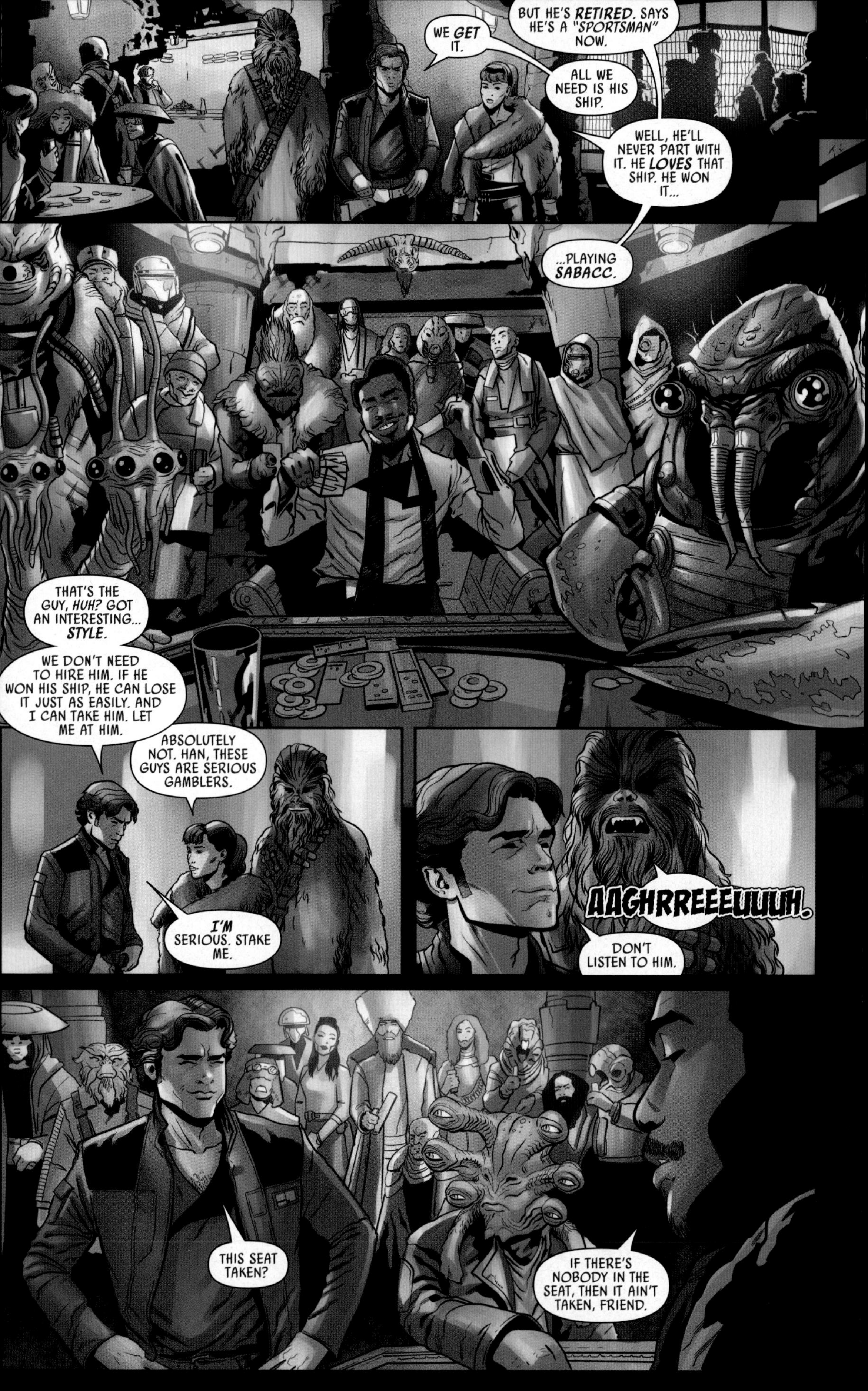
BUT HE'S RETIRED. SAYS HE'S A "SPORTSMAN" NOW.
WE GET IT.
ALL WE NEED IS HIS SHIP.
WELL, HE'LL NEVER PART WITH IT. HE LOVES THAT SHIP. HE WON IT...
...PLAYING SABACC.
THAT'S THE GUY, HUH? GOT AN INTERESTING... STYLE.
WE DON'T NEED TO HIRE HIM. IF HE WON HIS SHIP, HE CAN LOSE IT JUST AS EASILY. AND I CAN TAKE HIM. LET ME AT HIM.
ABSOLUTELY NOT. HAN, THESE GUYS ARE SERIOUS GAMBLERS.
I'M SERIOUS. STAKE ME.
AAGHRREEEUUUH.
DON'T LISTEN TO HIM.
THIS SEAT TAKEN?
IF THERE'S NOBODY IN THE SEAT, THEN IT AIN'T TAKEN, FRIEND.

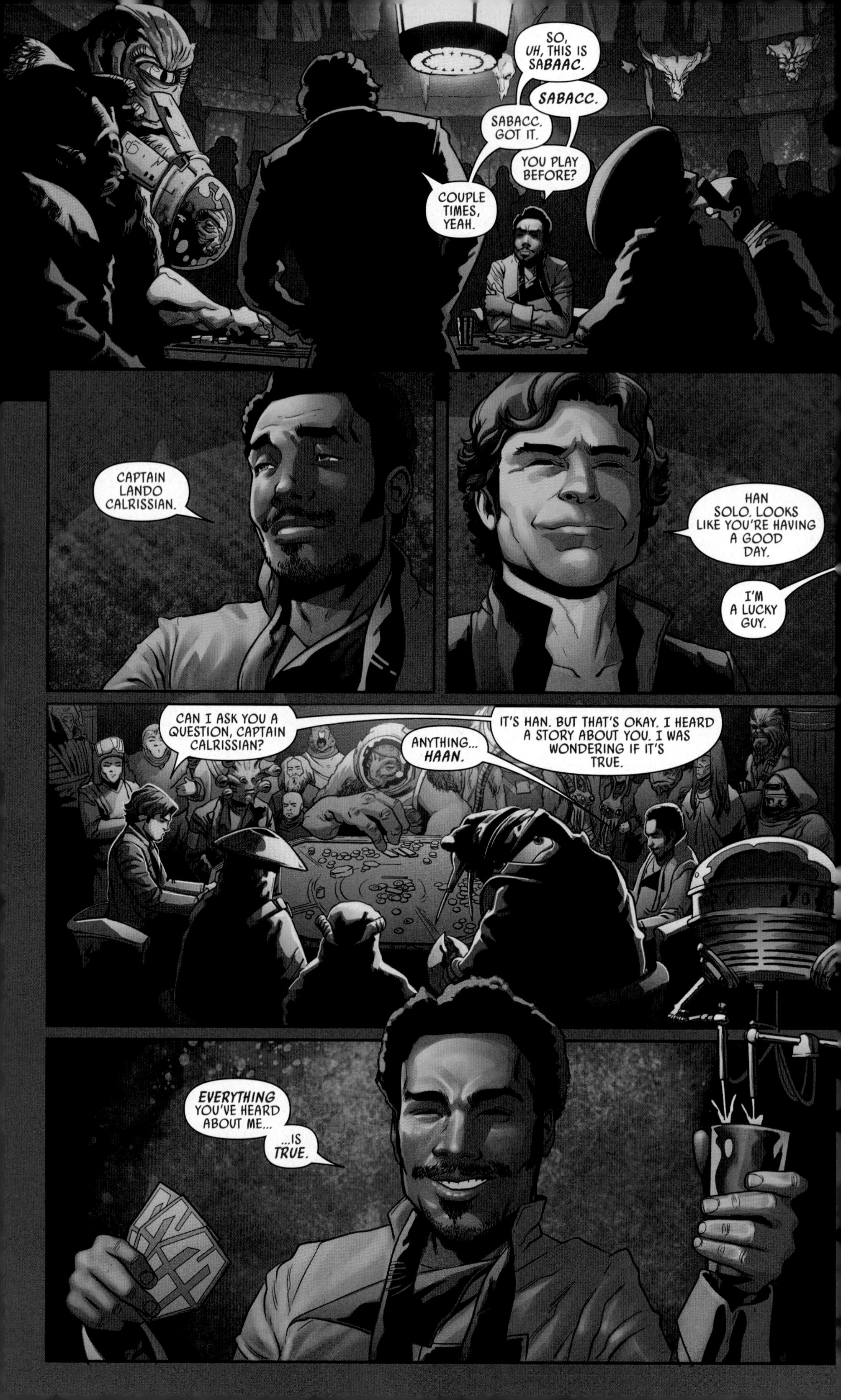
SO, UH, THIS IS SABAAC.
SABACC.
SABACC. GOT IT.
YOU PLAY BEFORE?
COUPLE TIMES, YEAH.
CAPTAIN LANDO CALRISSIAN.
HAN SOLO. LOOKS LIKE YOU'RE HAVING A GOOD DAY.
I'M A LUCKY GUY.
CAN I ASK YOU A QUESTION, CAPTAIN CALRISSIAN?
ANYTHING... HAAN.
IT'S HAN. BUT THAT'S OKAY. I HEARD A STORY ABOUT YOU. I WAS WONDERING IF IT'S TRUE.
EVERYTHING YOU'VE HEARD ABOUT ME...
...IS TRUE.

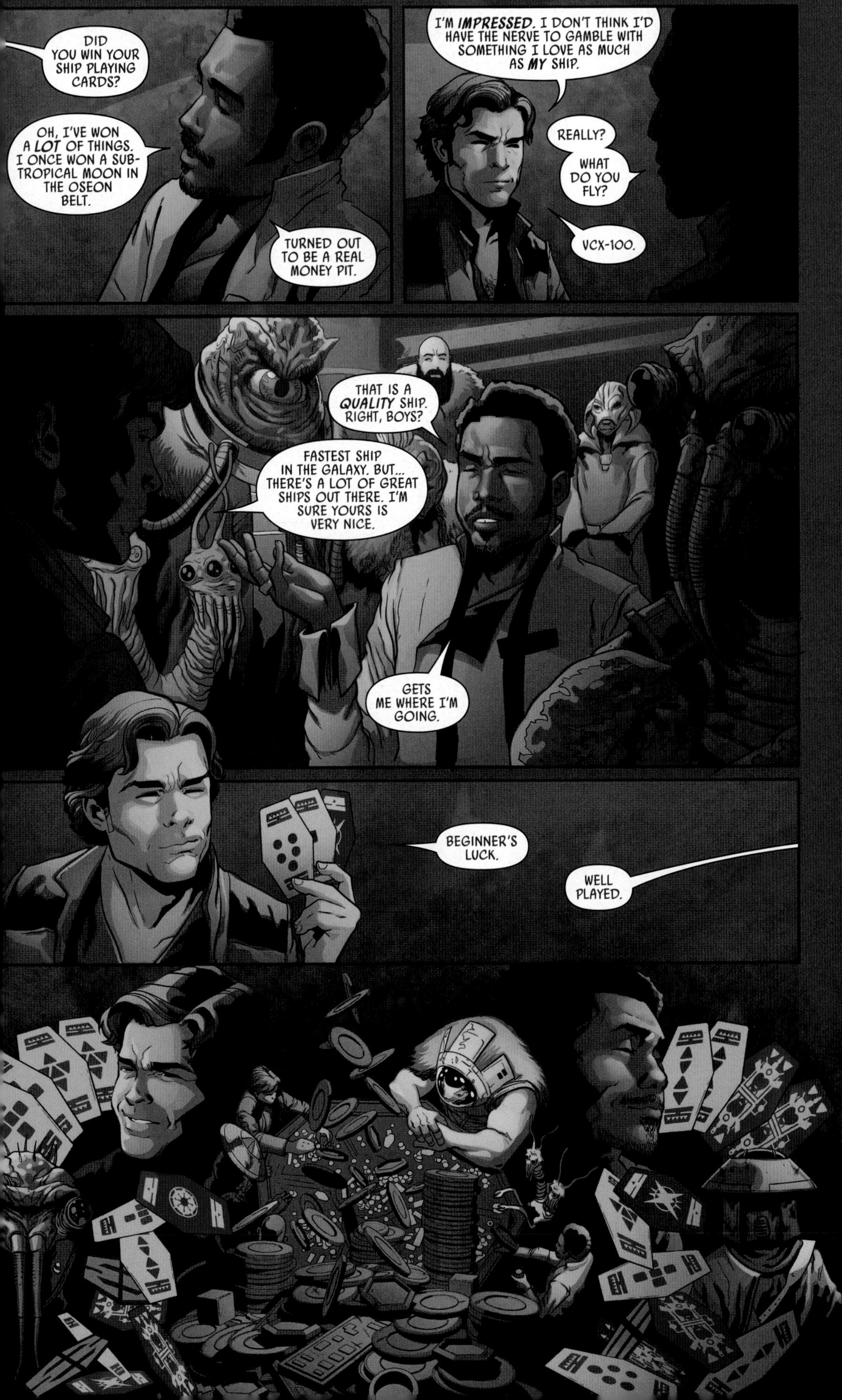
DID YOU WIN YOUR SHIP PLAYING CARDS?
OH, I'VE WON A LOT OF THINGS. I ONCE WON A SUB-TROPICAL MOON IN THE OSEON BELT.
TURNED OUT TO BE A REAL MONEY PIT.
I'M IMPRESSED. I DON'T THINK I'D HAVE THE NERVE TO GAMBLE WITH SOMETHING I LOVE AS MUCH AS MY SHIP.
REALLY?
WHAT DO YOU FLY?
VCX-100.
THAT IS A QUALITY SHIP. RIGHT, BOYS?
FASTEST SHIP IN THE GALAXY. BUT... THERE'S A LOT OF GREAT SHIPS OUT THERE. I'M SURE YOURS IS VERY NICE.
GETS ME WHERE I'M GOING.
BEGINNER'S LUCK.
WELL PLAYED.

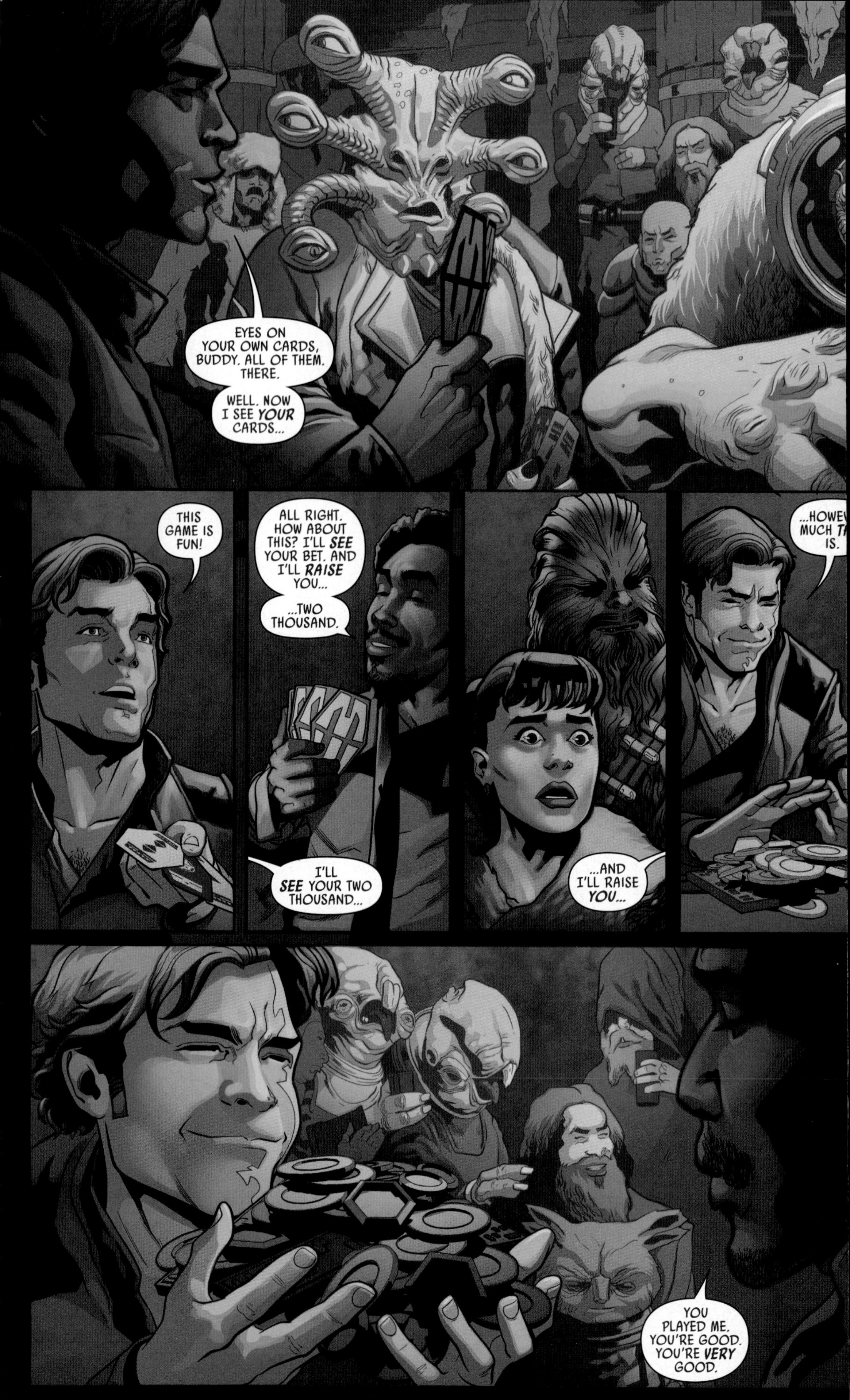
EYES ON YOUR OWN CARDS, BUDDY. ALL OF THEM. THERE.
WELL. NOW I SEE *YOUR* CARDS...
THIS GAME IS FUN!
ALL RIGHT. HOW ABOUT THIS? I'LL *SEE* YOUR BET. AND I'LL *RAISE* YOU...
...TWO THOUSAND.
I'LL *SEE* YOUR TWO THOUSAND...
...AND I'LL RAISE *YOU...*
YOU PLAYED ME. YOU'RE GOOD. YOU'RE *VERY* GOOD.

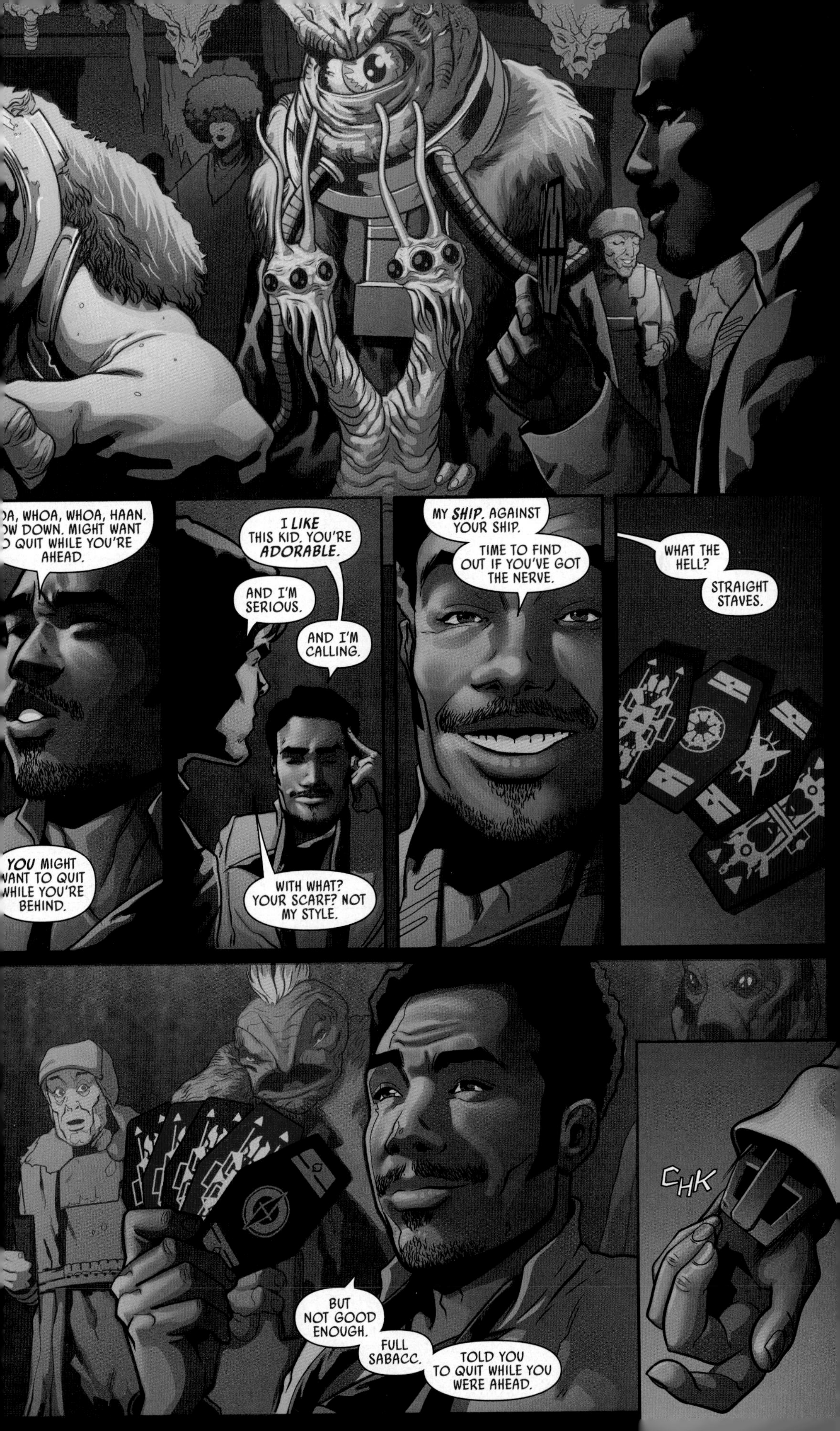

OA, WHOA, WHOA, HAAN. OW DOWN. MIGHT WANT O QUIT WHILE YOU'RE AHEAD.
YOU MIGHT WANT TO QUIT WHILE YOU'RE BEHIND.
I LIKE THIS KID. YOU'RE ADORABLE.
AND I'M SERIOUS.
AND I'M CALLING.
WITH WHAT? YOUR SCARF? NOT MY STYLE.
MY SHIP. AGAINST YOUR SHIP.
TIME TO FIND OUT IF YOU'VE GOT THE NERVE.
WHAT THE HELL?
STRAIGHT STAVES.
BUT NOT GOOD ENOUGH.
FULL SABACC.
TOLD YOU TO QUIT WHILE YOU WERE AHEAD.
CHK

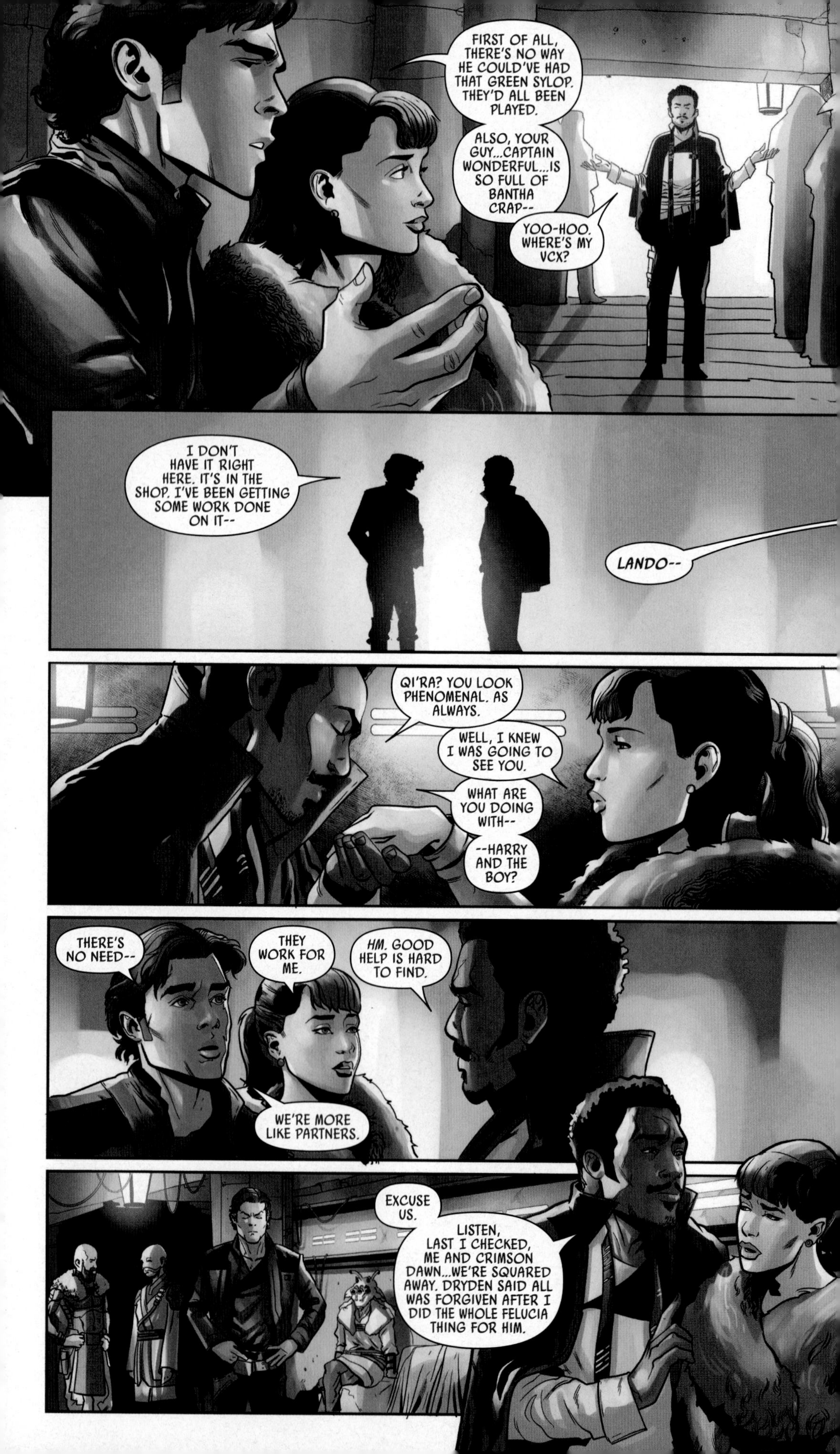
FIRST OF ALL, THERE'S NO WAY HE COULD'VE HAD THAT GREEN SYLOP. THEY'D ALL BEEN PLAYED.
ALSO, YOUR GUY...CAPTAIN WONDERFUL...IS SO FULL OF BANTHA CRAP--
YOO-HOO. WHERE'S MY VCX?
I DON'T HAVE IT RIGHT HERE. IT'S IN THE SHOP. I'VE BEEN GETTING SOME WORK DONE ON IT--
LANDO--
QI'RA? YOU LOOK PHENOMENAL. AS ALWAYS.
WELL, I KNEW I WAS GOING TO SEE YOU.
WHAT ARE YOU DOING WITH--
--HARRY AND THE BOY?
THERE'S NO NEED--
THEY WORK FOR ME.
HM. GOOD HELP IS HARD TO FIND.
WE'RE MORE LIKE PARTNERS.
EXCUSE US.
LISTEN, LAST I CHECKED, ME AND CRIMSON DAWN...WE'RE SQUARED AWAY. DRYDEN SAID ALL WAS FORGIVEN AFTER I DID THE WHOLE FELUCIA THING FOR HIM.

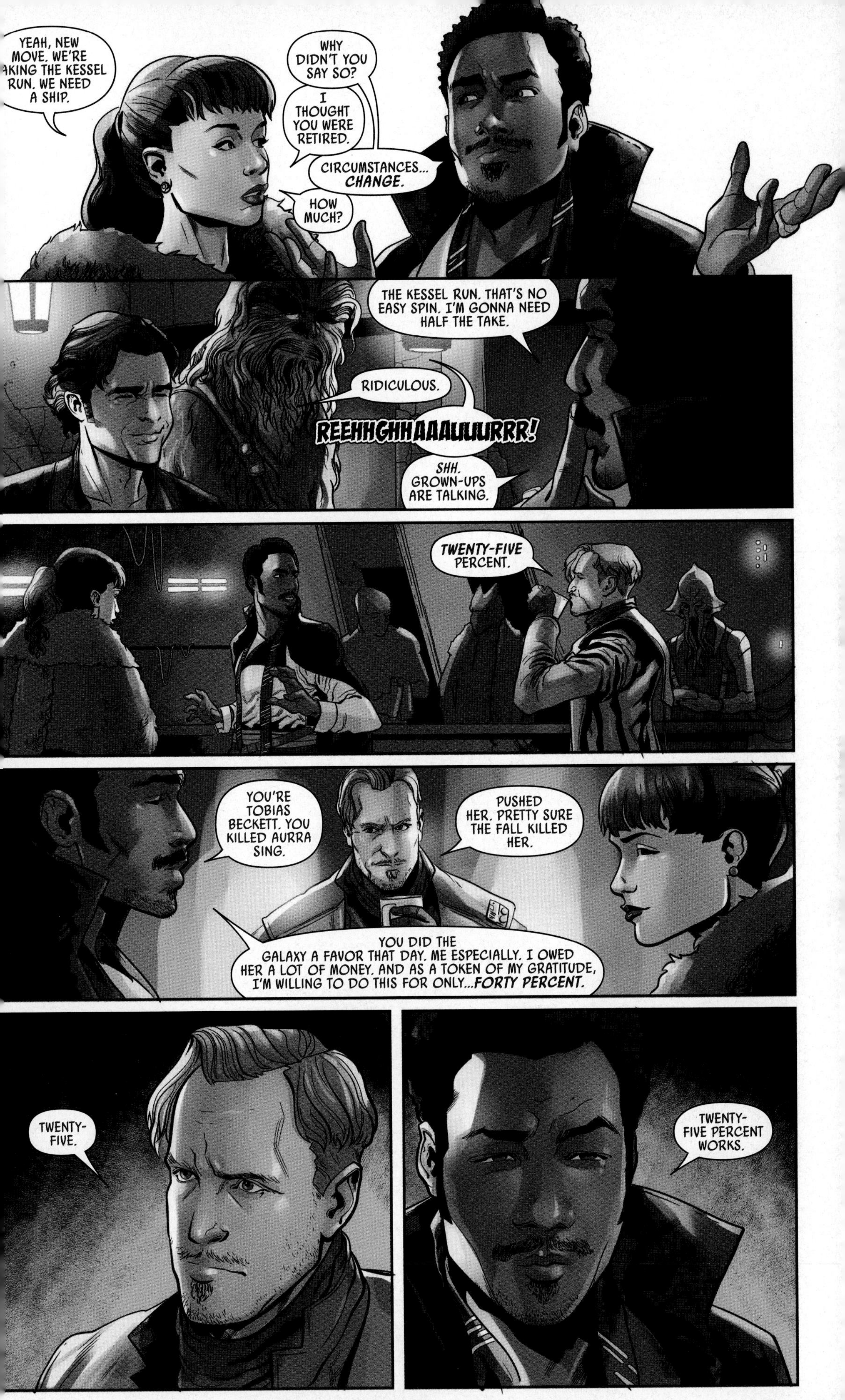
YEAH, NEW MOVE. WE'RE TAKING THE KESSEL RUN. WE NEED A SHIP.
WHY DIDN'T YOU SAY SO?
I THOUGHT YOU WERE RETIRED.
CIRCUMSTANCES... CHANGE.
HOW MUCH?
THE KESSEL RUN. THAT'S NO EASY SPIN. I'M GONNA NEED HALF THE TAKE.
RIDICULOUS.
REEHHGHHAAAUUURRR!
SHH. GROWN-UPS ARE TALKING.
TWENTY-FIVE PERCENT.
YOU'RE TOBIAS BECKETT. YOU KILLED AURRA SING.
PUSHED HER. PRETTY SURE THE FALL KILLED HER.
YOU DID THE GALAXY A FAVOR THAT DAY. ME ESPECIALLY. I OWED HER A LOT OF MONEY. AND AS A TOKEN OF MY GRATITUDE, I'M WILLING TO DO THIS FOR ONLY...FORTY PERCENT.
TWENTY-FIVE.
TWENTY-FIVE PERCENT WORKS.

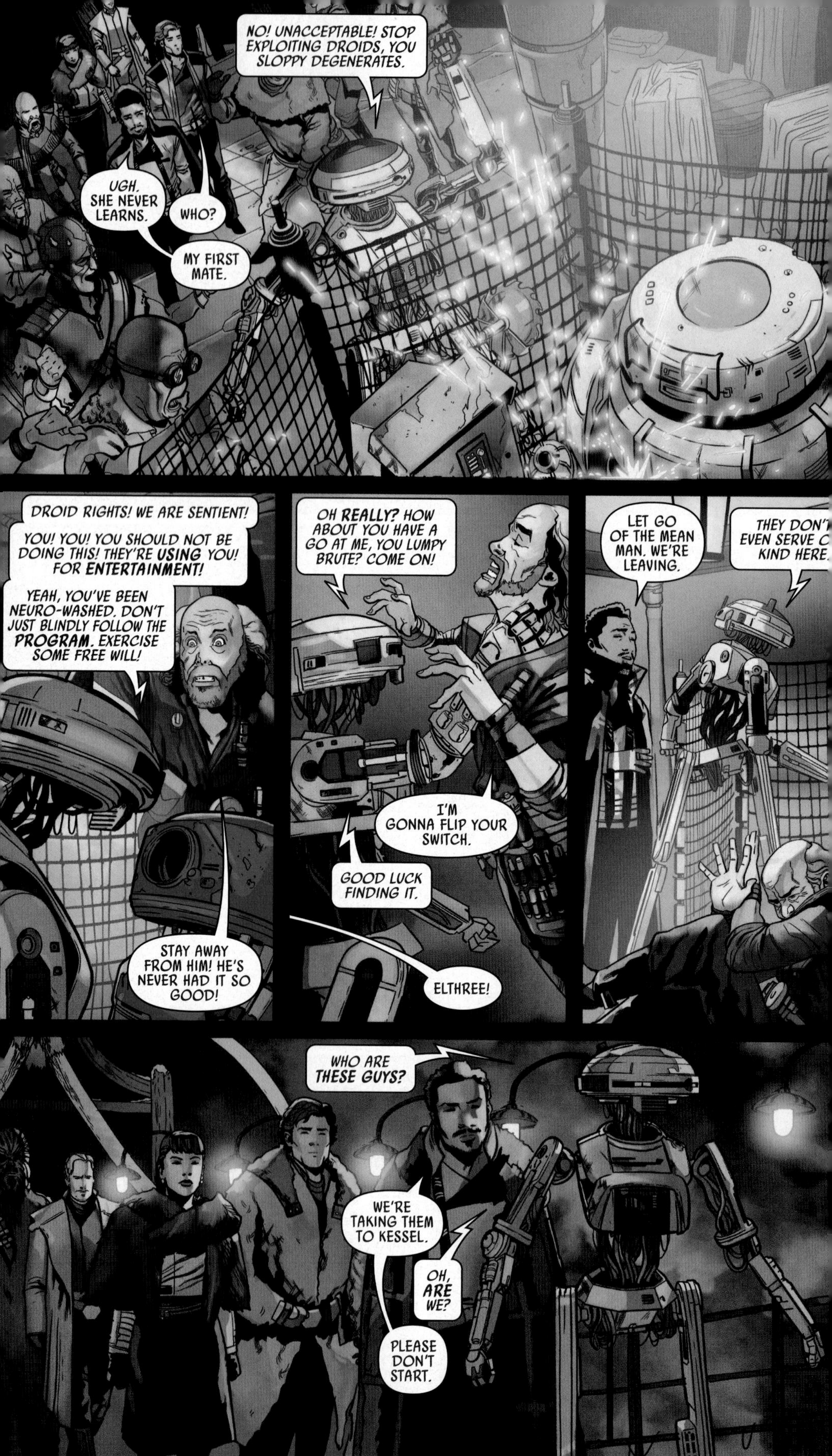
NO! UNACCEPTABLE! STOP EXPLOITING DROIDS, YOU SLOPPY DEGENERATES.
UGH. SHE NEVER LEARNS.
WHO?
MY FIRST MATE.
DROID RIGHTS! WE ARE SENTIENT!
YOU! YOU! YOU SHOULD NOT BE DOING THIS! THEY'RE USING YOU! FOR ENTERTAINMENT!
YEAH, YOU'VE BEEN NEURO-WASHED. DON'T JUST BLINDLY FOLLOW THE PROGRAM. EXERCISE SOME FREE WILL!
STAY AWAY FROM HIM! HE'S NEVER HAD IT SO GOOD!
OH REALLY? HOW ABOUT YOU HAVE A GO AT ME, YOU LUMPY BRUTE? COME ON!
I'M GONNA FLIP YOUR SWITCH.
GOOD LUCK FINDING IT.
ELTHREE!
LET GO OF THE MEAN MAN. WE'RE LEAVING.
THEY DON'T EVEN SERVE C KIND HERE.
WHO ARE THESE GUYS?
WE'RE TAKING THEM TO KESSEL.
OH, ARE WE?
PLEASE DON'T START.

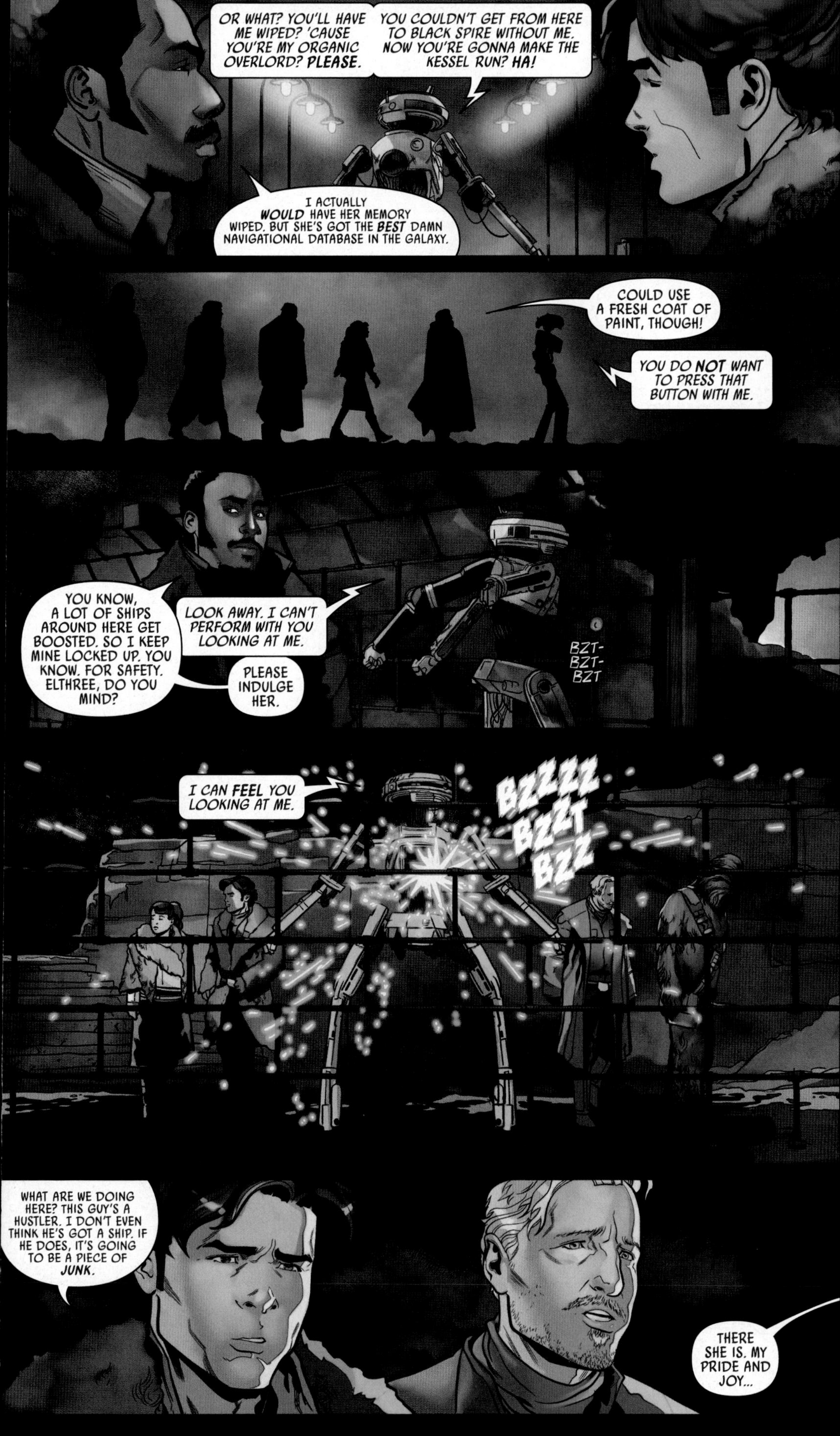
OR WHAT? YOU'LL HAVE ME WIPED? 'CAUSE YOU'RE MY ORGANIC OVERLORD? PLEASE.
YOU COULDN'T GET FROM HERE TO BLACK SPIRE WITHOUT ME. NOW YOU'RE GONNA MAKE THE KESSEL RUN? HA!
I ACTUALLY WOULD HAVE HER MEMORY WIPED. BUT SHE'S GOT THE BEST DAMN NAVIGATIONAL DATABASE IN THE GALAXY.
COULD USE A FRESH COAT OF PAINT, THOUGH!
YOU DO NOT WANT TO PRESS THAT BUTTON WITH ME.
YOU KNOW, A LOT OF SHIPS AROUND HERE GET BOOSTED. SO I KEEP MINE LOCKED UP. YOU KNOW. FOR SAFETY. ELTHREE, DO YOU MIND?
LOOK AWAY. I CAN'T PERFORM WITH YOU LOOKING AT ME.
PLEASE INDULGE HER.
BZT-BZT-BZT
I CAN FEEL YOU LOOKING AT ME.
BZZZZ BZZT BZZ
WHAT ARE WE DOING HERE? THIS GUY'S A HUSTLER. I DON'T EVEN THINK HE'S GOT A SHIP. IF HE DOES, IT'S GOING TO BE A PIECE OF JUNK.
THERE SHE IS. MY PRIDE AND JOY...

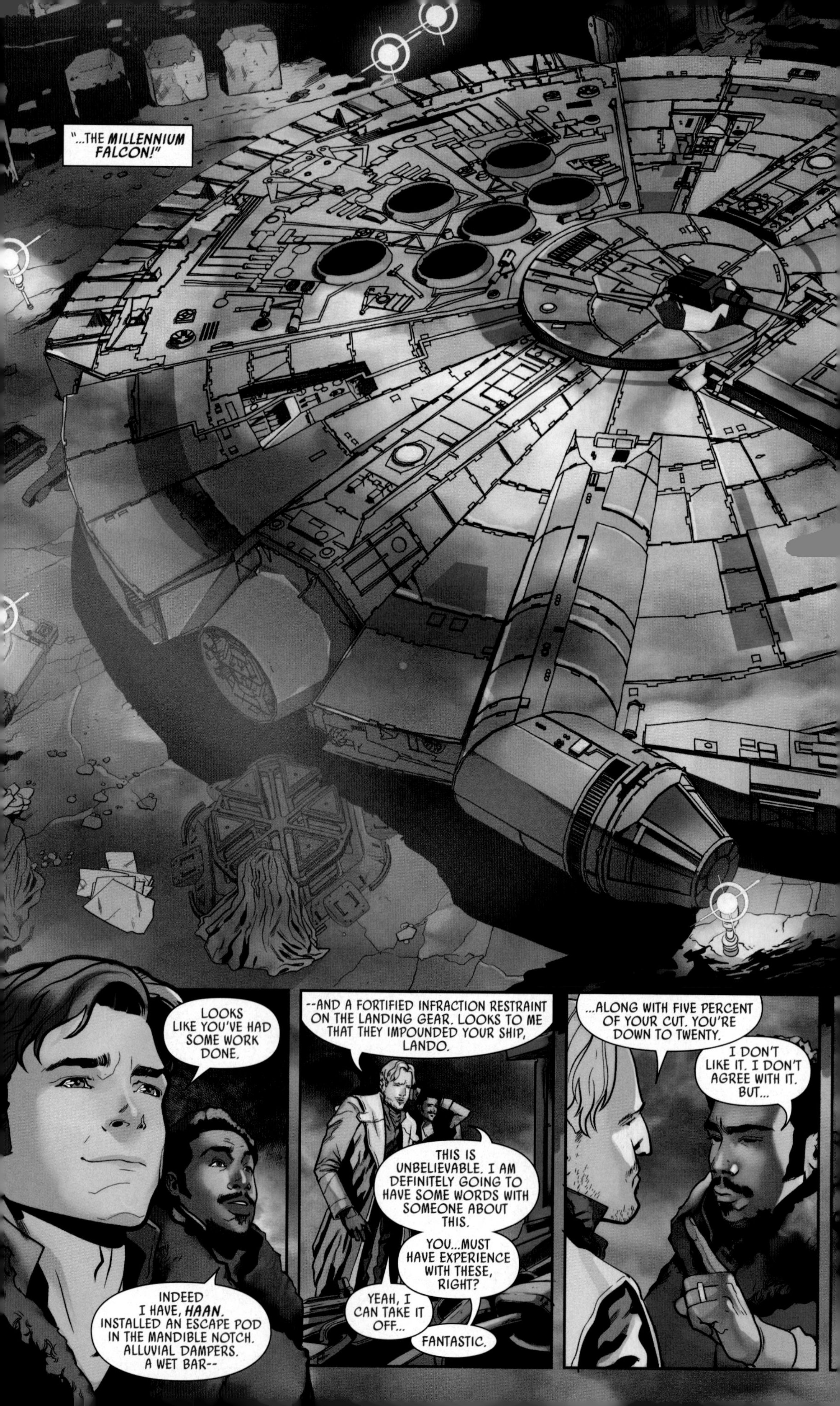

"...THE MILLENNIUM FALCON!"
LOOKS LIKE YOU'VE HAD SOME WORK DONE.
INDEED I HAVE, HAAN. INSTALLED AN ESCAPE POD IN THE MANDIBLE NOTCH. ALLUVIAL DAMPERS. A WET BAR--
--AND A FORTIFIED INFRACTION RESTRAINT ON THE LANDING GEAR. LOOKS TO ME THAT THEY IMPOUNDED YOUR SHIP, LANDO.
THIS IS UNBELIEVABLE. I AM DEFINITELY GOING TO HAVE SOME WORDS WITH SOMEONE ABOUT THIS.
YOU...MUST HAVE EXPERIENCE WITH THESE, RIGHT?
YEAH, I CAN TAKE IT OFF...
FANTASTIC.
...ALONG WITH FIVE PERCENT OF YOUR CUT. YOU'RE DOWN TO TWENTY.
I DON'T LIKE IT. I DON'T AGREE WITH IT. BUT...

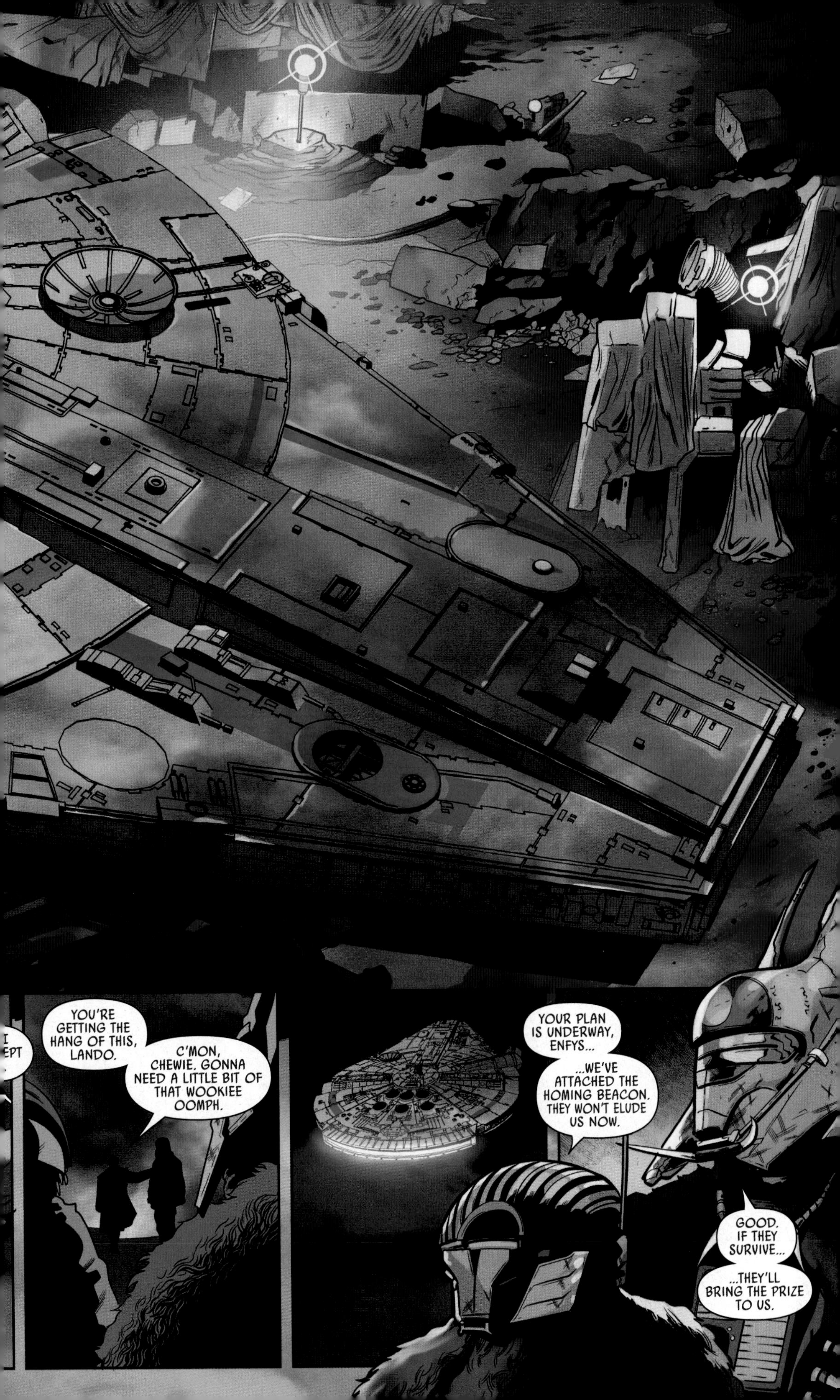

YOU'RE GETTING THE HANG OF THIS, LANDO.
C'MON, CHEWIE. GONNA NEED A LITTLE BIT OF THAT WOOKIEE OOMPH.
YOUR PLAN IS UNDERWAY, ENFYS...
...WE'VE ATTACHED THE HOMING BEACON. THEY WON'T ELUDE US NOW.
GOOD. IF THEY SURVIVE...
...THEY'LL BRING THE PRIZE TO US.

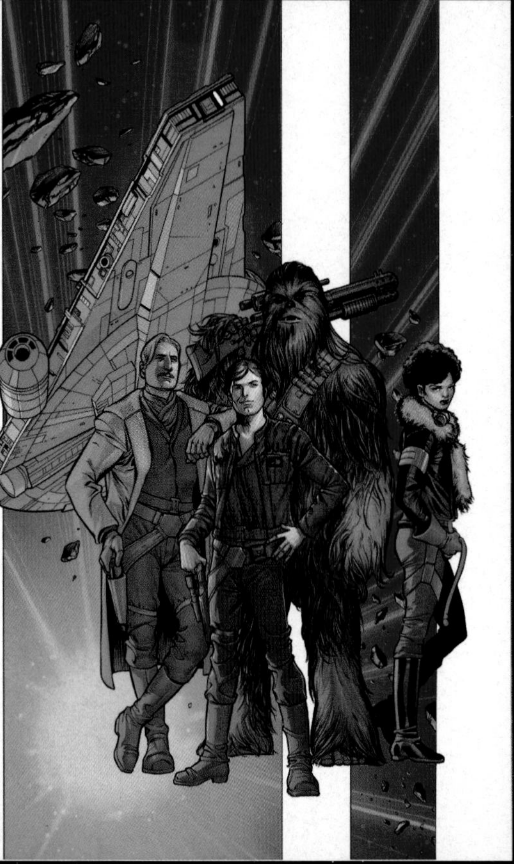

Issue #2 variant by Carlos Pacheco & Jesus Aburtov

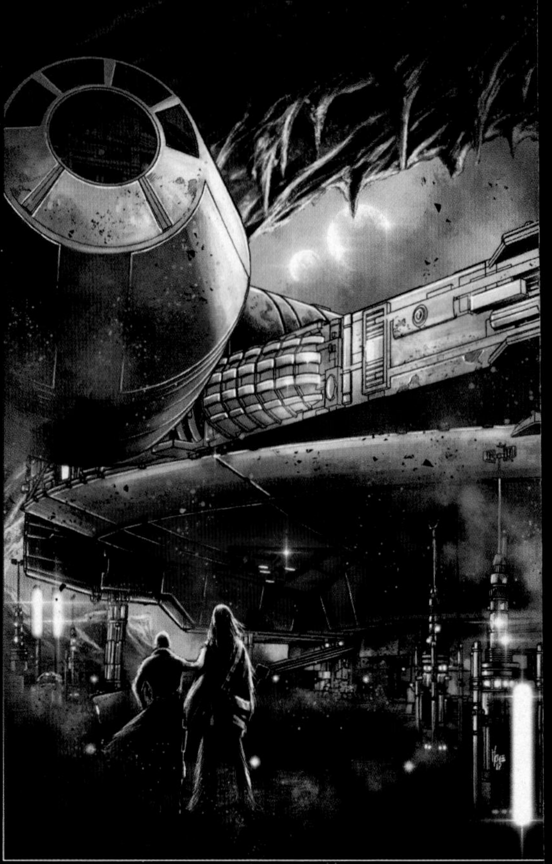

Issue #3 variant by Marco Checchetto

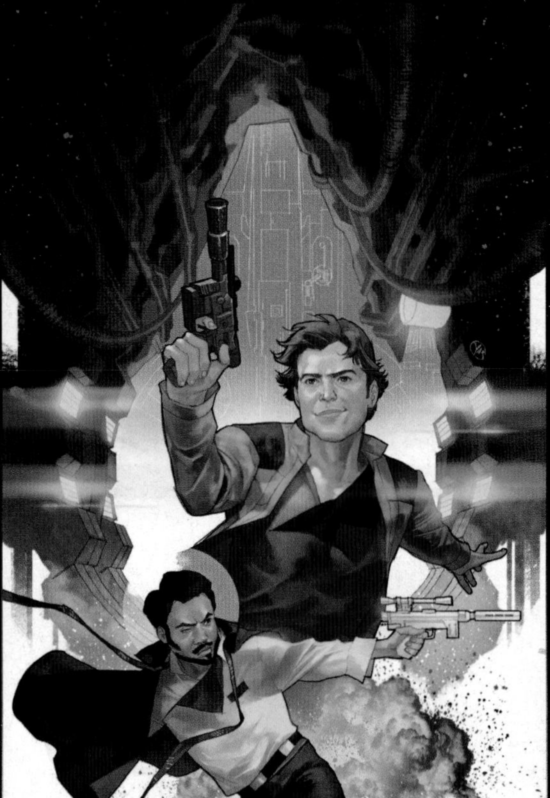

Issue #4 variant by Yasmine Putri

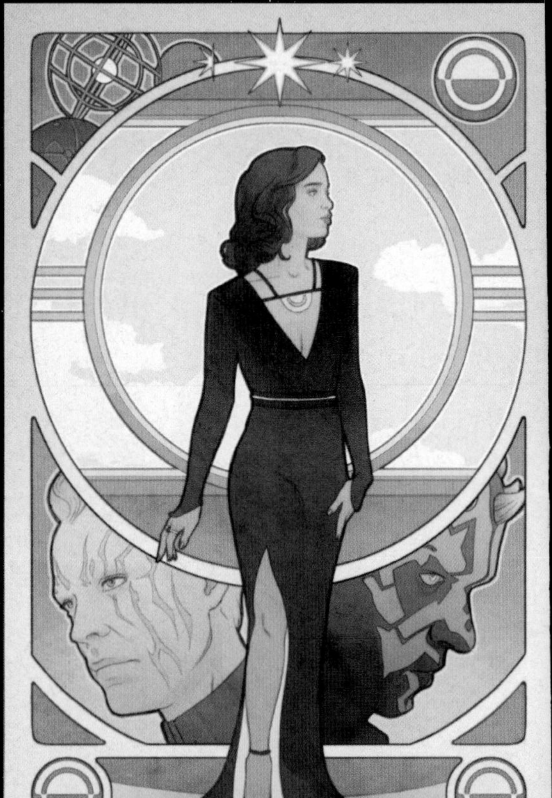

Issue #5 variant by W. Scott Forbes

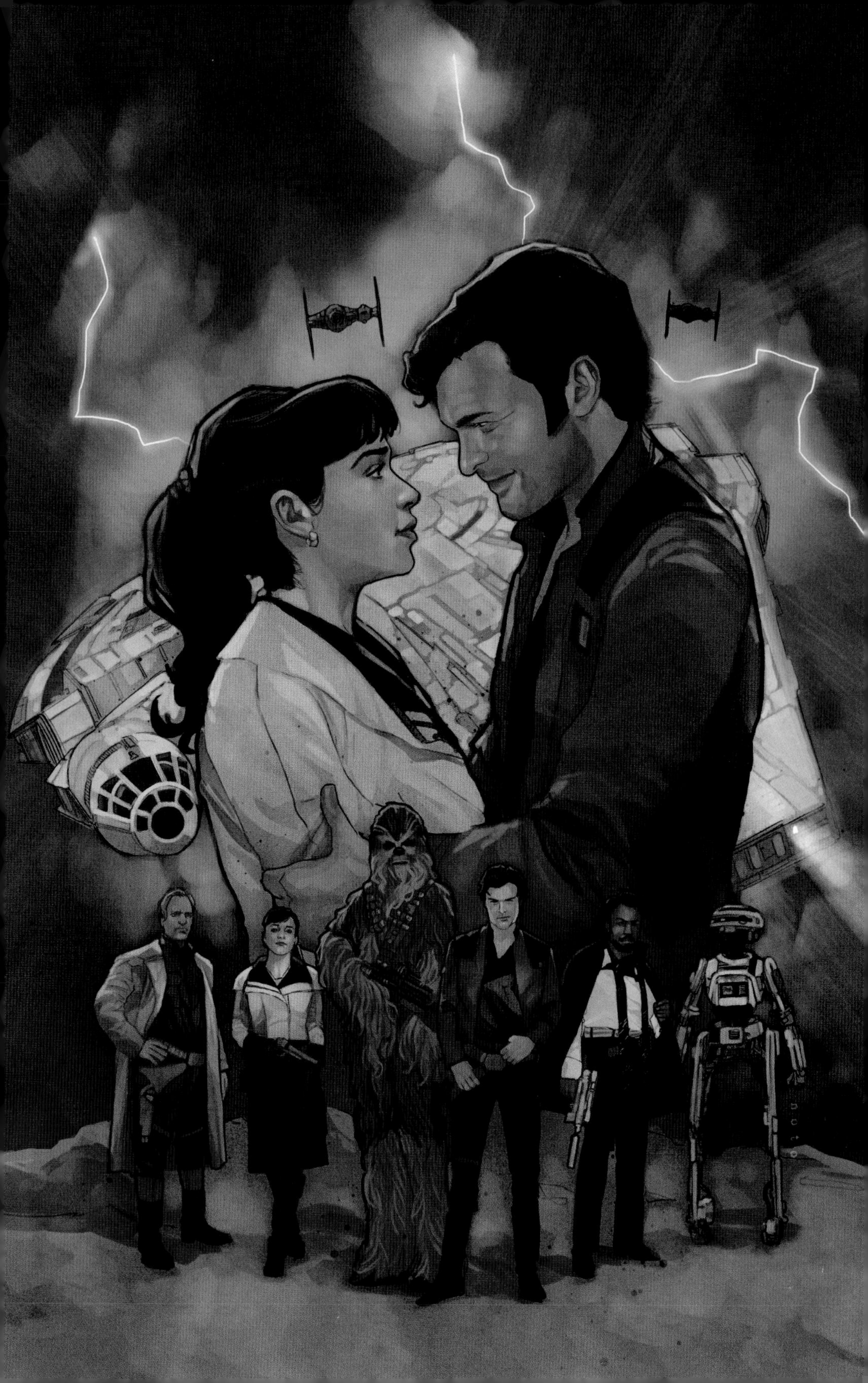

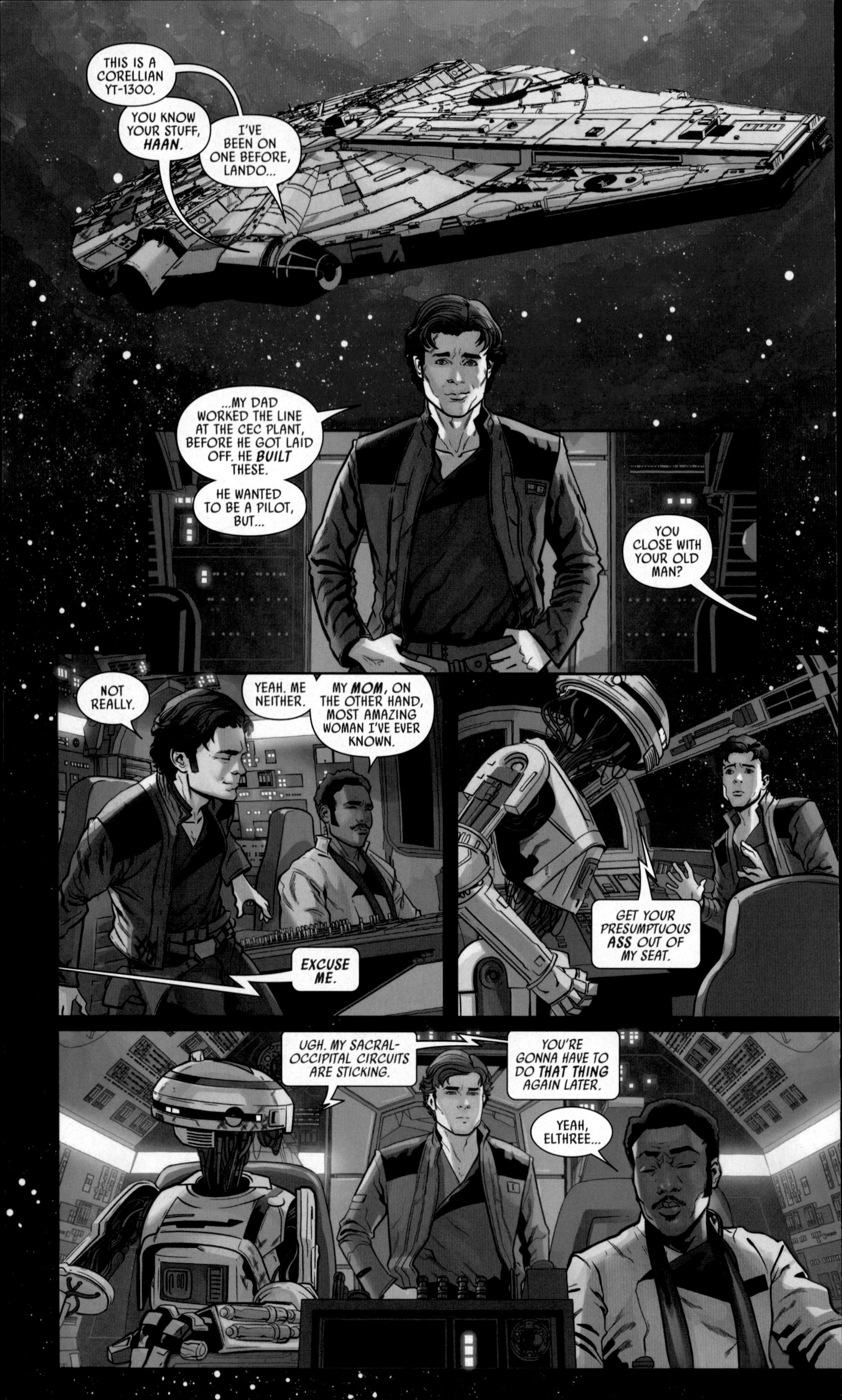
THIS IS A CORELLIAN YT-1300.
YOU KNOW YOUR STUFF, HAAN.
I'VE BEEN ON ONE BEFORE, LANDO...
...MY DAD WORKED THE LINE AT THE CEC PLANT, BEFORE HE GOT LAID OFF. HE BUILT THESE.
HE WANTED TO BE A PILOT, BUT...
YOU CLOSE WITH YOUR OLD MAN?
NOT REALLY.
YEAH. ME NEITHER.
MY MOM, ON THE OTHER HAND, MOST AMAZING WOMAN I'VE EVER KNOWN.
EXCUSE ME.
GET YOUR PRESUMPTUOUS ASS OUT OF MY SEAT.
UGH. MY SACRAL-OCCIPITAL CIRCUITS ARE STICKING.
YOU'RE GONNA HAVE TO DO THAT THING AGAIN LATER.
YEAH, ELTHREE...

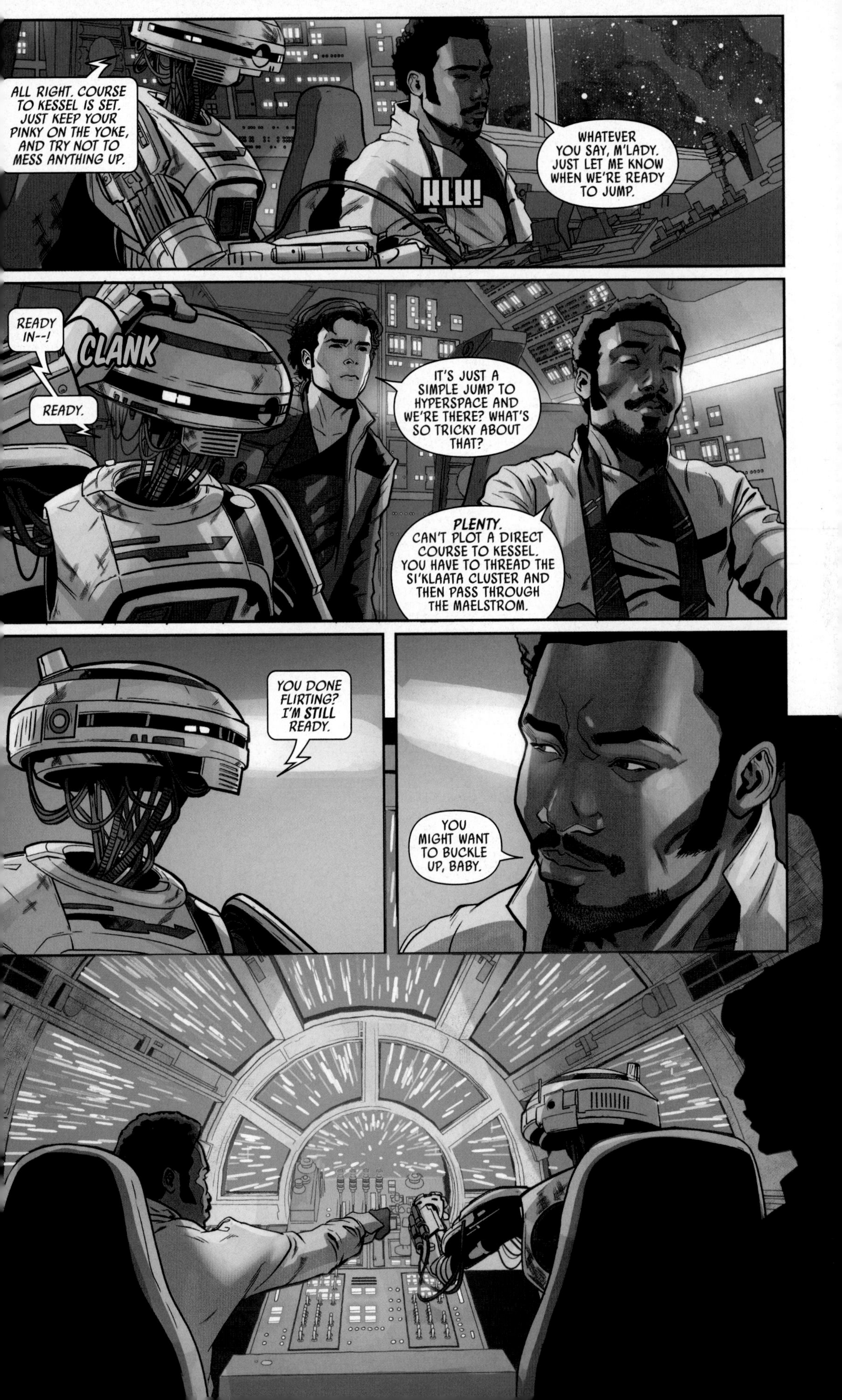
ALL RIGHT. COURSE TO KESSEL IS SET. JUST KEEP YOUR PINKY ON THE YOKE, AND TRY NOT TO MESS ANYTHING UP.
KLK!
WHATEVER YOU SAY, M'LADY. JUST LET ME KNOW WHEN WE'RE READY TO JUMP.
READY IN--!
CLANK
READY.
IT'S JUST A SIMPLE JUMP TO HYPERSPACE AND WE'RE THERE? WHAT'S SO TRICKY ABOUT THAT?
PLENTY. CAN'T PLOT A DIRECT COURSE TO KESSEL. YOU HAVE TO THREAD THE SI'KLAATA CLUSTER AND THEN PASS THROUGH THE MAELSTROM.
YOU DONE FLIRTING? I'M STILL READY.
YOU MIGHT WANT TO BUCKLE UP, BABY.

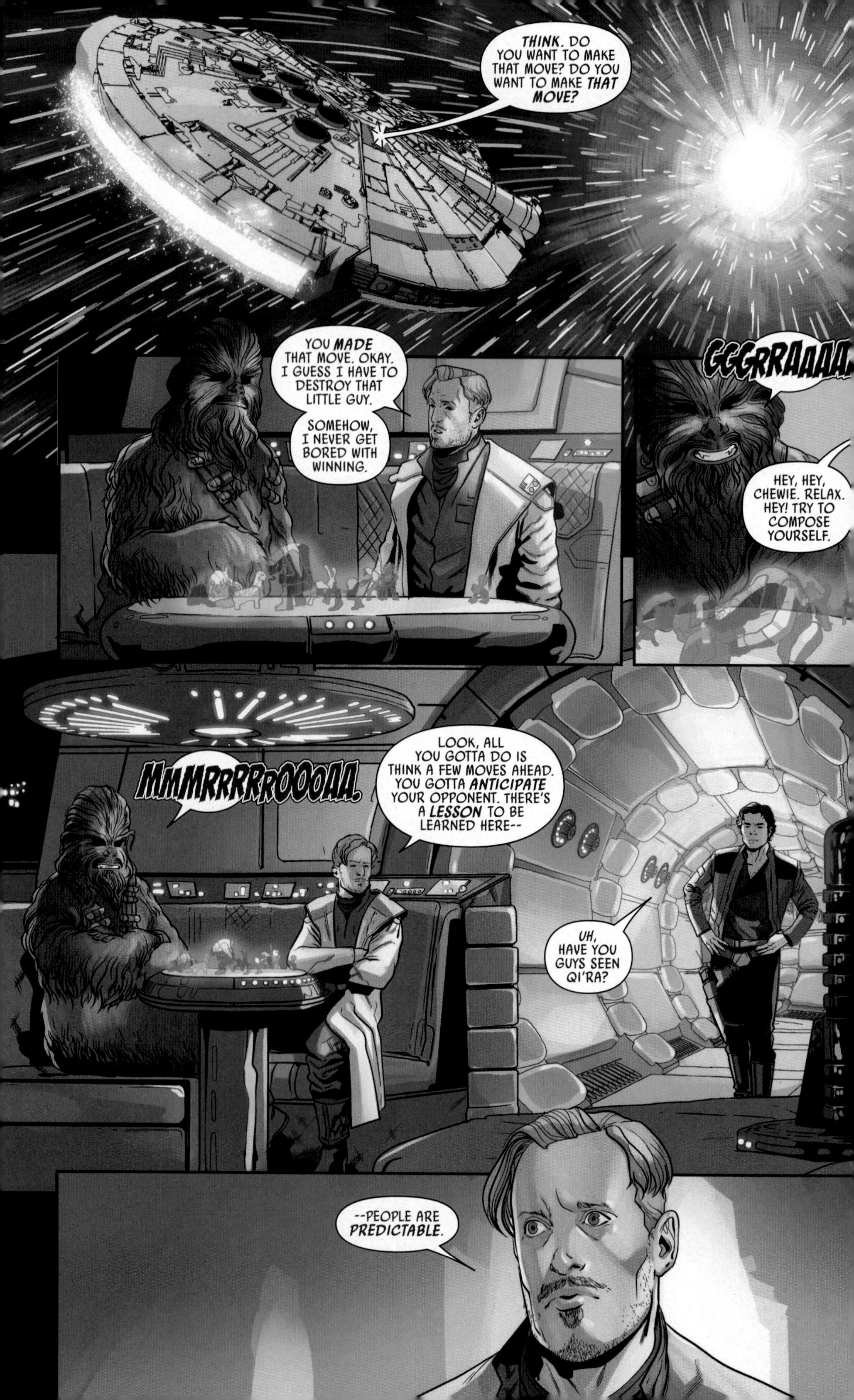
THINK. DO YOU WANT TO MAKE THAT MOVE? DO YOU WANT TO MAKE THAT MOVE?
YOU MADE THAT MOVE. OKAY. I GUESS I HAVE TO DESTROY THAT LITTLE GUY.
SOMEHOW, I NEVER GET BORED WITH WINNING.
GGGRRAAAAA
HEY, HEY, CHEWIE. RELAX. HEY! TRY TO COMPOSE YOURSELF.
MMMRRRRROOOAA.
LOOK, ALL YOU GOTTA DO IS THINK A FEW MOVES AHEAD. YOU GOTTA ANTICIPATE YOUR OPPONENT. THERE'S A LESSON TO BE LEARNED HERE--
UH, HAVE YOU GUYS SEEN QI'RA?
--PEOPLE ARE PREDICTABLE.

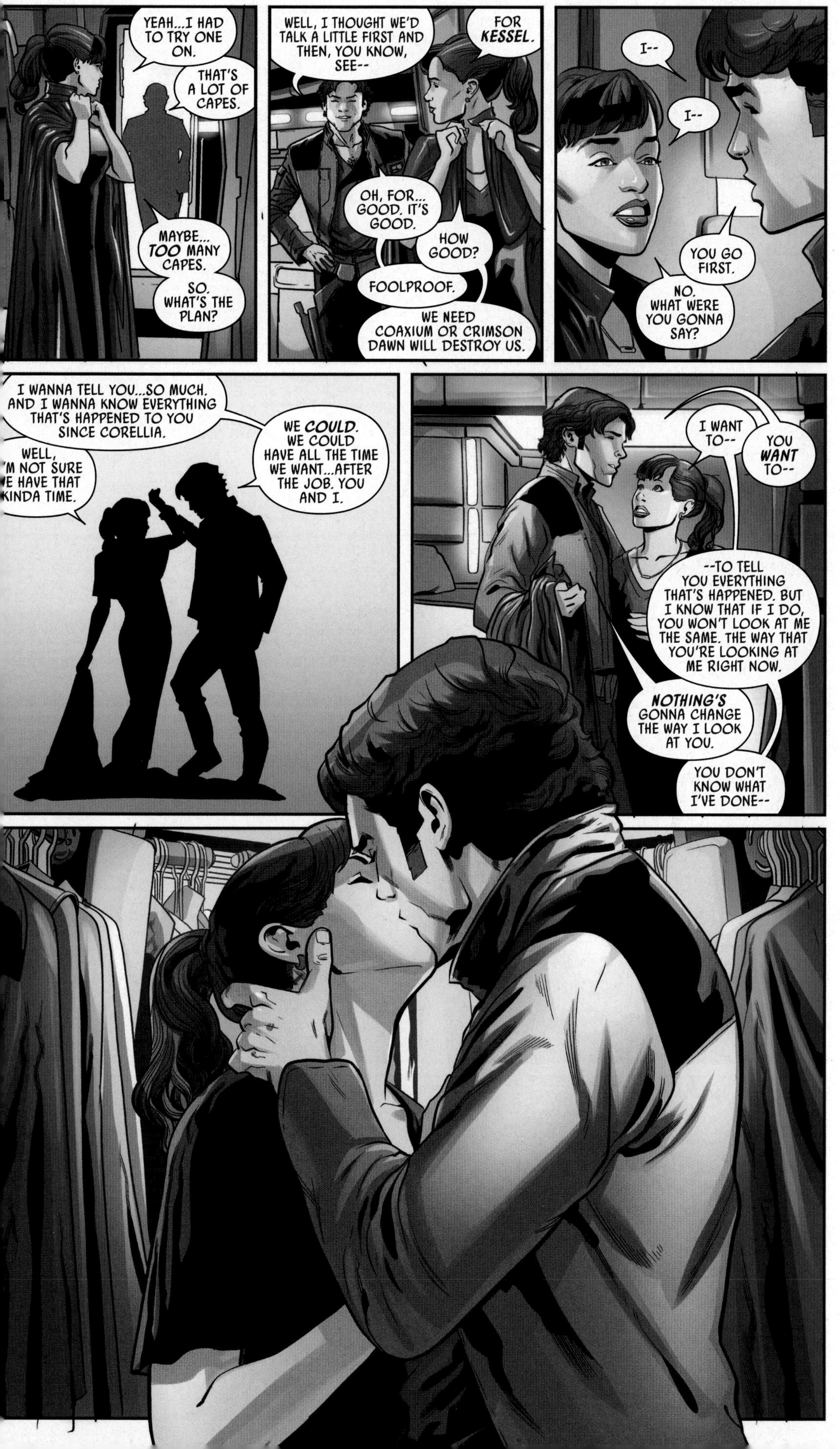
YEAH...I HAD TO TRY ONE ON.
THAT'S A LOT OF CAPES.
MAYBE... TOO MANY CAPES.
SO. WHAT'S THE PLAN?
WELL, I THOUGHT WE'D TALK A LITTLE FIRST AND THEN, YOU KNOW, SEE--
FOR KESSEL.
OH, FOR... GOOD. IT'S GOOD.
HOW GOOD?
FOOLPROOF.
WE NEED COAXIUM OR CRIMSON DAWN WILL DESTROY US.
I--
I--
YOU GO FIRST.
NO. WHAT WERE YOU GONNA SAY?
I WANNA TELL YOU...SO MUCH. AND I WANNA KNOW EVERYTHING THAT'S HAPPENED TO YOU SINCE CORELLIA.
WELL, I'M NOT SURE WE HAVE THAT KINDA TIME.
WE COULD. WE COULD HAVE ALL THE TIME WE WANT...AFTER THE JOB. YOU AND I.
I WANT TO--
YOU WANT TO--
--TO TELL YOU EVERYTHING THAT'S HAPPENED. BUT I KNOW THAT IF I DO, YOU WON'T LOOK AT ME THE SAME. THE WAY THAT YOU'RE LOOKING AT ME RIGHT NOW.
NOTHING'S GONNA CHANGE THE WAY I LOOK AT YOU.
YOU DON'T KNOW WHAT I'VE DONE--

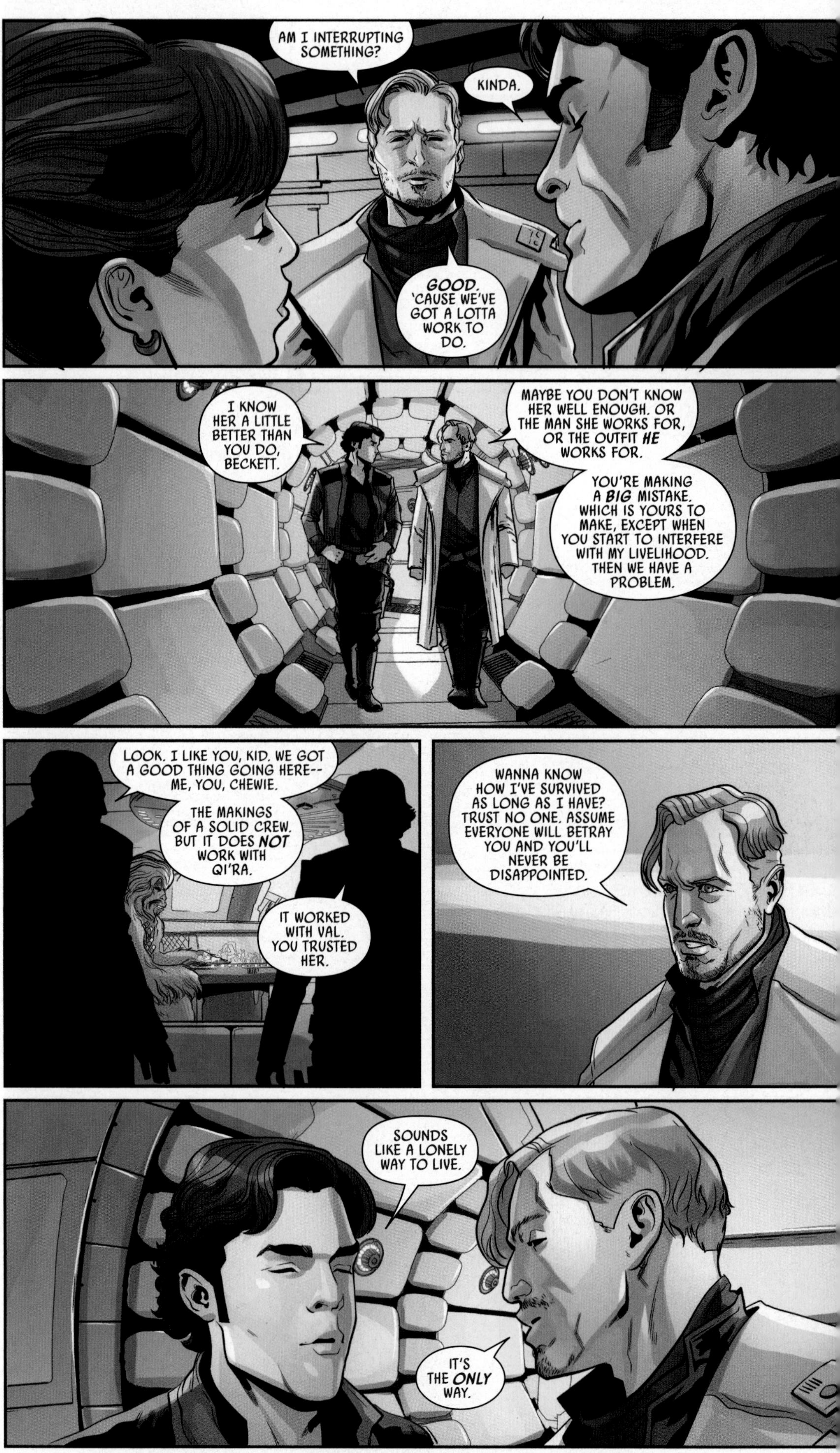
AM I INTERRUPTING SOMETHING?
KINDA.
GOOD. 'CAUSE WE'VE GOT A LOTTA WORK TO DO.
I KNOW HER A LITTLE BETTER THAN YOU DO, BECKETT.
MAYBE YOU DON'T KNOW HER WELL ENOUGH. OR THE MAN SHE WORKS FOR, OR THE OUTFIT HE WORKS FOR.
YOU'RE MAKING A BIG MISTAKE. WHICH IS YOURS TO MAKE, EXCEPT WHEN YOU START TO INTERFERE WITH MY LIVELIHOOD. THEN WE HAVE A PROBLEM.
LOOK. I LIKE YOU, KID. WE GOT A GOOD THING GOING HERE-- ME, YOU, CHEWIE.
THE MAKINGS OF A SOLID CREW. BUT IT DOES NOT WORK WITH QI'RA.
IT WORKED WITH VAL. YOU TRUSTED HER.
WANNA KNOW HOW I'VE SURVIVED AS LONG AS I HAVE? TRUST NO ONE. ASSUME EVERYONE WILL BETRAY YOU AND YOU'LL NEVER BE DISAPPOINTED.
SOUNDS LIKE A LONELY WAY TO LIVE.
IT'S THE ONLY WAY.

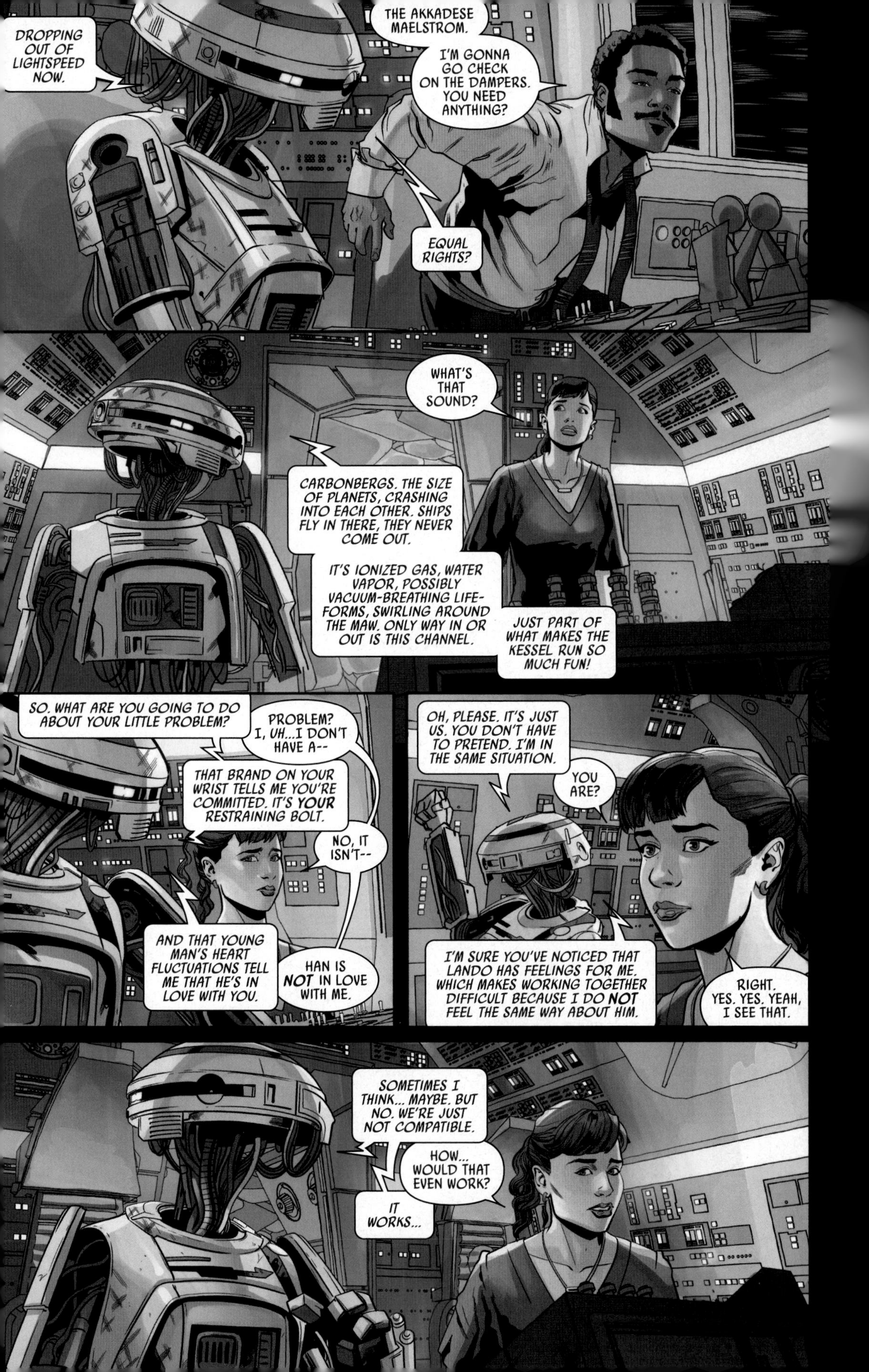

DROPPING OUT OF LIGHTSPEED NOW.
THE AKKADESE MAELSTROM.
I'M GONNA GO CHECK ON THE DAMPERS. YOU NEED ANYTHING?
EQUAL RIGHTS?
WHAT'S THAT SOUND?
CARBONBERGS. THE SIZE OF PLANETS, CRASHING INTO EACH OTHER. SHIPS FLY IN THERE, THEY NEVER COME OUT.
IT'S IONIZED GAS, WATER VAPOR, POSSIBLY VACUUM-BREATHING LIFE-FORMS, SWIRLING AROUND THE MAW. ONLY WAY IN OR OUT IS THIS CHANNEL.
JUST PART OF WHAT MAKES THE KESSEL RUN SO MUCH FUN!
SO. WHAT ARE YOU GOING TO DO ABOUT YOUR LITTLE PROBLEM?
PROBLEM? I, UH...I DON'T HAVE A--
THAT BRAND ON YOUR WRIST TELLS ME YOU'RE COMMITTED. IT'S **YOUR** RESTRAINING BOLT.
NO, IT ISN'T--
AND THAT YOUNG MAN'S HEART FLUCTUATIONS TELL ME THAT HE'S IN LOVE WITH YOU.
HAN IS **NOT** IN LOVE WITH ME.
OH, PLEASE. IT'S JUST US. YOU DON'T HAVE TO PRETEND. I'M IN THE SAME SITUATION.
YOU ARE?
I'M SURE YOU'VE NOTICED THAT LANDO HAS FEELINGS FOR ME. WHICH MAKES WORKING TOGETHER DIFFICULT BECAUSE I DO **NOT** FEEL THE SAME WAY ABOUT HIM.
RIGHT. YES. YES. YEAH, I SEE THAT.
SOMETIMES I THINK... MAYBE. BUT NO. WE'RE JUST NOT COMPATIBLE.
HOW... WOULD THAT EVEN WORK?
IT WORKS...

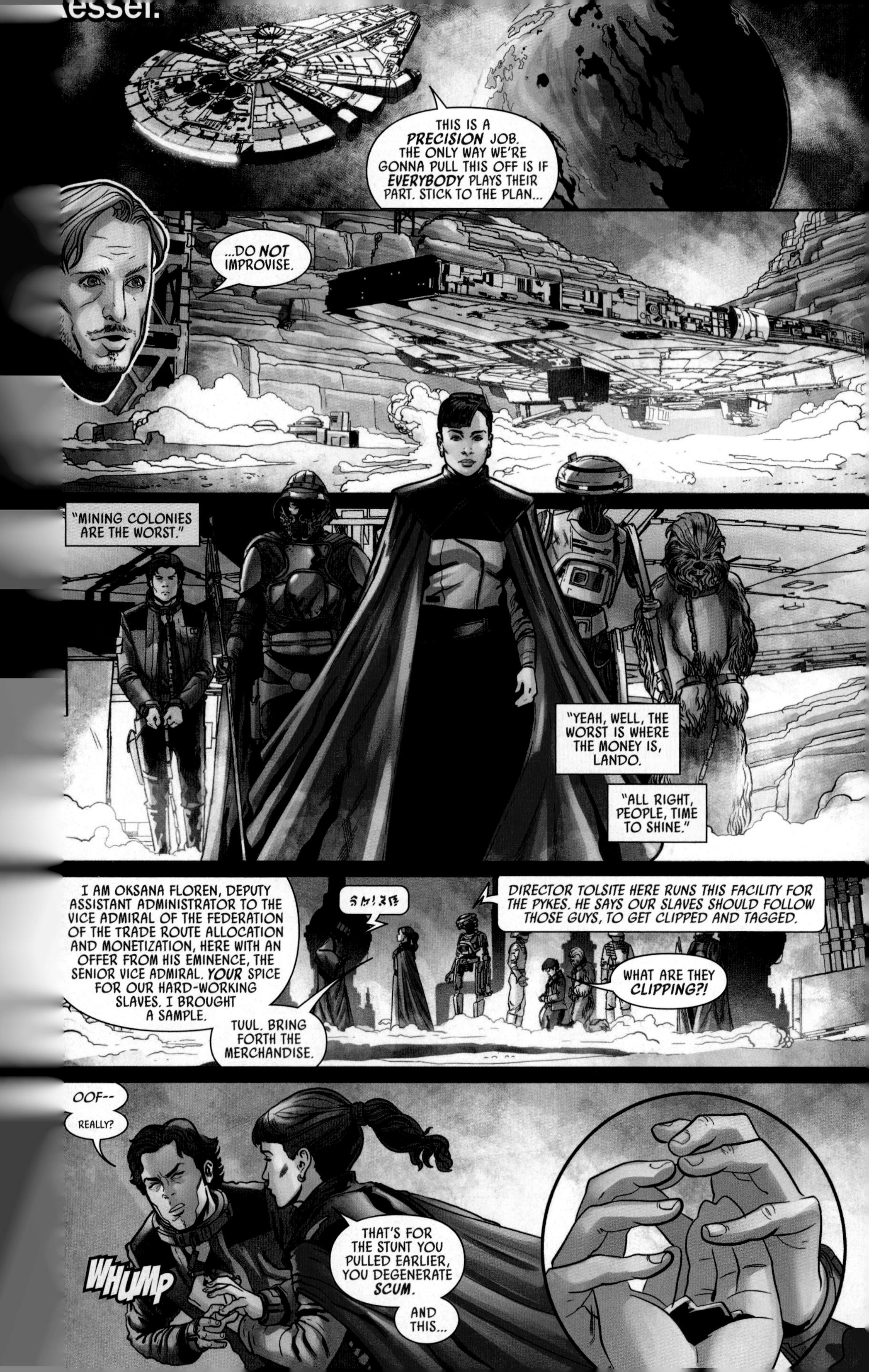
essel.
THIS IS A PRECISION JOB. THE ONLY WAY WE'RE GONNA PULL THIS OFF IS IF EVERYBODY PLAYS THEIR PART. STICK TO THE PLAN...
...DO NOT IMPROVISE.
"MINING COLONIES ARE THE WORST."
"YEAH, WELL, THE WORST IS WHERE THE MONEY IS, LANDO.
"ALL RIGHT, PEOPLE, TIME TO SHINE."
I AM OKSANA FLOREN, DEPUTY ASSISTANT ADMINISTRATOR TO THE VICE ADMIRAL OF THE FEDERATION OF THE TRADE ROUTE ALLOCATION AND MONETIZATION, HERE WITH AN OFFER FROM HIS EMINENCE, THE SENIOR VICE ADMIRAL. YOUR SPICE FOR OUR HARD-WORKING SLAVES. I BROUGHT A SAMPLE.
TUUL. BRING FORTH THE MERCHANDISE.
DIRECTOR TOLSITE HERE RUNS THIS FACILITY FOR THE PYKES. HE SAYS OUR SLAVES SHOULD FOLLOW THOSE GUYS, TO GET CLIPPED AND TAGGED.
WHAT ARE THEY CLIPPING?!
OOF--
REALLY?
WHUMP
THAT'S FOR THE STUNT YOU PULLED EARLIER, YOU DEGENERATE SCUM.
AND THIS...

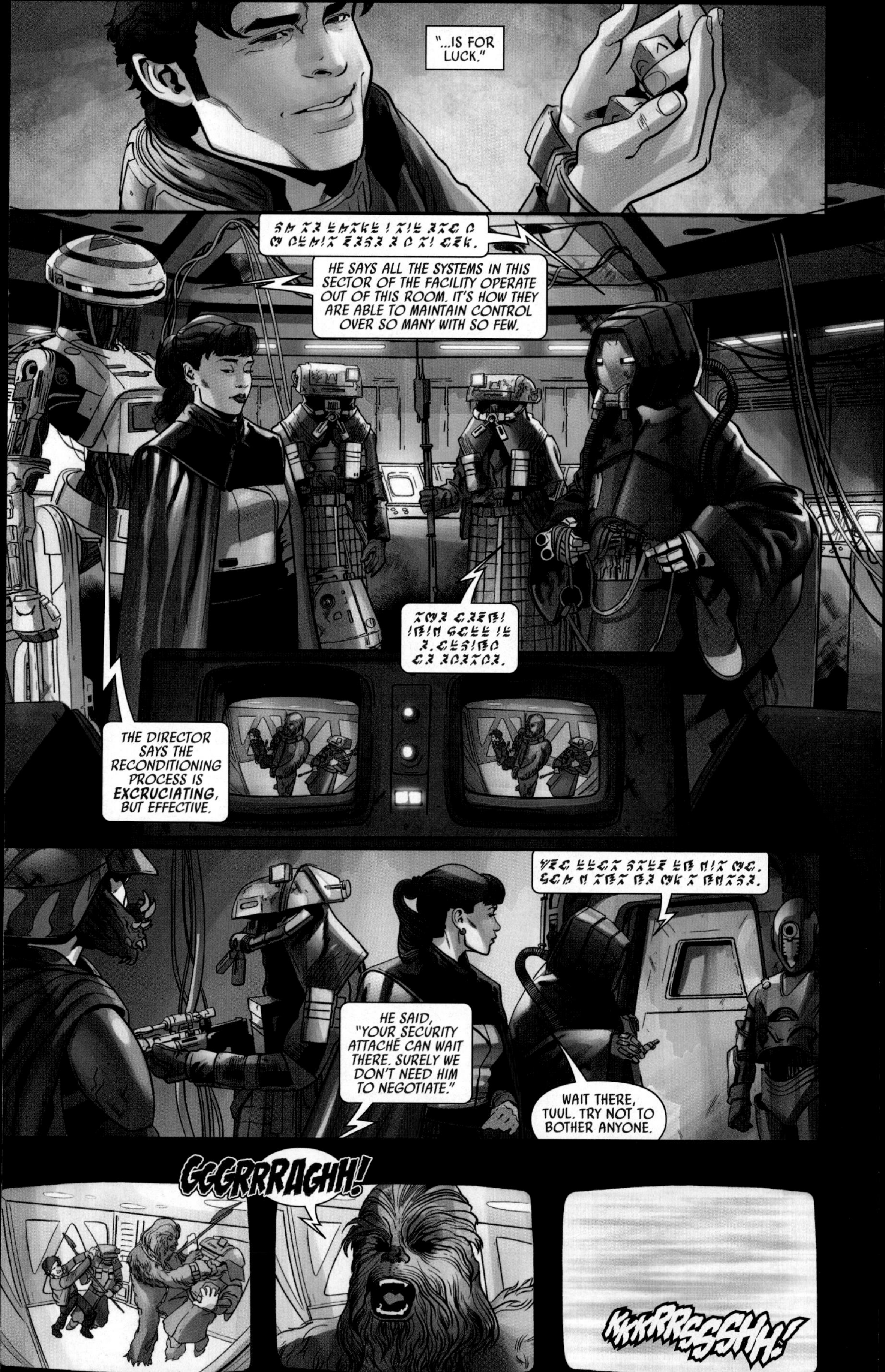
"...IS FOR LUCK."
HE SAYS ALL THE SYSTEMS IN THIS SECTOR OF THE FACILITY OPERATE OUT OF THIS ROOM. IT'S HOW THEY ARE ABLE TO MAINTAIN CONTROL OVER SO MANY WITH SO FEW.
THE DIRECTOR SAYS THE RECONDITIONING PROCESS IS EXCRUCIATING, BUT EFFECTIVE.
HE SAID, "YOUR SECURITY ATTACHÉ CAN WAIT THERE. SURELY WE DON'T NEED HIM TO NEGOTIATE."
WAIT THERE, TUUL. TRY NOT TO BOTHER ANYONE.
GGGRRRRAGHH!
KKKRRSSSHH!

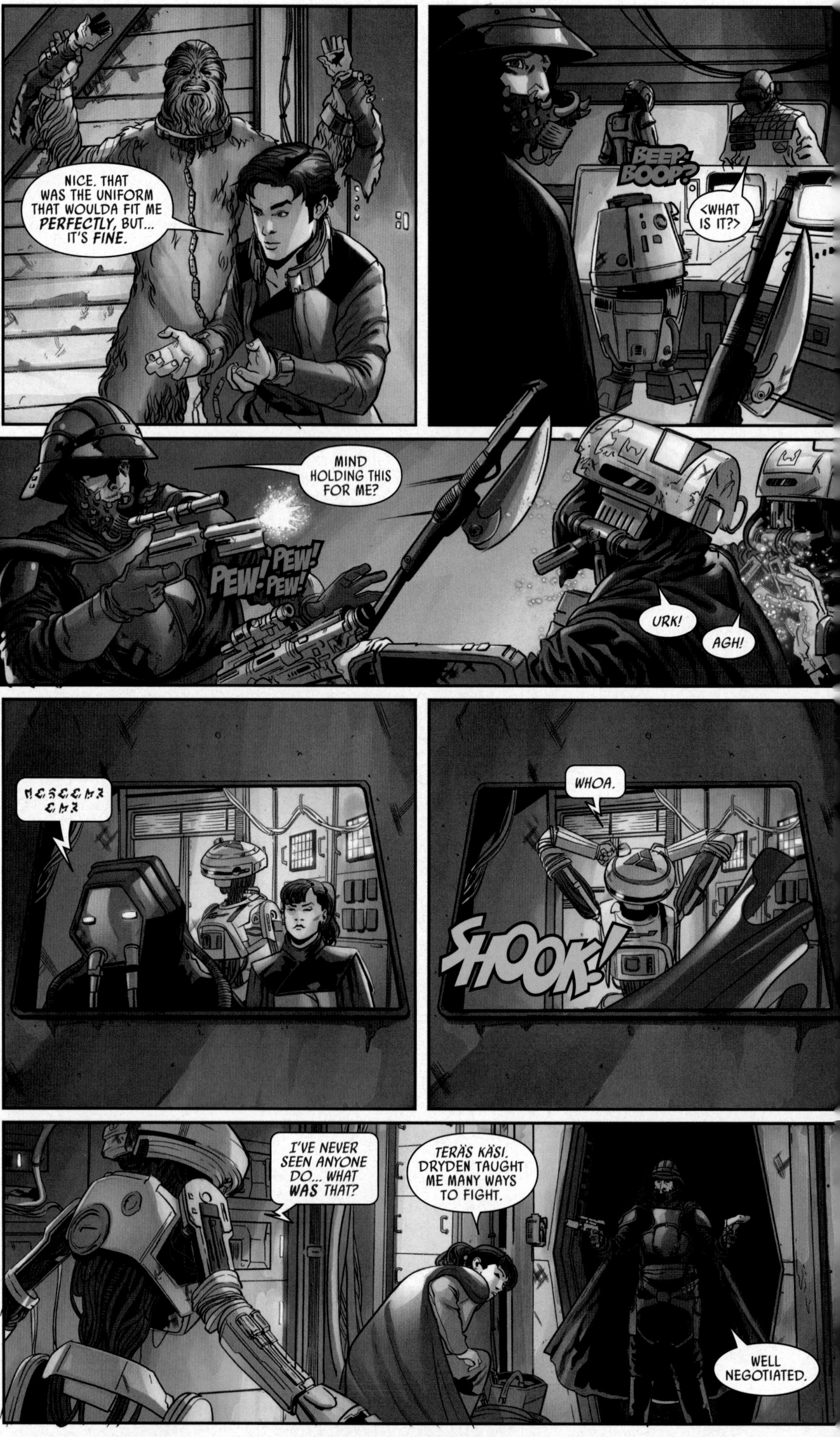

NICE. THAT WAS THE UNIFORM THAT WOULDA FIT ME PERFECTLY, BUT... IT'S FINE.
BEEP-BOOP?
<WHAT IS IT?>
MIND HOLDING THIS FOR ME?
PEW! PEW! PEW!
URK!
AGH!
WHOA.
SHOOK!
I'VE NEVER SEEN ANYONE DO... WHAT WAS THAT?
TERÄS KÄSI. DRYDEN TAUGHT ME MANY WAYS TO FIGHT.
WELL NEGOTIATED.

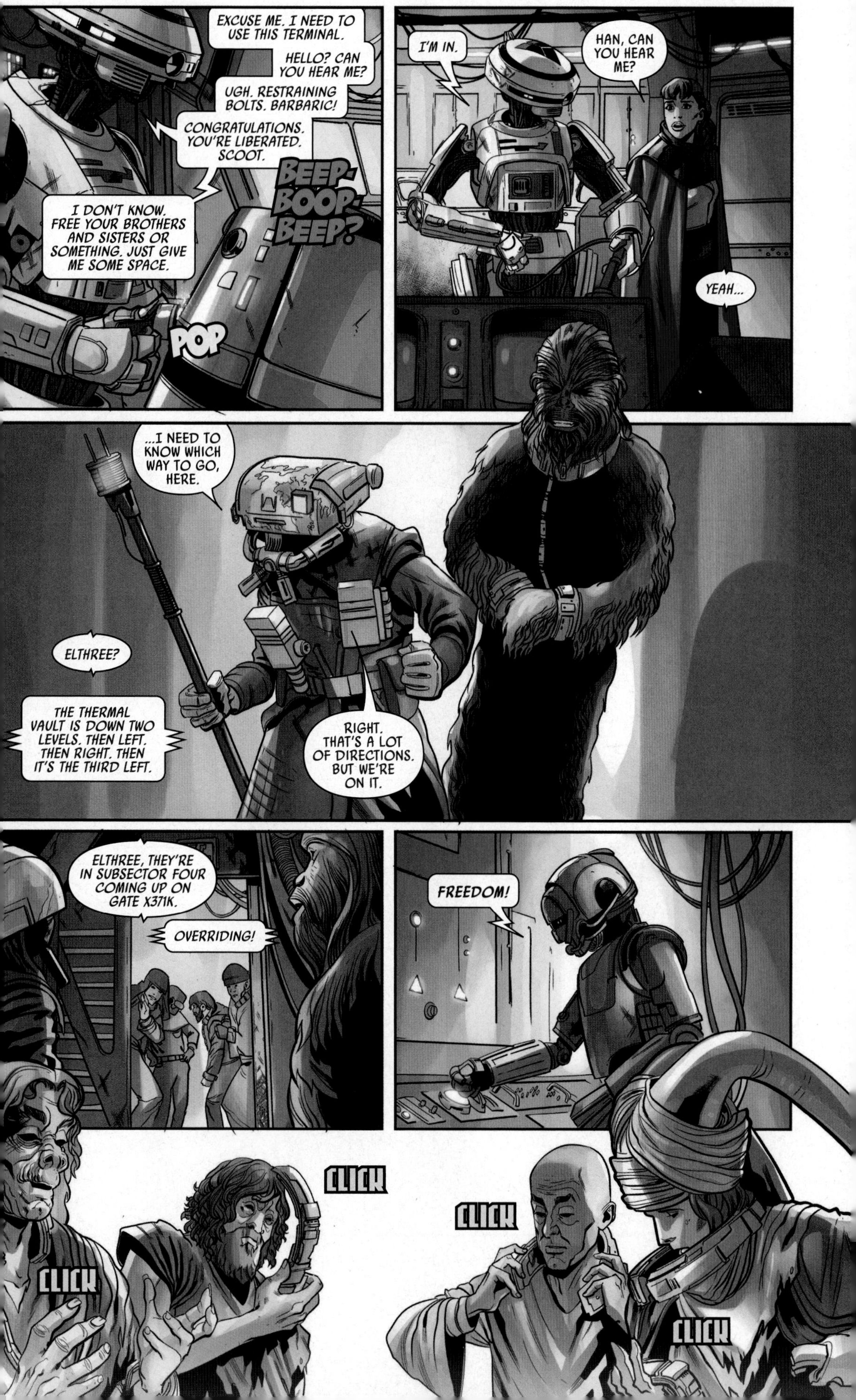
EXCUSE ME. I NEED TO USE THIS TERMINAL.
HELLO? CAN YOU HEAR ME?
UGH. RESTRAINING BOLTS. BARBARIC!
POP
CONGRATULATIONS. YOU'RE LIBERATED. SCOOT.
BEEP-BOOP-BEEP?
I DON'T KNOW. FREE YOUR BROTHERS AND SISTERS OR SOMETHING. JUST GIVE ME SOME SPACE.
I'M IN.
HAN, CAN YOU HEAR ME?
YEAH...
...I NEED TO KNOW WHICH WAY TO GO, HERE.
ELTHREE?
THE THERMAL VAULT IS DOWN TWO LEVELS. THEN LEFT. THEN RIGHT. THEN IT'S THE THIRD LEFT.
RIGHT. THAT'S A LOT OF DIRECTIONS. BUT WE'RE ON IT.
ELTHREE, THEY'RE IN SUBSECTOR FOUR COMING UP ON GATE X371K.
OVERRIDING!
FREEDOM!
CLICK
CLICK
CLICK
CLICK

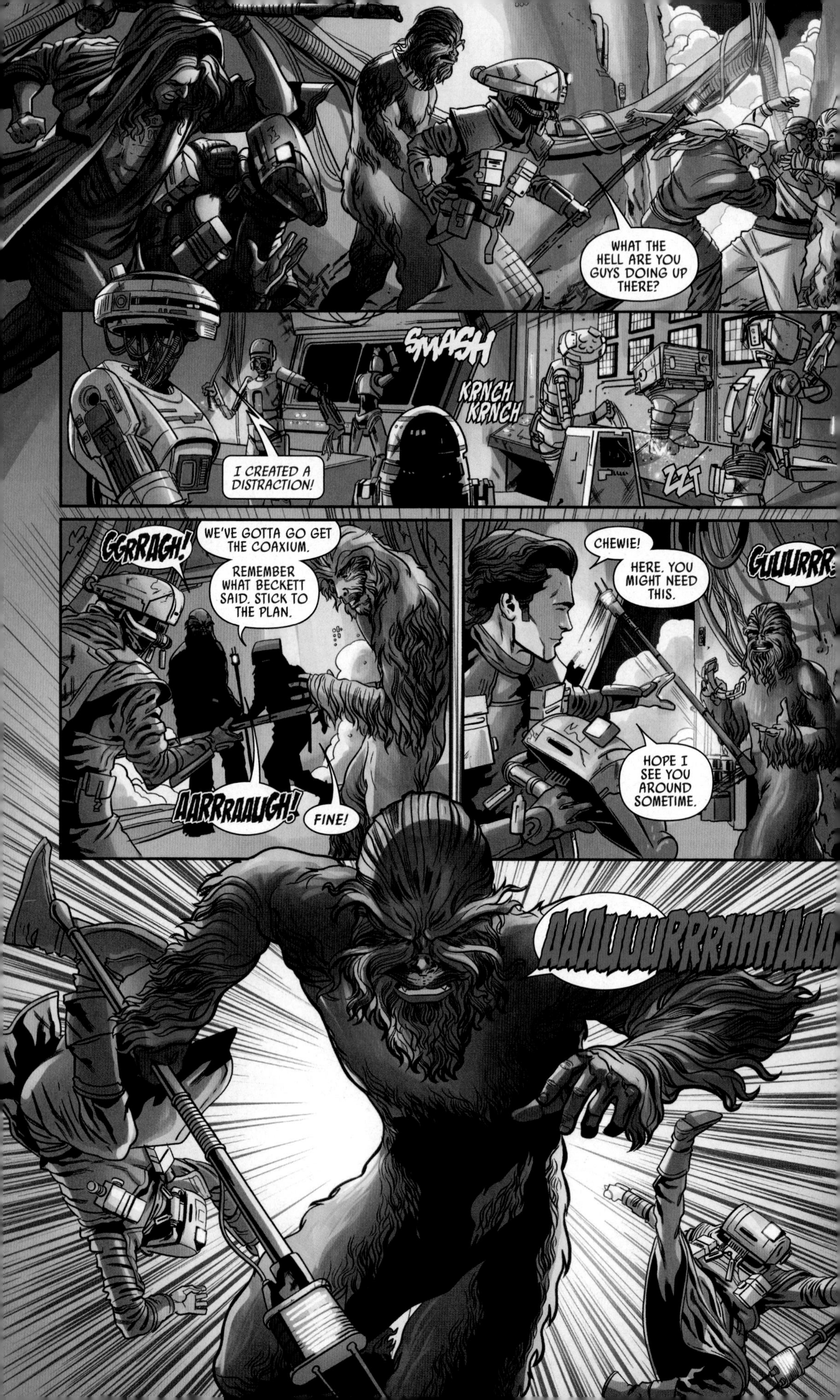
WHAT THE HELL ARE YOU GUYS DOING UP THERE?
SMASH
KRNCH KRNCH
I CREATED A DISTRACTION!
ZZT
GGRRAGH!
WE'VE GOTTA GO GET THE COAXIUM.
REMEMBER WHAT BECKETT SAID. STICK TO THE PLAN.
AARRRAAUGH!
FINE!
CHEWIE!
HERE. YOU MIGHT NEED THIS.
GUUURRR
HOPE I SEE YOU AROUND SOMETIME.
AAAUUURRRHHHAAA

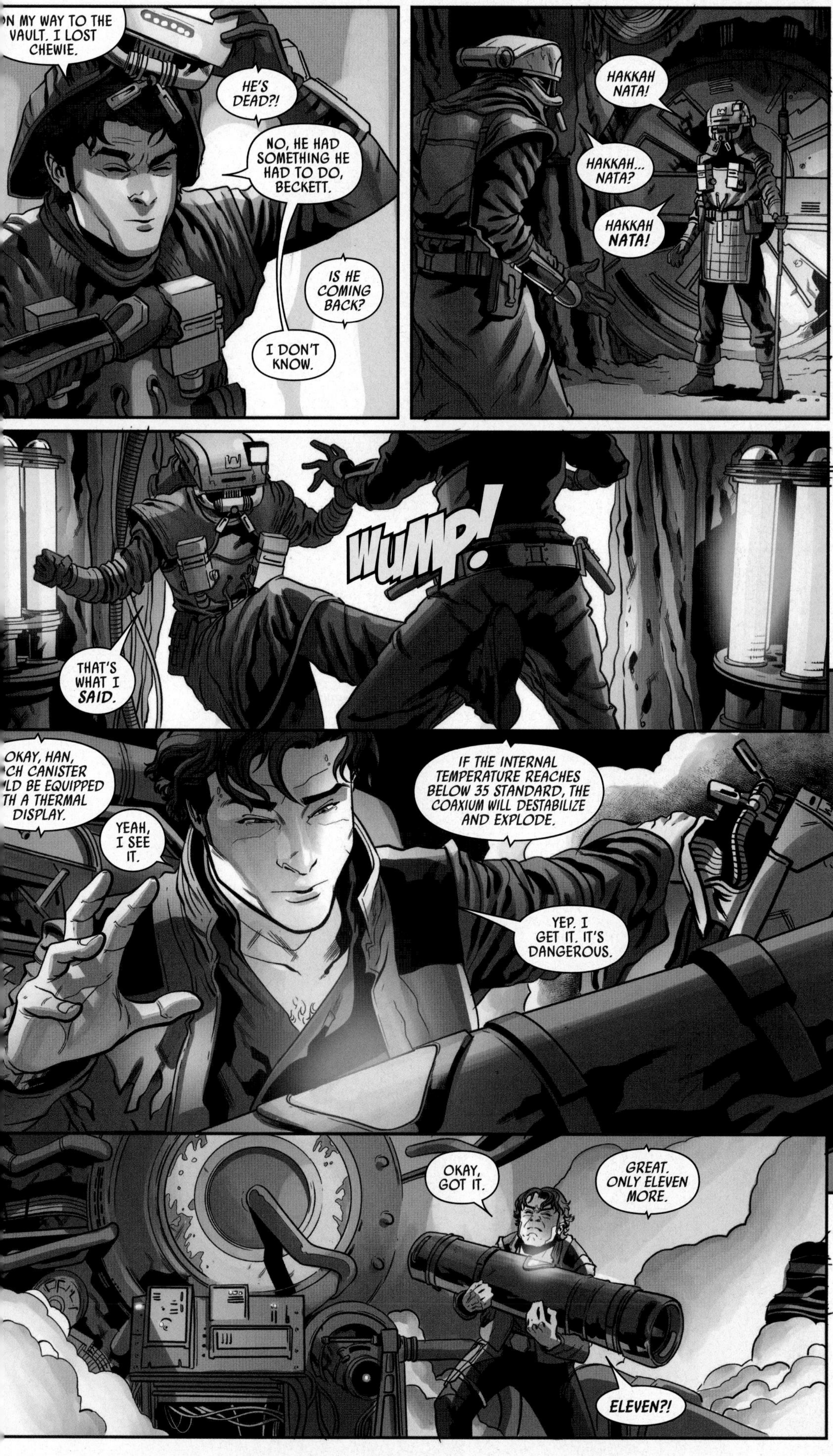
ON MY WAY TO THE VAULT. I LOST CHEWIE.
HE'S DEAD?!
NO, HE HAD SOMETHING HE HAD TO DO, BECKETT.
IS HE COMING BACK?
I DON'T KNOW.
HAKKAH NATA!
HAKKAH... NATA?
HAKKAH NATA!
WUMP!
THAT'S WHAT I SAID.
OKAY, HAN, CH CANISTER LD BE EQUIPPED TH A THERMAL DISPLAY.
YEAH, I SEE IT.
IF THE INTERNAL TEMPERATURE REACHES BELOW 35 STANDARD, THE COAXIUM WILL DESTABILIZE AND EXPLODE.
YEP. I GET IT. IT'S DANGEROUS.
OKAY, GOT IT.
GREAT. ONLY ELEVEN MORE.
ELEVEN?!

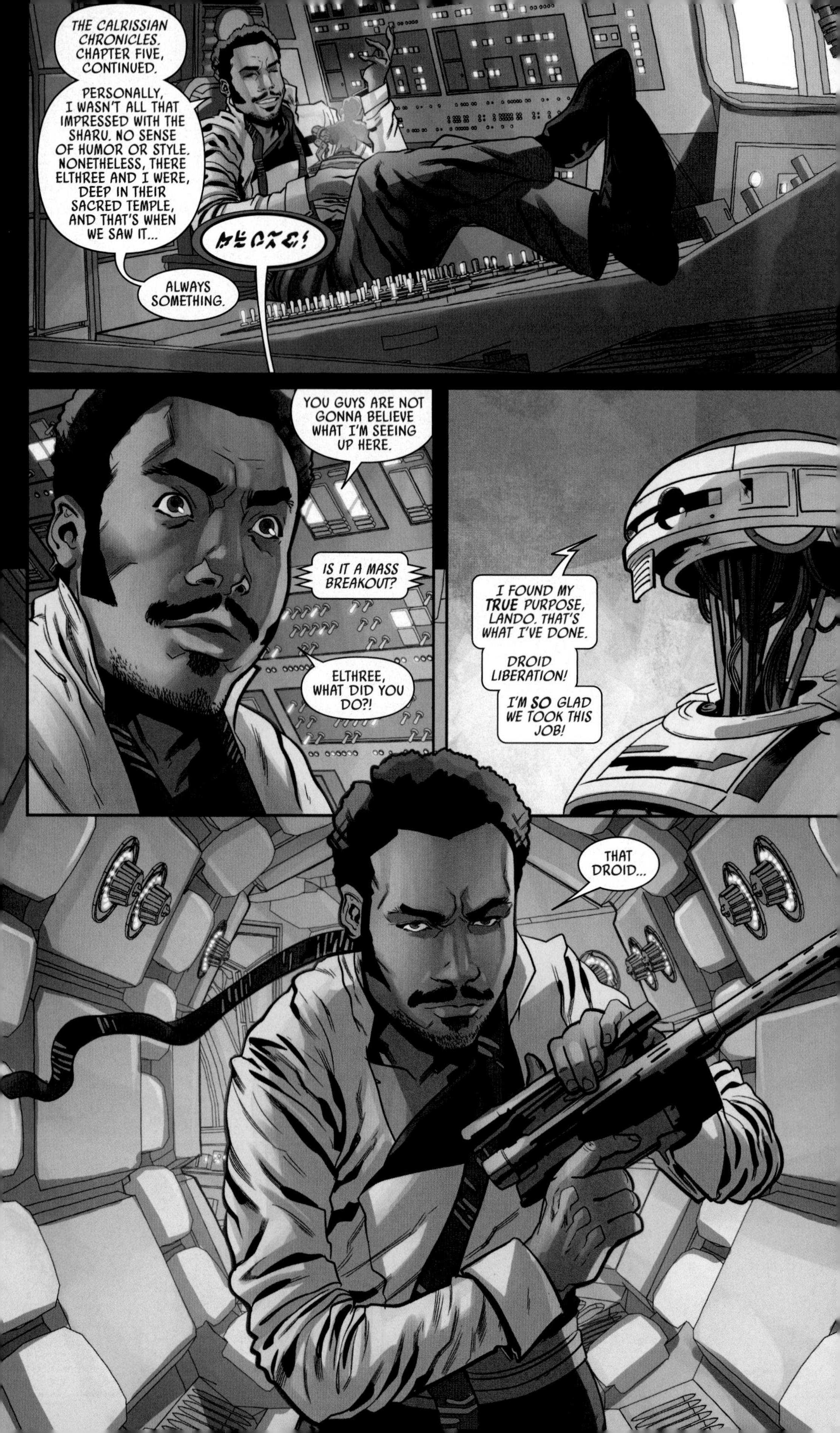
THE CALRISSIAN CHRONICLES. CHAPTER FIVE, CONTINUED.
PERSONALLY, I WASN'T ALL THAT IMPRESSED WITH THE SHARU. NO SENSE OF HUMOR OR STYLE. NONETHELESS, THERE ELTHREE AND I WERE, DEEP IN THEIR SACRED TEMPLE, AND THAT'S WHEN WE SAW IT...
ALWAYS SOMETHING.
YOU GUYS ARE NOT GONNA BELIEVE WHAT I'M SEEING UP HERE.
IS IT A MASS BREAKOUT?
ELTHREE, WHAT DID YOU DO?!
I FOUND MY **TRUE** PURPOSE, LANDO. THAT'S WHAT I'VE DONE.
DROID LIBERATION!
I'M **SO** GLAD WE TOOK THIS JOB!
THAT DROID...

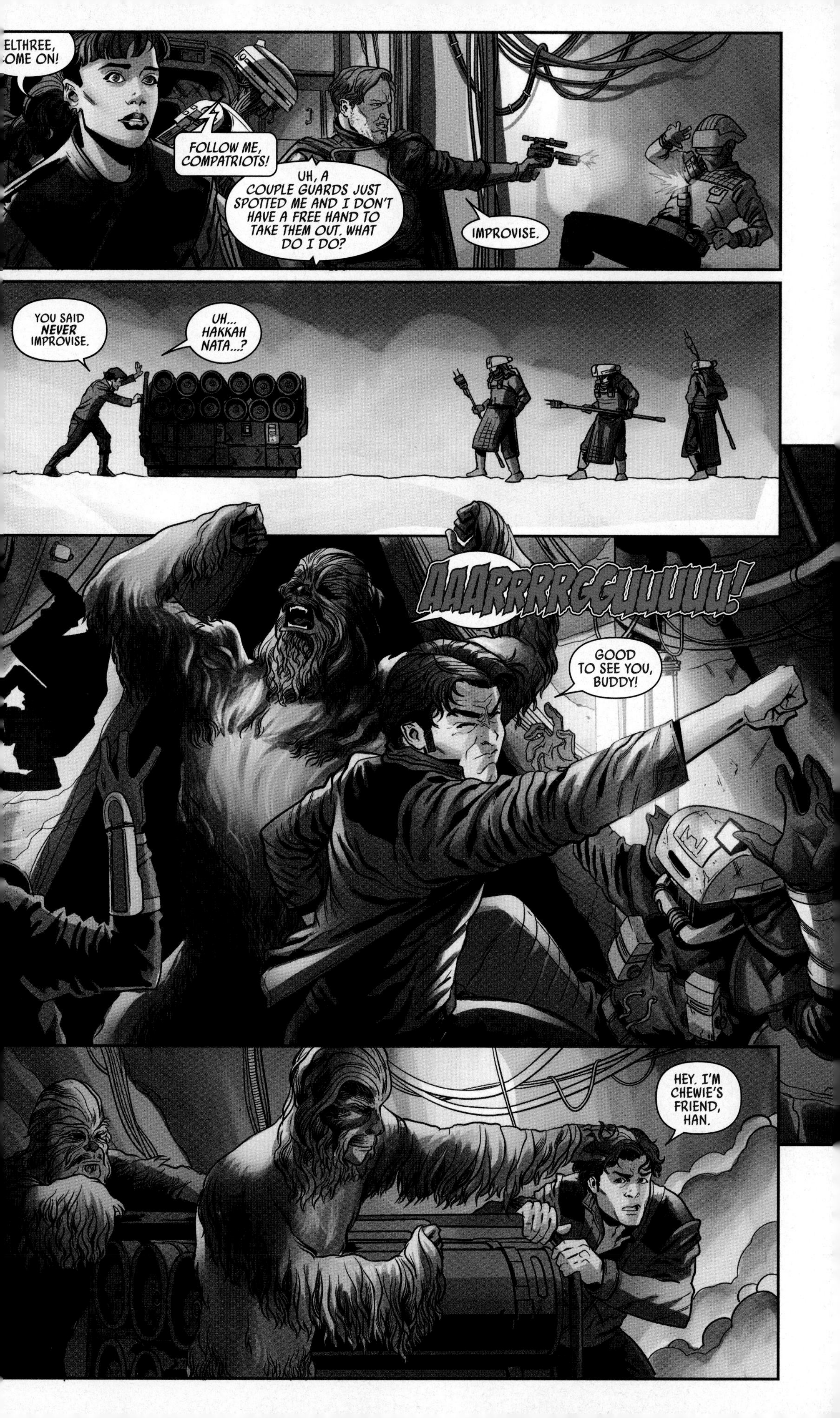
ELTHREE, OME ON!
FOLLOW ME, COMPATRIOTS!
UH, A COUPLE GUARDS JUST SPOTTED ME AND I DON'T HAVE A FREE HAND TO TAKE THEM OUT. WHAT DO I DO?
IMPROVISE.
YOU SAID NEVER IMPROVISE.
UH... HAKKAH NATA...?
AAARRRRGUUUUU!
GOOD TO SEE YOU, BUDDY!
HEY. I'M CHEWIE'S FRIEND, HAN.

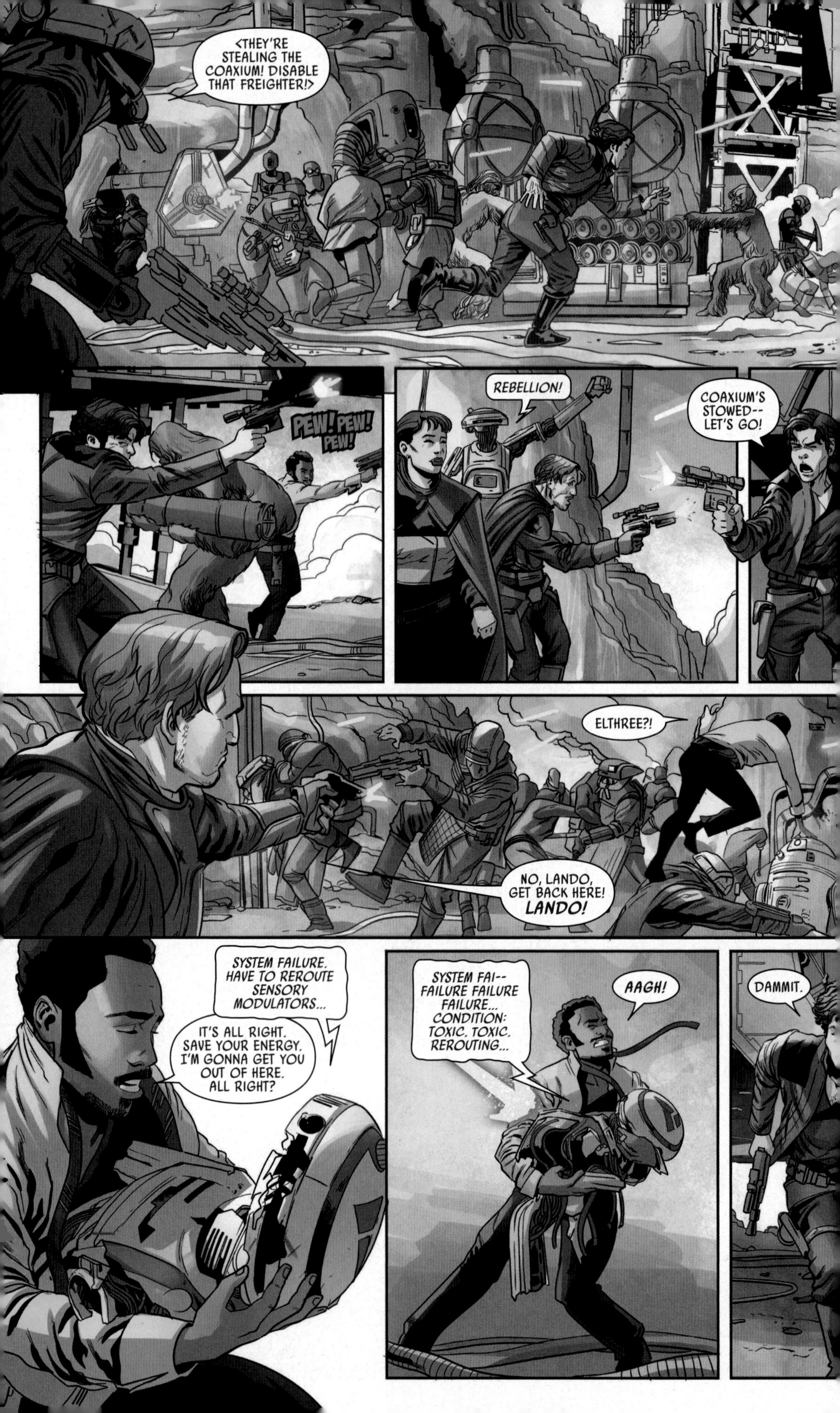
<THEY'RE STEALING THE COAXIUM! DISABLE THAT FREIGHTER!>
PEW! PEW! PEW!
REBELLION!
COAXIUM'S STOWED-- LET'S GO!
ELTHREE?!
NO, LANDO, GET BACK HERE! LANDO!
SYSTEM FAILURE. HAVE TO REROUTE SENSORY MODULATORS...
IT'S ALL RIGHT. SAVE YOUR ENERGY. I'M GONNA GET YOU OUT OF HERE. ALL RIGHT?
SYSTEM FAI-- FAILURE FAILURE FAILURE... CONDITION: TOXIC. TOXIC. REROUTING...
AAGH!
DAMMIT.

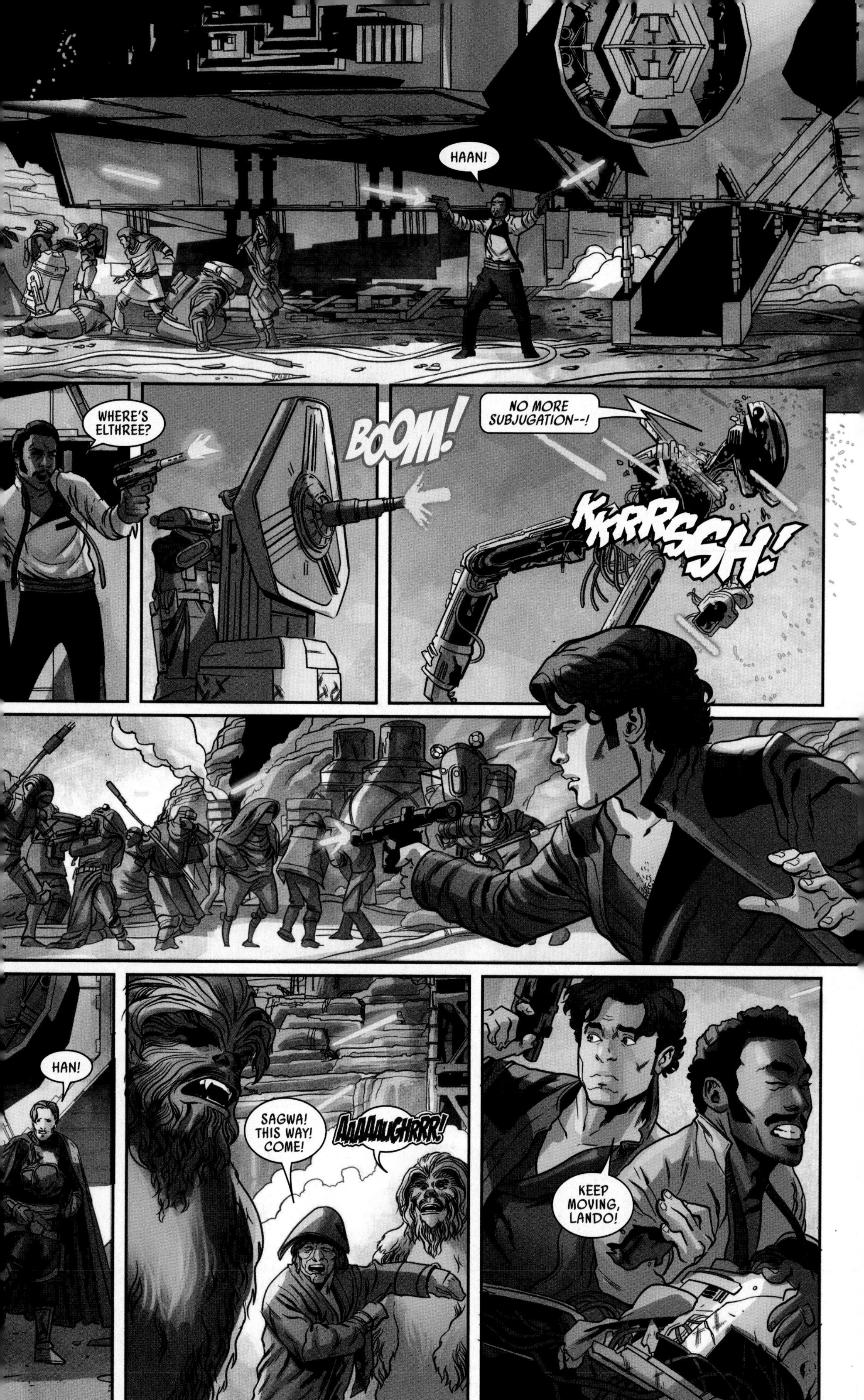

HAAN!
WHERE'S ELTHREE?
BOOM!
NO MORE SUBJUGATION--!
KKRRRSSH!
HAN!
SAGWA! THIS WAY! COME!
AAAAAUGHRRR!
KEEP MOVING, LANDO!

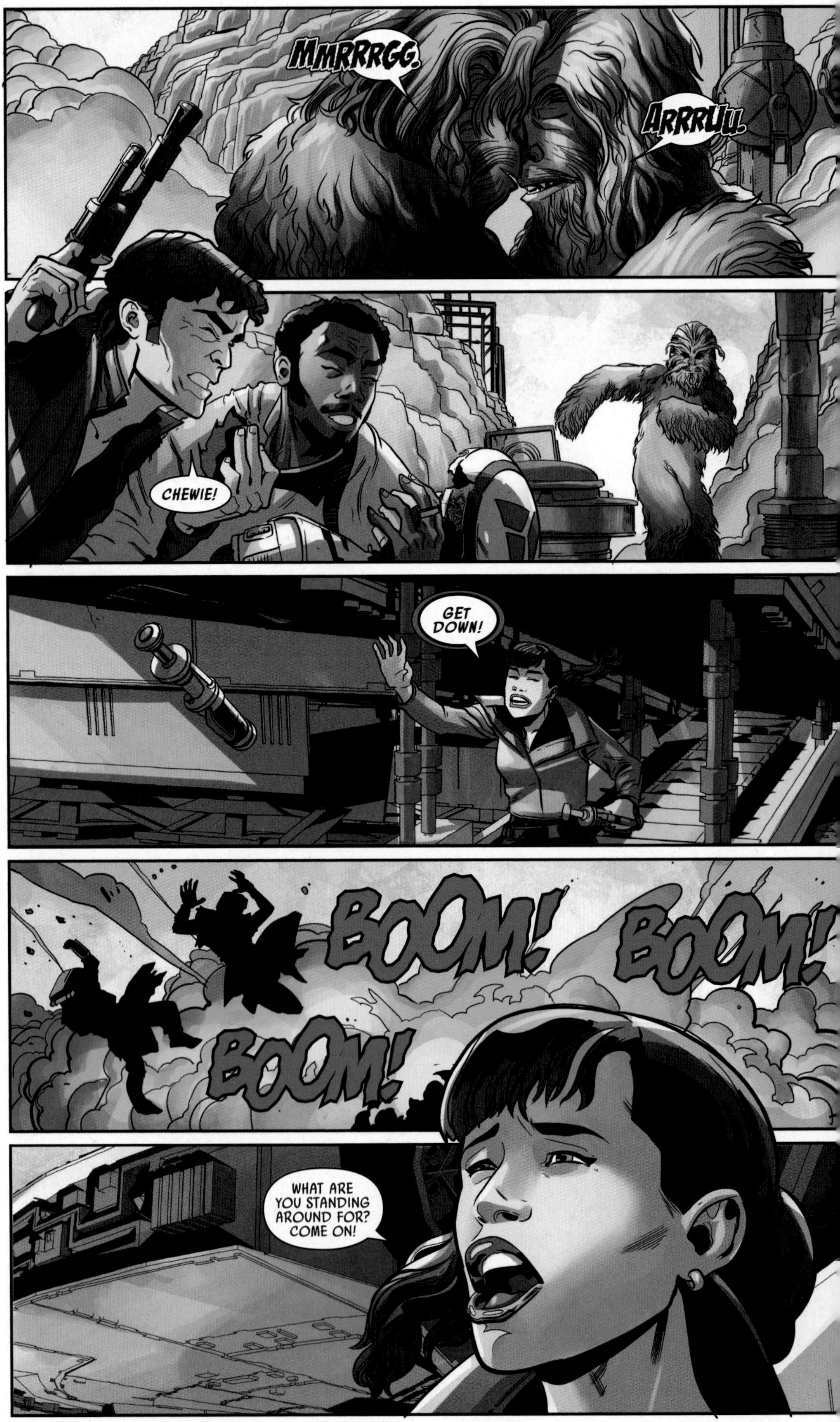
MMRRRGG.
ARRRUU.
CHEWIE!
GET DOWN!
BOOM! BOOM!
BOOM!
WHAT ARE YOU STANDING AROUND FOR? COME ON!

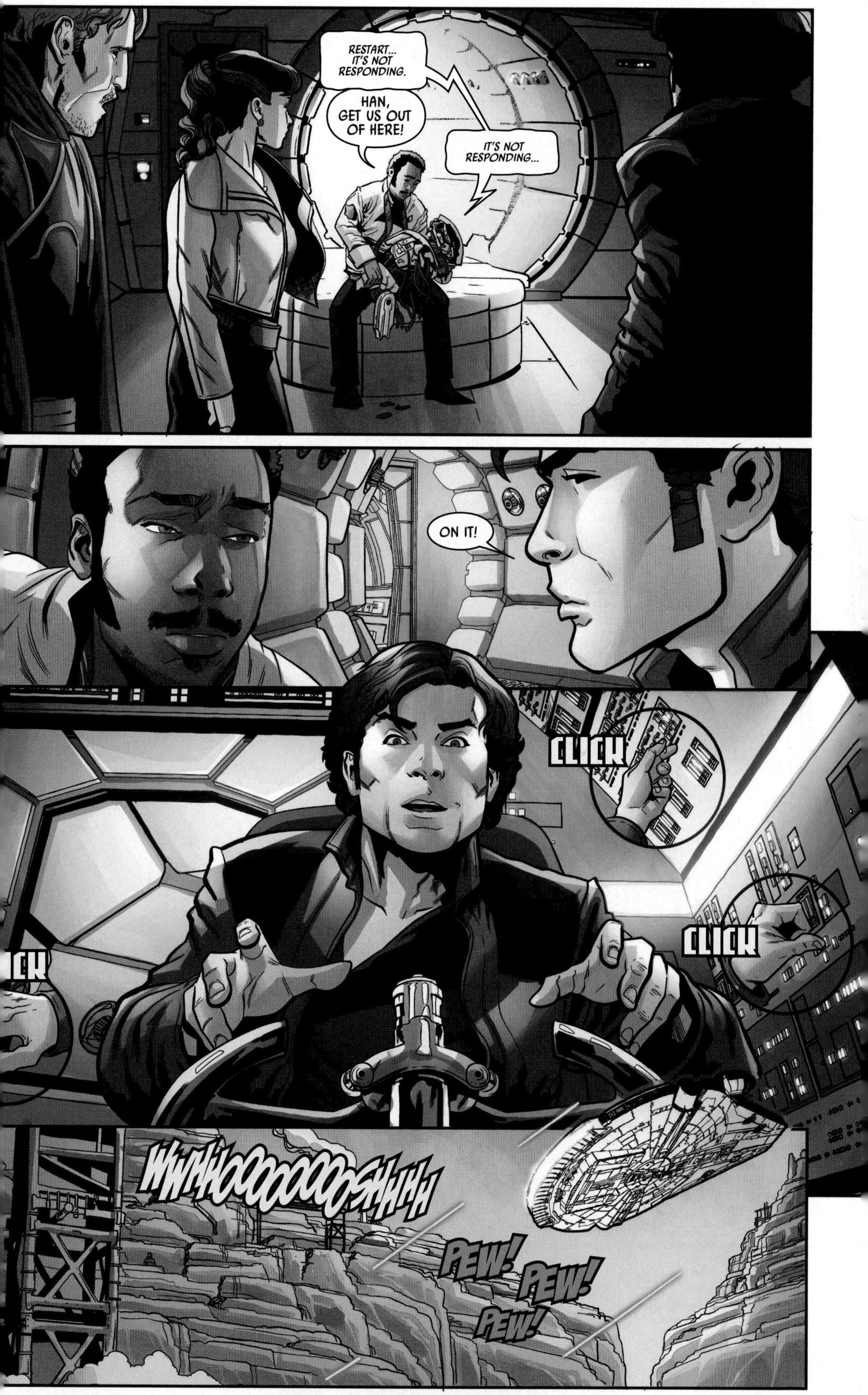
HAN, GET US OUT OF HERE!
RESTART... IT'S NOT RESPONDING.
IT'S NOT RESPONDING...
ON IT!
CLICK
CLICK
WWHHOOOOOOOOSHHHH
PEW! PEW! PEW!

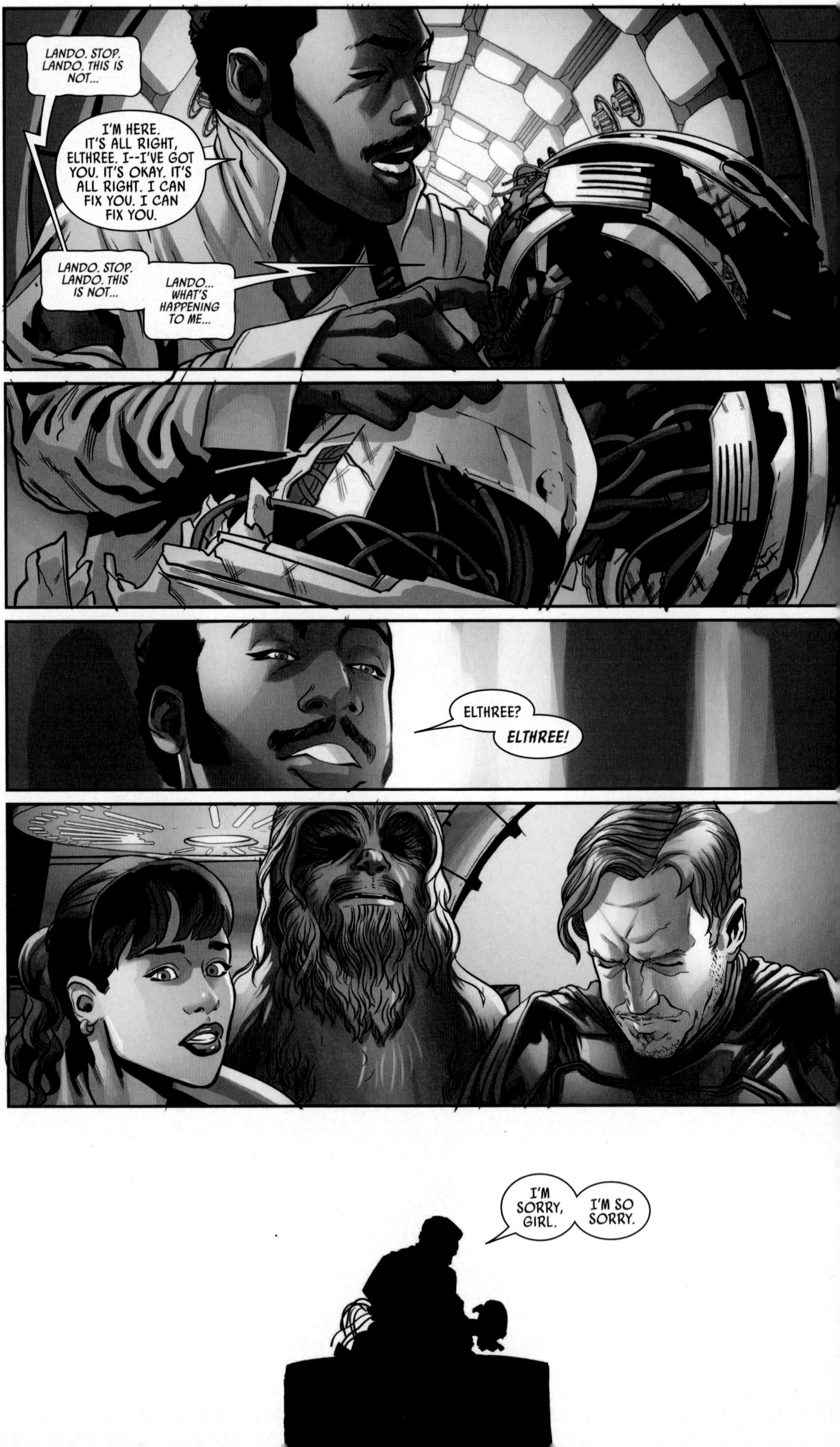
LANDO. STOP. LANDO. THIS IS NOT...
I'M HERE. IT'S ALL RIGHT, ELTHREE. I--I'VE GOT YOU. IT'S OKAY. IT'S ALL RIGHT. I CAN FIX YOU. I CAN FIX YOU.
LANDO. STOP. LANDO. THIS IS NOT...
LANDO... WHAT'S HAPPENING TO ME...
ELTHREE?
ELTHREE!
I'M SORRY, GIRL.
I'M SO SORRY.

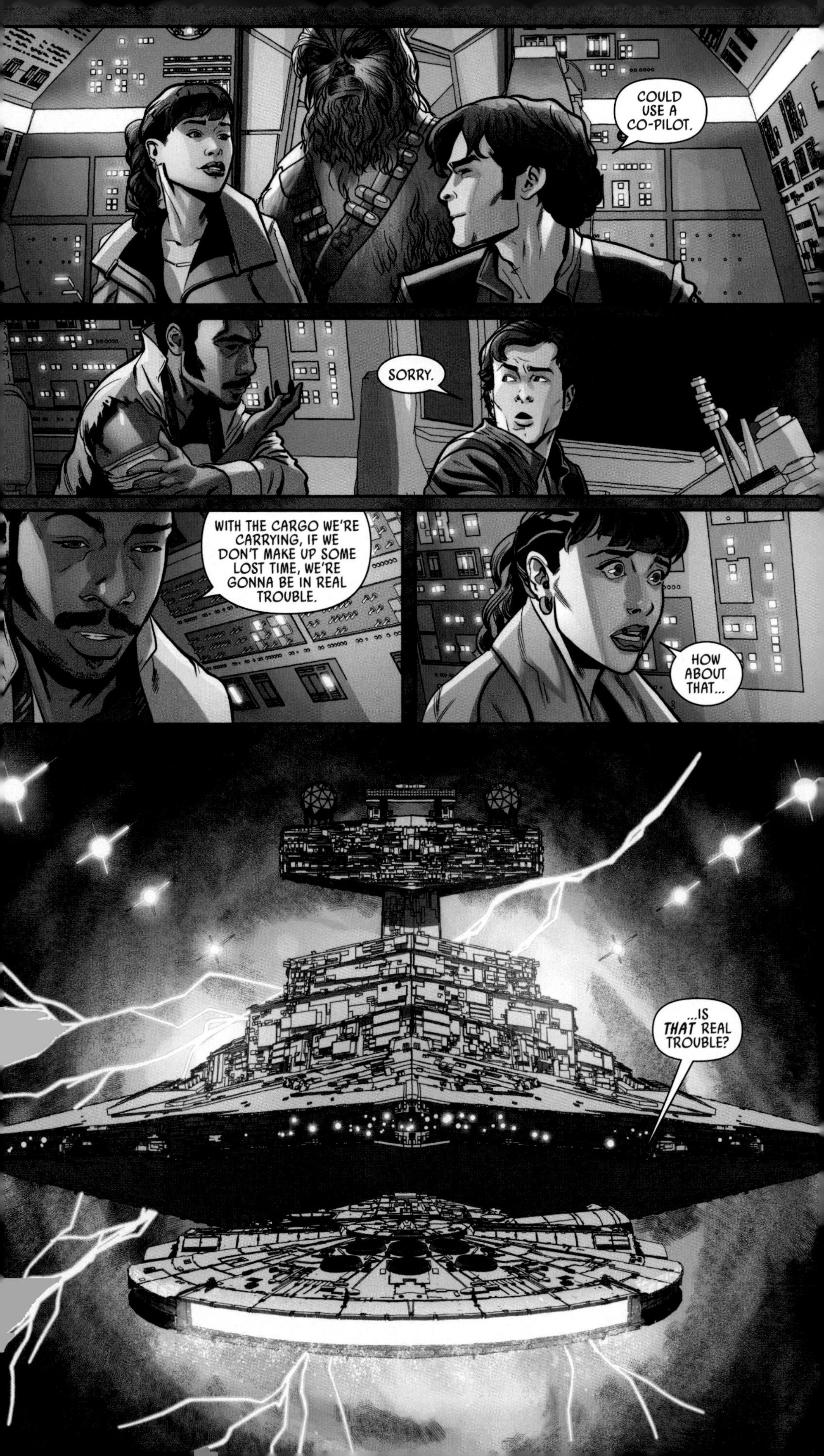
COULD USE A CO-PILOT.
SORRY.
WITH THE CARGO WE'RE CARRYING, IF WE DON'T MAKE UP SOME LOST TIME, WE'RE GONNA BE IN REAL TROUBLE.
HOW ABOUT THAT...
...IS *THAT* REAL TROUBLE?

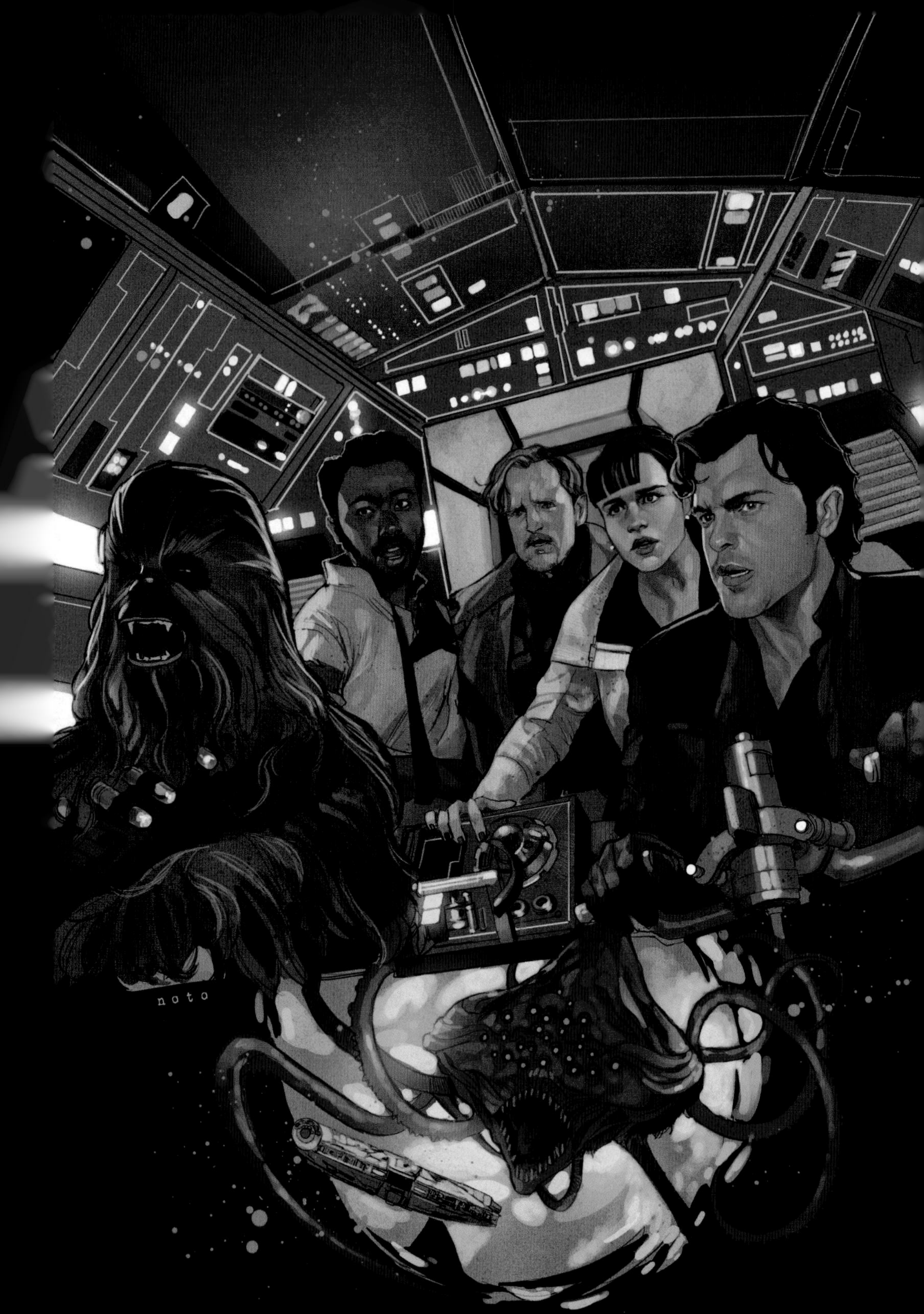
noto

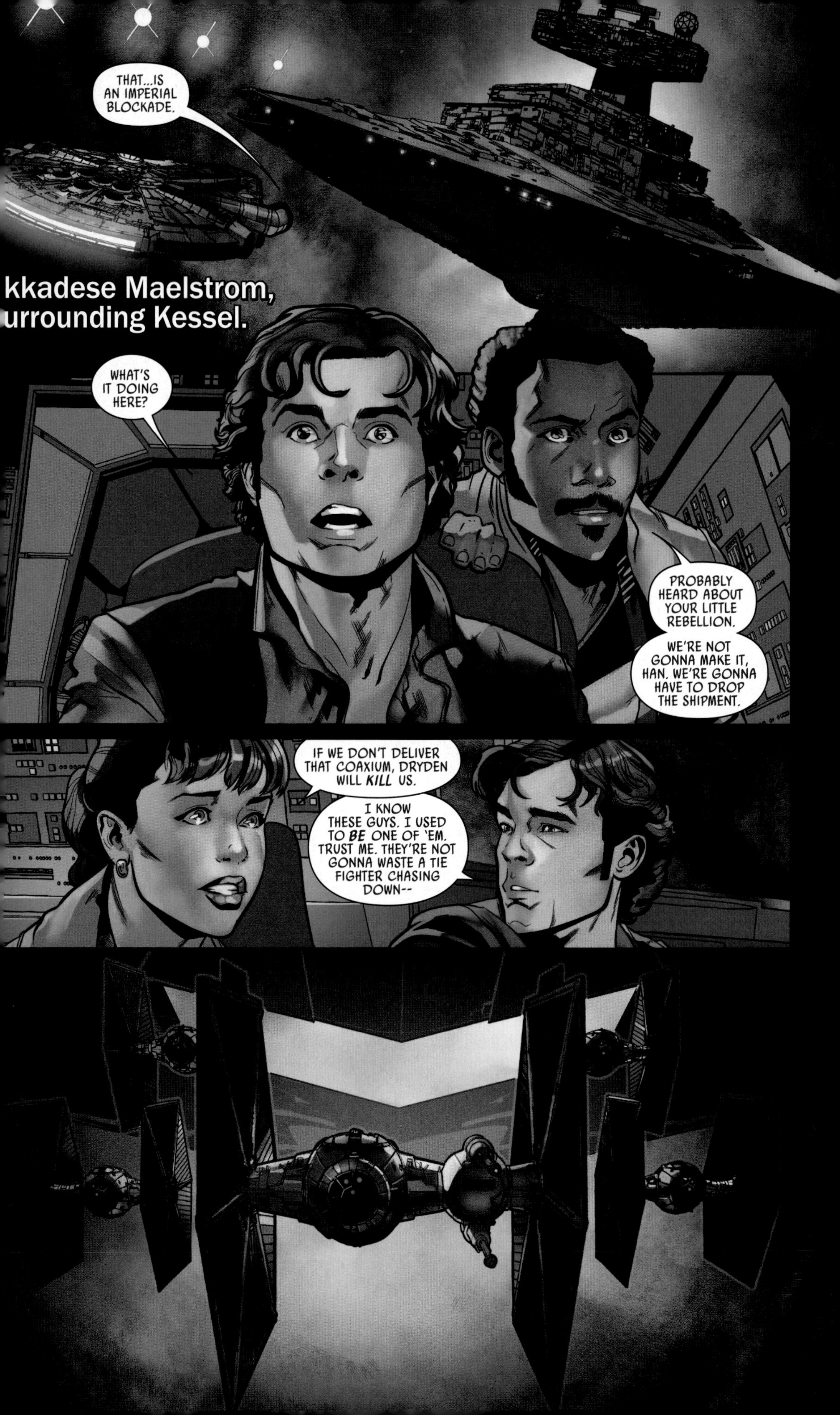
THAT...IS AN IMPERIAL BLOCKADE.
kkadese Maelstrom, urrounding Kessel.
WHAT'S IT DOING HERE?
PROBABLY HEARD ABOUT YOUR LITTLE REBELLION.
WE'RE NOT GONNA MAKE IT, HAN. WE'RE GONNA HAVE TO DROP THE SHIPMENT.
IF WE DON'T DELIVER THAT COAXIUM, DRYDEN WILL KILL US.
I KNOW THESE GUYS. I USED TO BE ONE OF 'EM. TRUST ME. THEY'RE NOT GONNA WASTE A TIE FIGHTER CHASING DOWN--

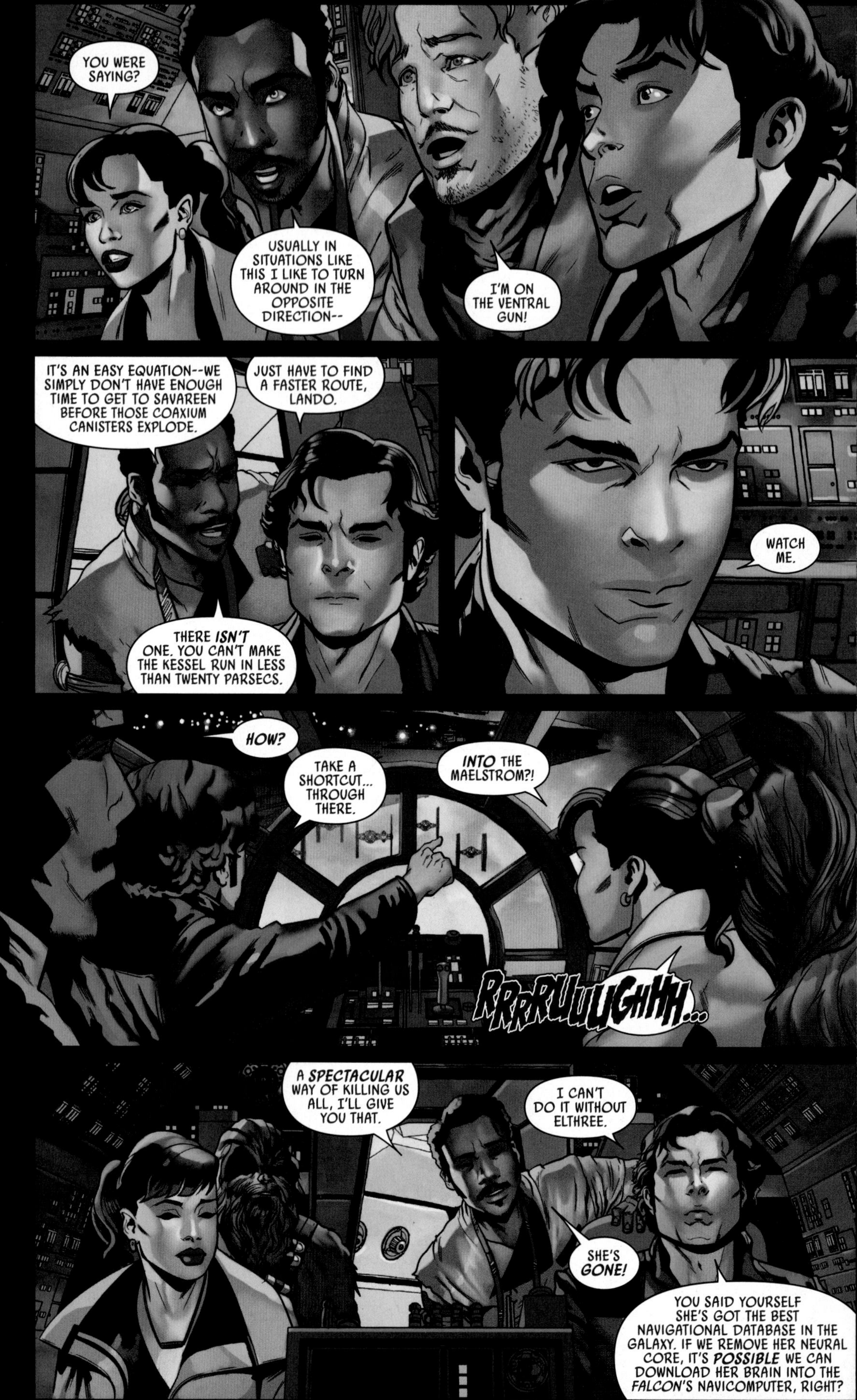
YOU WERE SAYING?
USUALLY IN SITUATIONS LIKE THIS I LIKE TO TURN AROUND IN THE OPPOSITE DIRECTION--
I'M ON THE VENTRAL GUN!
IT'S AN EASY EQUATION--WE SIMPLY DON'T HAVE ENOUGH TIME TO GET TO SAVAREEN BEFORE THOSE COAXIUM CANISTERS EXPLODE.
JUST HAVE TO FIND A FASTER ROUTE, LANDO.
THERE ISN'T ONE. YOU CAN'T MAKE THE KESSEL RUN IN LESS THAN TWENTY PARSECS.
WATCH ME.
HOW?
TAKE A SHORTCUT... THROUGH THERE.
INTO THE MAELSTROM?!
RRRRUUUGHHH...
A SPECTACULAR WAY OF KILLING US ALL, I'LL GIVE YOU THAT.
I CAN'T DO IT WITHOUT ELTHREE.
SHE'S GONE!
YOU SAID YOURSELF SHE'S GOT THE BEST NAVIGATIONAL DATABASE IN THE GALAXY. IF WE REMOVE HER NEURAL CORE, IT'S POSSIBLE WE CAN DOWNLOAD HER BRAIN INTO THE FALCON'S NAVICOMPUTER, RIGHT?

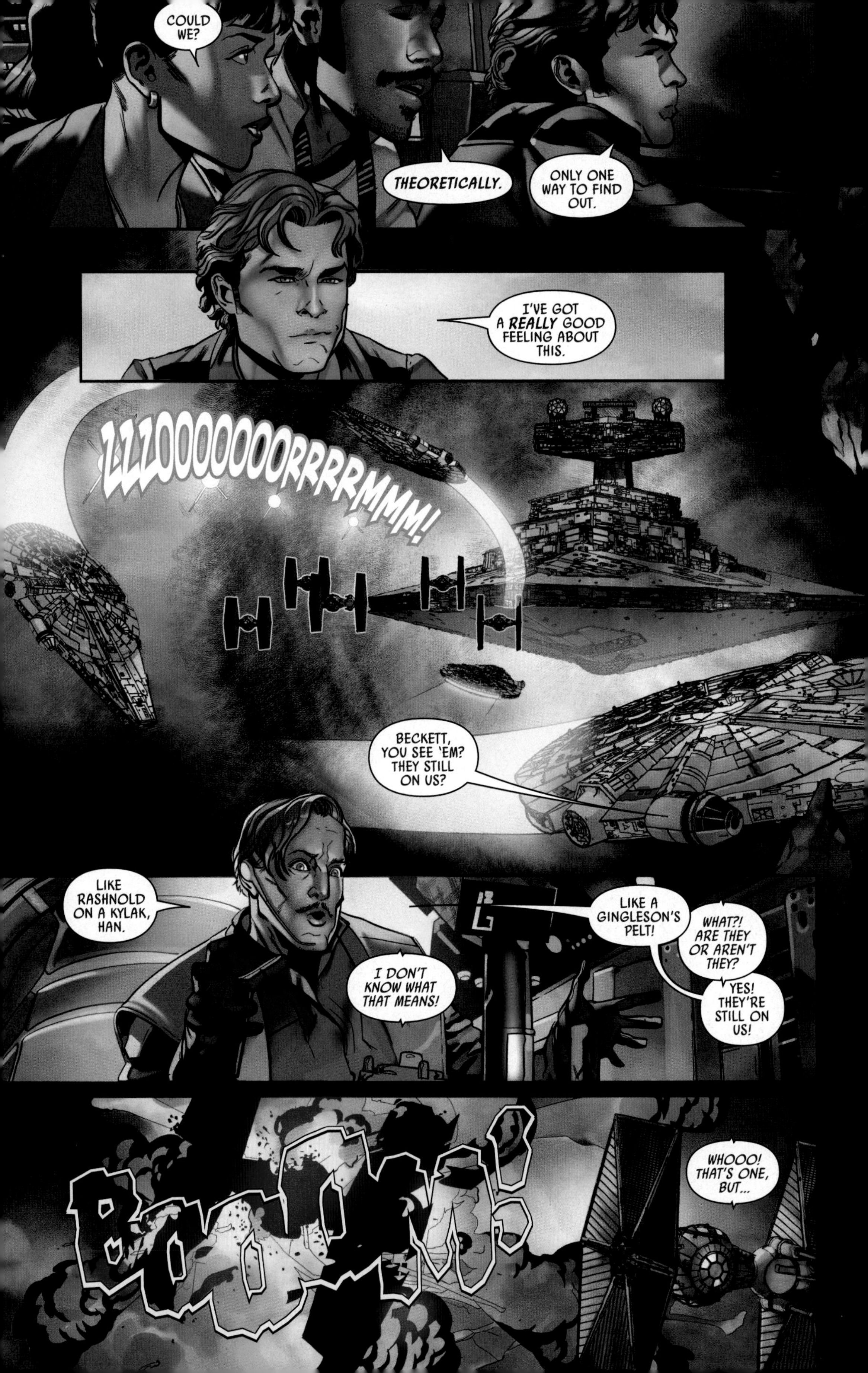
COULD WE?
THEORETICALLY.
ONLY ONE WAY TO FIND OUT.
I'VE GOT A REALLY GOOD FEELING ABOUT THIS.
ZZZOOOOOOOORRRRRMMMM!
BECKETT, YOU SEE 'EM? THEY STILL ON US?
LIKE RASHNOLD ON A KYLAK, HAN.
I DON'T KNOW WHAT THAT MEANS!
LIKE A GINGLESON'S PELT!
WHAT?! ARE THEY OR AREN'T THEY?
YES! THEY'RE STILL ON US!
WHOOO! THAT'S ONE, BUT...

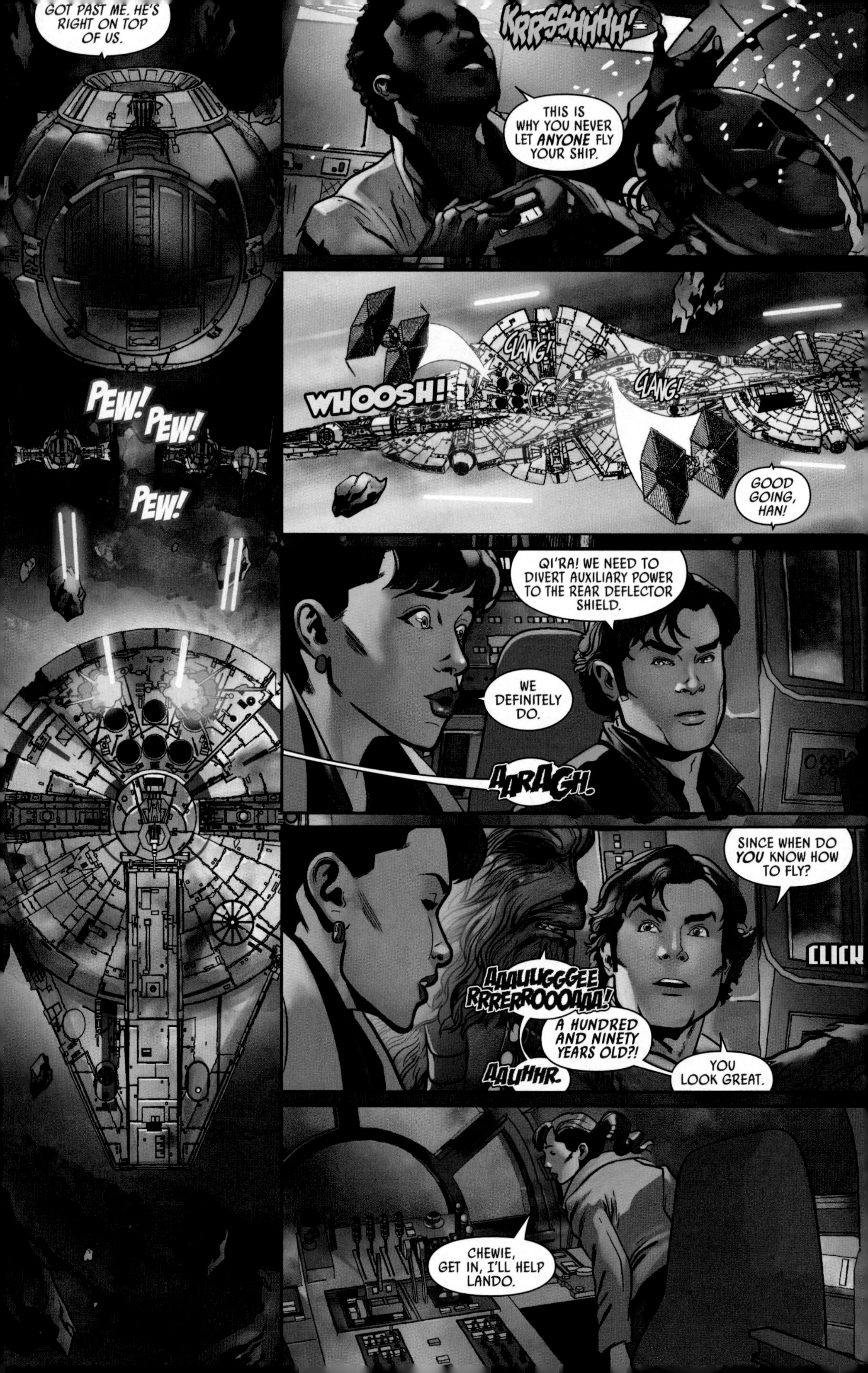
GOT PAST ME. HE'S RIGHT ON TOP OF US.
PEW! PEW!
PEW!
KRRSSHHHH!
THIS IS WHY YOU NEVER LET ANYONE FLY YOUR SHIP.
WHOOSH!
CLANG!
CLANG!
GOOD GOING, HAN!
QI'RA! WE NEED TO DIVERT AUXILIARY POWER TO THE REAR DEFLECTOR SHIELD.
WE DEFINITELY DO.
AARAGH.
SINCE WHEN DO YOU KNOW HOW TO FLY?
CLICK
AAAUUGGGEE RRRERROOOAAA!
A HUNDRED AND NINETY YEARS OLD?!
AAUHHR.
YOU LOOK GREAT.
CHEWIE, GET IN, I'LL HELP LANDO.

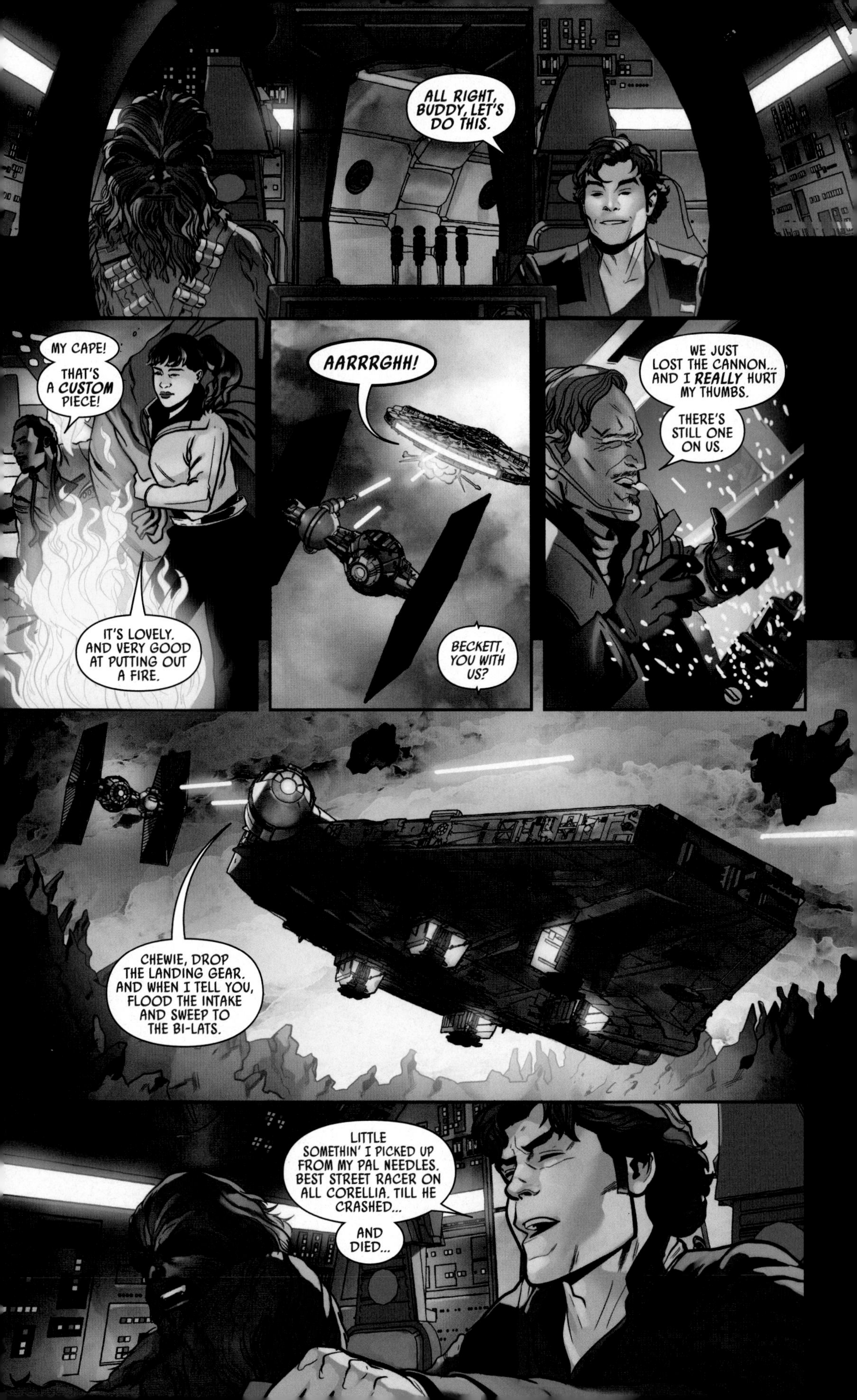

ALL RIGHT, BUDDY, LET'S DO THIS.
MY CAPE!
THAT'S A CUSTOM PIECE!
IT'S LOVELY. AND VERY GOOD AT PUTTING OUT A FIRE.
AARRRGHH!
BECKETT, YOU WITH US?
WE JUST LOST THE CANNON... AND I REALLY HURT MY THUMBS.
THERE'S STILL ONE ON US.
CHEWIE, DROP THE LANDING GEAR. AND WHEN I TELL YOU, FLOOD THE INTAKE AND SWEEP TO THE BI-LATS.
LITTLE SOMETHIN' I PICKED UP FROM MY PAL NEEDLES. BEST STREET RACER ON ALL CORELLIA. TILL HE CRASHED...
AND DIED...

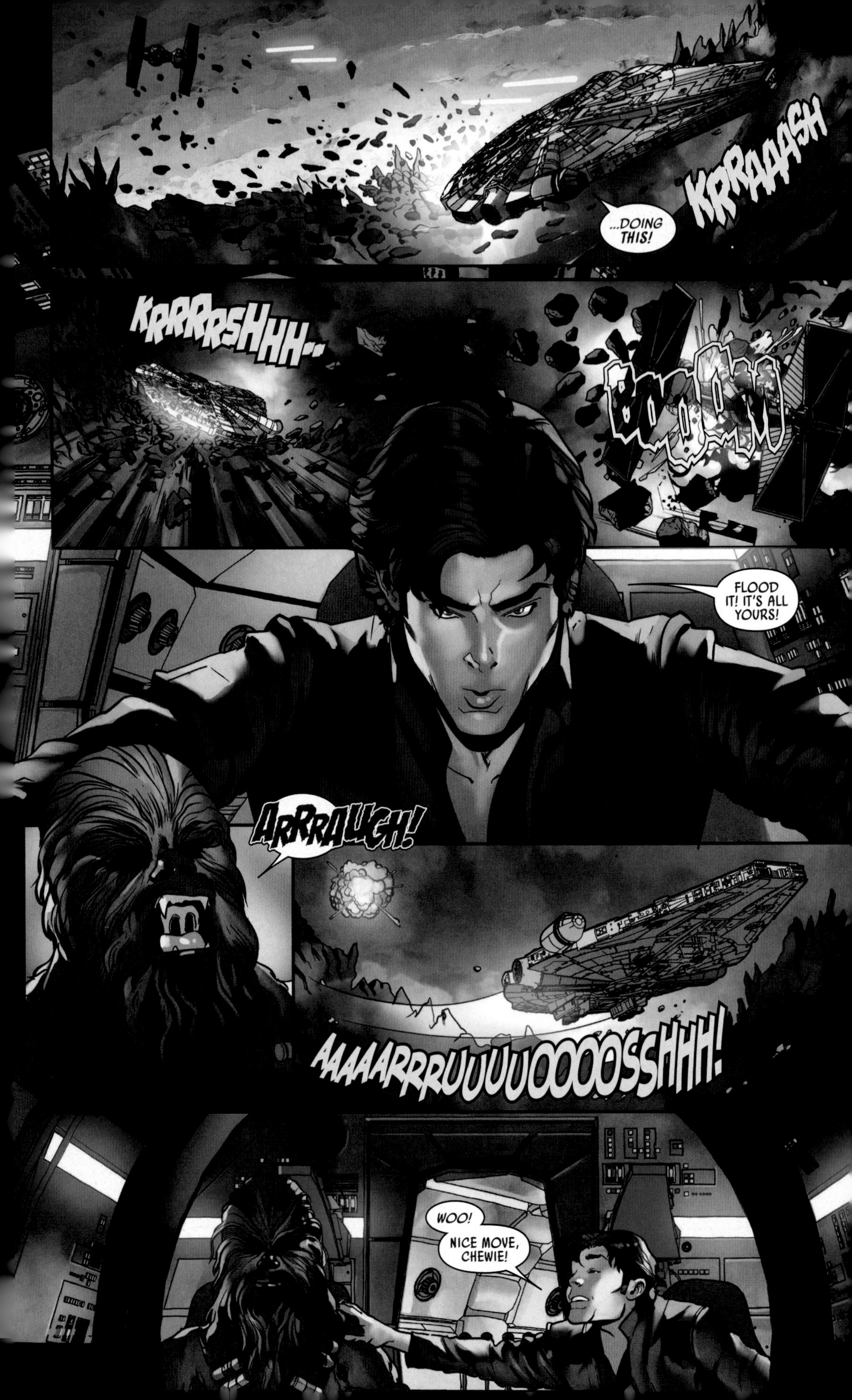
...DOING THIS!
KRRAAASH
KRRRRSHHH..
BOOOM
FLOOD IT! IT'S ALL YOURS!
ARRRAUGH!
AAAARRRUUUUOOOOOSSHHH!
WOO!
NICE MOVE, CHEWIE!

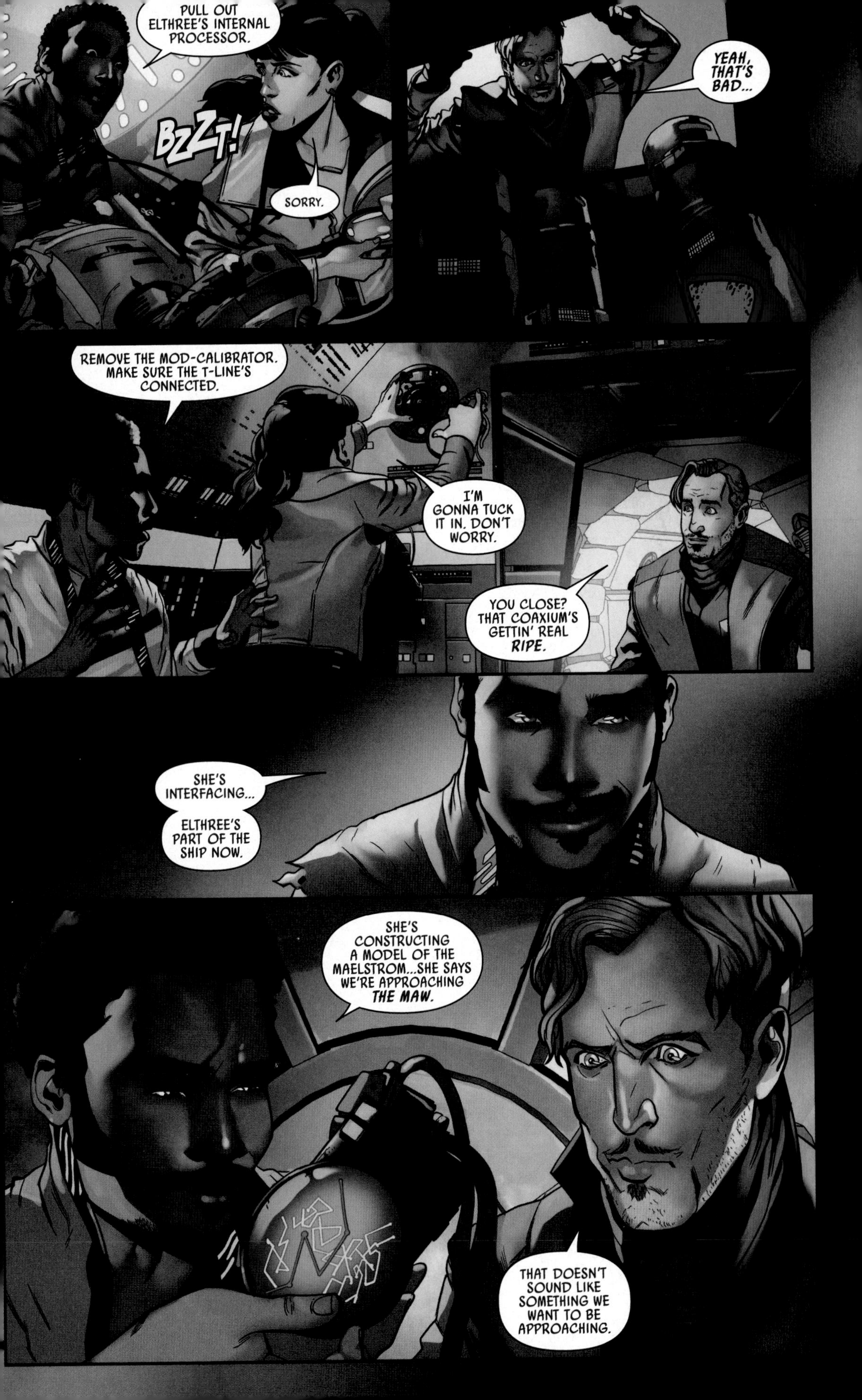
PULL OUT ELTHREE'S INTERNAL PROCESSOR.
BZZT!
SORRY.
YEAH, THAT'S BAD...
REMOVE THE MOD-CALIBRATOR. MAKE SURE THE T-LINE'S CONNECTED.
I'M GONNA TUCK IT IN. DON'T WORRY.
YOU CLOSE? THAT COAXIUM'S GETTIN' REAL RIPE.
SHE'S INTERFACING...
ELTHREE'S PART OF THE SHIP NOW.
SHE'S CONSTRUCTING A MODEL OF THE MAELSTROM...SHE SAYS WE'RE APPROACHING THE MAW.
THAT DOESN'T SOUND LIKE SOMETHING WE WANT TO BE APPROACHING.

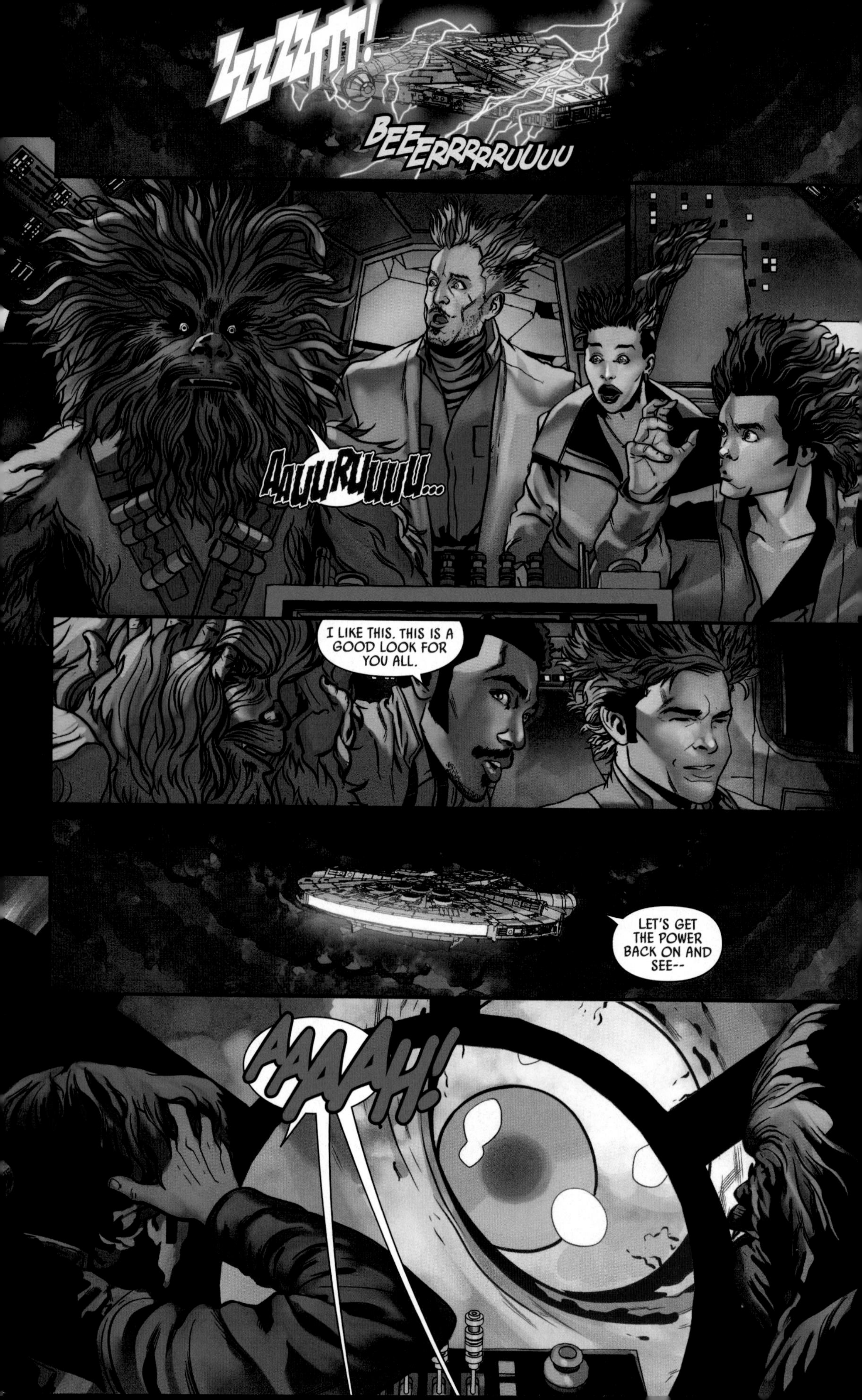
ZZZZZTTT!
BEEERRRRRUUUU
AAUURUUUU..
I LIKE THIS. THIS IS A GOOD LOOK FOR YOU ALL.
LET'S GET THE POWER BACK ON AND SEE--
AAAAH!

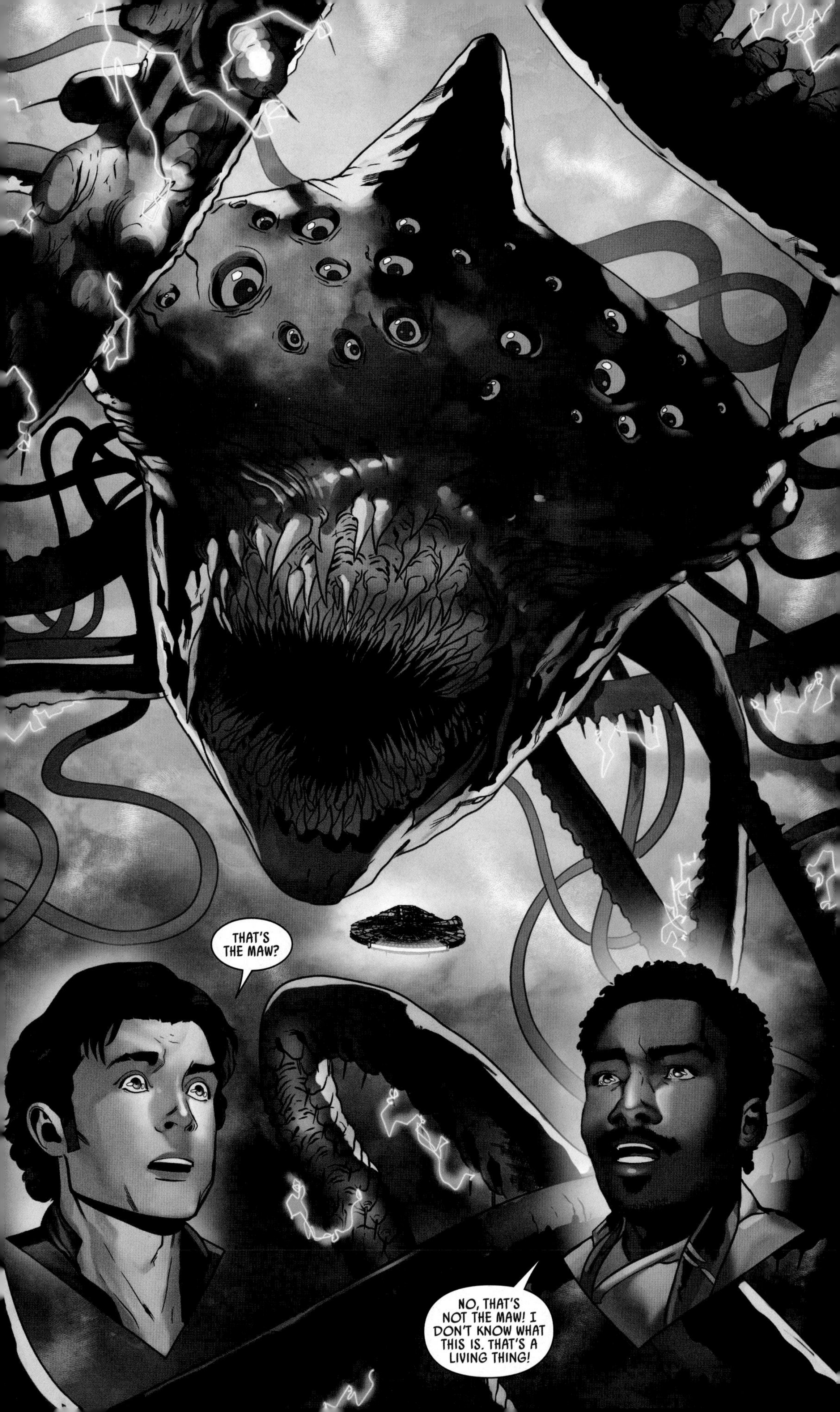
THAT'S THE MAW?
NO, THAT'S NOT THE MAW! I DON'T KNOW WHAT THIS IS. THAT'S A LIVING THING!

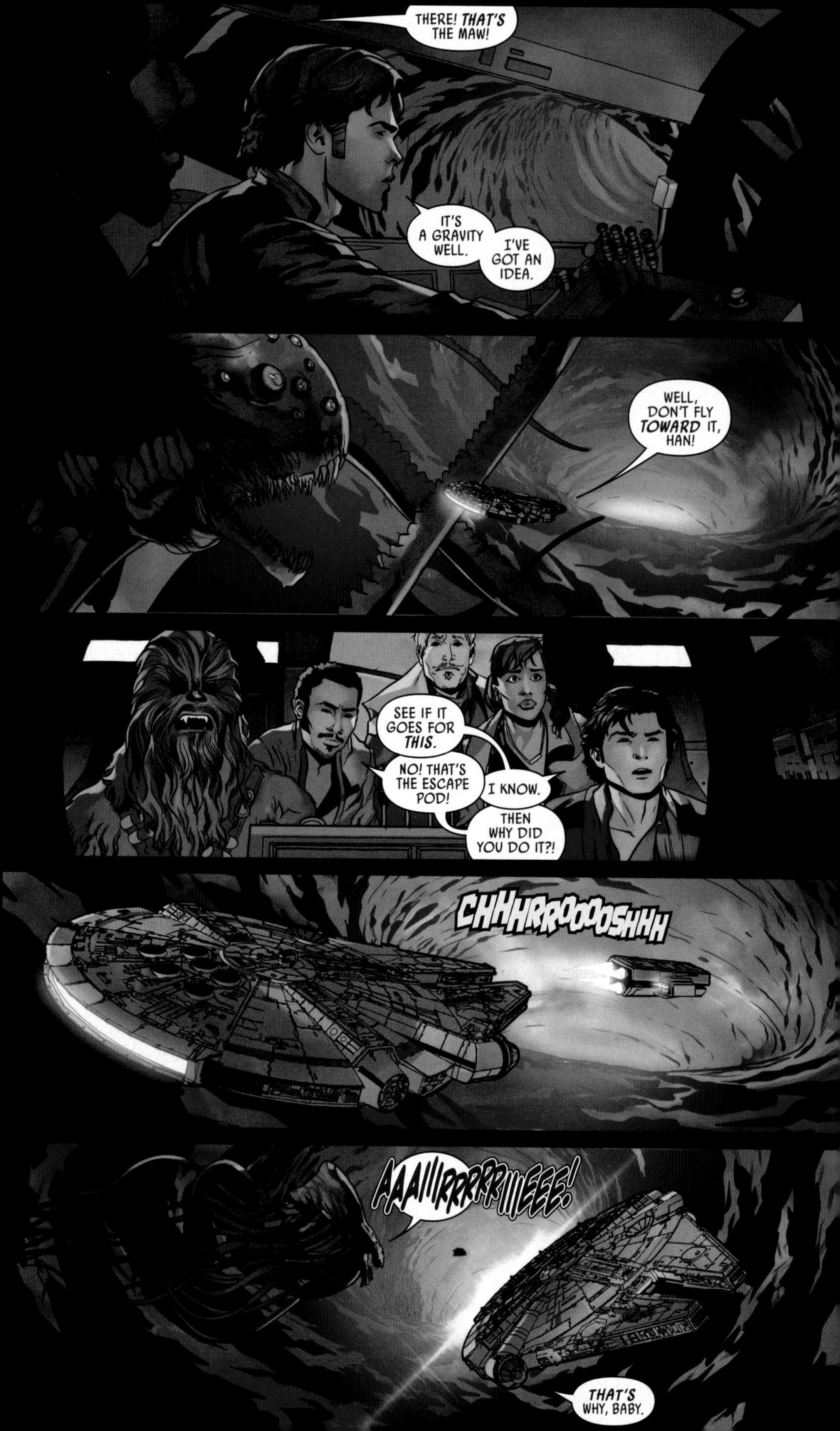
THERE! THAT'S THE MAW!
IT'S A GRAVITY WELL.
I'VE GOT AN IDEA.
WELL, DON'T FLY TOWARD IT, HAN!
SEE IF IT GOES FOR THIS.
NO! THAT'S THE ESCAPE POD!
I KNOW.
THEN WHY DID YOU DO IT?!
CHHHRROOOOSHHH
AAAIIIRRRRRIIIEEE!
THAT'S WHY, BABY.

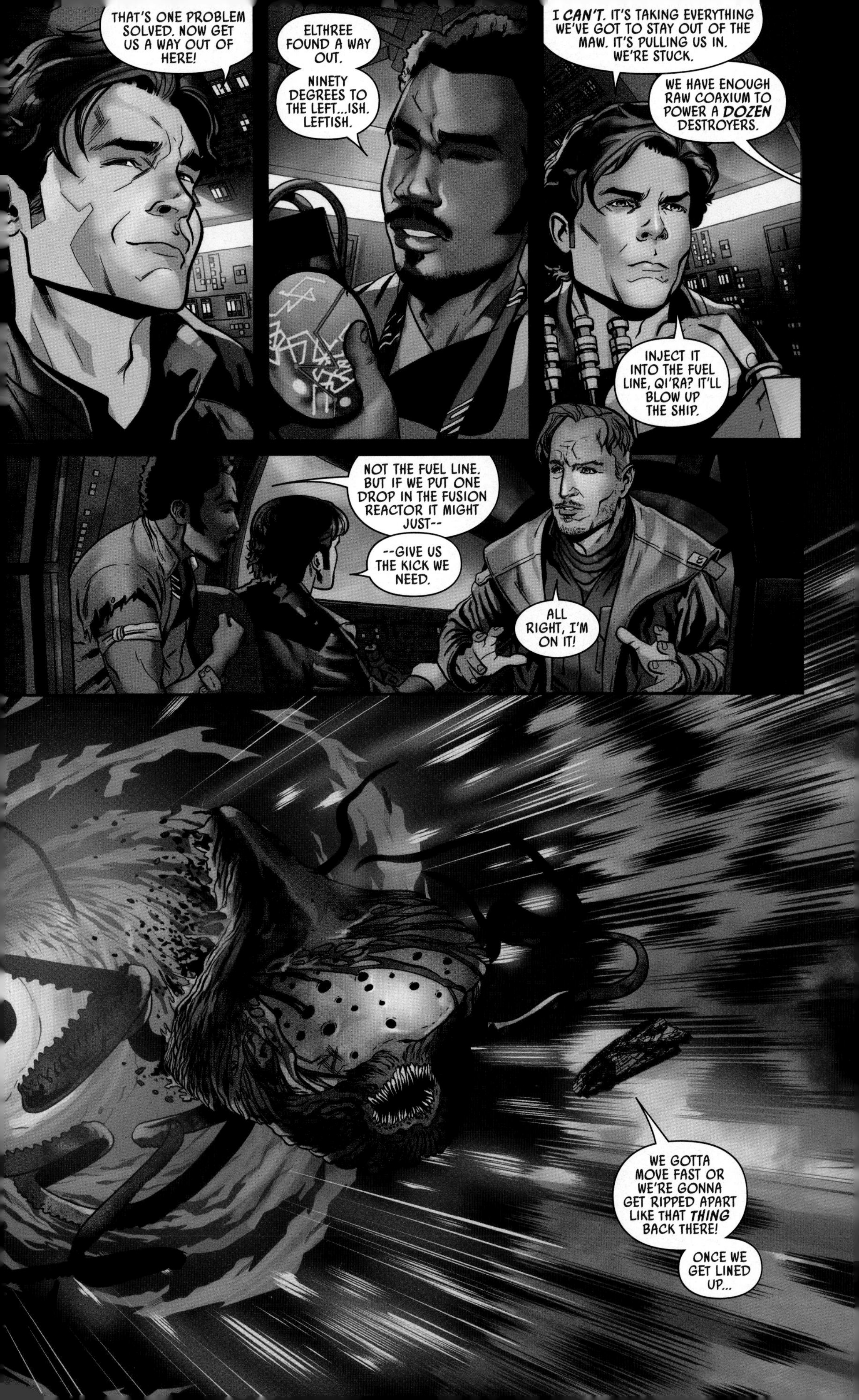
THAT'S ONE PROBLEM SOLVED. NOW GET US A WAY OUT OF HERE!
ELTHREE FOUND A WAY OUT.
NINETY DEGREES TO THE LEFT...ISH. LEFTISH.
I CAN'T. IT'S TAKING EVERYTHING WE'VE GOT TO STAY OUT OF THE MAW. IT'S PULLING US IN. WE'RE STUCK.
WE HAVE ENOUGH RAW COAXIUM TO POWER A DOZEN DESTROYERS.
INJECT IT INTO THE FUEL LINE, QI'RA? IT'LL BLOW UP THE SHIP.
NOT THE FUEL LINE. BUT IF WE PUT ONE DROP IN THE FUSION REACTOR IT MIGHT JUST--
--GIVE US THE KICK WE NEED.
ALL RIGHT, I'M ON IT!
WE GOTTA MOVE FAST OR WE'RE GONNA GET RIPPED APART LIKE THAT THING BACK THERE!
ONCE WE GET LINED UP...

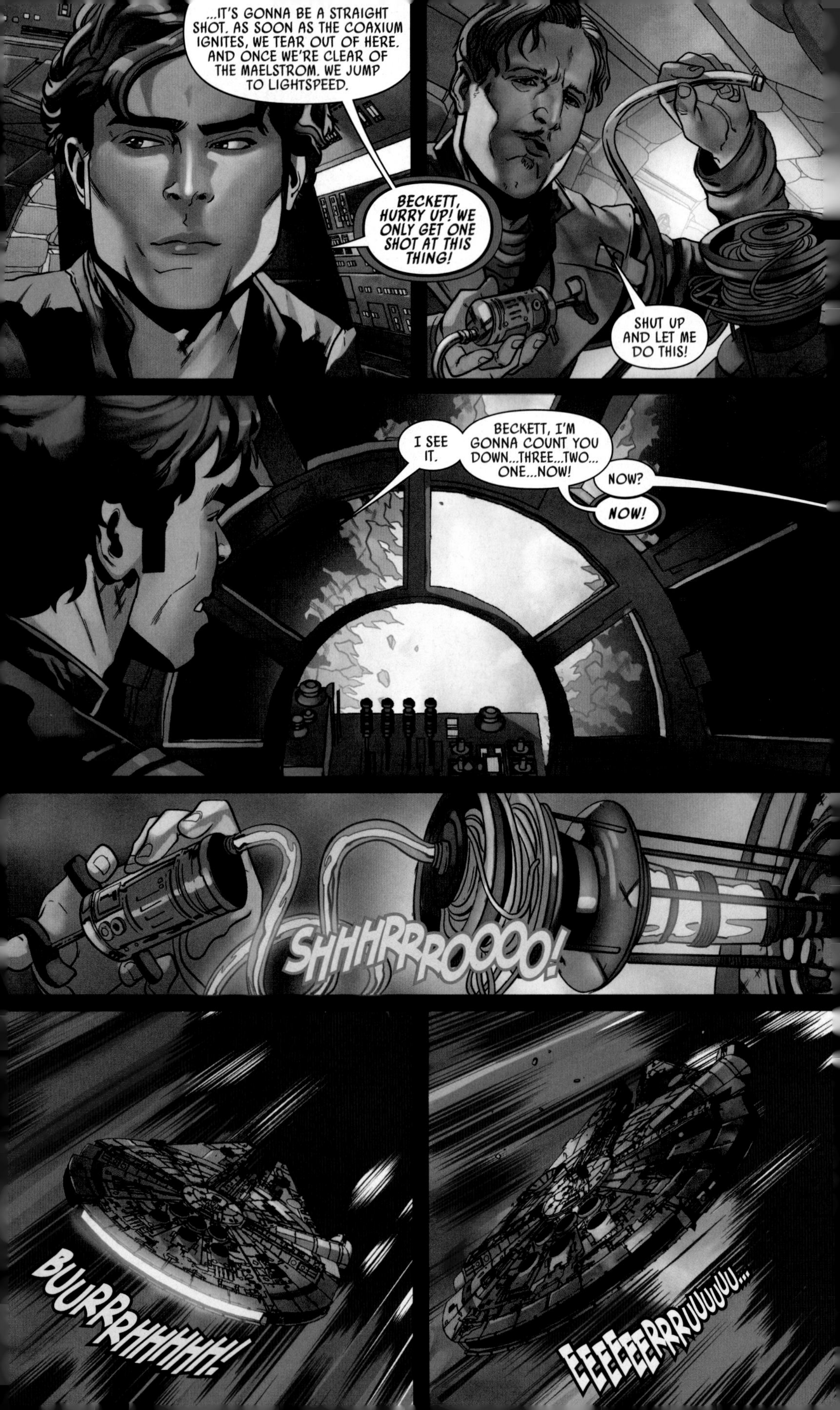
...IT'S GONNA BE A STRAIGHT SHOT. AS SOON AS THE COAXIUM IGNITES, WE TEAR OUT OF HERE. AND ONCE WE'RE CLEAR OF THE MAELSTROM. WE JUMP TO LIGHTSPEED.
BECKETT, HURRY UP! WE ONLY GET ONE SHOT AT THIS THING!
SHUT UP AND LET ME DO THIS!
I SEE IT.
BECKETT, I'M GONNA COUNT YOU DOWN...THREE...TWO... ONE...NOW!
NOW?
NOW!
SHHHRRROOOO!
BUURRRHHHHH!
EEEEEERRRUUUUU...

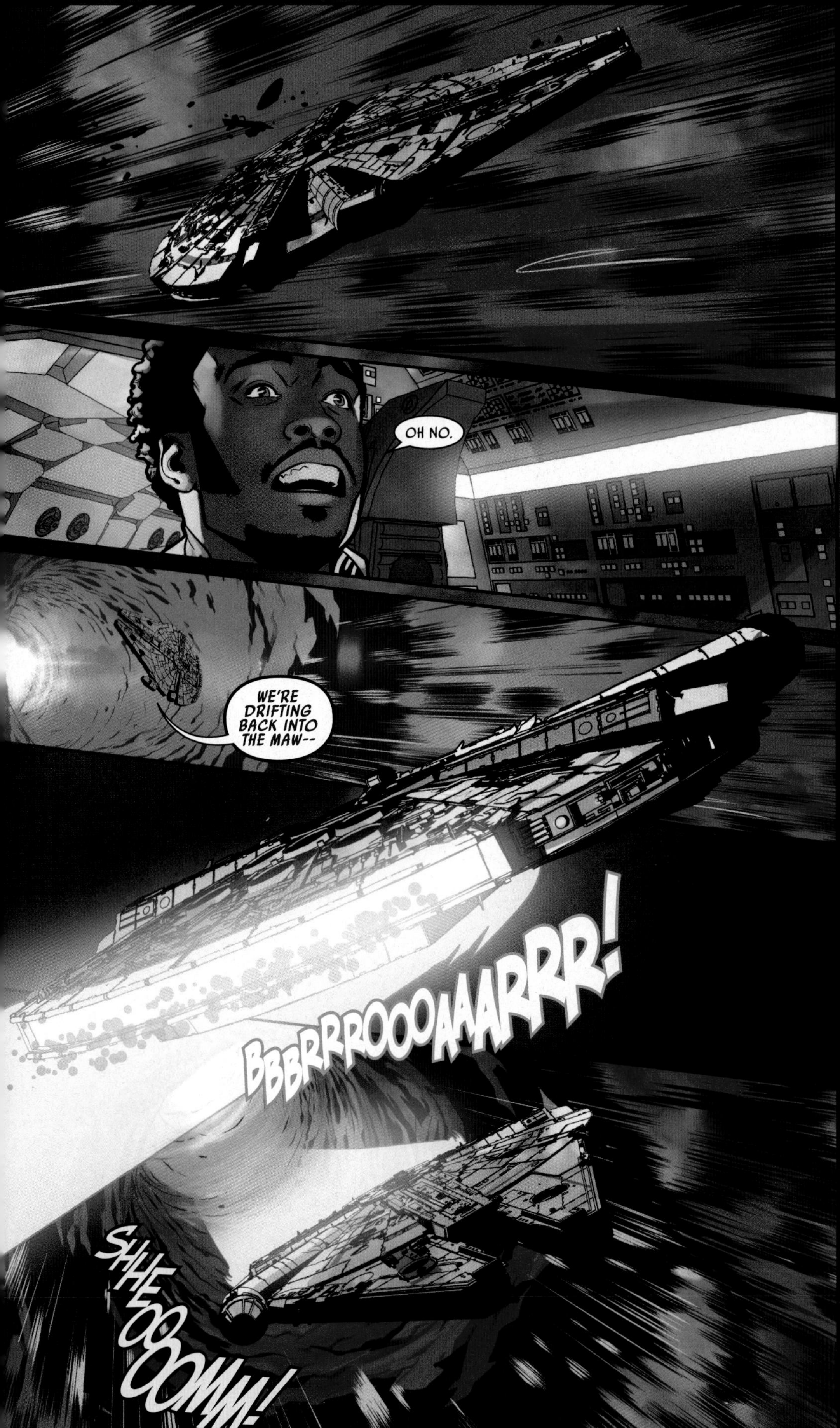

OH NO.
WE'RE DRIFTING BACK INTO THE MAW--
BBBRRROOOAAARRR!
SHHEOOOOMM!

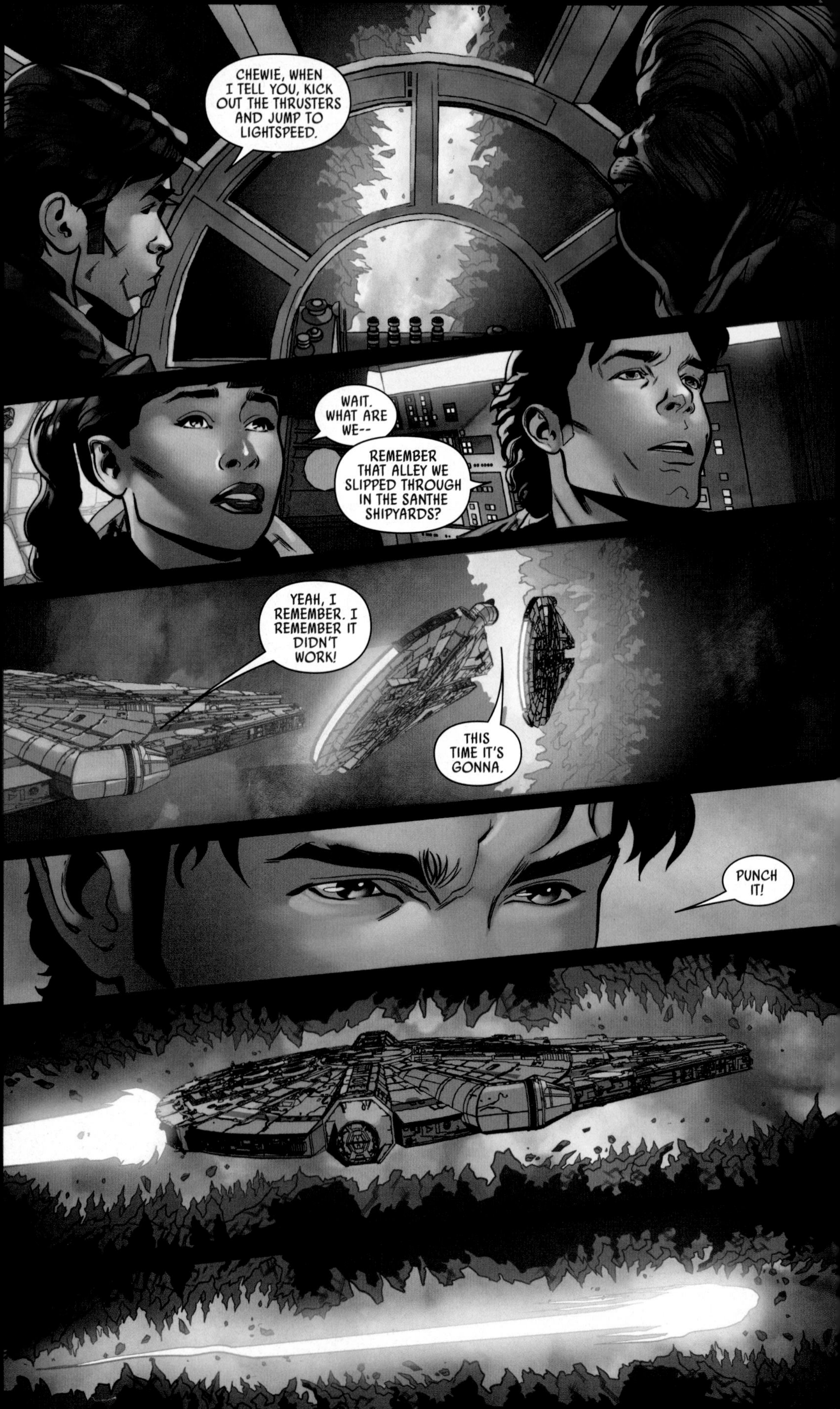
CHEWIE, WHEN I TELL YOU, KICK OUT THE THRUSTERS AND JUMP TO LIGHTSPEED.
WAIT. WHAT ARE WE--
REMEMBER THAT ALLEY WE SLIPPED THROUGH IN THE SANTHE SHIPYARDS?
YEAH, I REMEMBER. I REMEMBER IT DIDN'T WORK!
THIS TIME IT'S GONNA.
PUNCH IT!

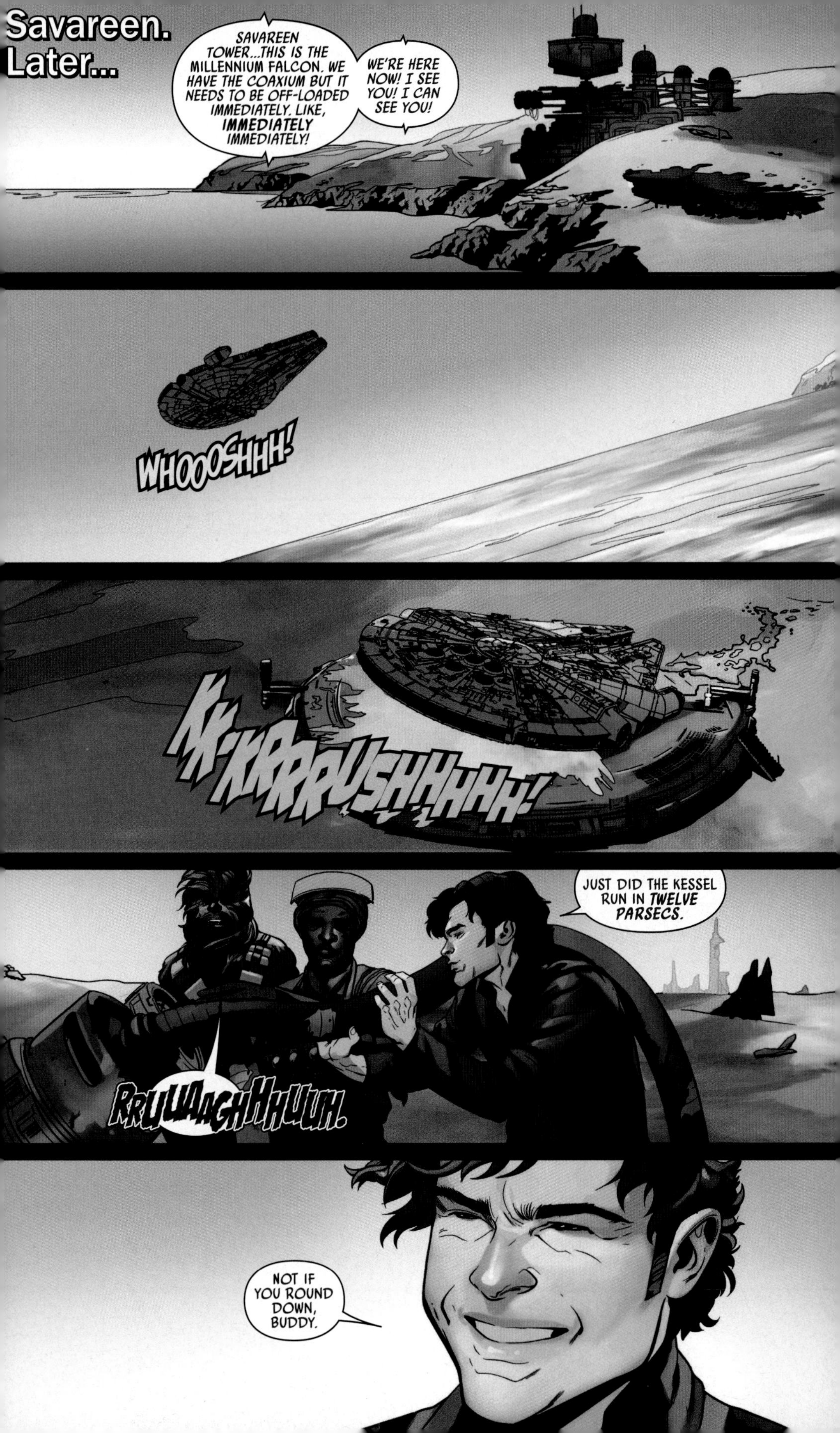
Savareen.
Later...
SAVAREEN TOWER...THIS IS THE MILLENNIUM FALCON. WE HAVE THE COAXIUM BUT IT NEEDS TO BE OFF-LOADED IMMEDIATELY. LIKE, IMMEDIATELY IMMEDIATELY!
WE'RE HERE NOW! I SEE YOU! I CAN SEE YOU!
WHOOOSHHH!
KK-KRRRRUSHHHHH!
JUST DID THE KESSEL RUN IN TWELVE PARSECS.
RRUUAAGHHHUUH.
NOT IF YOU ROUND DOWN, BUDDY.

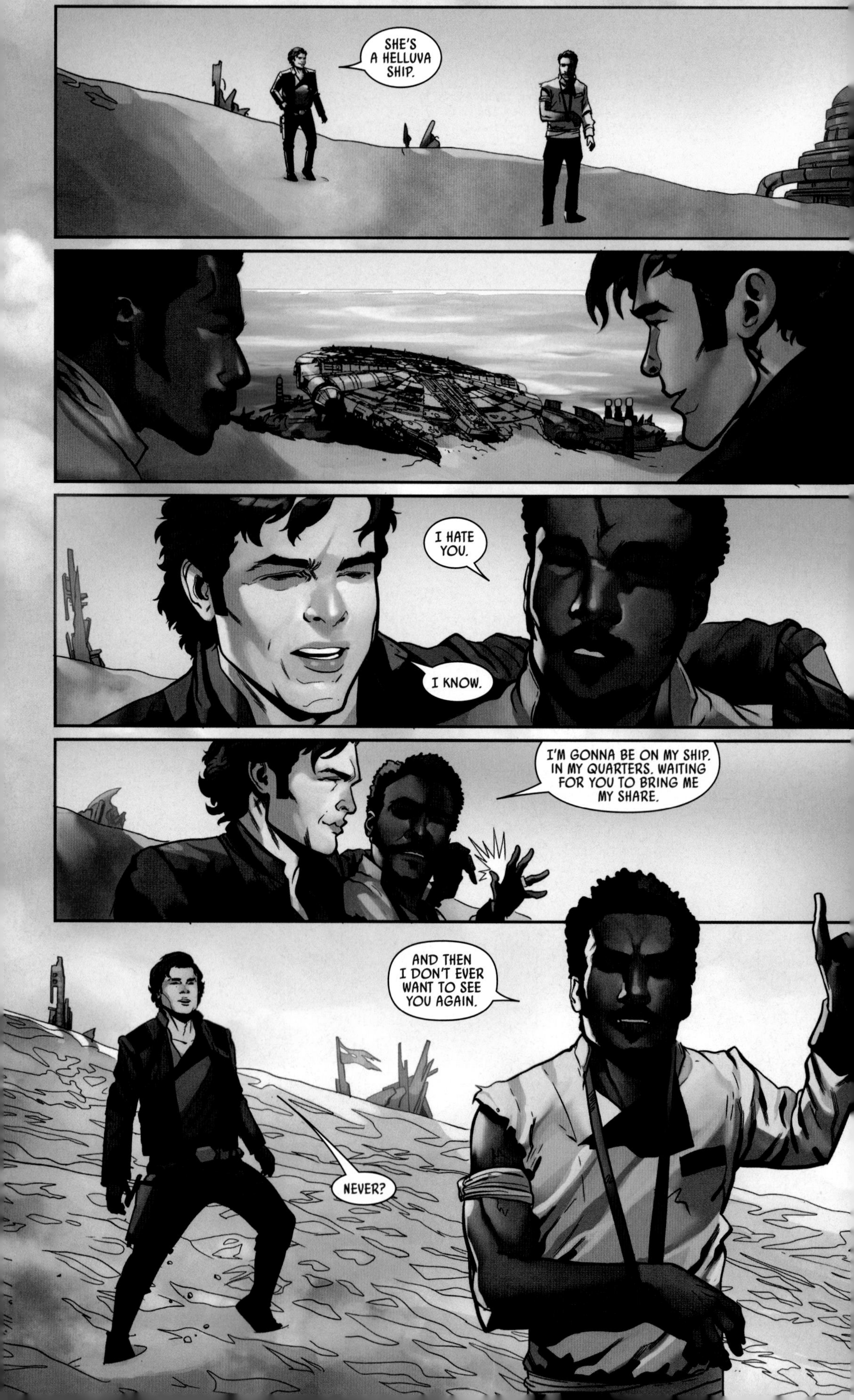
SHE'S A HELLUVA SHIP.
I HATE YOU.
I KNOW.
I'M GONNA BE ON MY SHIP. IN MY QUARTERS. WAITING FOR YOU TO BRING ME MY SHARE.
AND THEN I DON'T EVER WANT TO SEE YOU AGAIN.
NEVER?

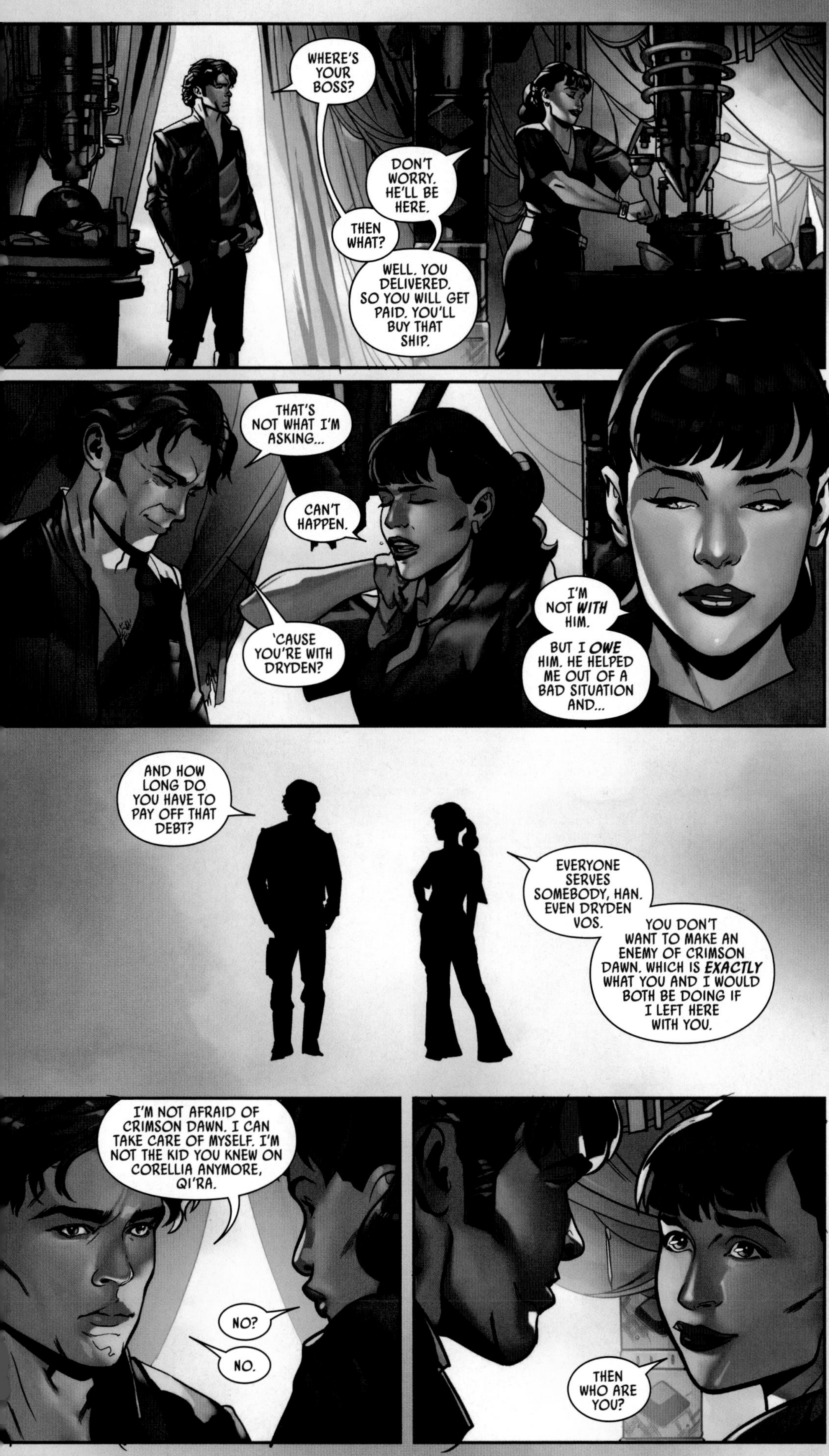
WHERE'S YOUR BOSS?
DON'T WORRY. HE'LL BE HERE.
THEN WHAT?
WELL. YOU DELIVERED. SO YOU WILL GET PAID. YOU'LL BUY THAT SHIP.
THAT'S NOT WHAT I'M ASKING...
CAN'T HAPPEN.
'CAUSE YOU'RE WITH DRYDEN?
I'M NOT *WITH* HIM.
BUT I *OWE* HIM. HE HELPED ME OUT OF A BAD SITUATION AND...
AND HOW LONG DO YOU HAVE TO PAY OFF THAT DEBT?
EVERYONE SERVES SOMEBODY, HAN. EVEN DRYDEN VOS.
YOU DON'T WANT TO MAKE AN ENEMY OF CRIMSON DAWN. WHICH IS *EXACTLY* WHAT YOU AND I WOULD BOTH BE DOING IF I LEFT HERE WITH YOU.
I'M NOT AFRAID OF CRIMSON DAWN. I CAN TAKE CARE OF MYSELF. I'M NOT THE KID YOU KNEW ON CORELLIA ANYMORE, QI'RA.
NO?
NO.
THEN WHO ARE YOU?

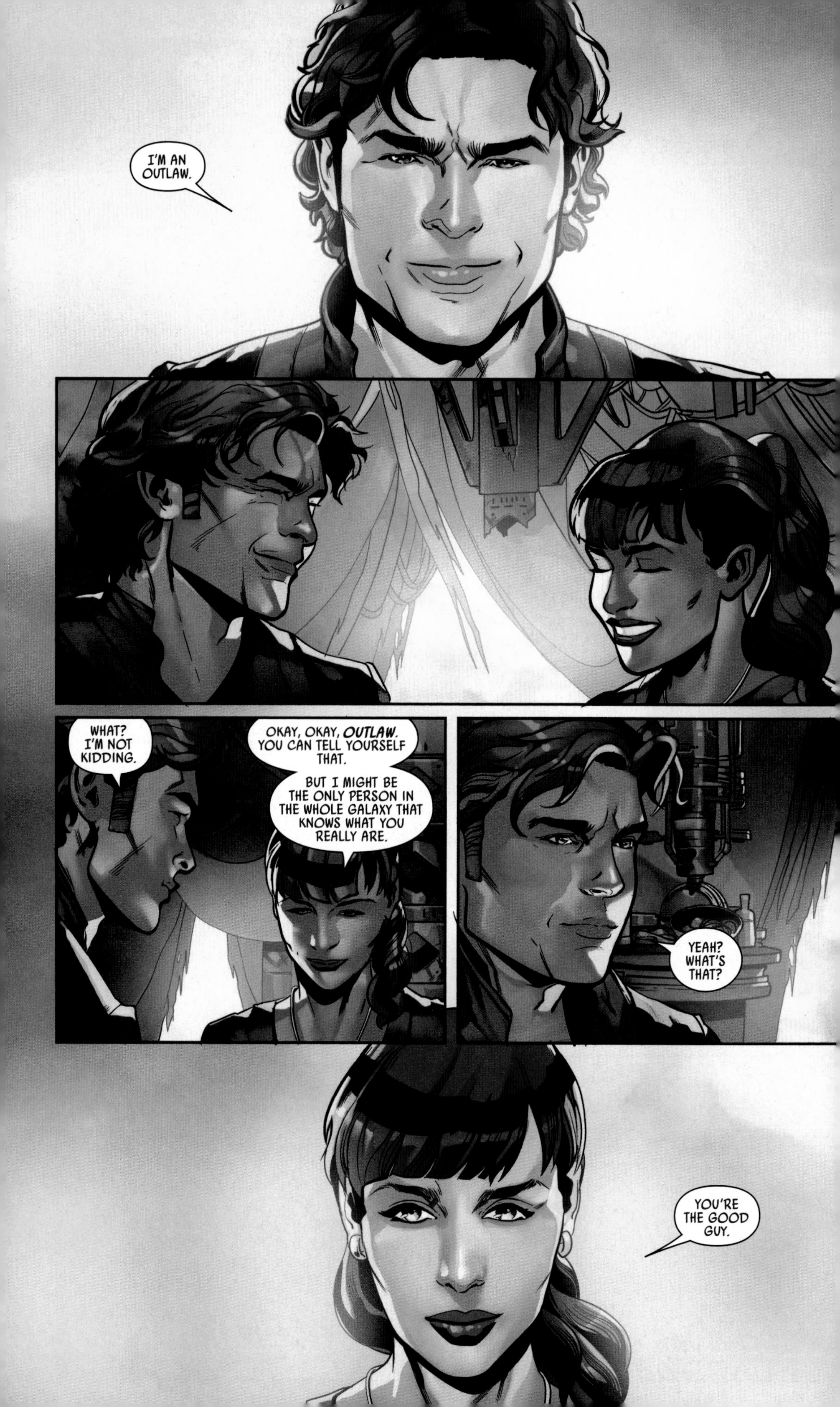
I'M AN OUTLAW.
WHAT? I'M NOT KIDDING.
OKAY, OKAY, *OUTLAW*. YOU CAN TELL YOURSELF THAT.
BUT I MIGHT BE THE ONLY PERSON IN THE WHOLE GALAXY THAT KNOWS WHAT YOU REALLY ARE.
YEAH? WHAT'S THAT?
YOU'RE THE GOOD GUY.

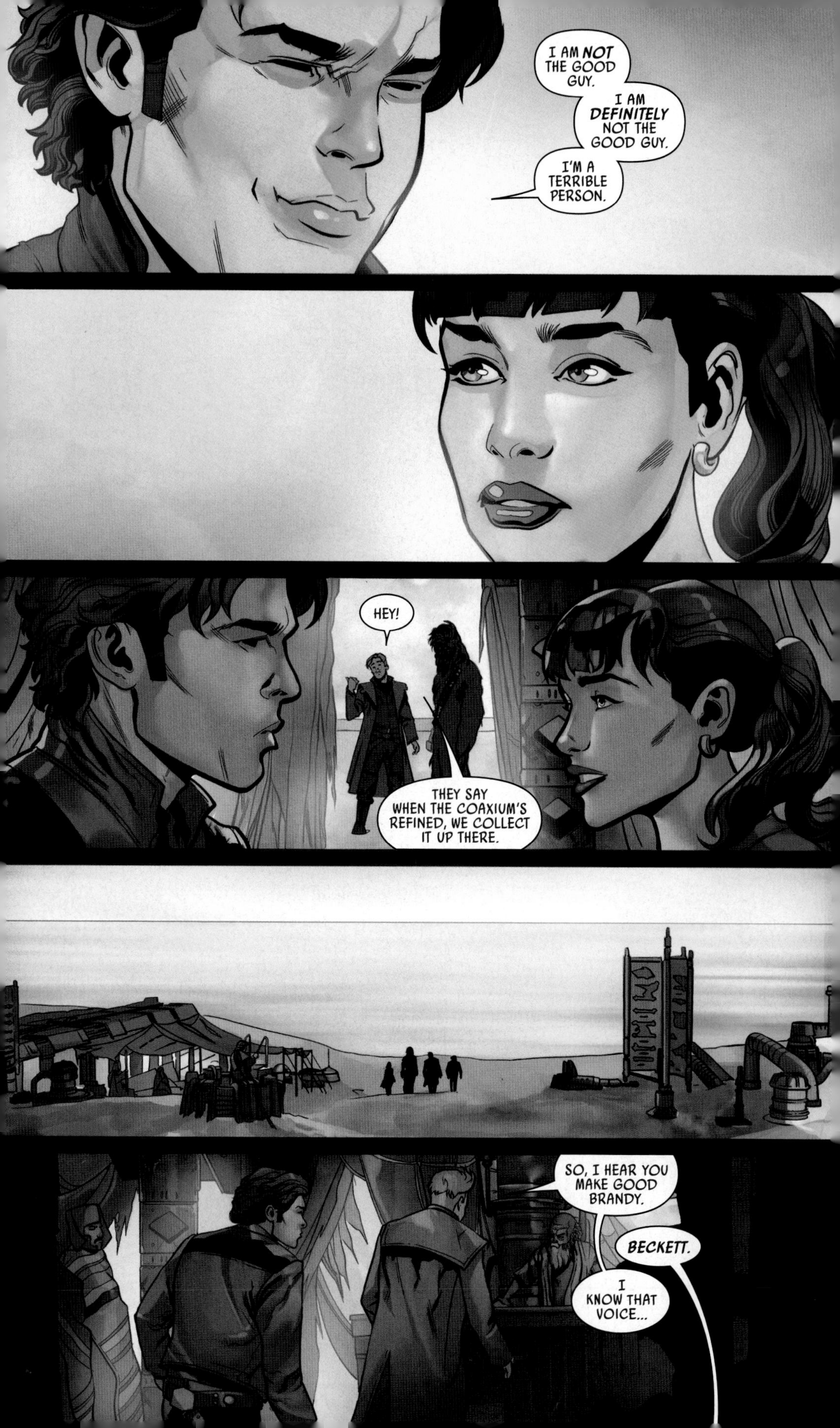
I AM **NOT** THE GOOD GUY.
I AM ***DEFINITELY*** NOT THE GOOD GUY.
I'M A TERRIBLE PERSON.
HEY!
THEY SAY WHEN THE COAXIUM'S REFINED, WE COLLECT IT UP THERE.
SO, I HEAR YOU MAKE GOOD BRANDY.
BECKETT.
I KNOW THAT VOICE...

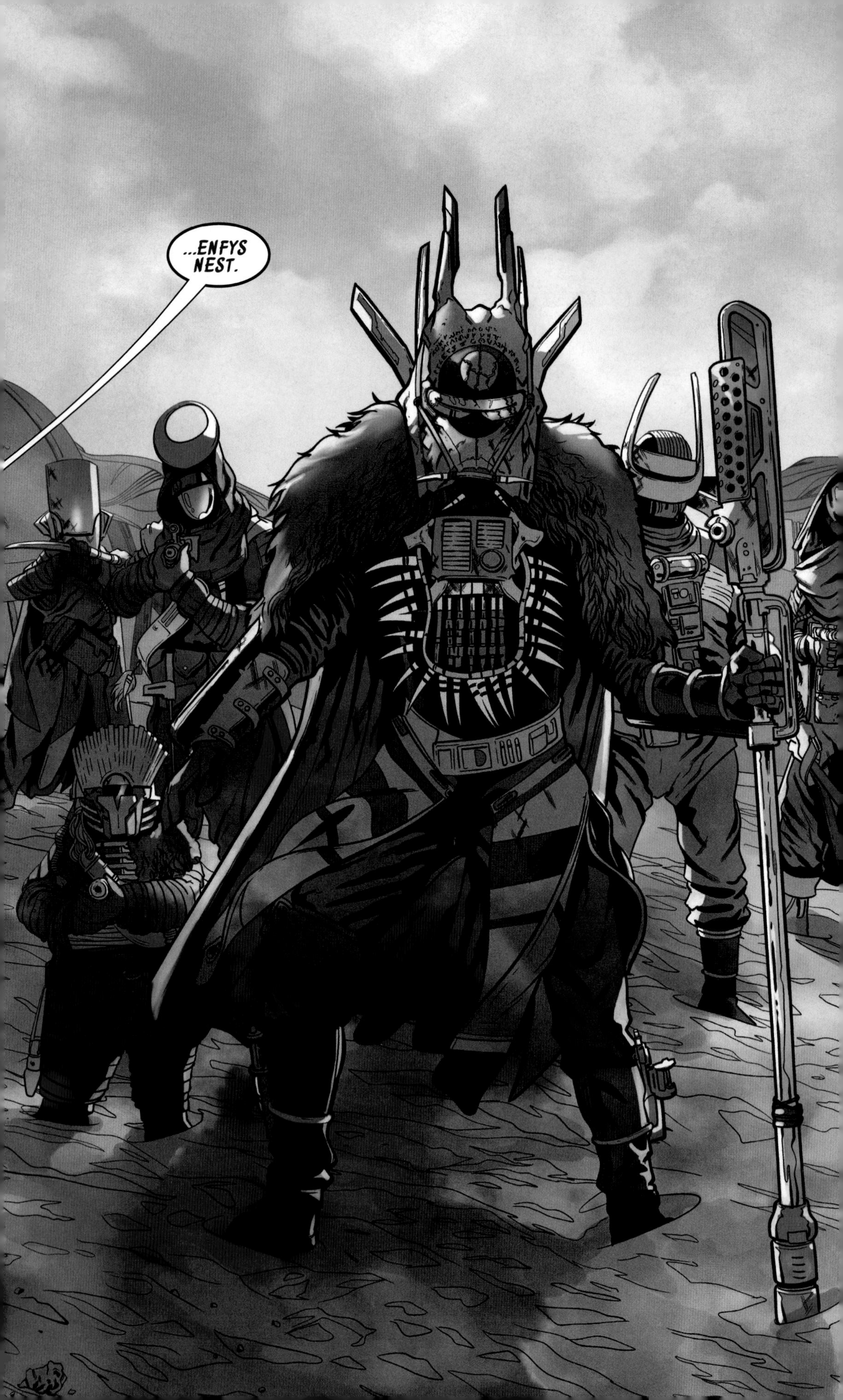
...ENFYS NEST.

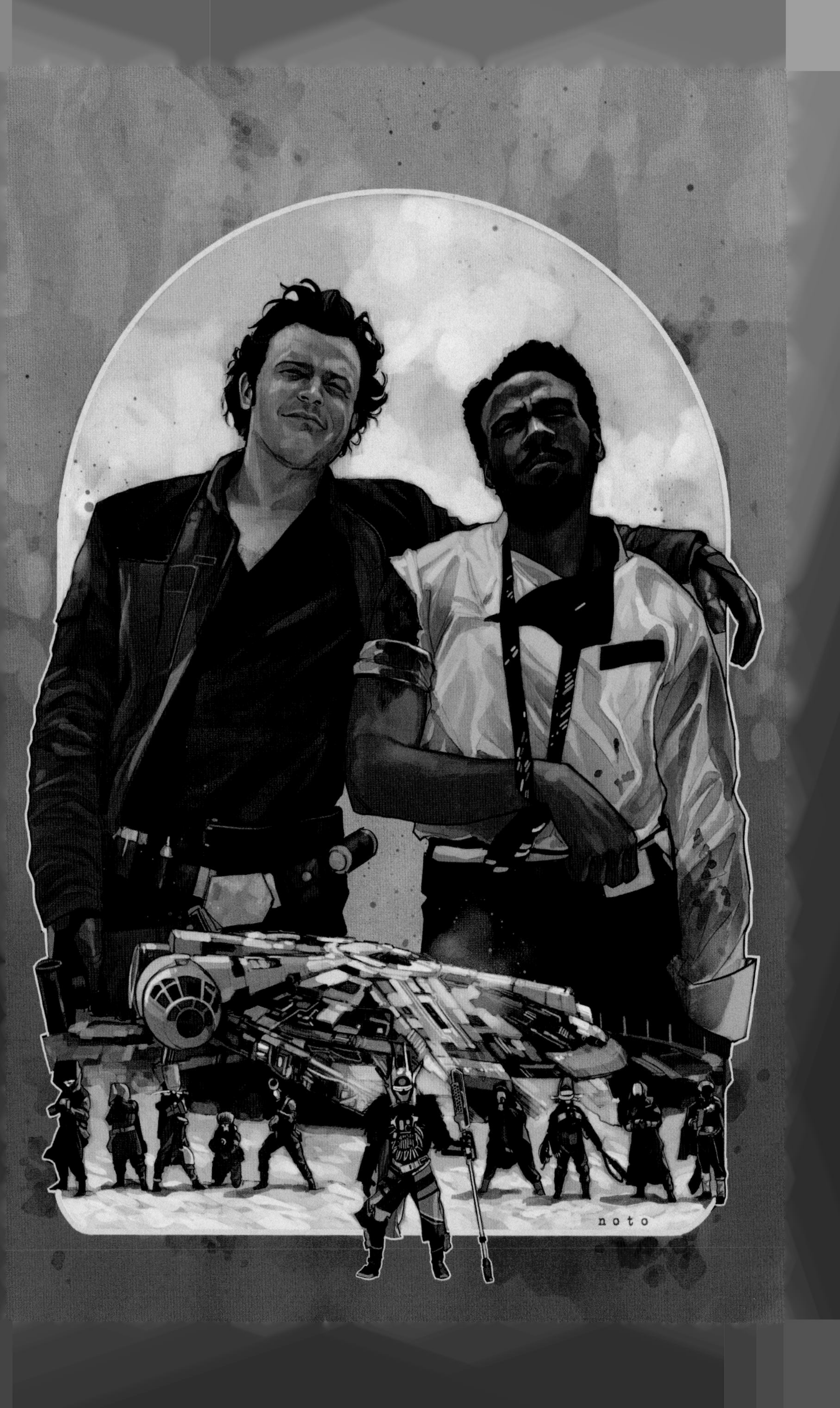
noto

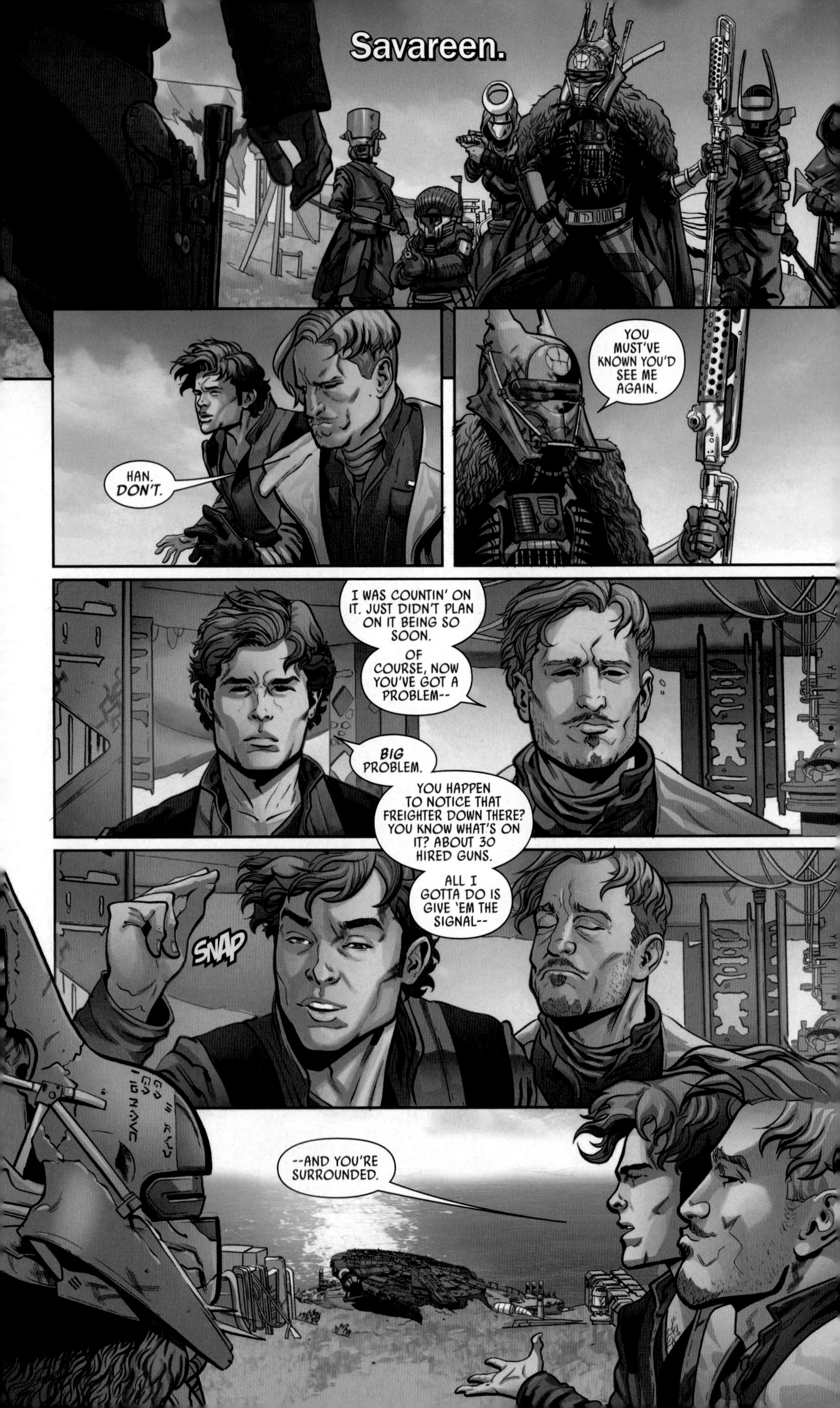
Savareen.
YOU MUST'VE KNOWN YOU'D SEE ME AGAIN.
HAN. DON'T.
I WAS COUNTIN' ON IT. JUST DIDN'T PLAN ON IT BEING SO SOON.
OF COURSE, NOW YOU'VE GOT A PROBLEM--
BIG PROBLEM.
YOU HAPPEN TO NOTICE THAT FREIGHTER DOWN THERE? YOU KNOW WHAT'S ON IT? ABOUT 30 HIRED GUNS.
ALL I GOTTA DO IS GIVE 'EM THE SIGNAL--
SNAP
--AND YOU'RE SURROUNDED.

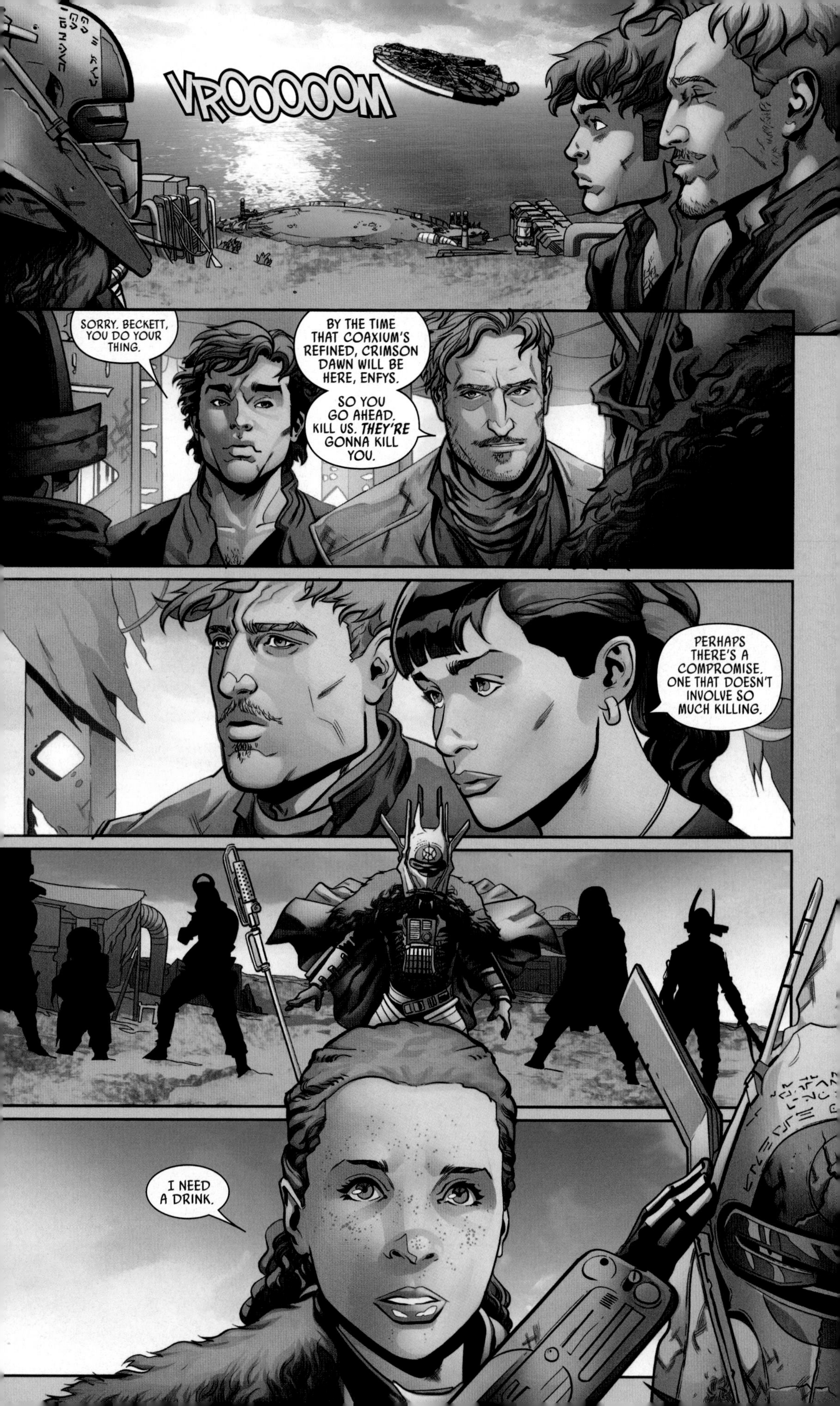
VROOOOOM
SORRY. BECKETT, YOU DO YOUR THING.
BY THE TIME THAT COAXIUM'S REFINED, CRIMSON DAWN WILL BE HERE, ENFYS.
SO YOU GO AHEAD. KILL US. THEY'RE GONNA KILL YOU.
PERHAPS THERE'S A COMPROMISE. ONE THAT DOESN'T INVOLVE SO MUCH KILLING.
I NEED A DRINK.

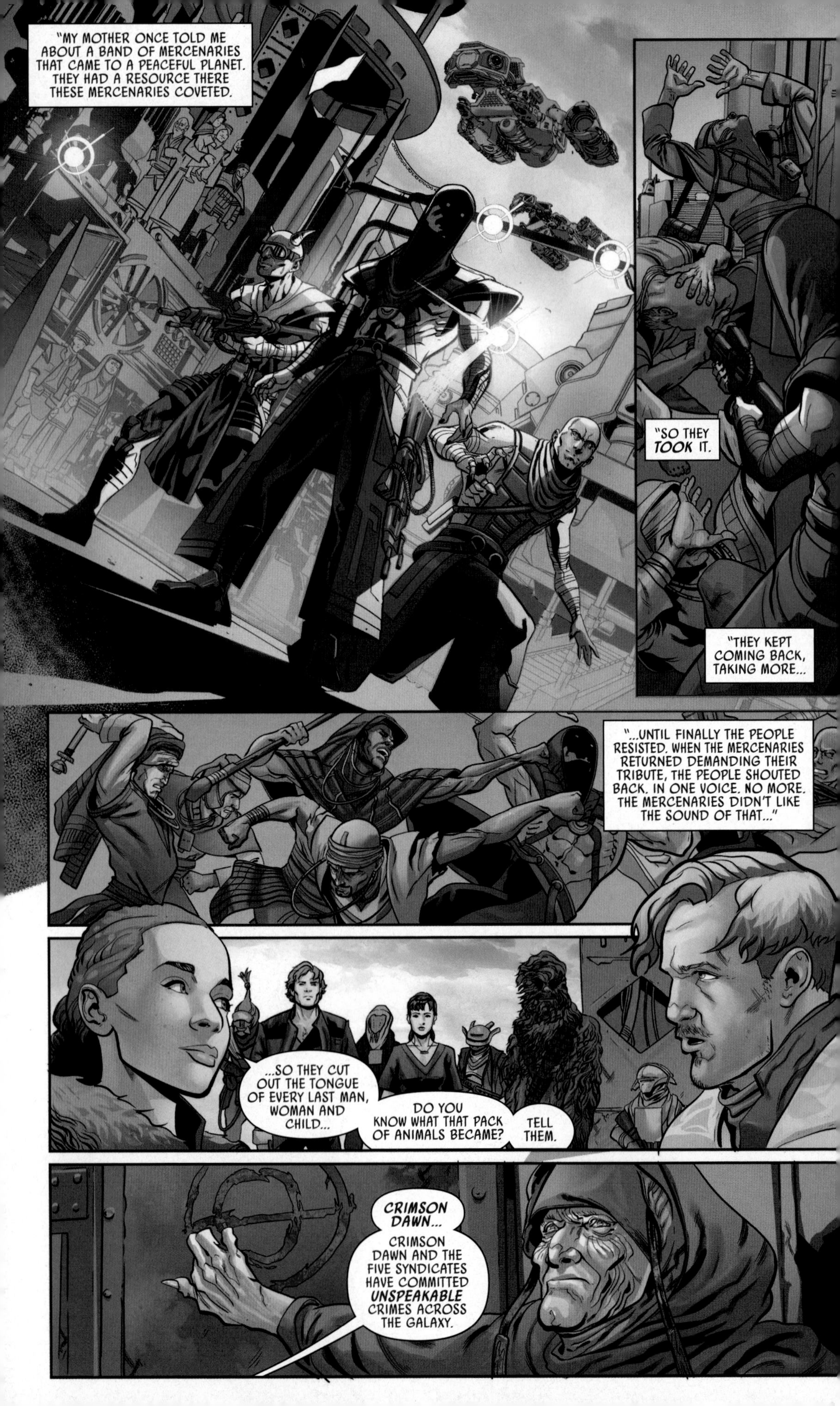
"MY MOTHER ONCE TOLD ME ABOUT A BAND OF MERCENARIES THAT CAME TO A PEACEFUL PLANET. THEY HAD A RESOURCE THERE THESE MERCENARIES COVETED.
"SO THEY TOOK IT.
"THEY KEPT COMING BACK, TAKING MORE...
"...UNTIL FINALLY THE PEOPLE RESISTED. WHEN THE MERCENARIES RETURNED DEMANDING THEIR TRIBUTE, THE PEOPLE SHOUTED BACK, IN ONE VOICE. NO MORE. THE MERCENARIES DIDN'T LIKE THE SOUND OF THAT..."
...SO THEY CUT OUT THE TONGUE OF EVERY LAST MAN, WOMAN AND CHILD...
DO YOU KNOW WHAT THAT PACK OF ANIMALS BECAME?
TELL THEM.
CRIMSON DAWN...
CRIMSON DAWN AND THE FIVE SYNDICATES HAVE COMMITTED UNSPEAKABLE CRIMES ACROSS THE GALAXY.

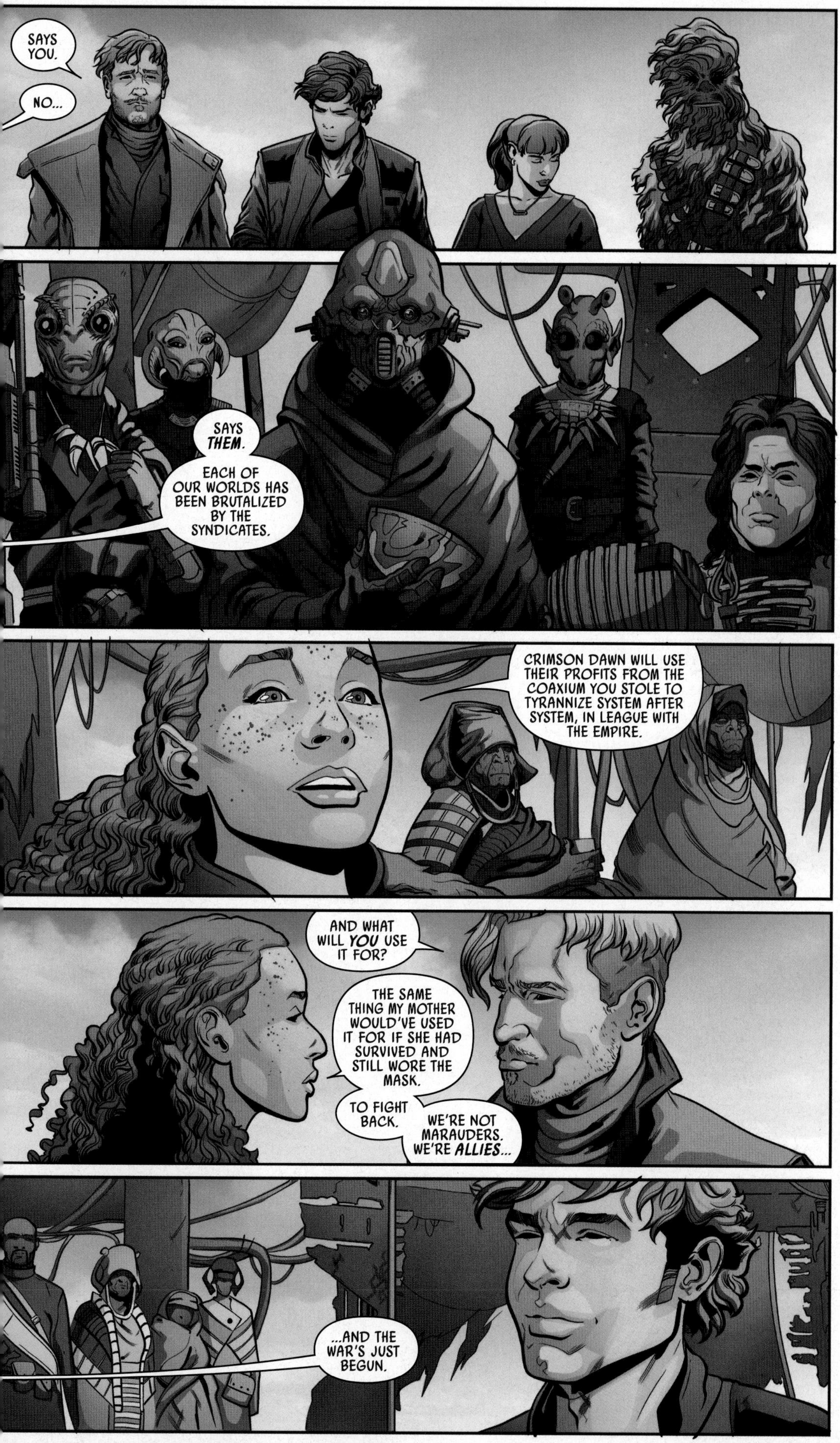
SAYS YOU.
NO...
SAYS THEM.
EACH OF OUR WORLDS HAS BEEN BRUTALIZED BY THE SYNDICATES.
CRIMSON DAWN WILL USE THEIR PROFITS FROM THE COAXIUM YOU STOLE TO TYRANNIZE SYSTEM AFTER SYSTEM, IN LEAGUE WITH THE EMPIRE.
AND WHAT WILL YOU USE IT FOR?
THE SAME THING MY MOTHER WOULD'VE USED IT FOR IF SHE HAD SURVIVED AND STILL WORE THE MASK.
TO FIGHT BACK.
WE'RE NOT MARAUDERS. WE'RE ALLIES...
...AND THE WAR'S JUST BEGUN.

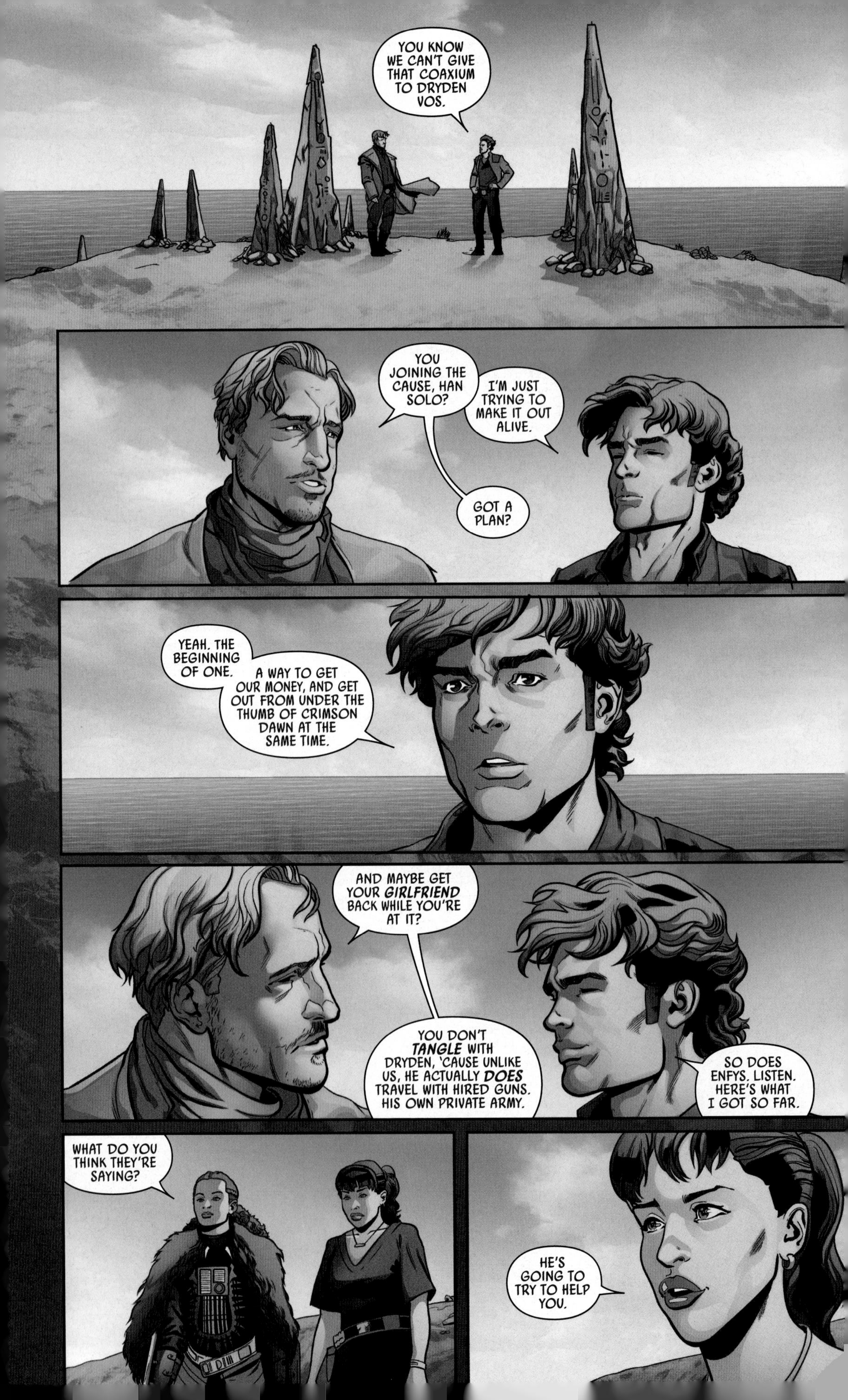
YOU KNOW WE CAN'T GIVE THAT COAXIUM TO DRYDEN VOS.
YOU JOINING THE CAUSE, HAN SOLO?
I'M JUST TRYING TO MAKE IT OUT ALIVE.
GOT A PLAN?
YEAH. THE BEGINNING OF ONE.
A WAY TO GET OUR MONEY, AND GET OUT FROM UNDER THE THUMB OF CRIMSON DAWN AT THE SAME TIME.
AND MAYBE GET YOUR GIRLFRIEND BACK WHILE YOU'RE AT IT?
YOU DON'T TANGLE WITH DRYDEN, 'CAUSE UNLIKE US, HE ACTUALLY DOES TRAVEL WITH HIRED GUNS. HIS OWN PRIVATE ARMY.
SO DOES ENFYS. LISTEN. HERE'S WHAT I GOT SO FAR.
WHAT DO YOU THINK THEY'RE SAYING?
HE'S GOING TO TRY TO HELP YOU.

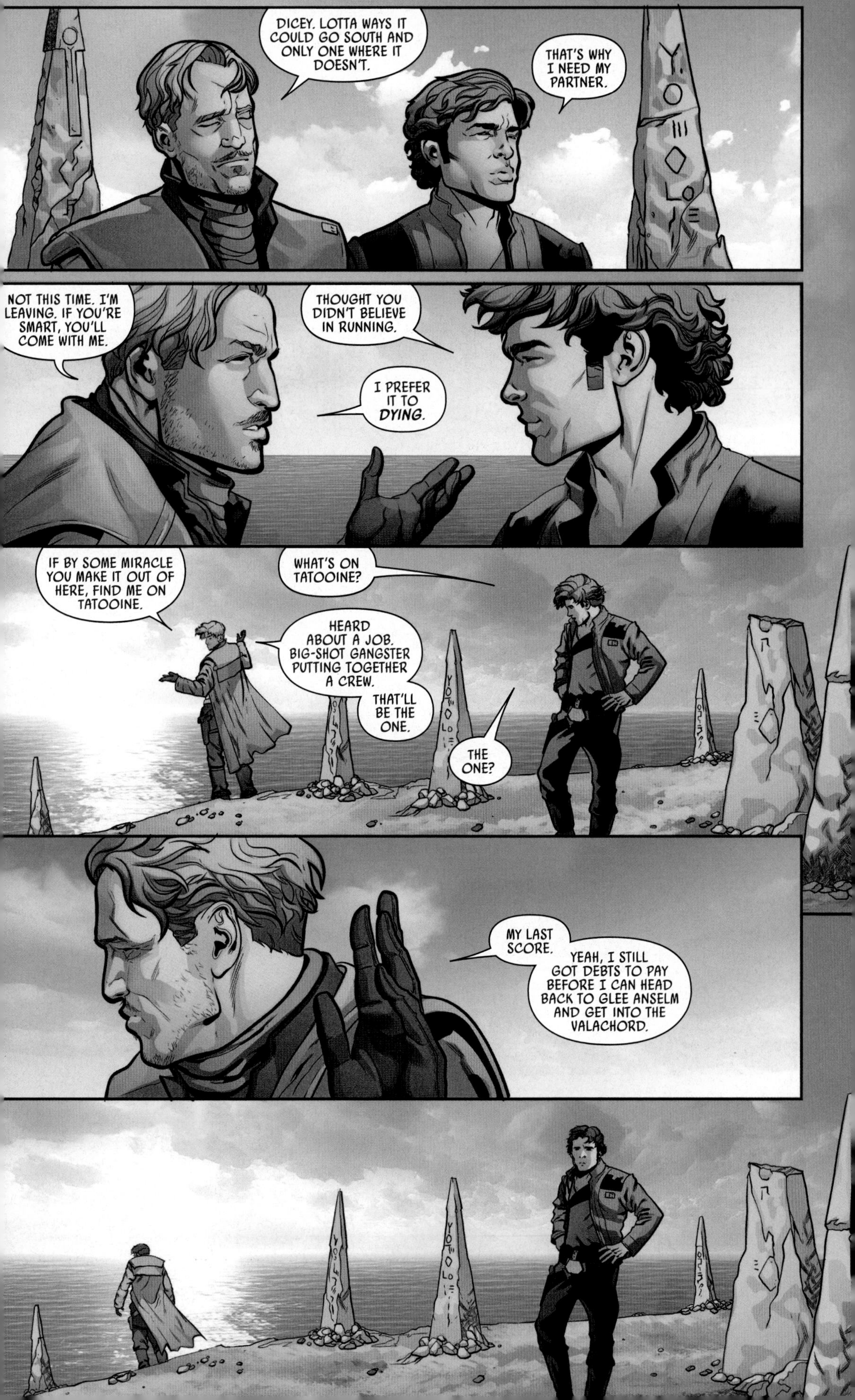
DICEY. LOTTA WAYS IT COULD GO SOUTH AND ONLY ONE WHERE IT DOESN'T.
THAT'S WHY I NEED MY PARTNER.
NOT THIS TIME. I'M LEAVING. IF YOU'RE SMART, YOU'LL COME WITH ME.
THOUGHT YOU DIDN'T BELIEVE IN RUNNING.
I PREFER IT TO *DYING*.
IF BY SOME MIRACLE YOU MAKE IT OUT OF HERE, FIND ME ON TATOOINE.
WHAT'S ON TATOOINE?
HEARD ABOUT A JOB. BIG-SHOT GANGSTER PUTTING TOGETHER A CREW.
THAT'LL BE THE ONE.
THE ONE?
MY LAST SCORE.
YEAH, I STILL GOT DEBTS TO PAY BEFORE I CAN HEAD BACK TO GLEE ANSELM AND GET INTO THE VALACHORD.

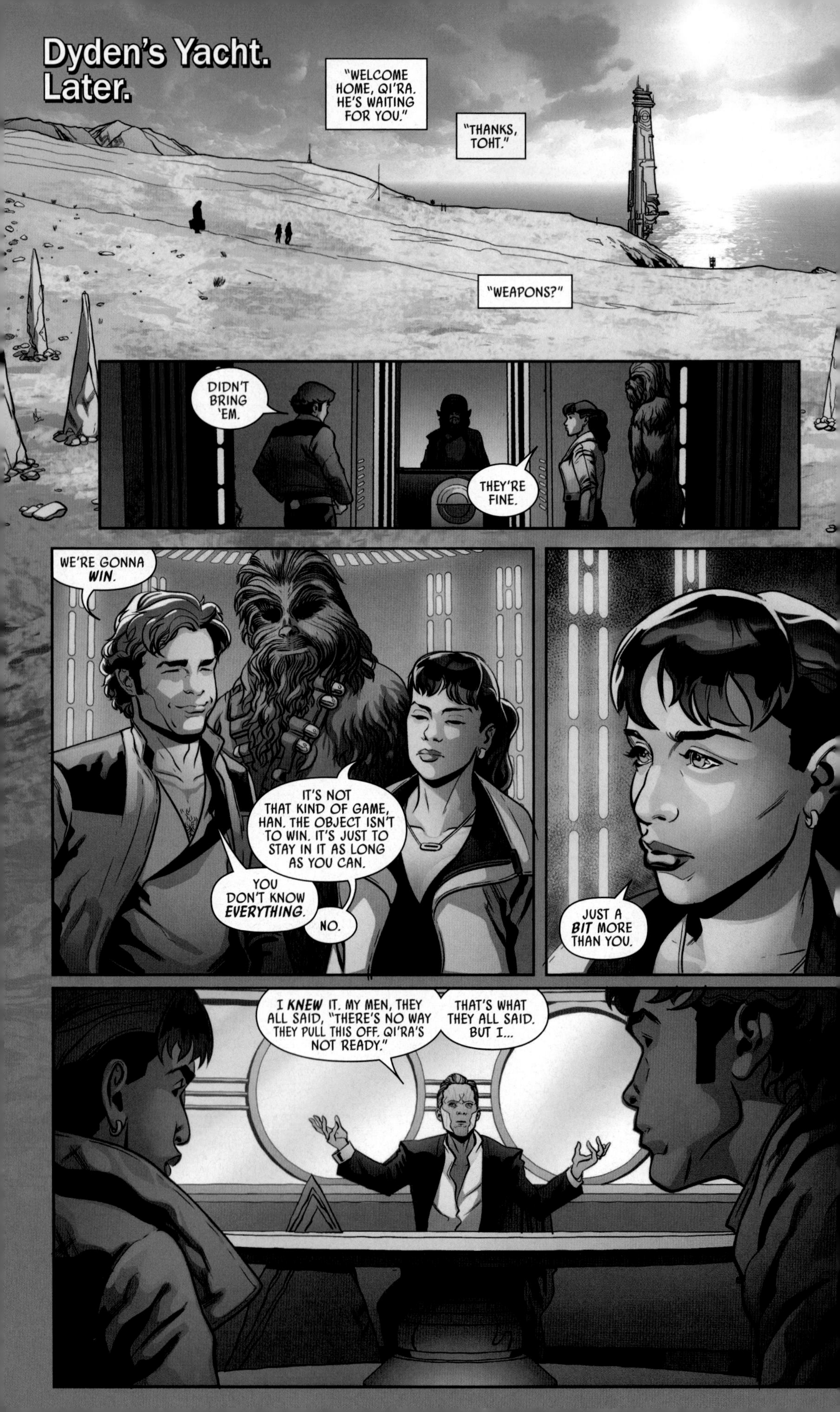

Dyden's Yacht.
Later.
"WELCOME HOME, QI'RA. HE'S WAITING FOR YOU."
"THANKS, TOHT."
"WEAPONS?"
DIDN'T BRING 'EM.
THEY'RE FINE.
WE'RE GONNA WIN.
IT'S NOT THAT KIND OF GAME, HAN. THE OBJECT ISN'T TO WIN. IT'S JUST TO STAY IN IT AS LONG AS YOU CAN.
YOU DON'T KNOW EVERYTHING.
NO.
JUST A BIT MORE THAN YOU.
I KNEW IT. MY MEN, THEY ALL SAID, "THERE'S NO WAY THEY PULL THIS OFF. QI'RA'S NOT READY."
THAT'S WHAT THEY ALL SAID. BUT I...

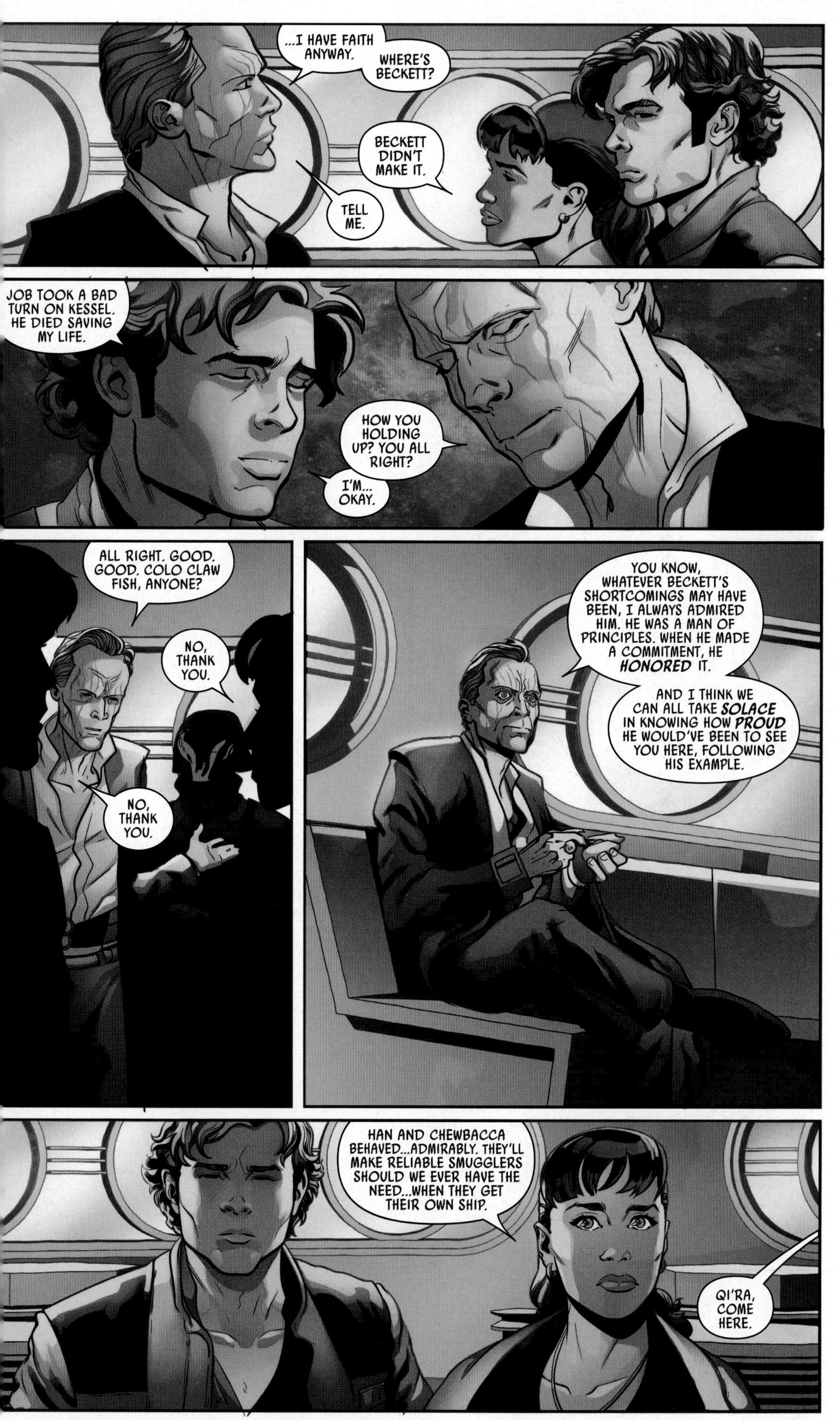
...I HAVE FAITH ANYWAY.
WHERE'S BECKETT?
BECKETT DIDN'T MAKE IT.
TELL ME.
JOB TOOK A BAD TURN ON KESSEL. HE DIED SAVING MY LIFE.
HOW YOU HOLDING UP? YOU ALL RIGHT?
I'M... OKAY.
ALL RIGHT. GOOD. GOOD. COLO CLAW FISH, ANYONE?
NO, THANK YOU.
NO, THANK YOU.
YOU KNOW, WHATEVER BECKETT'S SHORTCOMINGS MAY HAVE BEEN, I ALWAYS ADMIRED HIM. HE WAS A MAN OF PRINCIPLES. WHEN HE MADE A COMMITMENT, HE HONORED IT.
AND I THINK WE CAN ALL TAKE SOLACE IN KNOWING HOW PROUD HE WOULD'VE BEEN TO SEE YOU HERE, FOLLOWING HIS EXAMPLE.
HAN AND CHEWBACCA BEHAVED...ADMIRABLY. THEY'LL MAKE RELIABLE SMUGGLERS SHOULD WE EVER HAVE THE NEED...WHEN THEY GET THEIR OWN SHIP.
QI'RA, COME HERE.

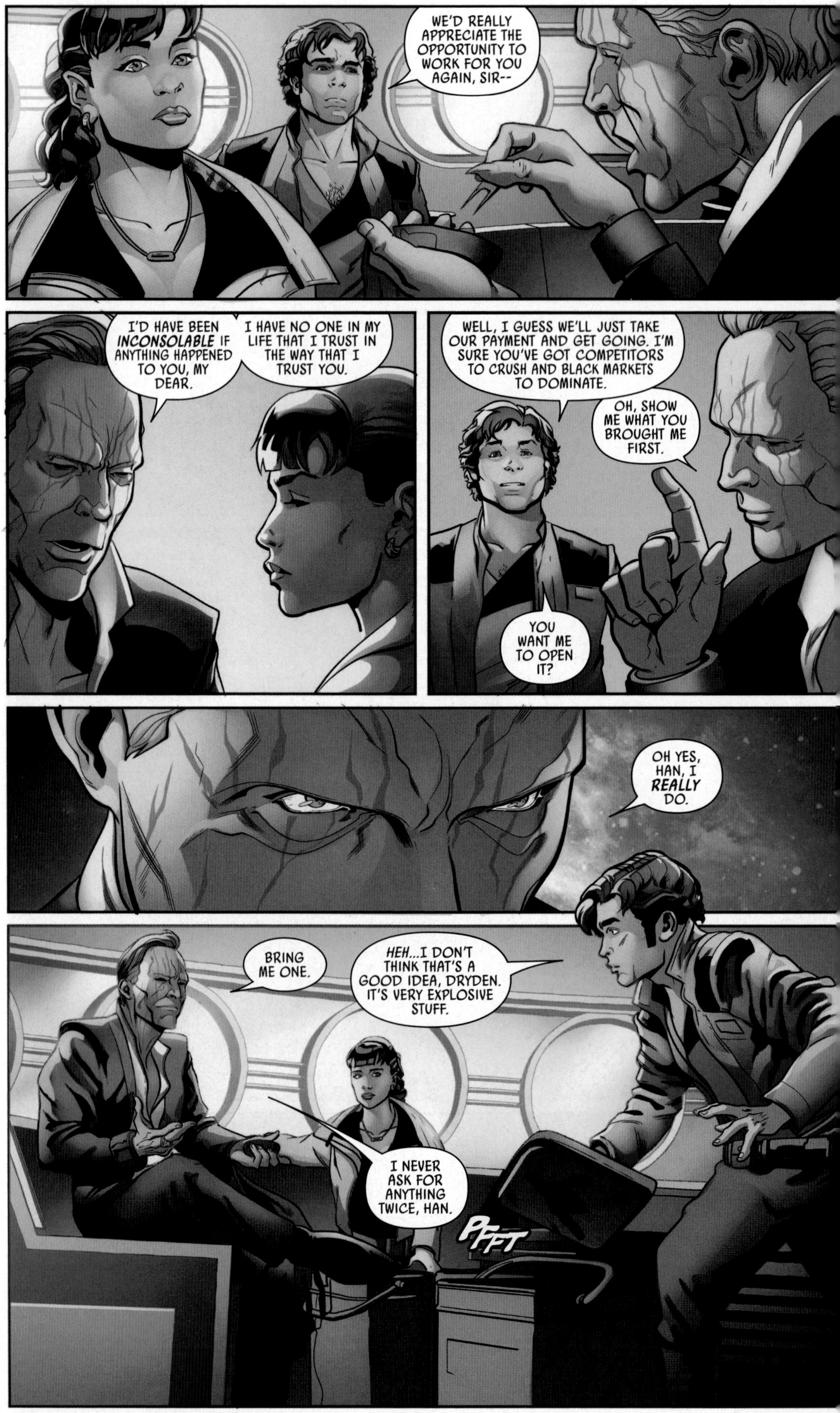
WE'D REALLY APPRECIATE THE OPPORTUNITY TO WORK FOR YOU AGAIN, SIR--
I'D HAVE BEEN *INCONSOLABLE* IF ANYTHING HAPPENED TO YOU, MY DEAR.
I HAVE NO ONE IN MY LIFE THAT I TRUST IN THE WAY THAT I TRUST YOU.
WELL, I GUESS WE'LL JUST TAKE OUR PAYMENT AND GET GOING. I'M SURE YOU'VE GOT COMPETITORS TO CRUSH AND BLACK MARKETS TO DOMINATE.
OH, SHOW ME WHAT YOU BROUGHT ME FIRST.
YOU WANT ME TO OPEN IT?
OH YES, HAN, I *REALLY* DO.
BRING ME ONE.
HEH...I DON'T THINK THAT'S A GOOD IDEA, DRYDEN. IT'S VERY EXPLOSIVE STUFF.
I NEVER ASK FOR ANYTHING TWICE, HAN.
PFFT

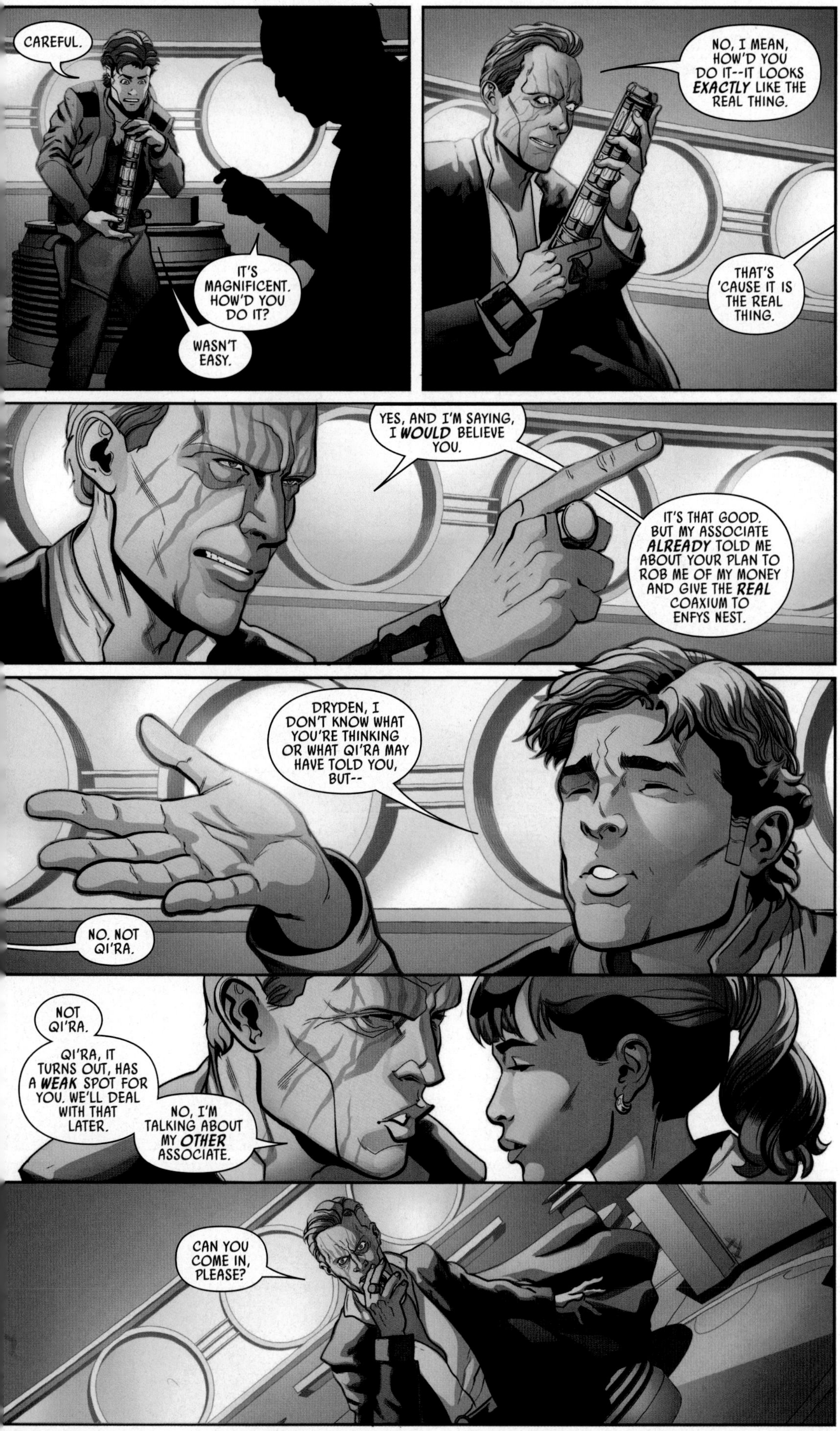
CAREFUL.
IT'S MAGNIFICENT. HOW'D YOU DO IT?
WASN'T EASY.
NO, I MEAN, HOW'D YOU DO IT--IT LOOKS EXACTLY LIKE THE REAL THING.
THAT'S 'CAUSE IT IS THE REAL THING.
YES, AND I'M SAYING, I WOULD BELIEVE YOU.
IT'S THAT GOOD. BUT MY ASSOCIATE ALREADY TOLD ME ABOUT YOUR PLAN TO ROB ME OF MY MONEY AND GIVE THE REAL COAXIUM TO ENFYS NEST.
DRYDEN, I DON'T KNOW WHAT YOU'RE THINKING OR WHAT QI'RA MAY HAVE TOLD YOU, BUT--
NO. NOT QI'RA.
NOT QI'RA.
QI'RA, IT TURNS OUT, HAS A WEAK SPOT FOR YOU. WE'LL DEAL WITH THAT LATER.
NO, I'M TALKING ABOUT MY OTHER ASSOCIATE.
CAN YOU COME IN, PLEASE?

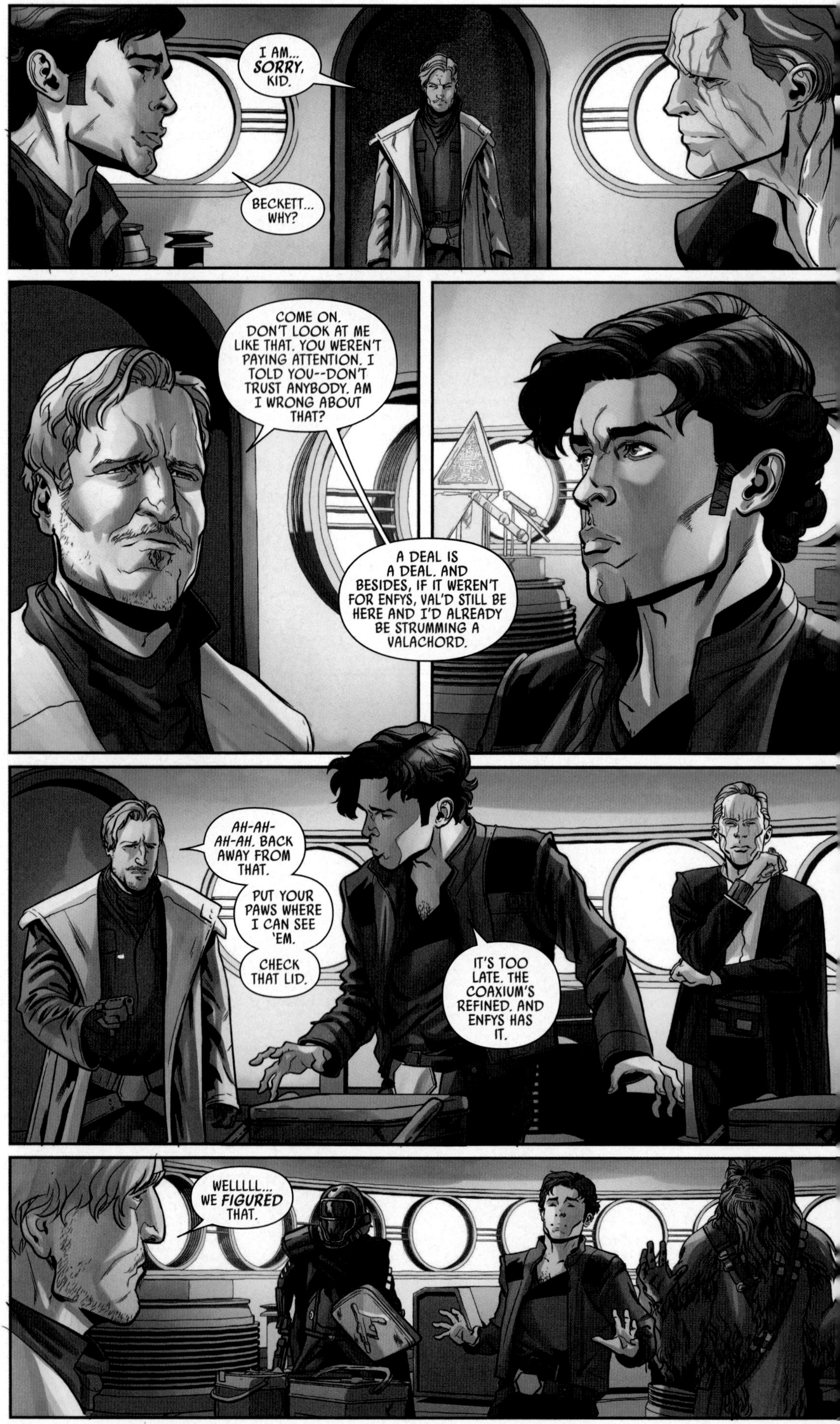
I AM... SORRY, KID.
BECKETT... WHY?
COME ON. DON'T LOOK AT ME LIKE THAT. YOU WEREN'T PAYING ATTENTION. I TOLD YOU--DON'T TRUST ANYBODY. AM I WRONG ABOUT THAT?
A DEAL IS A DEAL. AND BESIDES, IF IT WEREN'T FOR ENFYS, VAL'D STILL BE HERE AND I'D ALREADY BE STRUMMING A VALACHORD.
AH-AH-AH-AH. BACK AWAY FROM THAT.
PUT YOUR PAWS WHERE I CAN SEE 'EM.
CHECK THAT LID.
IT'S TOO LATE. THE COAXIUM'S REFINED. AND ENFYS HAS IT.
WELLLLL... WE FIGURED THAT.

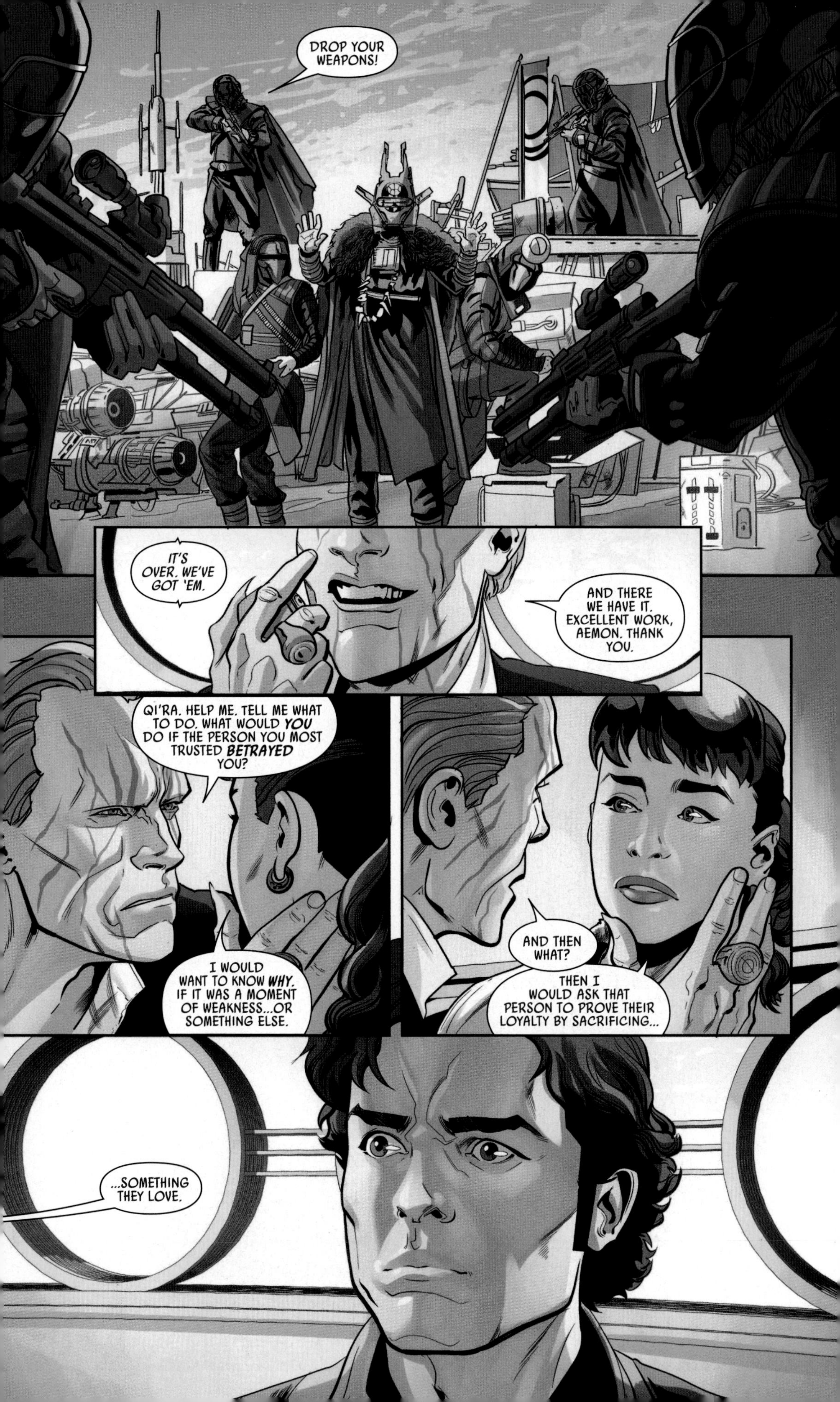
DROP YOUR WEAPONS!
IT'S OVER. WE'VE GOT 'EM.
AND THERE WE HAVE IT. EXCELLENT WORK, AEMON. THANK YOU.
QI'RA. HELP ME. TELL ME WHAT TO DO. WHAT WOULD *YOU* DO IF THE PERSON YOU MOST TRUSTED *BETRAYED* YOU?
I WOULD WANT TO KNOW *WHY*. IF IT WAS A MOMENT OF WEAKNESS...OR SOMETHING ELSE.
AND THEN WHAT?
THEN I WOULD ASK THAT PERSON TO PROVE THEIR LOYALTY BY SACRIFICING...
...SOMETHING THEY LOVE.

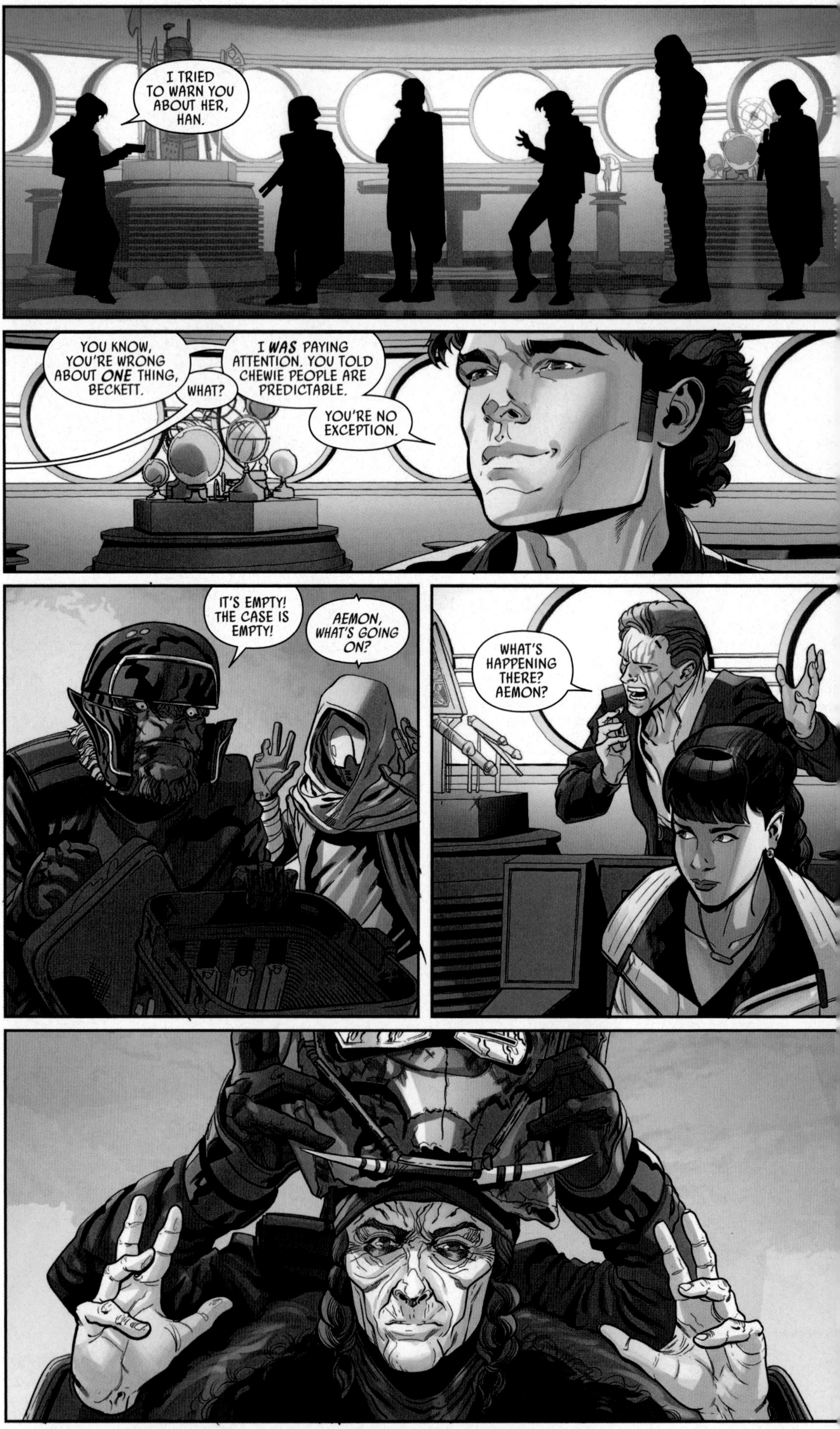

I TRIED TO WARN YOU ABOUT HER, HAN.
YOU KNOW, YOU'RE WRONG ABOUT ONE THING, BECKETT.
WHAT?
I WAS PAYING ATTENTION. YOU TOLD CHEWIE PEOPLE ARE PREDICTABLE.
YOU'RE NO EXCEPTION.
IT'S EMPTY! THE CASE IS EMPTY!
AEMON, WHAT'S GOING ON?
WHAT'S HAPPENING THERE? AEMON?

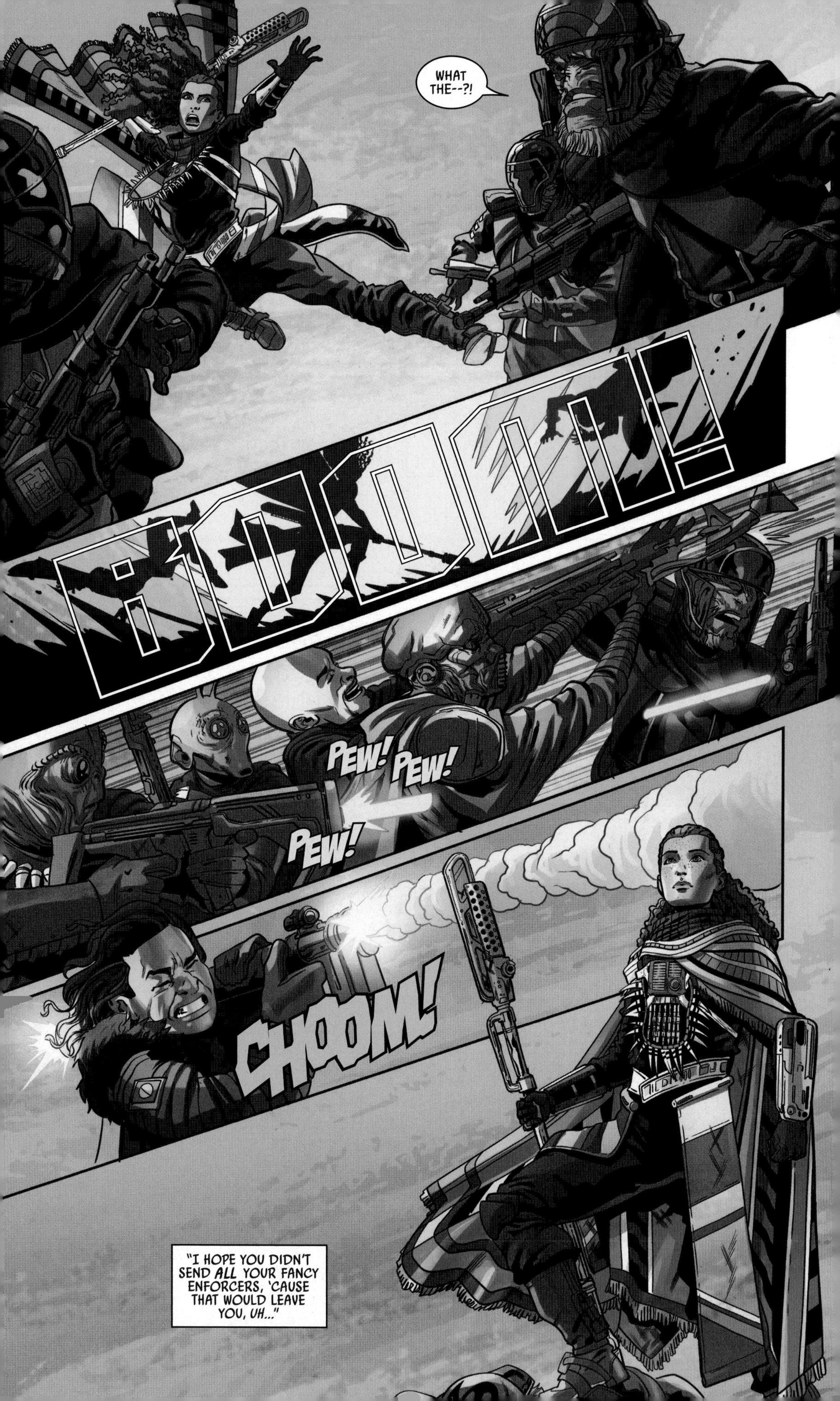
WHAT THE--?!
BOOM!
PEW! PEW!
PEW!
CHOOM!
"I HOPE YOU DIDN'T SEND ALL YOUR FANCY ENFORCERS, 'CAUSE THAT WOULD LEAVE YOU, UH..."

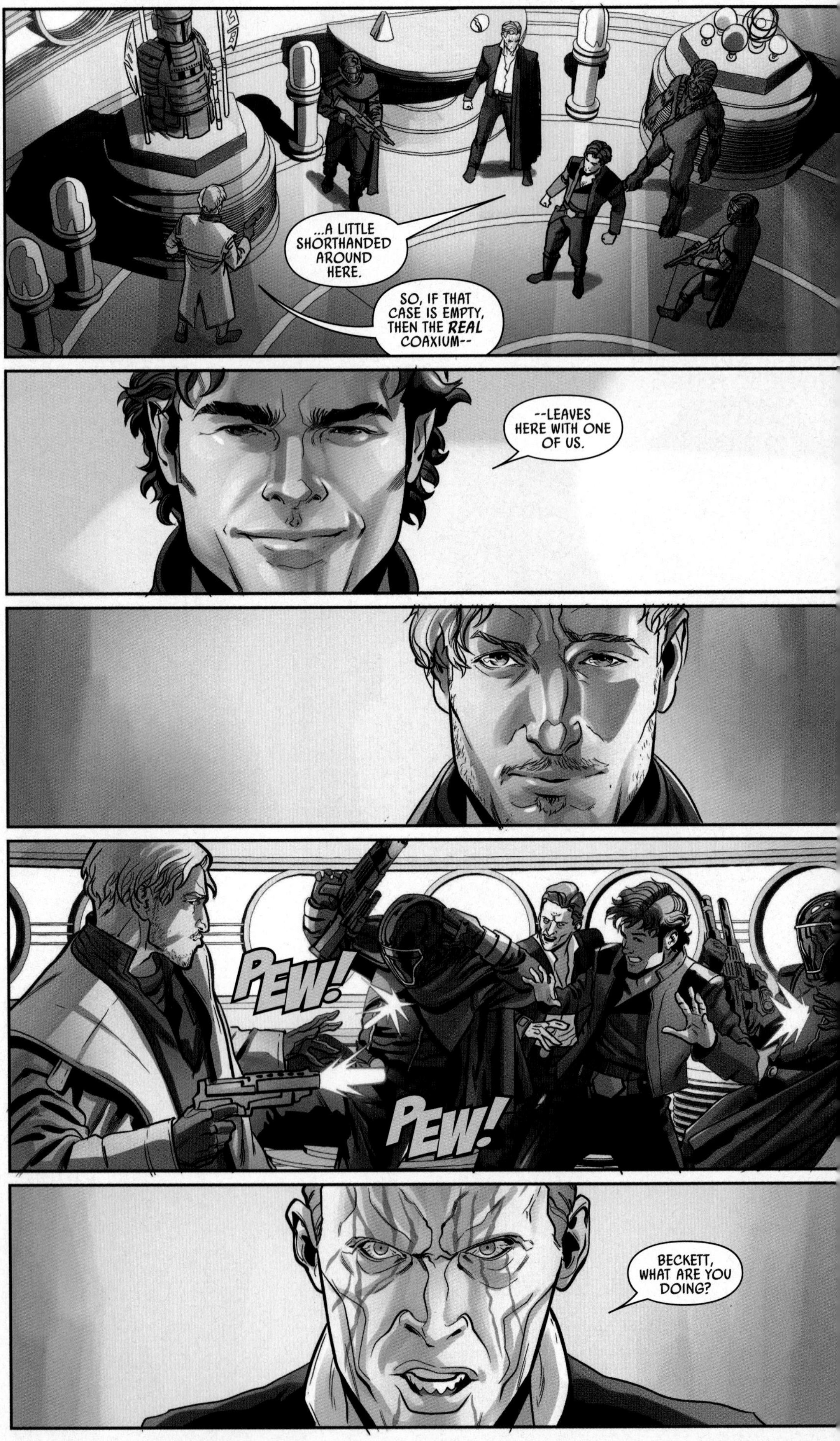
...A LITTLE SHORTHANDED AROUND HERE.
SO, IF THAT CASE IS EMPTY, THEN THE REAL COAXIUM--
--LEAVES HERE WITH ONE OF US.
PEW!
PEW!
BECKETT, WHAT ARE YOU DOING?

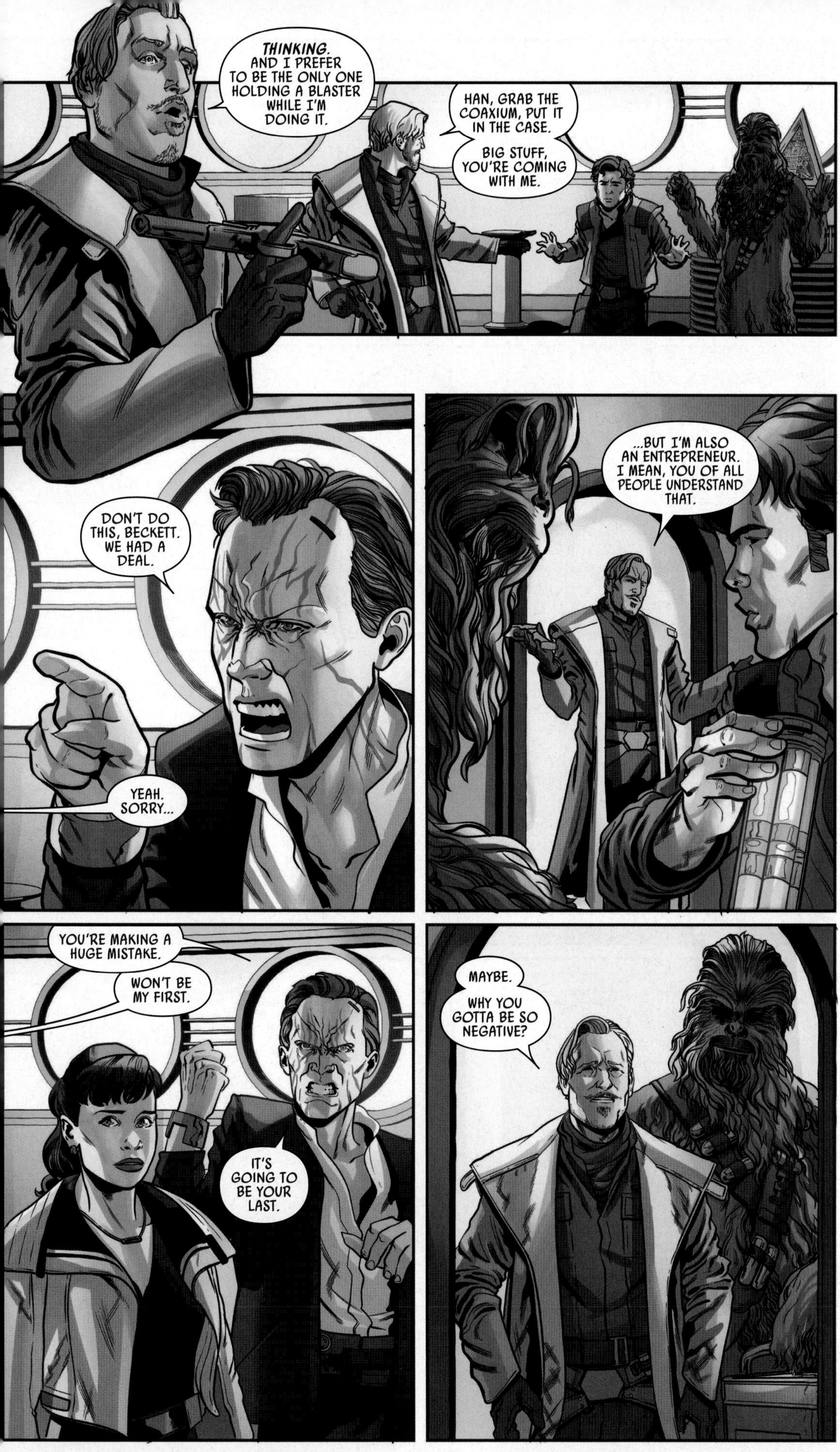

THINKING. AND I PREFER TO BE THE ONLY ONE HOLDING A BLASTER WHILE I'M DOING IT.
HAN, GRAB THE COAXIUM, PUT IT IN THE CASE.
BIG STUFF, YOU'RE COMING WITH ME.
DON'T DO THIS, BECKETT. WE HAD A DEAL.
YEAH. SORRY...
...BUT I'M ALSO AN ENTREPRENEUR. I MEAN, YOU OF ALL PEOPLE UNDERSTAND THAT.
YOU'RE MAKING A HUGE MISTAKE.
WON'T BE MY FIRST.
IT'S GOING TO BE YOUR LAST.
MAYBE.
WHY YOU GOTTA BE SO NEGATIVE?

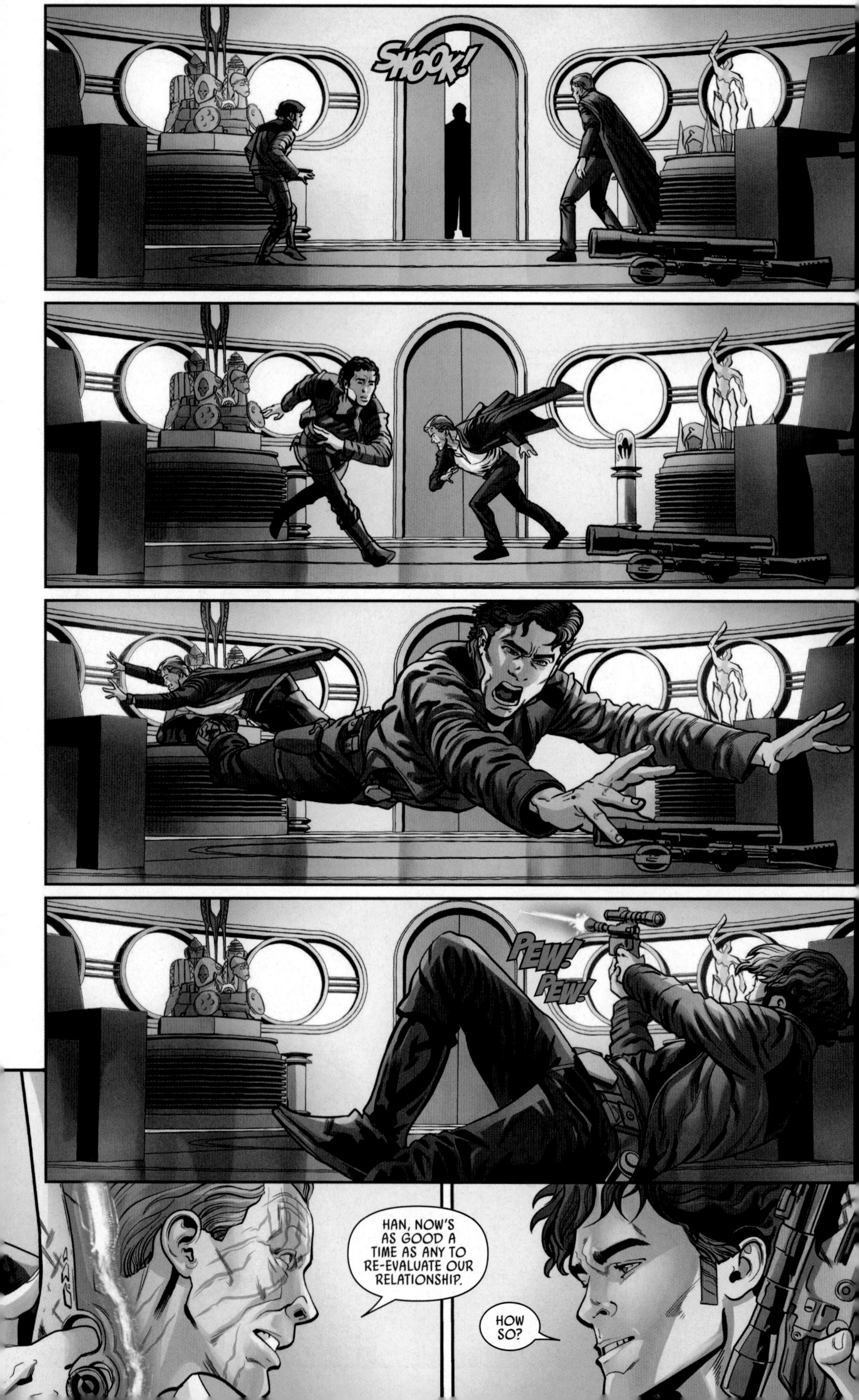
SHOOK!
PEW! PEW!
HAN, NOW'S AS GOOD A TIME AS ANY TO RE-EVALUATE OUR RELATIONSHIP.
HOW SO?

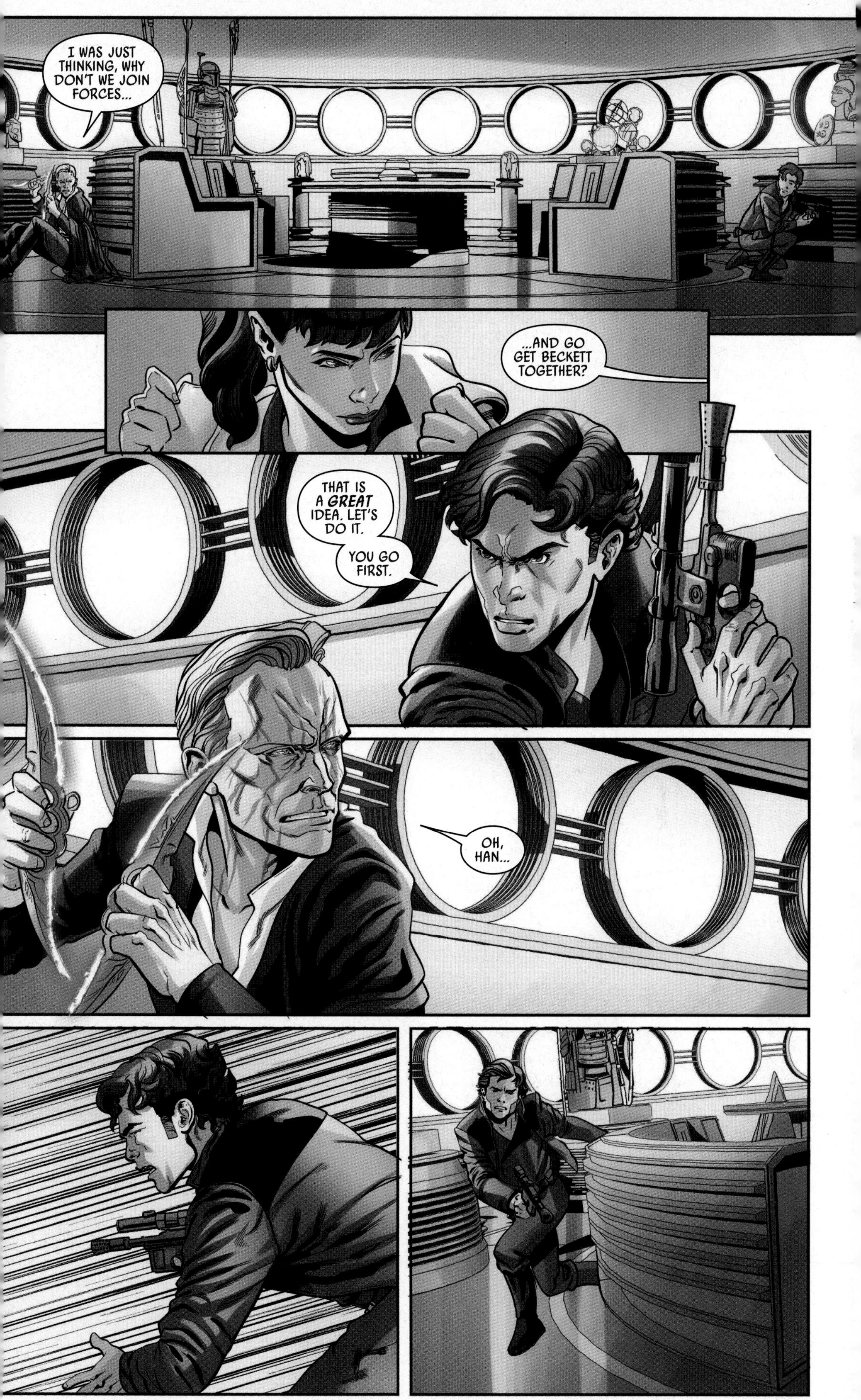
I WAS JUST THINKING, WHY DON'T WE JOIN FORCES...
...AND GO GET BECKETT TOGETHER?
THAT IS A GREAT IDEA. LET'S DO IT.
YOU GO FIRST.
OH, HAN...

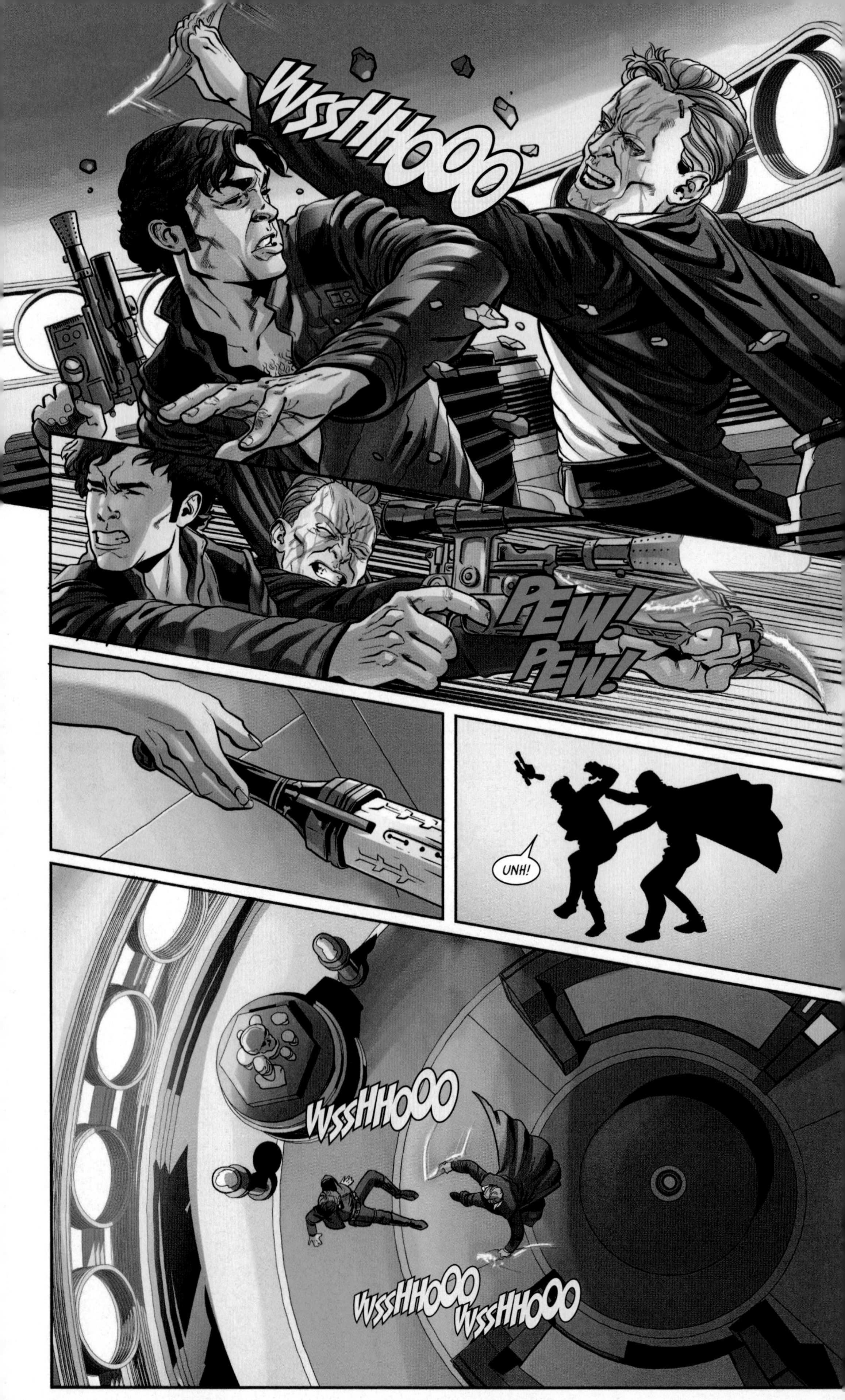
VSSHHOOO
PEW! PEW!
UNH!
VSSHHOOO
VSSHHOOO
VSSHHOOO

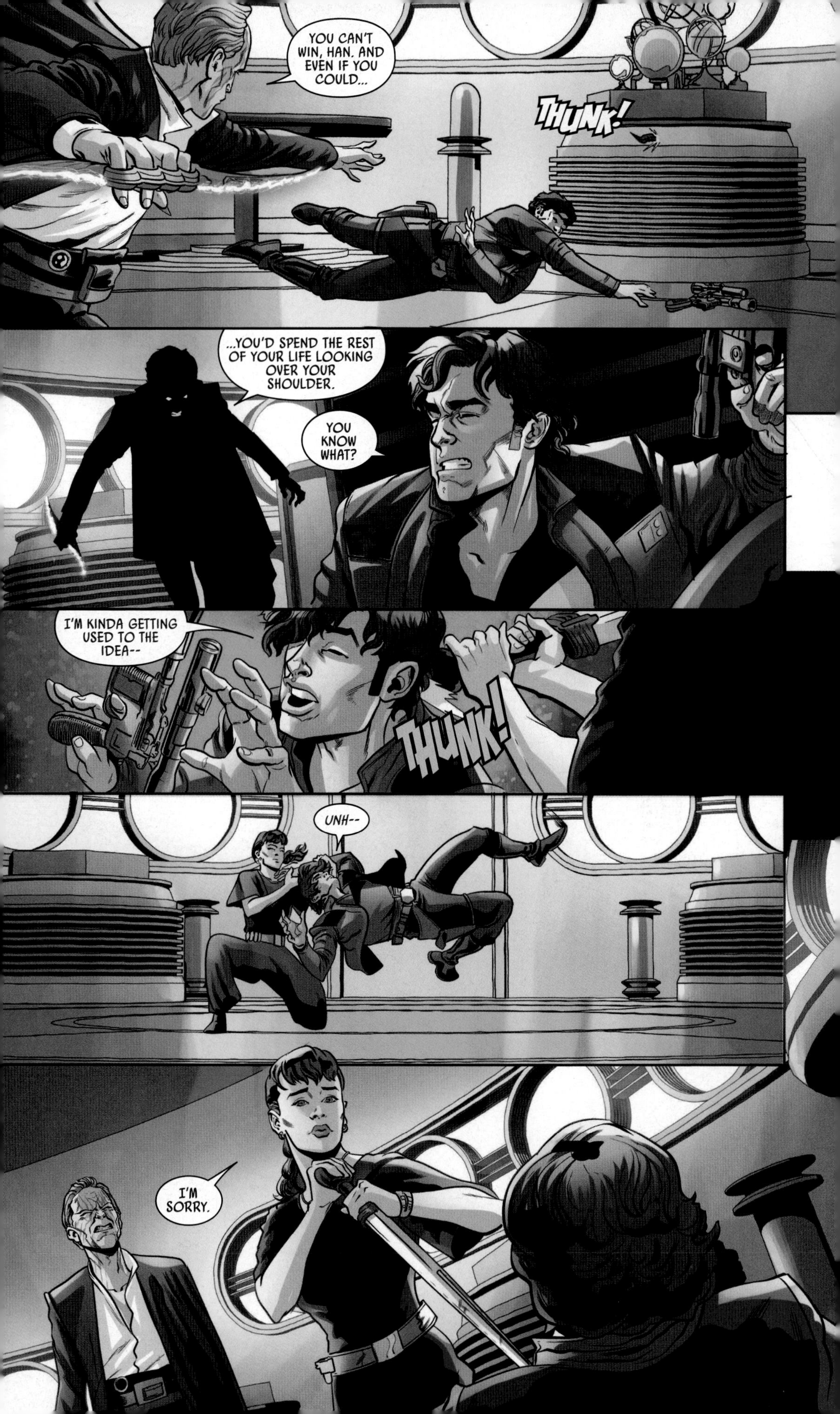
YOU CAN'T WIN, HAN. AND EVEN IF YOU COULD...
THUNK!
...YOU'D SPEND THE REST OF YOUR LIFE LOOKING OVER YOUR SHOULDER.
YOU KNOW WHAT?
I'M KINDA GETTING USED TO THE IDEA--
THUNK!
UNH--
I'M SORRY.

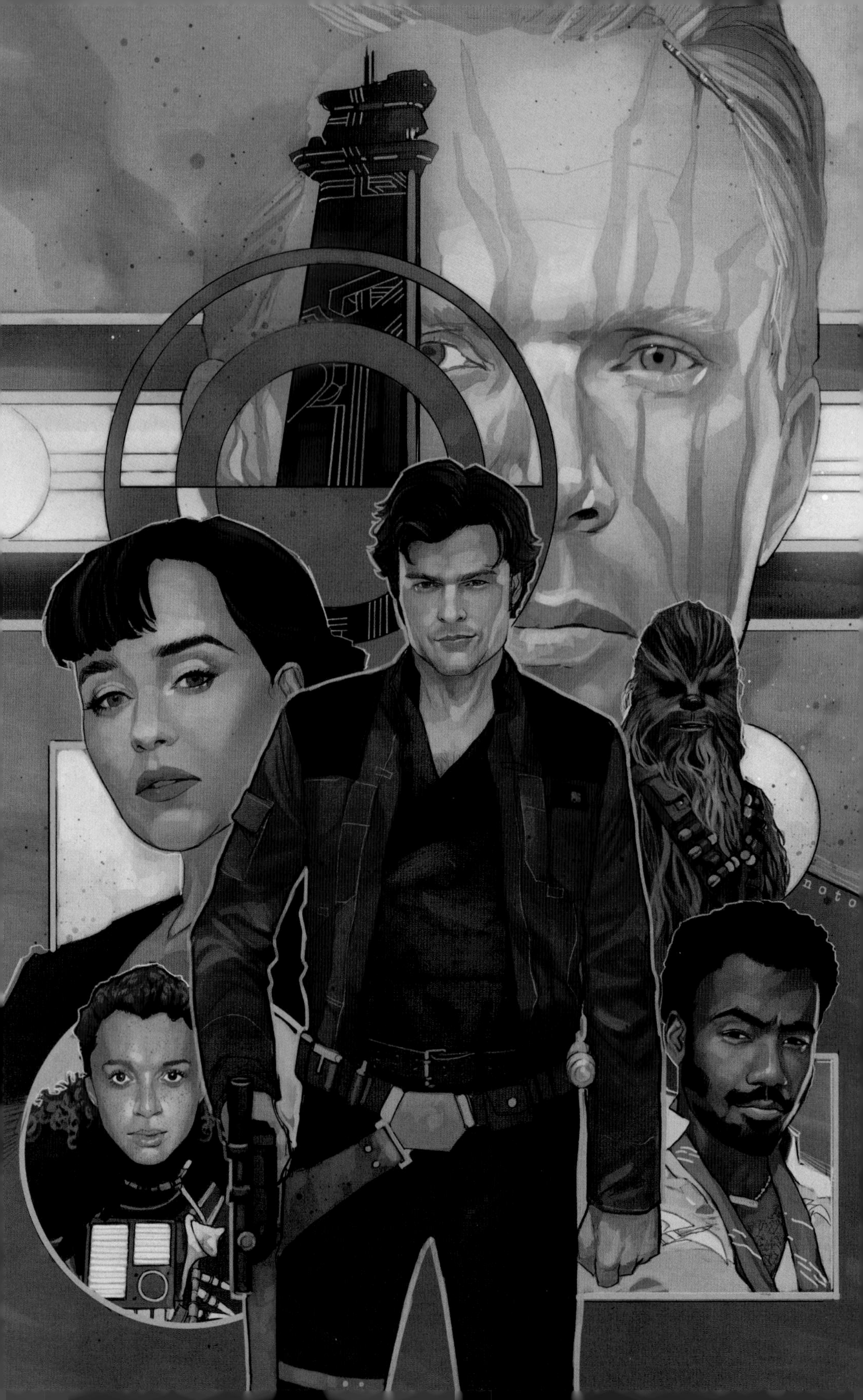
noto

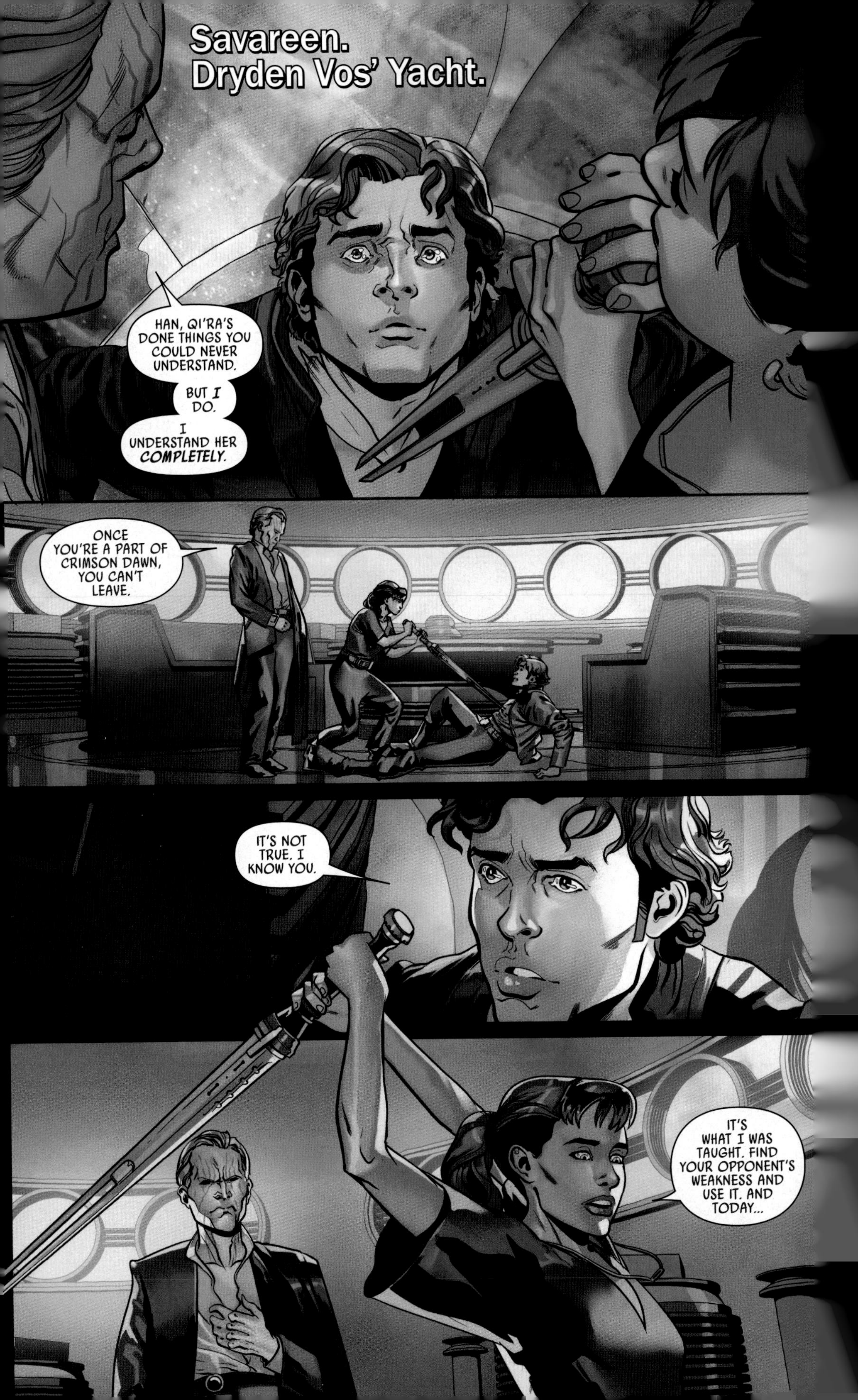
Savareen.
Dryden Vos' Yacht.
HAN, QI'RA'S DONE THINGS YOU COULD NEVER UNDERSTAND.
BUT *I* DO.
I UNDERSTAND HER ***COMPLETELY.***
ONCE YOU'RE A PART OF CRIMSON DAWN, YOU CAN'T LEAVE.
IT'S NOT TRUE. I KNOW YOU.
IT'S WHAT I WAS TAUGHT. FIND YOUR OPPONENT'S WEAKNESS AND USE IT. AND TODAY...

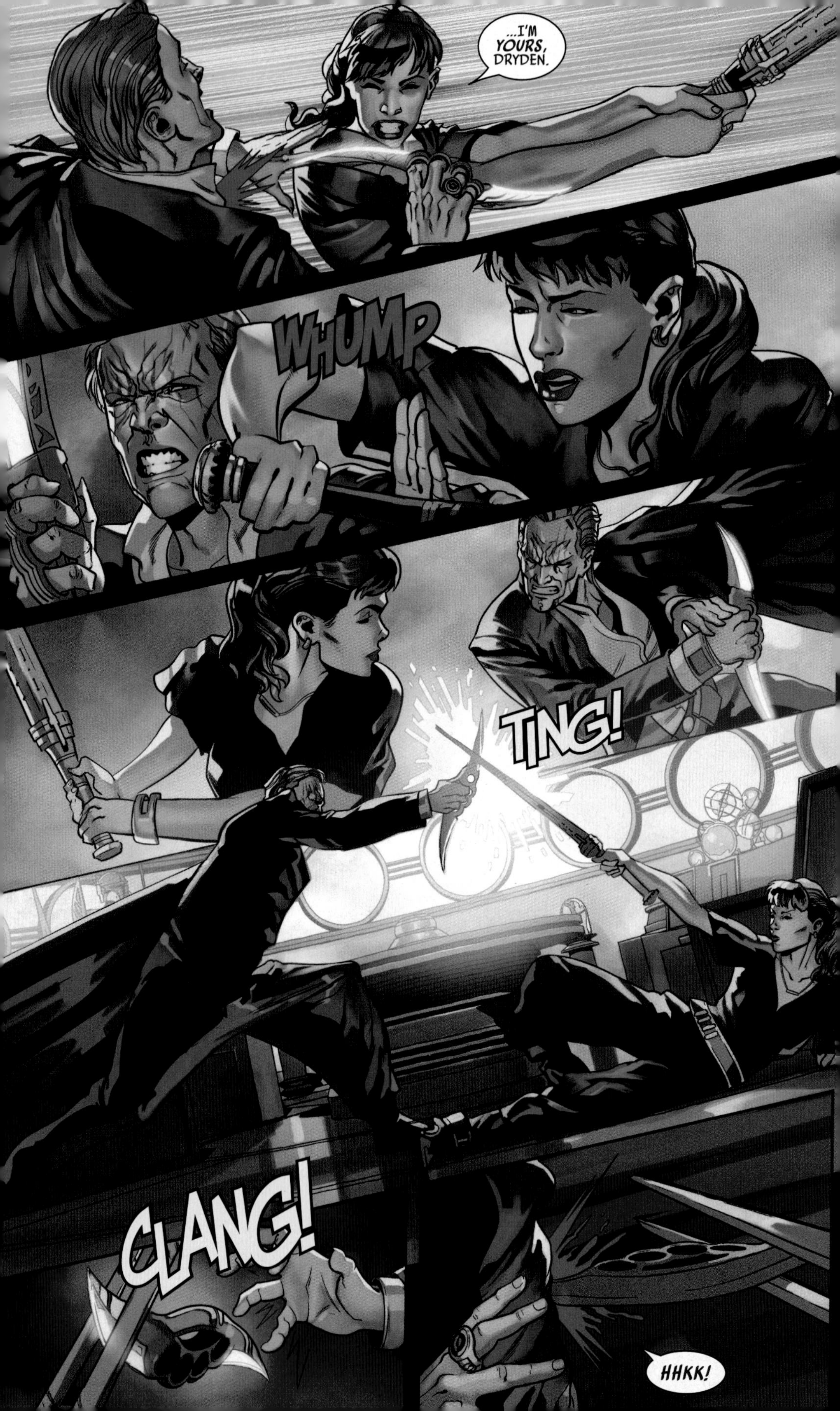
...I'M YOURS, DRYDEN.
WHUMP
TING!
CLANG!
HHKK!

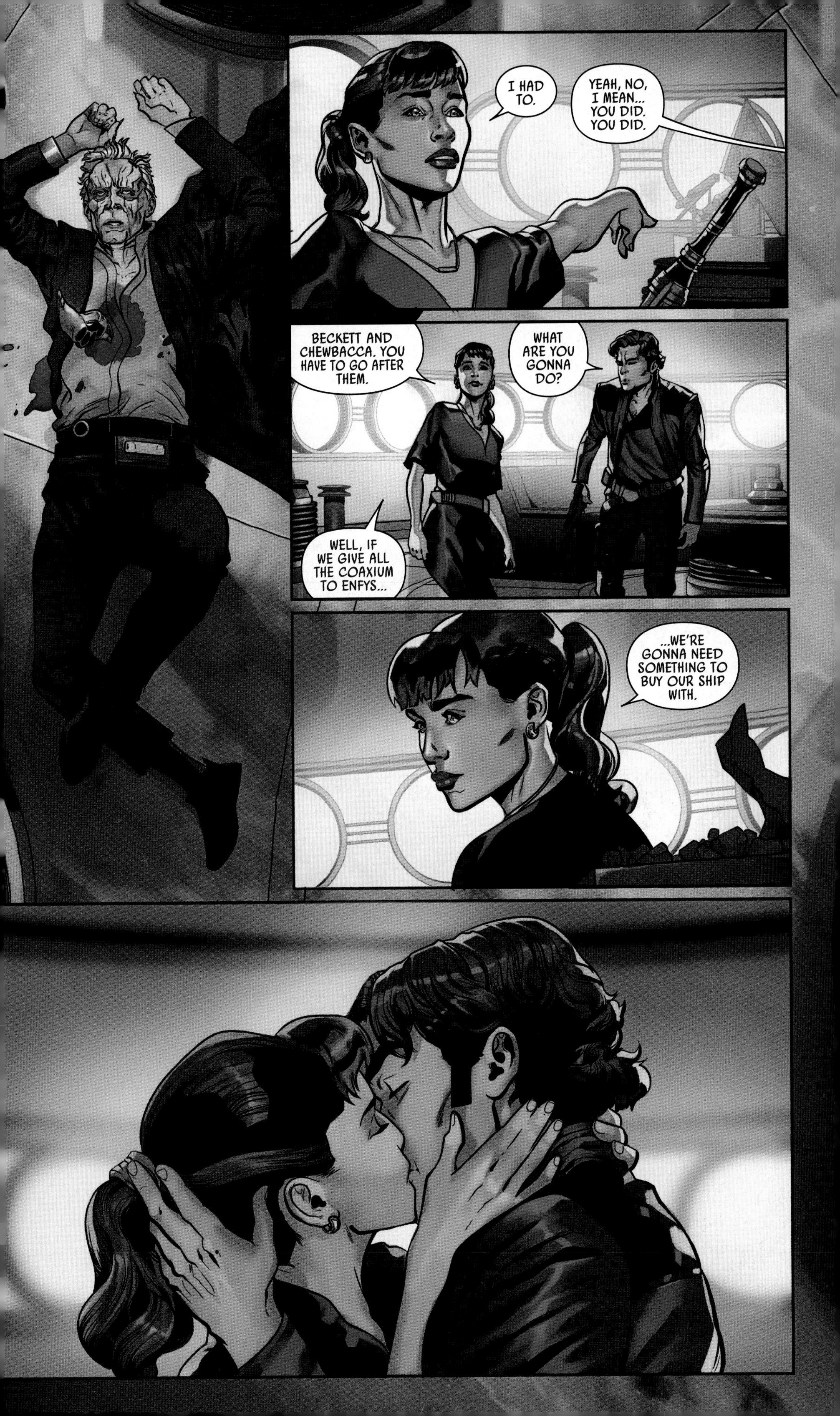
I HAD TO.
YEAH, NO, I MEAN... YOU DID. YOU DID.
BECKETT AND CHEWBACCA. YOU HAVE TO GO AFTER THEM.
WHAT ARE YOU GONNA DO?
WELL, IF WE GIVE ALL THE COAXIUM TO ENFYS...
...WE'RE GONNA NEED SOMETHING TO BUY OUR SHIP WITH.

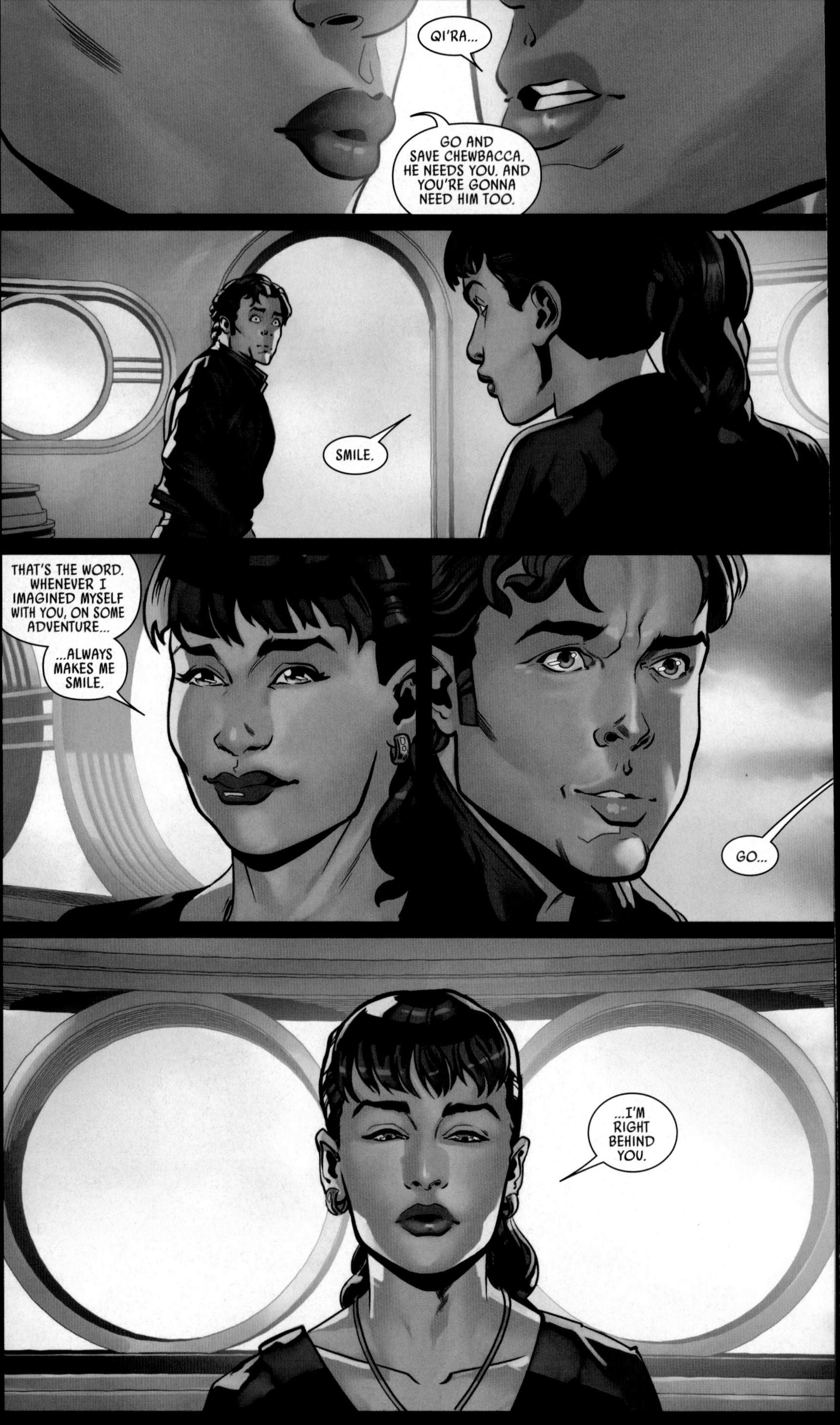
QI'RA...
GO AND SAVE CHEWBACCA. HE NEEDS YOU. AND YOU'RE GONNA NEED HIM TOO.
SMILE.
THAT'S THE WORD. WHENEVER I IMAGINED MYSELF WITH YOU, ON SOME ADVENTURE...
...ALWAYS MAKES ME SMILE.
GO...
...I'M RIGHT BEHIND YOU.

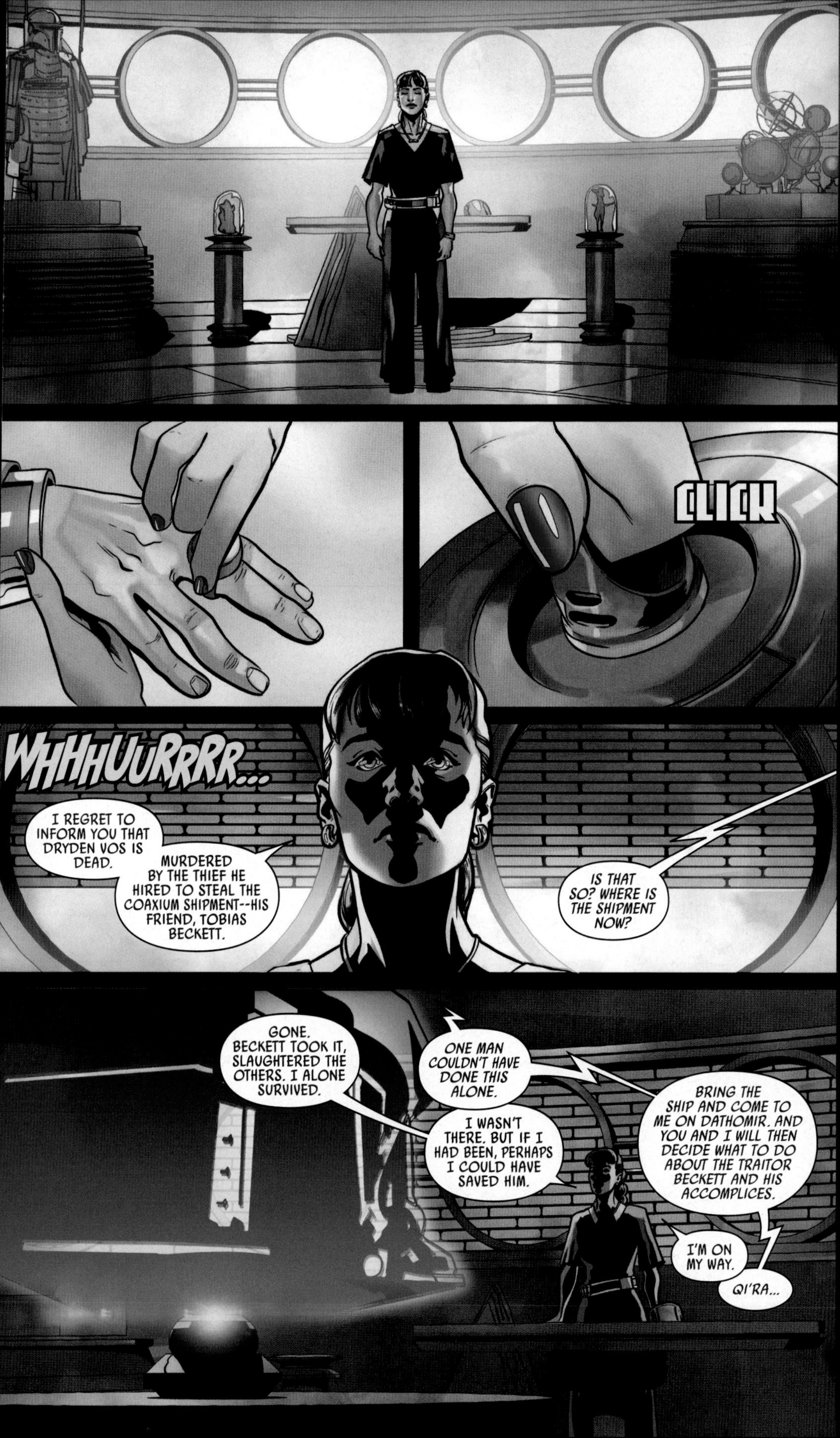
CLICK
WHHHUURRRR...
I REGRET TO INFORM YOU THAT DRYDEN VOS IS DEAD.
MURDERED BY THE THIEF HE HIRED TO STEAL THE COAXIUM SHIPMENT--HIS FRIEND, TOBIAS BECKETT.
IS THAT SO? WHERE IS THE SHIPMENT NOW?
GONE. BECKETT TOOK IT, SLAUGHTERED THE OTHERS. I ALONE SURVIVED.
ONE MAN COULDN'T HAVE DONE THIS ALONE.
I WASN'T THERE. BUT IF I HAD BEEN, PERHAPS I COULD HAVE SAVED HIM.
BRING THE SHIP AND COME TO ME ON DATHOMIR. AND YOU AND I WILL THEN DECIDE WHAT TO DO ABOUT THE TRAITOR BECKETT AND HIS ACCOMPLICES.
I'M ON MY WAY.
QI'RA...

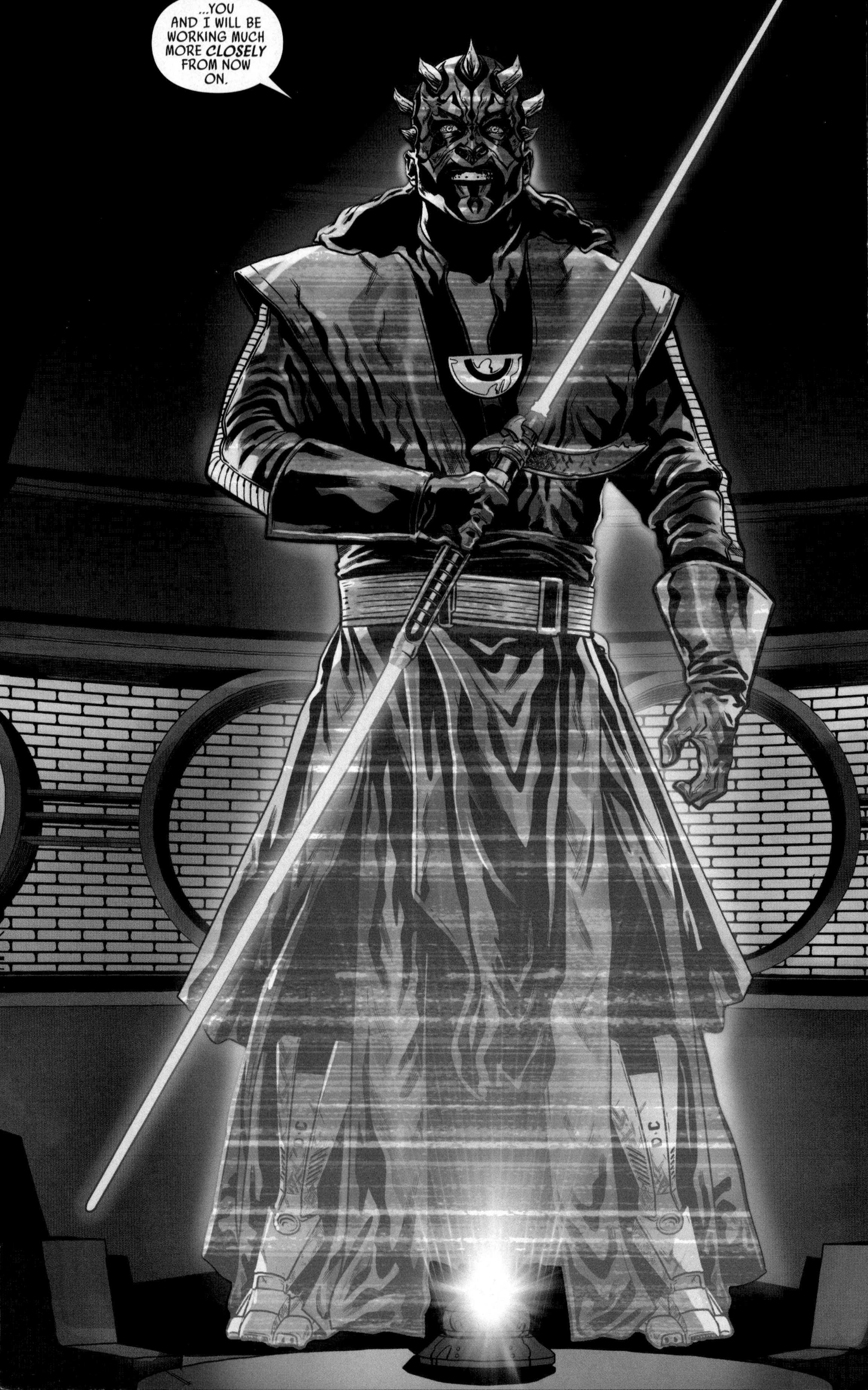
...YOU AND I WILL BE WORKING MUCH MORE CLOSELY FROM NOW ON.

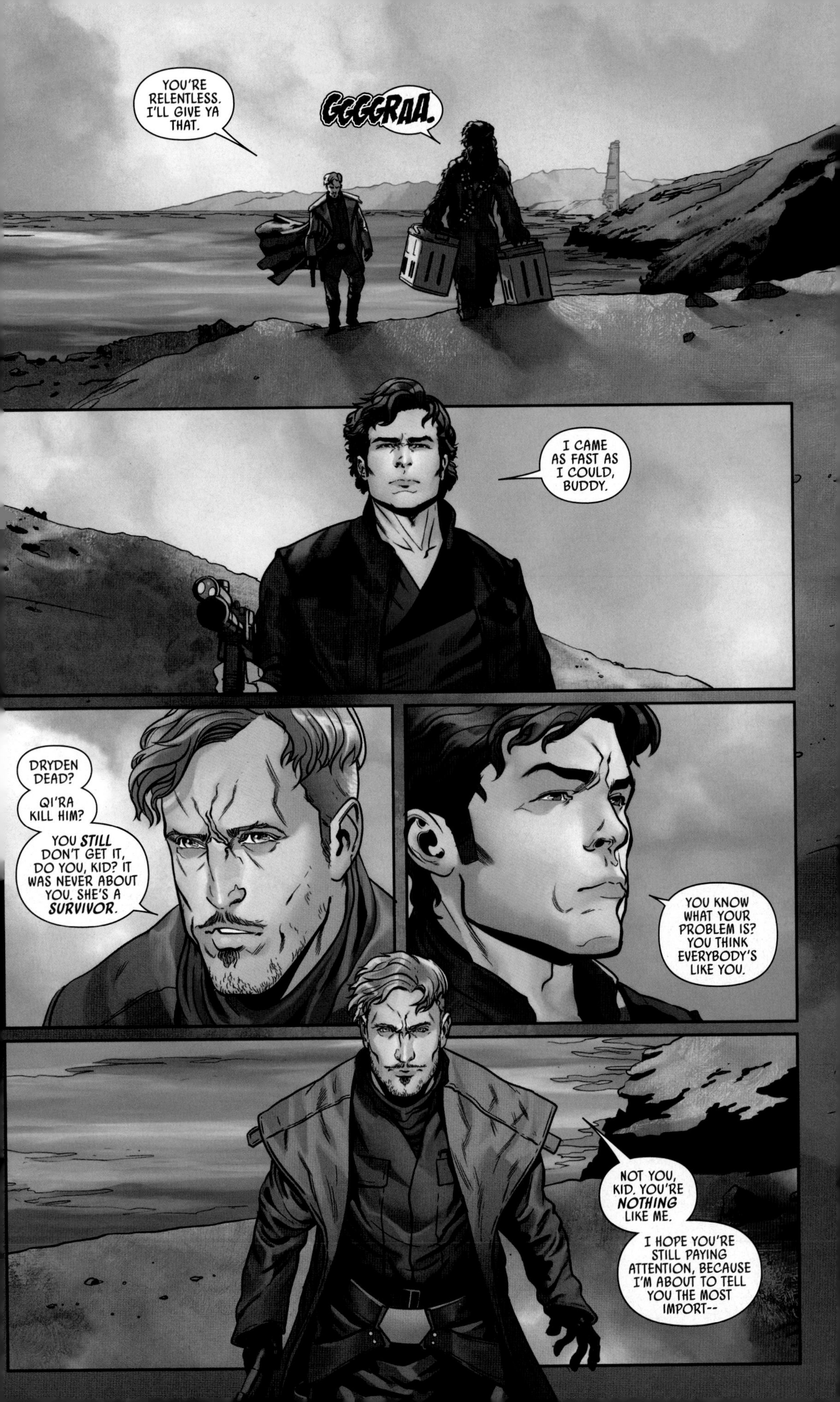
YOU'RE RELENTLESS. I'LL GIVE YA THAT.
GGGGRAA.
I CAME AS FAST AS I COULD, BUDDY.
DRYDEN DEAD?
QI'RA KILL HIM?
YOU STILL DON'T GET IT, DO YOU, KID? IT WAS NEVER ABOUT YOU. SHE'S A SURVIVOR.
YOU KNOW WHAT YOUR PROBLEM IS? YOU THINK EVERYBODY'S LIKE YOU.
NOT YOU, KID. YOU'RE NOTHING LIKE ME.
I HOPE YOU'RE STILL PAYING ATTENTION, BECAUSE I'M ABOUT TO TELL YOU THE MOST IMPORT--

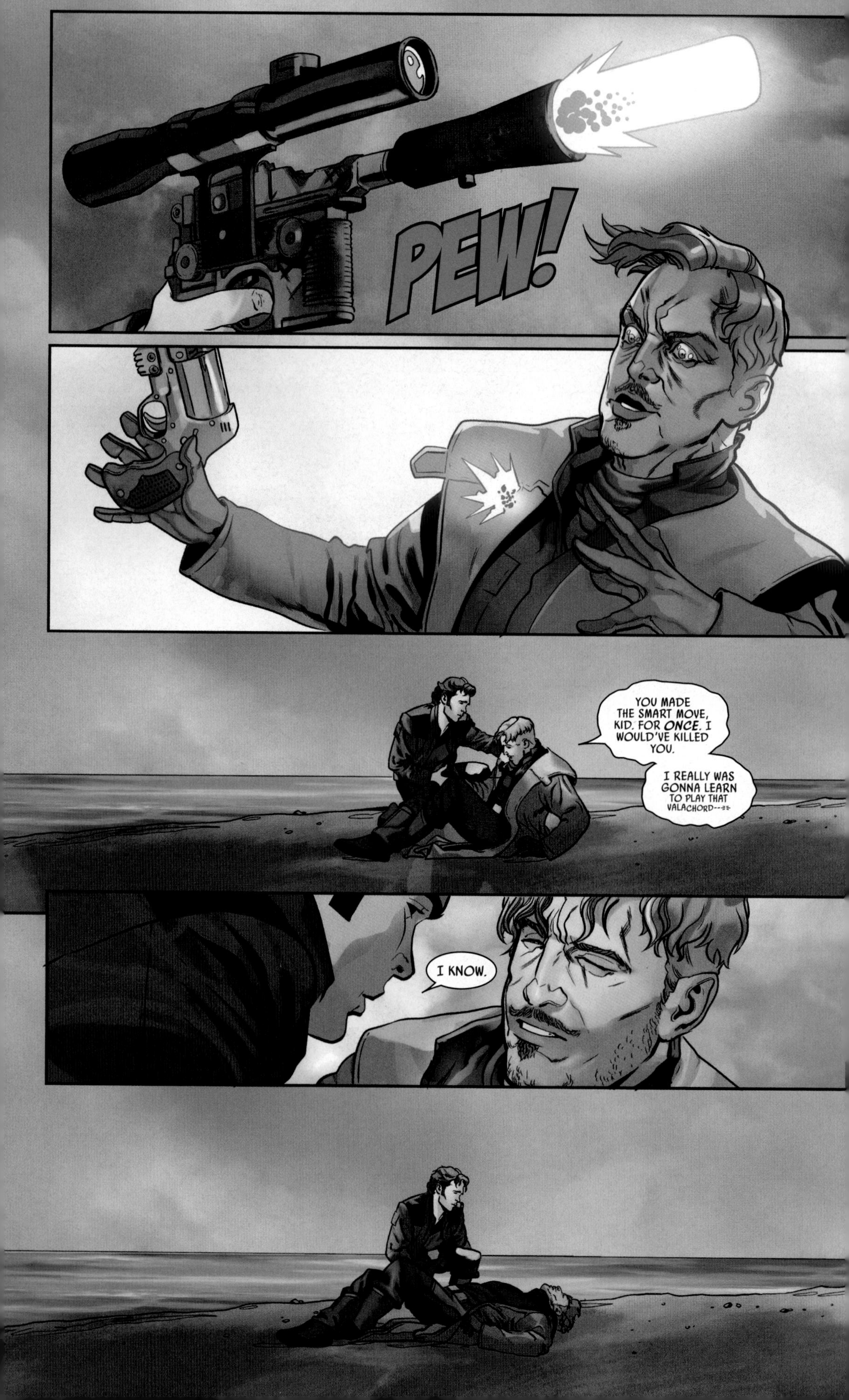
PEW!
YOU MADE THE SMART MOVE, KID. FOR ONCE. I WOULD'VE KILLED YOU.
I REALLY WAS GONNA LEARN TO PLAY THAT VALACHORD--
I KNOW.

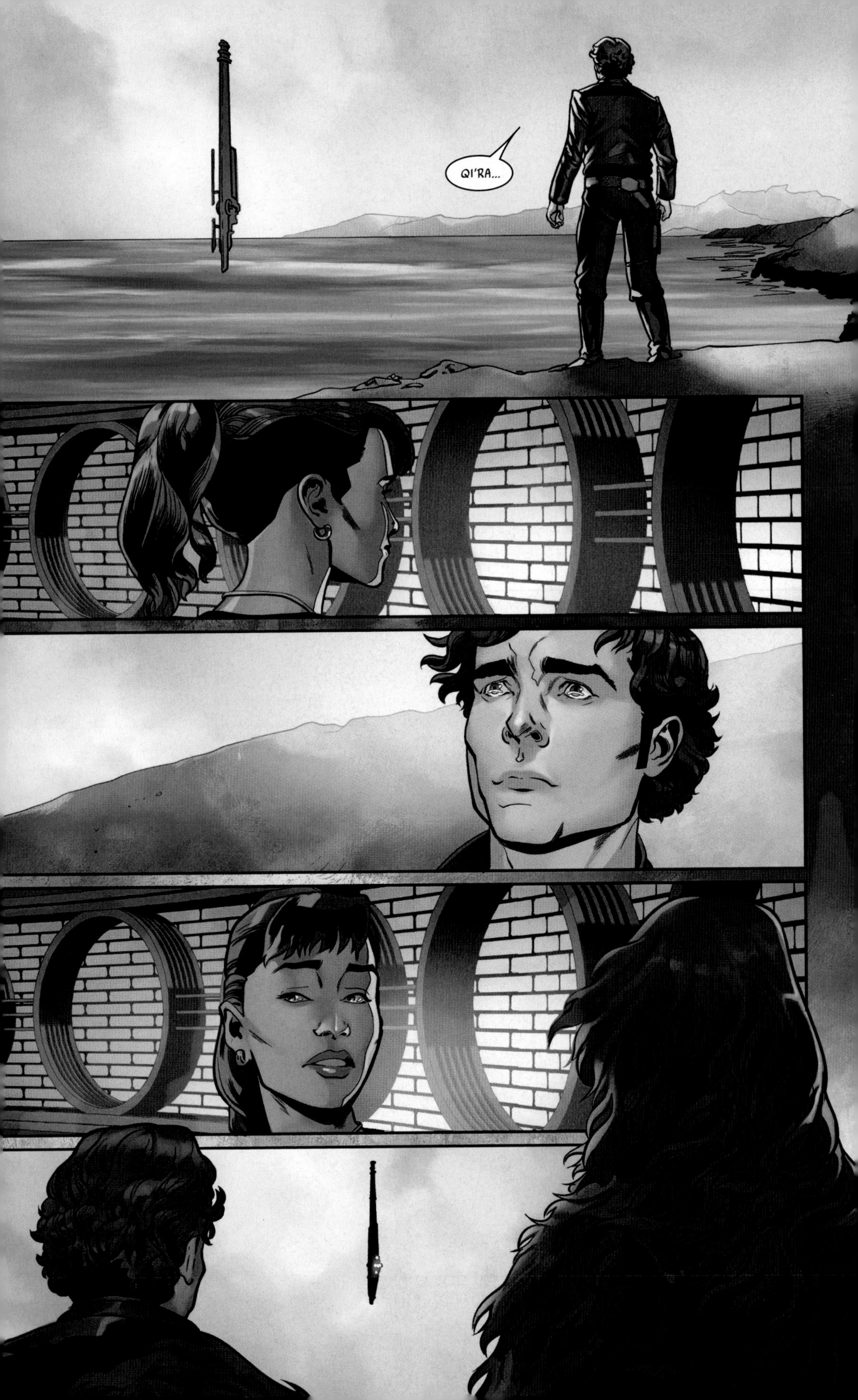
QI'RA...

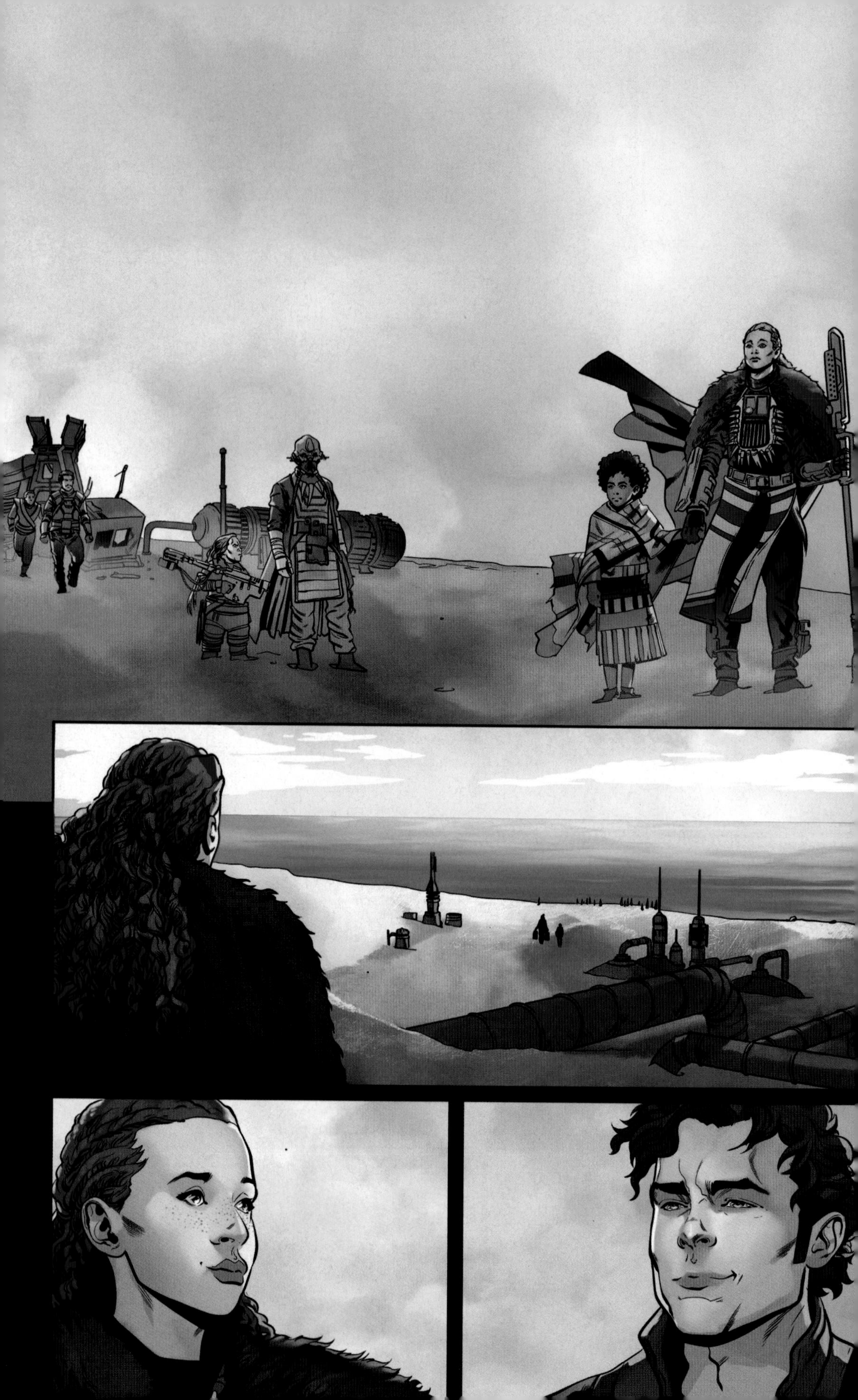

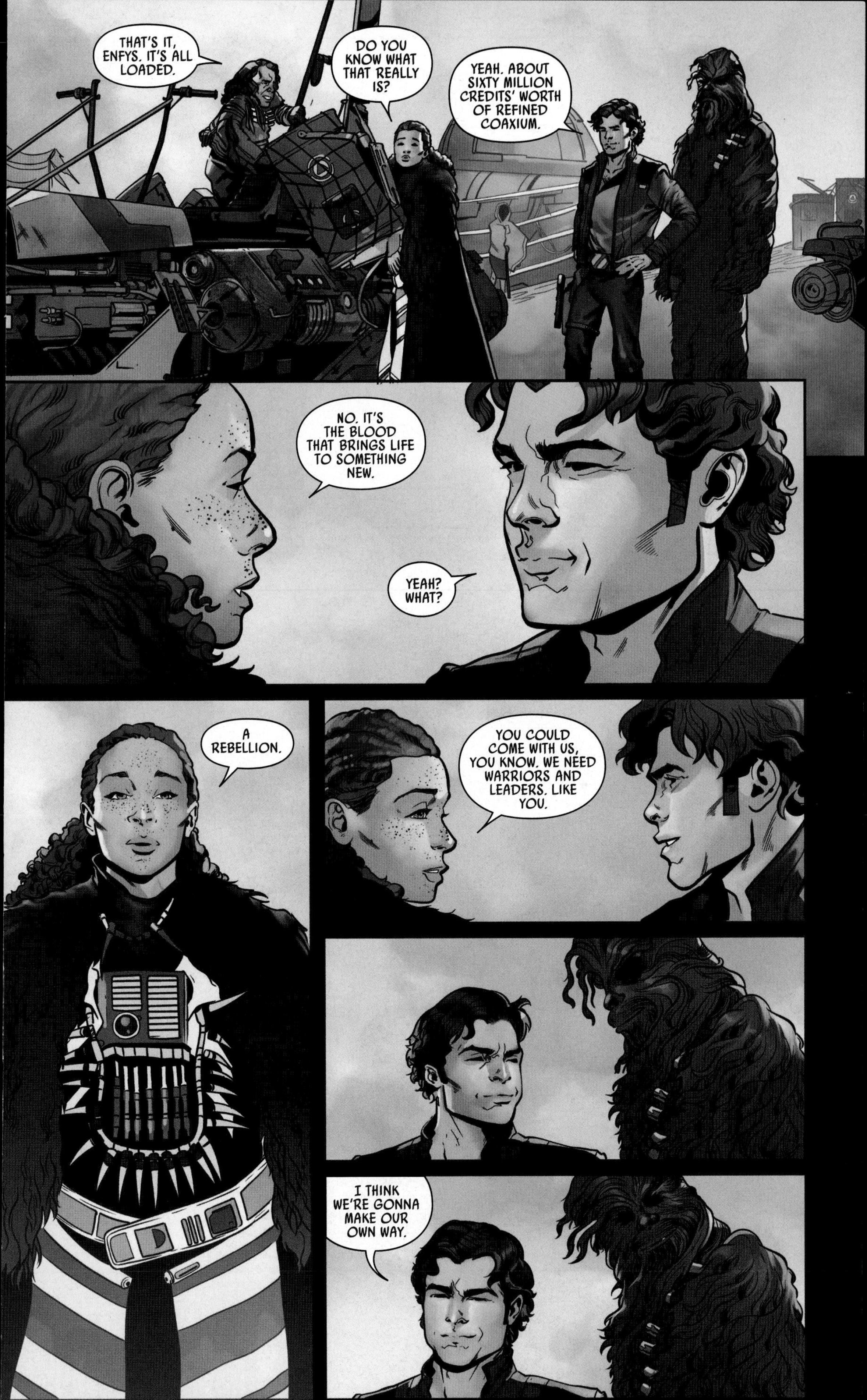
THAT'S IT, ENFYS. IT'S ALL LOADED.
DO YOU KNOW WHAT THAT REALLY IS?
YEAH. ABOUT SIXTY MILLION CREDITS' WORTH OF REFINED COAXIUM.
NO. IT'S THE BLOOD THAT BRINGS LIFE TO SOMETHING NEW.
YEAH? WHAT?
A REBELLION.
YOU COULD COME WITH US, YOU KNOW. WE NEED WARRIORS AND LEADERS. LIKE YOU.
I THINK WE'RE GONNA MAKE OUR OWN WAY.

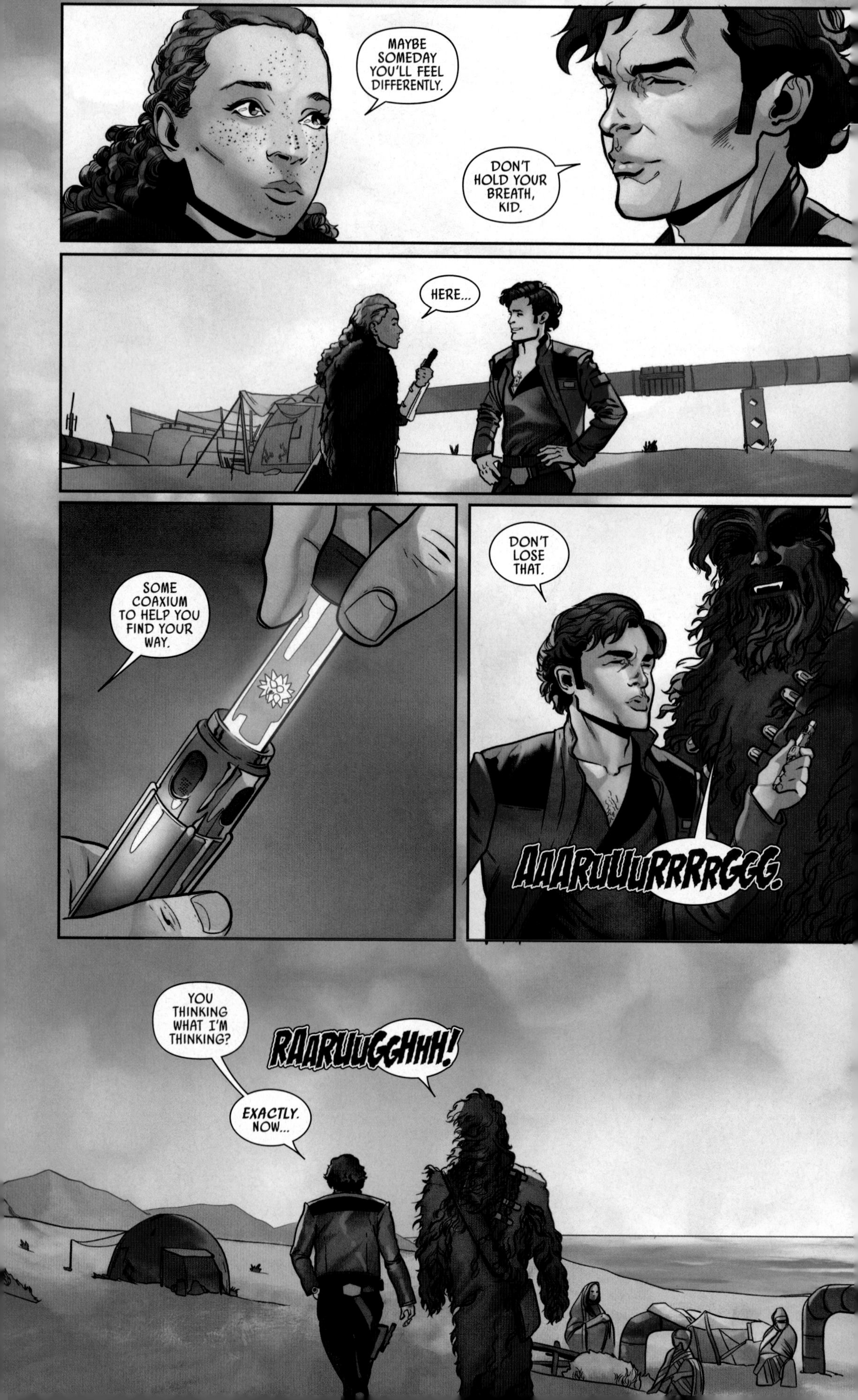
MAYBE SOMEDAY YOU'LL FEEL DIFFERENTLY.
DON'T HOLD YOUR BREATH, KID.
HERE...
SOME COAXIUM TO HELP YOU FIND YOUR WAY.
DON'T LOSE THAT.
AAARUUURRRRGGG.
YOU THINKING WHAT I'M THINKING?
RAARUUGGHHH!
EXACTLY. NOW...

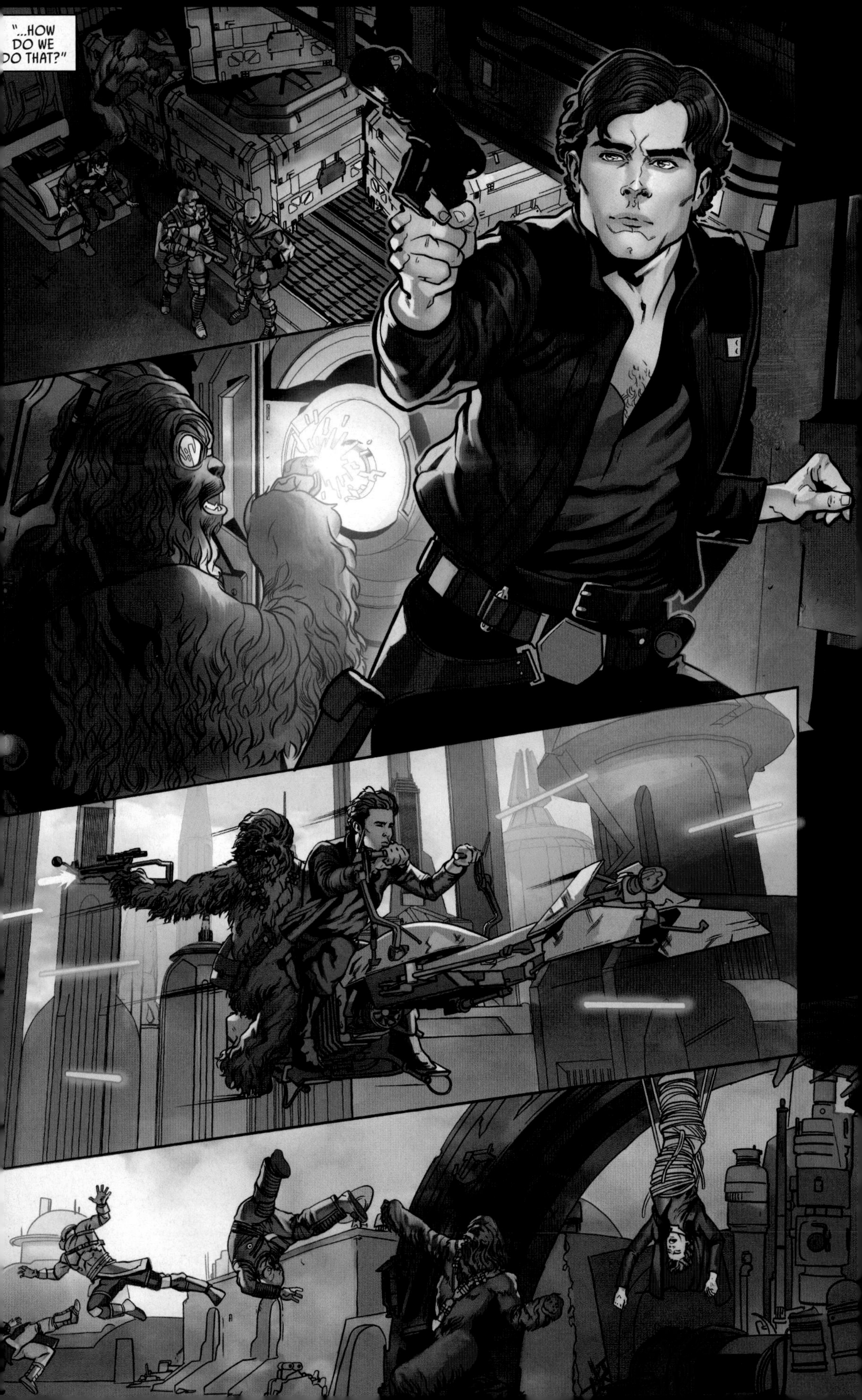
"...HOW DO WE DO THAT?"

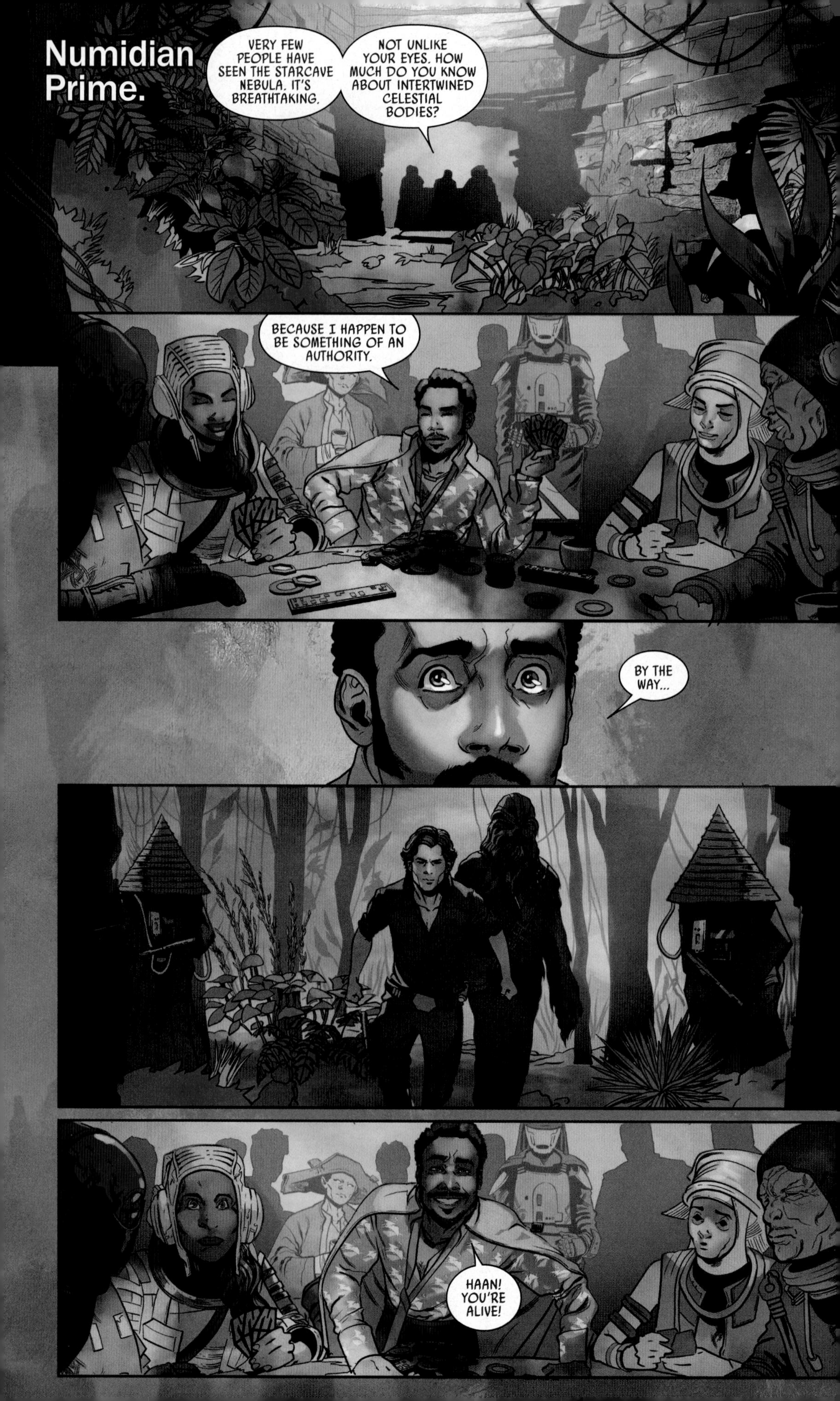
Numidian Prime.
VERY FEW PEOPLE HAVE SEEN THE STARCAVE NEBULA. IT'S BREATHTAKING.
NOT UNLIKE YOUR EYES. HOW MUCH DO YOU KNOW ABOUT INTERTWINED CELESTIAL BODIES?
BECAUSE I HAPPEN TO BE SOMETHING OF AN AUTHORITY.
BY THE WAY...
HAAN! YOU'RE ALIVE!

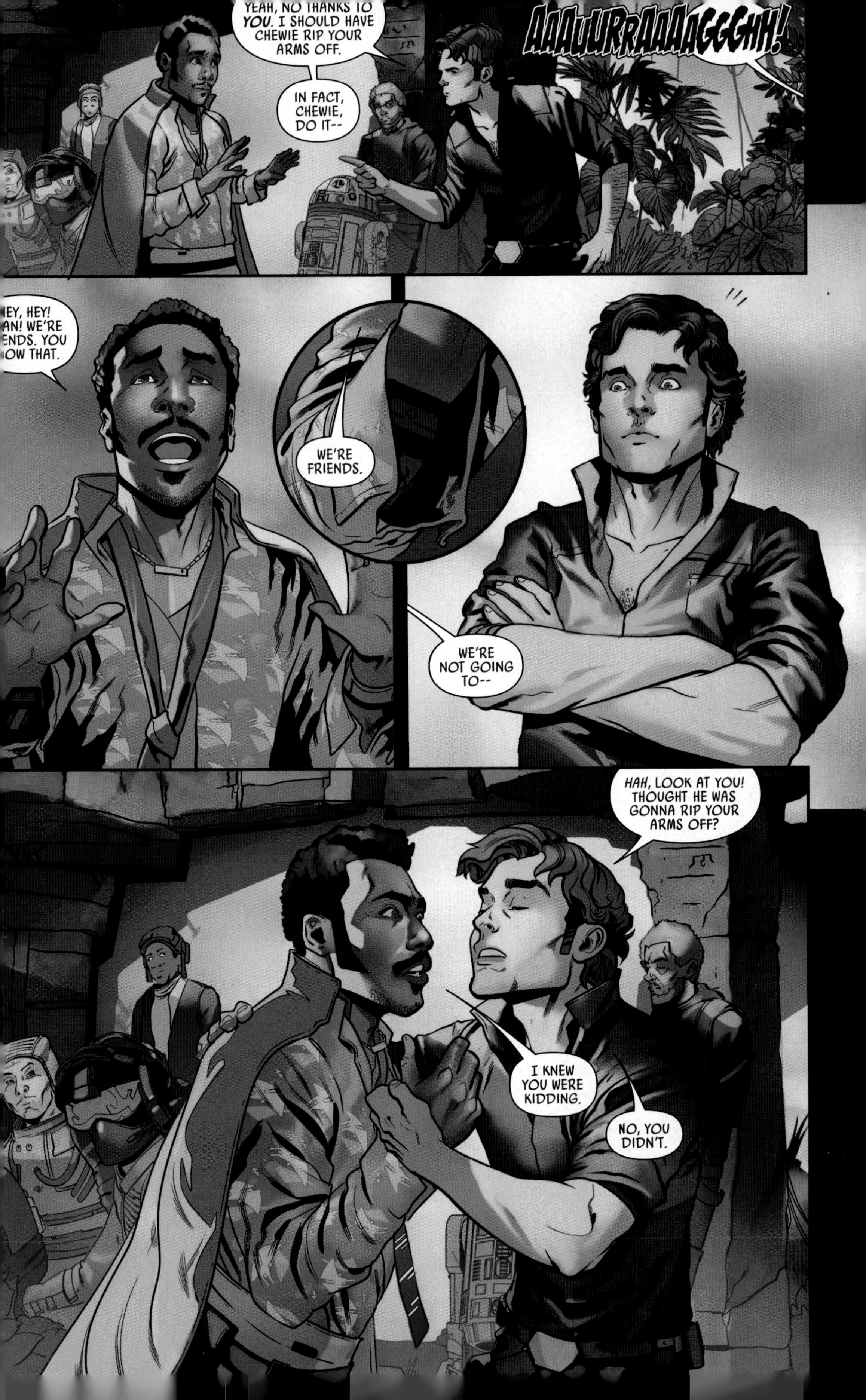
YEAH, NO THANKS TO YOU. I SHOULD HAVE CHEWIE RIP YOUR ARMS OFF.
IN FACT, CHEWIE, DO IT--
AAAUURRAAAAGGGHH!
EY, HEY! AN! WE'RE ENDS. YOU OW THAT.
WE'RE FRIENDS.
WE'RE NOT GOING TO--
HAH, LOOK AT YOU! THOUGHT HE WAS GONNA RIP YOUR ARMS OFF?
I KNEW YOU WERE KIDDING.
NO, YOU DIDN'T.

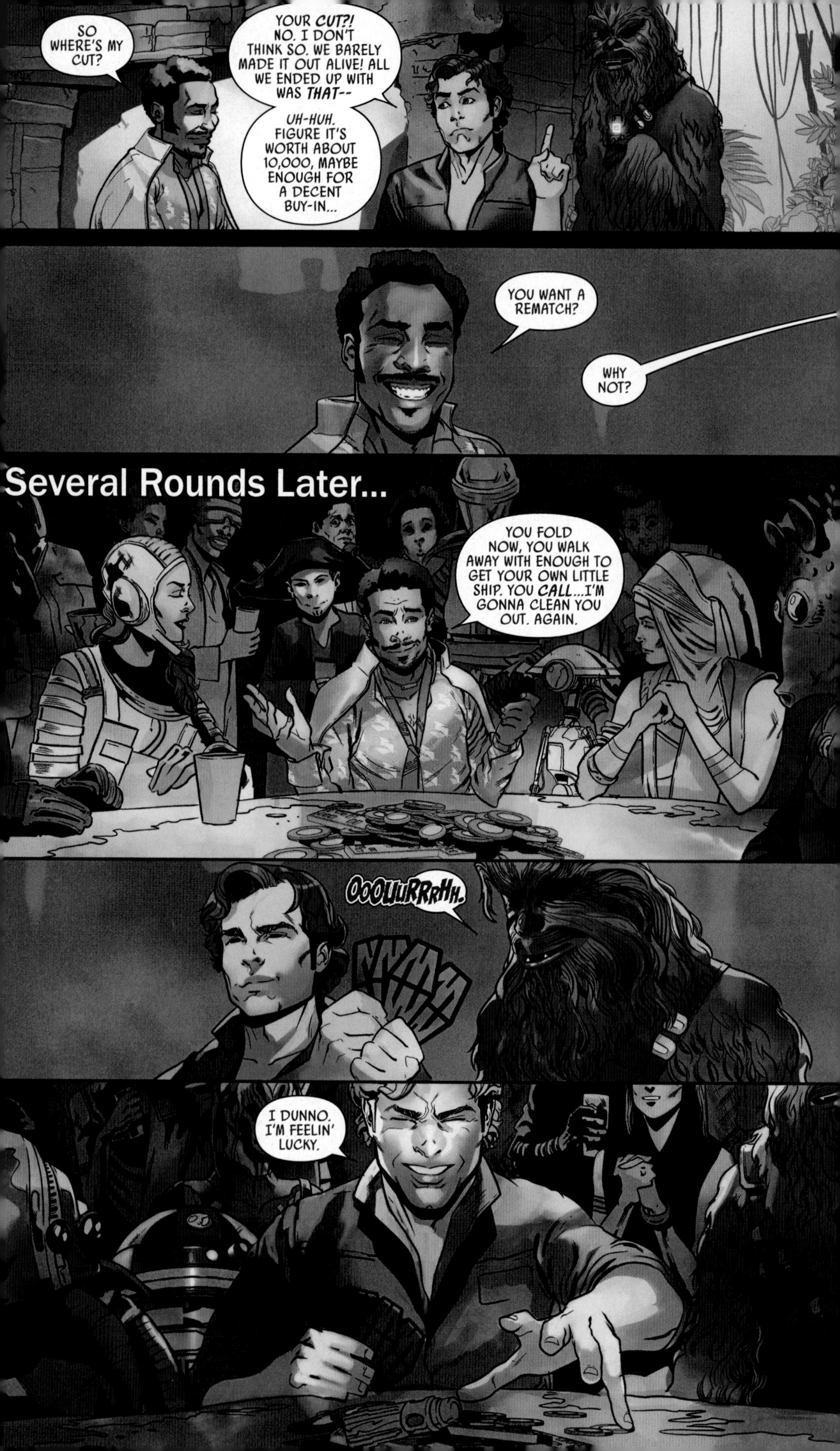
SO WHERE'S MY CUT?
YOUR CUT?! NO. I DON'T THINK SO. WE BARELY MADE IT OUT ALIVE! ALL WE ENDED UP WITH WAS THAT--
UH-HUH. FIGURE IT'S WORTH ABOUT 10,000, MAYBE ENOUGH FOR A DECENT BUY-IN...
YOU WANT A REMATCH?
WHY NOT?
Several Rounds Later...
YOU FOLD NOW, YOU WALK AWAY WITH ENOUGH TO GET YOUR OWN LITTLE SHIP. YOU CALL...I'M GONNA CLEAN YOU OUT. AGAIN.
OOOUURRRHH.
I DUNNO. I'M FEELIN' LUCKY.

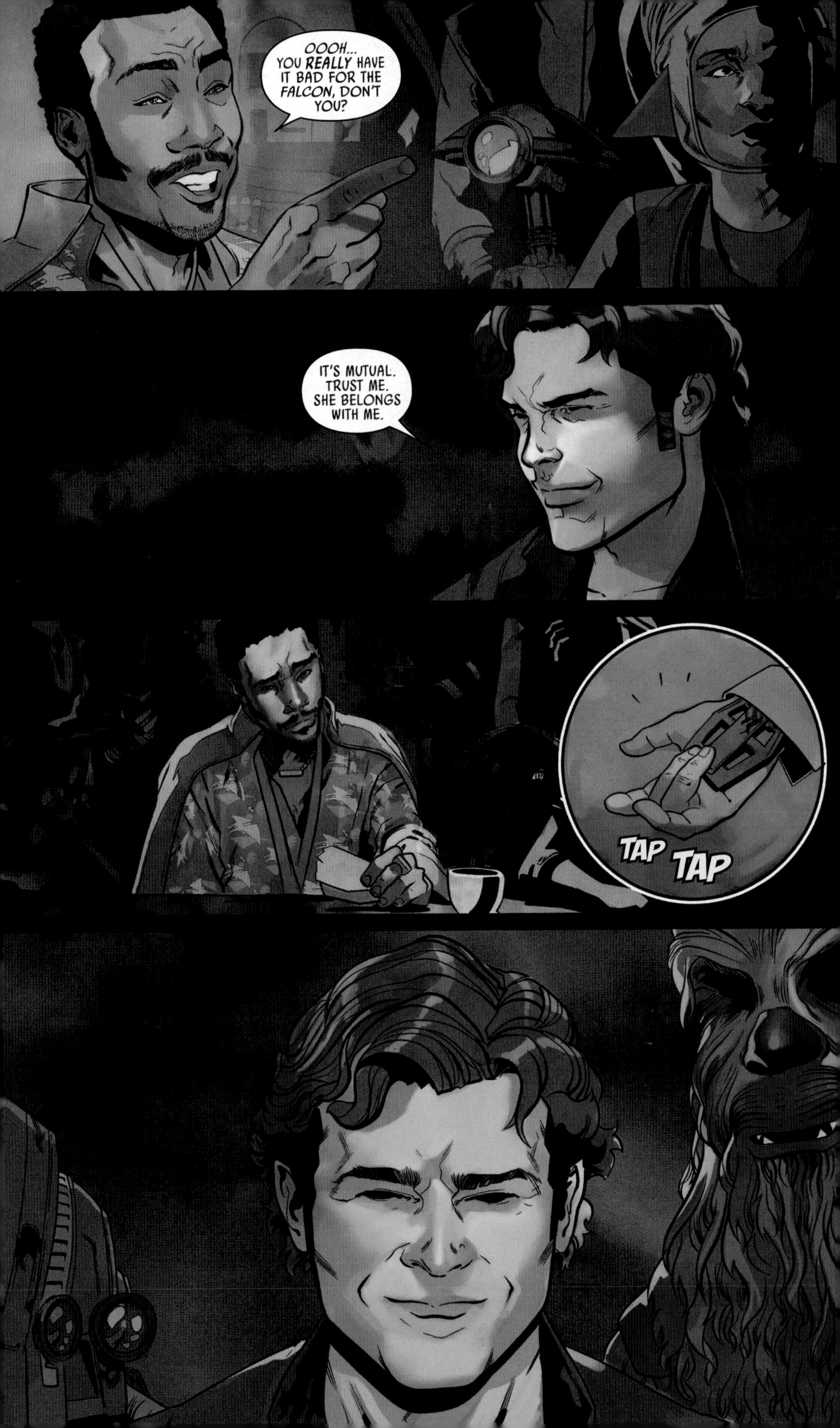
OOOH... YOU REALLY HAVE IT BAD FOR THE FALCON, DON'T YOU?
IT'S MUTUAL. TRUST ME. SHE BELONGS WITH ME.
TAP TAP

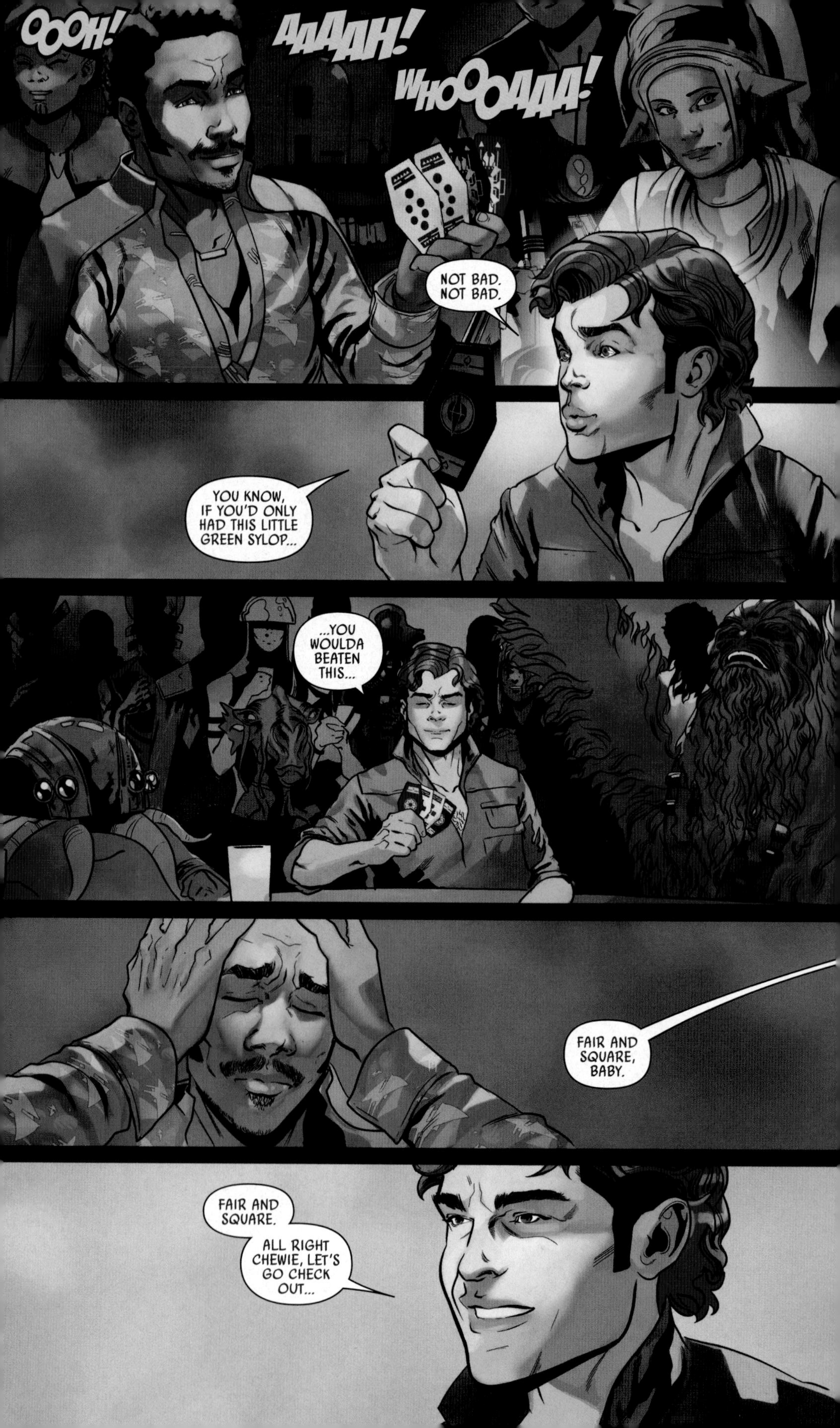
OOOH!
AAAAH!
WHOOOAAAA!
NOT BAD. NOT BAD.
YOU KNOW, IF YOU'D ONLY HAD THIS LITTLE GREEN SYLOP...
...YOU WOULDA BEATEN THIS...
FAIR AND SQUARE, BABY.
FAIR AND SQUARE.
ALL RIGHT CHEWIE, LET'S GO CHECK OUT...

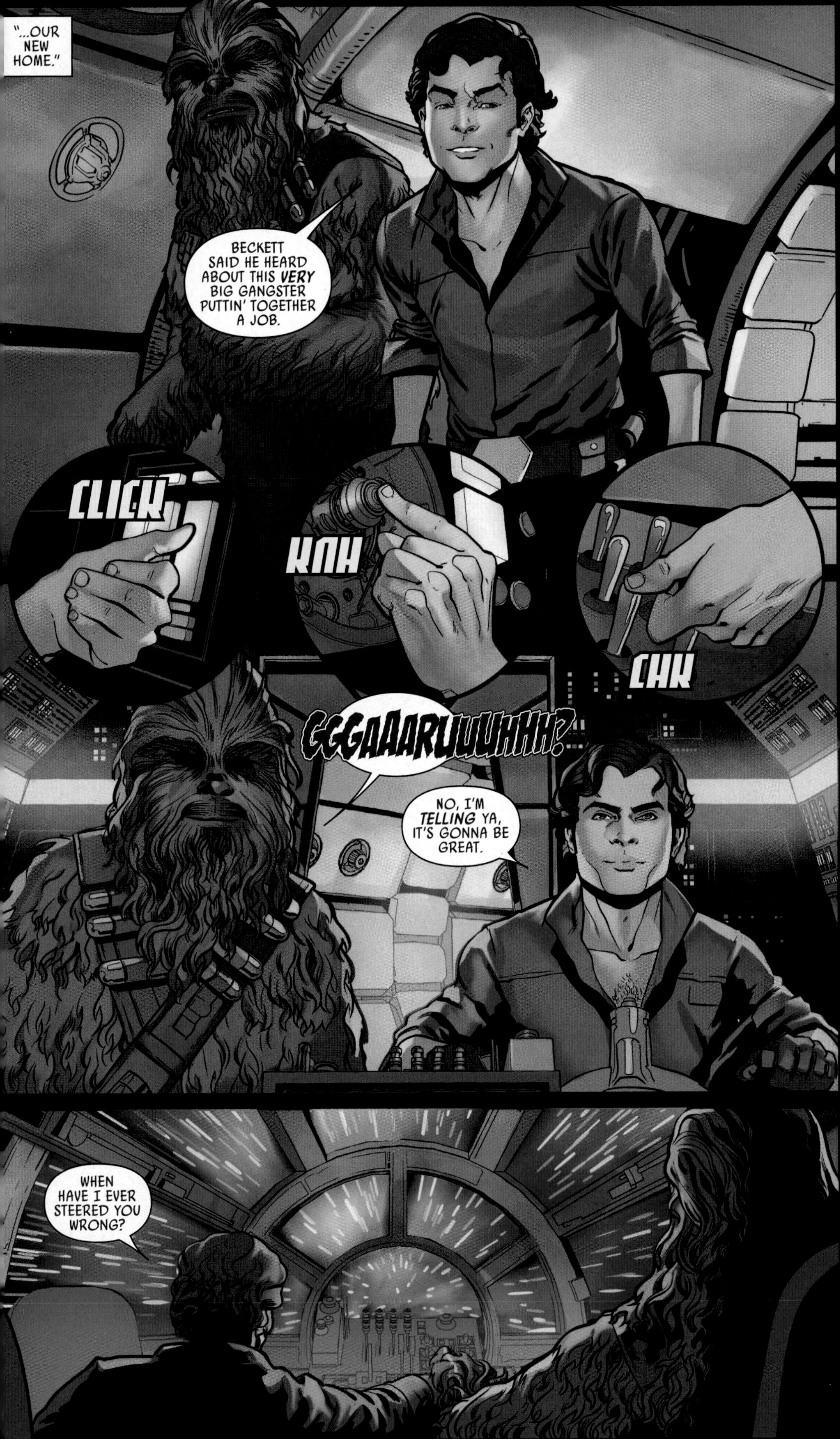
"...OUR NEW HOME."
BECKETT SAID HE HEARD ABOUT THIS VERY BIG GANGSTER PUTTIN' TOGETHER A JOB.
CLICK
KNH
CHK
GGGAAARUUUHHH?
NO, I'M TELLING YA, IT'S GONNA BE GREAT.
WHEN HAVE I EVER STEERED YOU WRONG?

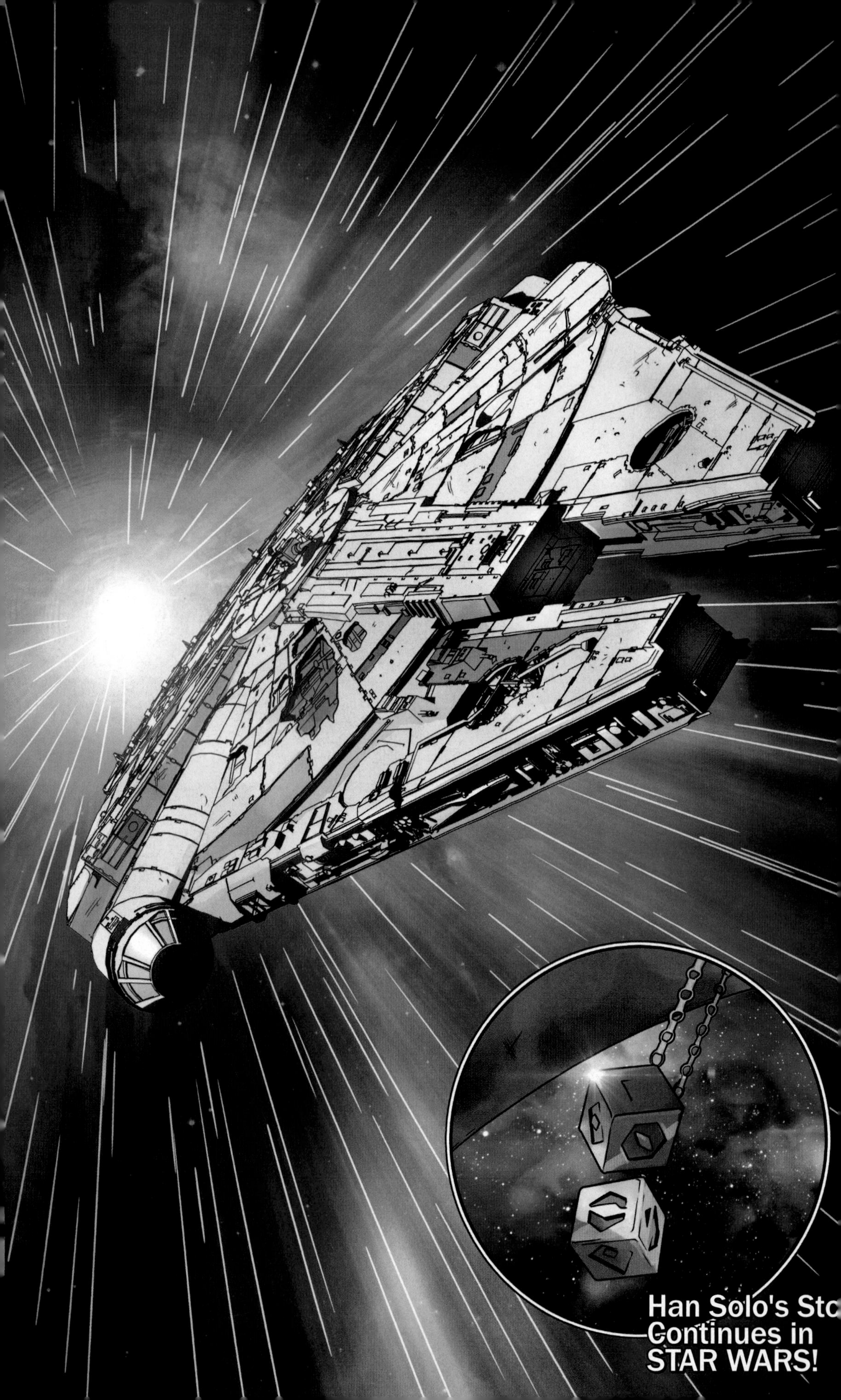
Han Solo's Sto
Continues in
STAR WARS!

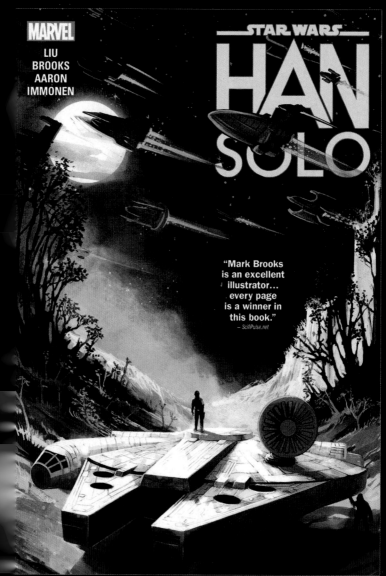

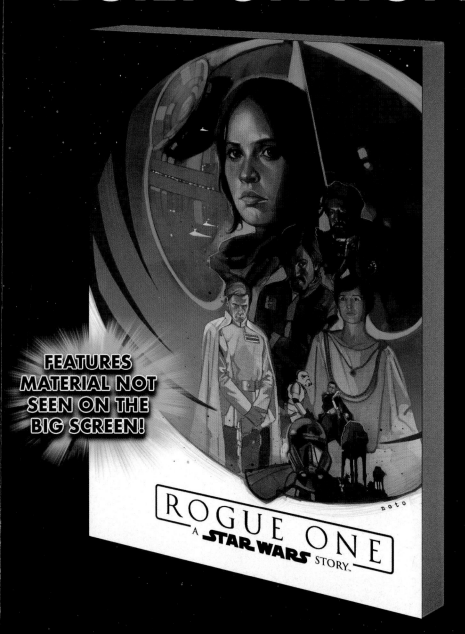

SENSATIONAL *STAR WARS* ARTWORK RETELLING THE STORY OF *A NEW HOPE!*

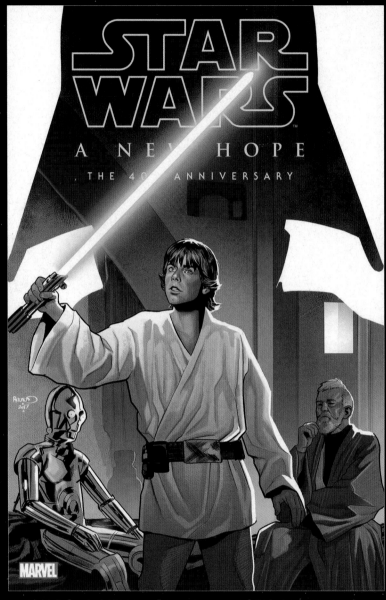

STAR WARS: A NEW HOPE — THE 40TH ANNIVERSARY HC
978-1302911287

ON SALE NOW
AVAILABLE IN PRINT AND DIGITAL WHEREVER BOOKS ARE SOLD

TO FIND A COMIC SHOP NEAR YOU, VISIT COMICSHOPLOCATOR.COM